Material London,

NEW CULTURAL STUDIES

Series Editors

Joan DeJean
Carroll Smith-Rosenberg
Peter Stallybrass
Gary A. Tomlinson

A complete list of books in the series
is available from the publisher.

Material London, ca. 1600

Edited by Lena Cowen Orlin

PENN

University of Pennsylvania Press

Philadelphia

10 9 8 7 6 5 4 3 2 1

Published by
University of Pennsylvania Press
Philadelphia, Pennsylvania 19104-4011

Library of Congress Cataloging-in-Publication Data
Material London, ca. 1600 / edited by Lena Cowen Orlin.
    p.   cm. — (New cultural studies)
    Includes bibliographical references and index.
    ISBN 0-8122-3540-1 (cloth : alk. paper). — ISBN 0-8122-1721-7 (pbk. : alk. paper)
    1. London (England) — History — 16th century.   2. London (England) — history — 17th
century.   3. Material culture — England — London.   I. Title: Material London, ca. 1600.
II. Orlin, Lena Cowen.   III. Series.

DA680 .M38 2000
942.105′5 — dc21

99-054378

Contents

Illustrations

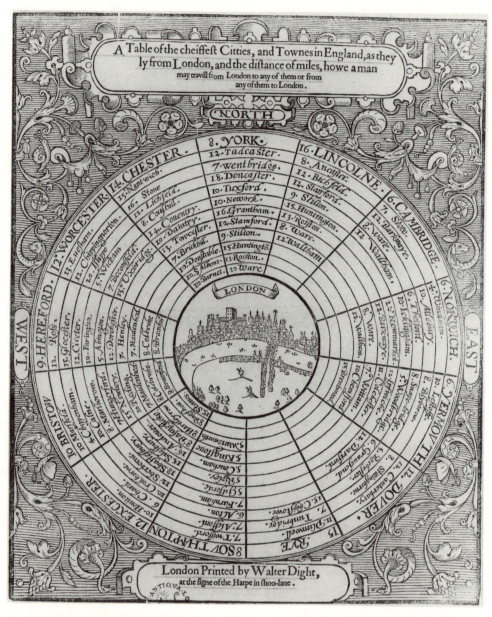

1.1. "A Table of the cheiffest Citties, and Townes in England, as they ly from London," a broadside printed "ca. 1600" (STC 10021.7; Lemon 106). By permission of the Society of Antiquaries of London.

I

Introduction

Lena Cowen Orlin

"A Table of the cheiffest Citties, and Townes in England," a broadside printed about 1600, acknowledges that there were other urban centers in England besides London—thirteen of them, including York, Lincoln, Norwich, and Bristol (fig. 1.1).[1] Estimating that there were also as many as eight hundred market towns, A. L. Beier and Roger Finlay conclude that "the country was not devoid of possible competitors to London."[2] The "Table" represents relatively few of these, however, and all are defined by their distance from the central cityscape, "as they ly from London." The broadside's mileages are organized to allow for multiple manipulations of the data. Thus, because York is 8 miles from Tadcaster, which is 12 miles from Wentbridge, which is 7 miles from Doncaster, and so on, it can be concluded somewhat laboriously that York is 150 miles from London. It is also possible to calculate the distances from London to Doncaster (123 miles), from York to Wentbridge (20 miles), from Doncaster to Tadcaster (19 miles), and so on. But if this textual information must be puzzled out, the visual message of the broadside is clear at a glance: all English roads lead from London. Other towns and cities are laid out in concentric circles, as if on an imaginary astronomical chart, with London as the radiant sun for this crowded system of lesser planets and reduplicative asteroids.

The mileages given in the "Table" are inaccurate by modern maps and measures, but they were evidently fairly standard for the time. In a great manuscript miscellany compiled a few years after the "Table" was printed, Thomas Trevelyon copied a chart for the geography of England, "How a man may journey from any notable towne in England, to the Citie of London" (fig. 1.2 shows one of five folio pages).[3] The miscellany is a lavishly illustrated one, but in this case Trevelyon employed the textual format he seems to have preferred for such other densely informative charts as those on "the age of the moon," "aspects of planets," "moveable feasts," and also, notably, "A Table of

from royston to barkway. .4 4 m̃
from barkway to puckeridge, .s. mile
from puckeridge to ware, .s. mile
from ware to waltham, .8. mile
from waltham to london, .12. mile

From couentry to oxford, .9. mile

from couentry to southam, .10. mile
from southam to banbury, .10. mile
from banbury to woodstocke, .12. mile
from woodstocke to oxford, .12. mile

From oxford to london, .47. mile

from oxford to whatlybridge, s. mile
from whatlybridge to tetsworth, s. mile
from tetsworth to stokenchurch.s. mile
from stokenchurch to wickam, .s. mile
from wickam to beconsfield, .s. mile
from beconsfield to vxbridge, .7. mile
from vxbridge to london, .is. mile

From saint dauids to london, .212. mile

from S. dauids to oxford, .12. mile
from oxford to carmarden, .24. mile
from carmarden to newton, .12. mile
from newton to lanbury .10. mile
from lanbury to brecknock, 16. mile
from brecknock to hay, .10. mile
from hay, to herreford, .14. mile
from herreford to rosse, .19. mile
from rosse to glocester, .12. mile
from glocester to chichester, .is. mile
from chicheffer to farington, .12. mile
from farington to abington, .10. mile
from abington to dorchester, .s. mile
from dorcester to henley, .12. mile
from henley to maidenhead, .7. mile
from maidenhead to colbrooke, .7. mile
from colbrooke to hounslow, .s. mile
from hounslow to london, .10. mile

from carmarthen to london, .157. mile

from carmarthen to laundoury, .20. mile

from laundouery to belthe, .14. mile
from belthe to preston, .12. mile
from preston to worcester, .26. mile
from worcester to euesham, .12. mile
from euesham to chipping norton, 14. mile
from chipping norton to islip, .12. mile
from islip to wickham, .20. mile
from wickham to beconsfield, .s. mile
from beconsfield to vxbridge, .7. mile
from vxbridge to london, .is. mile

From carnaruan to chester and so to london .199. mile

from carnaruan to conaway, .14. mile
from conaway to denbigh, .11. mile
from denbigh to flint, .12. mile
from flint to chester, .10. mile
from chester to wich, .is. mile
from wich to stone, .is. mile
from stone to lichfield, .18. mile
from lichfield to colesill, .12. mile
from colesill to couentry, .8. mile
from couentry to deuentry, .14. mile
from deuentry to tocester, .10. mile
from tocester to stony stratford, .6. mile
from stony stratford to brickhill, .7. mile
from brickhill to dunstable, .7. mile
from dunstable to S. albones, .10. mile
from S. albones to barnet, .10. mile
from barnet to london, .10. mile

From bristow to london, .97. mile

from bristow to maxesfall, .10. mile
from maxesfall to chipnam, .10. mile
from chipnam to marleborow, .is. mile
from marleborow to hungerford, 8. mile
from hungerford to newbury, .7. mile
from newbury to reading, .is. mile
from reading to maidenhead, .10. mile
from maydenhead to colbrooke, .7. mile
from Colbrooke to london, .is. mile

From bristoll to cambridge

from bristoll to sadbery, .10. mile

1.2 "How a man may journey from any notable towne in England, to the Citie of London," from Thomas Trevelyon's manuscript miscellany, "Epitome of ancient and modern history" (ca. 1606). Folger MS V.b. 232, fol. 35v.

the Rhombe and Distaunce, of some of the most famous Cities of the world, from the Honourable Citie of London" (fig. 1.3). While "How a man may journey" repeats much of the information presented in the printed broadside, Trevelyon evidently consulted an independent source in incorporating more towns and more routes than the broadside's design allowed for. Despite the greater complexity of his data, Trevelyon also had a single organizing principle. In his chart, many journeys are punctuated with the catch phrase, "and so to london," or, even more concisely, "to london."

Although the mileages in both the broadside and the miscellany can be calculated in both directions, in the former the emphasis is on travel *from* London, while in the latter the direction of default is the journey *to* London. The journey *to* is that with which history has traditionally been most preoccupied. The essential fuel for early modern London's engines was the great number of people who migrated there from the hinterlands, seeking to improve their material conditions and swelling the capital's population. By 1600 London had overtaken all European centers except Naples and Paris demographically; by 1700 it would eclipse these two cities, as well, achieving parity with the great metropolis of Constantinople. In 1600, London was thus thoroughly established as the English national lodestone. All roads and many dreams led to London.

Thomas Platter wrote in 1599 that "London is the capital of England and so superior to other English towns that London is not said to be in England, but rather England to be in London."[4] This is a fantasy to which many local, regional, and urban studies of sixteenth- and seventeenth-century England have appropriately given the lie.[5] Nonetheless, London retains a position in academic discourse to match the power it held in the early modern imagination. London had many guises: prehistoric settlement, Roman occupation, medieval city, and modern conurbation; capital city, seat of national government, and home of the monarch; great port of trade (unlike other European national capitals); cultural center, with a near monopoly on printing and publishing; emergent center of industry and of empire. Simply to review London's multiple identities is metonymically to call a roll of academic disciplines and subdisciplines: archaeology, urban studies, sociology, cultural anthropology, political history, intellectual history, court studies, economic history, literary history, the history of the book, and the history of art and architecture. Studies in all these areas have at one time or another taken London as their subject.[6]

The authors in this volume represent most of the fields cited above. Their essays are grouped in five sections which point up themes that cut across these disciplines. The contributors to Part I wrestle most comprehensively and

A Table of the Rhombe and Distaunce. of some of the most famous Cities of the world. from the Honorable Citie of London.

Names of the Cities.	Rhombe or poynt of the Compase,	Distance in miles	Sune riseth H M		Longest day Hour	Minnig
Quinzay,	East by South.	5300.	8.—52.	A	14. —	52.
Calecut.	Sou, Ea, by, East.	4840.	5.—48.	A	12. —	40.
Virginia,	West, Sou, West.	3650.	5.—32.	Po.	14. —	28.
Babilon.	East, Sou, East,	2710.	3.—46.	A	14 —	14.
Ierusalem.	Sou, Eeast, by East,	2320.	3.—6.	A	14. —	14.
Grand Cair.	Sou, East by East	2260.	2.—50.	A	14. —	2.
Alexandria,	Sou, East, by, East	2120,	2.—36.	A	14. —	6.
Moscove.	East, by, North,	1620.	2.—58.	A	14.17. —	8.
Constantinaple,	East, Sou, East,	1480.	2.—22.	A	17.15. —	24.
Athens,	Sou, East, by, East,	1440.	2.—2.	A	is 14. —	52,
Colmogro,	Nar, East, by, East,	1380.	2.—28.	A	20. —	6,
Marocco,	South, by, West,	1290,	0.—24.	Po.	14. —	13.
Rome.	South, East,	896.	1. 6.	A	is. —	4.
Siuell,	South, Westerly,	880.	0.—31.	Po.	14. —	40.
Lisbone	South, South, West,	830.	0.—33.	Po.	14. —	44.
Vienn	East, South, East,	776,	1.—18.	A	is. —	56.
Venice.	South, East, by, East,	720,	1.—4.	A	is. —	32.
Prage,	East, by, South,	640	1.—5.	A	16. —	10
Copenhge.	North, East, by, East,	510.	0.—50.	A	17. —	22,
Marcellis.	South, East, by, South,	450,	0.—32.	A	is. —	16.
Geneua,	South, East,	440,	0.—32.	A	is. —	34.
Burdeaux,	South, Easterly,	390,	0.—1.	A	is. —	26,
Rochell.	South, Westerly,	340,	0.—2.	Po.	is. —	36.
Dublin,	North, West, by, North	290,	0.—36,	Po.	16. —	44.
Edenbrough,	North, Nor, West,	286,	0.—16.	Po.	16 17. —	22.
Paris	South, East, by, South	240.	0.—14.	A	16. —	0.
Antwerpe,	East, South, East,	220.	0.—22.	A	16. —	16.
Middleborow.	Easte,	142.	0.—24.	A	16. —	25.

This former Table consisteth, 5 Columnes: the first whereof, conteineth, the names of Cities: the second, the rhombe or poynt of the Compasse they beare, from London. The third, the destaunce of each of them from the sayd Citie: the fourth the tyme of sune rysing before it douth at london. the 5. the longest day in these plaeces.

1.3. "A Table of the Rhombe and Distaunce, of some of the most famous Cities of the world, from the Honourable Citie of London," from Thomas Trevelyon's manuscript miscellany, "Epitome of ancient and modern history" (ca. 1606). Folger MS V.b. 232, fol. 24v.

directly with the larger "Meanings of Material London." Some consequences of London's role as a trade center are explored in Part II, "Consumer Culture: Domesticating Foreign Fashion." Part III, "Subjects of the City," deals with social hierarchies and with the ways in which social change constituted particularly urban sensibilities and subjectivities around 1600. The concerns of Part IV are the city's "Diversions and Display," its conspicuous consumptions, cosmopolitan tastes, and ready amusements. Part V, "Building the City," describes structures built, rebuilt, and unbuilt in the great population boom of the sixteenth and seventeenth centuries.

Contributors to the collection were not given assignments, nor was there any design that they should jointly compile a comprehensive view of London's history and representation. Those goals have been admirably fulfilled by A. L. Beier and Roger Finlay's *London, 1500–1700: The Making of the Metropolis* and by Lawrence Manley's *Literature and Culture in Early Modern London.*[7] Similarly, there was no intention of duplicating volumes that have consolidated the more frequently encountered approaches to London as the center of early modern English political culture and of theatrical culture, such as Linda Levy Peck's *Mental World of the Jacobean Court* and David L. Smith, Richard Strier, and David Bevington's *Theatrical City: Culture, Theater, and Politics in London, 1576–1649.*[8]

Instead, this collection began with a topic that aimed to be both sufficiently nondirective to allow for contributions from a wide range of disciplines — from anthropology and archaeology to literature and the fine arts — and also specific enough for a multivalent cogency. With one important variation, the process of compiling the volume followed the format for the American television game show *Jeopardy*. In the game, a category is established, an answer is revealed, and contestants are challenged to formulate the question appropriate to the given category which would result in the prescribed answer. The authors in this volume all undertook to question the same answer: "Material London, ca. 1600." In their disciplinary training, research interests, methodological practices, theoretical stances, and political convictions, however, each author constituted her or his own category. Thus each posed a different question. As it historically has done so often before, London once again proved its richness, throwing off multiple instances of interest and meaning. Because the process exposed some of the ways in which different academic cultures shape assumptions as well as conclusions, many of these are metameanings.

Among the larger issues of the volume are those concentrated in the three terms of the organizing topic: "material," "London," and "ca. 1600." Each of these terms is drawn into contention, and each comes most sharply into focus in one of the three essays of Part I. Derek Keene is the first to interrogate the chronological parameters "ca. 1600"; Alan Sinfield theorizes the meanings of the "material"; and David Harris Sacks initiates a volume-long discussion of the definition of "London."

Perhaps the most unexpected of the controversies engaged by this volume is that regarding its chronological referent, 1600. The date requires no justification among scholars of literary and political history, coinciding as it roughly does with the midpoint of William Shakespeare's playwriting career and with the end of the Elizabethan era and the inauguration of empire. Sacks fairly represents the sense of epoch with which people in these two fields are familiar. But Shakespeare never takes center stage here (appearing primarily as one in the company of theatrical entrepreneurs whose material progress Andrew Gurr charts), nor does Elizabeth I, nor does James I. These virtual non-appearances constitute one of the symptoms of the volume's revisionist nature, as the stories that have long dominated London's theatrical and political annals give ground to other ways of making meaning in our historical narratives.

By contesting the usual academic inclination to emphasize the radical singularity of any place or date under construction, Derek Keene poses a persuasive challenge to our habits of periodization. In "Material London in Time and Space," he argues that 1600 was not a moment of material re-definition for London. The demographic and commercial characteristics of sixteenth-century London were already well in place in the thirteenth century, and London's ascendance to the status of a world capital in 1700 was by no means an inevitable development of its position in 1600. Keene thus holds no brief for London "ca. 1600." John Schofield, who combines archaeological, documentary, and pictorial evidence for his survey of "The Topography and Buildings of London, ca. 1600," agrees with Keene that at the turn of the seventeenth century London remained essentially medieval, particularly as compared with urban centers on the Continent. Schofield recognizes the important architectural consequences of London's demographic explosion, as neighborhoods took on distinct characters, development pushed the urban bounds outward, properties of dissolved monasteries were adapted for city use, and public works and civic improvements were undertaken. But while many London structures of 1600 were unusual in the English context because of the city's peculiar functions and facilities, they were nonetheless not up to the Renaissance standards of great urban centers on the Continent. By such estimations as Keene's and Schofield's, in 1600 London had not yet made the material leap to modernity.

In "Building, Buying, and Collecting in London, 1600–1625," Linda Levy Peck carries Schofield's story of the built environment further into the seventeenth century, and she similarly recognizes London's comparative provincialism. The English urban elite had to look beyond London to the Continent for the architectural designs, paintings, and sculptures that London life had given them a taste for but that the London market did not yet provide. Nonetheless, in Peck's estimation the 1603 accession of James I marks an important turning point. The self-conceptualizations and material ambitions of English aristocrats were significantly transformed as they learned to cultivate European tastes, to desire personal splendor, and to develop a collecting culture. Correspondingly, Ann Rosalind Jones and Peter Stallybrass emphasize that London culture was remade in the early seventeenth century through the importation of styles from other countries. In " 'Rugges of London and the Diuell's Band': Irish Mantles and Yellow Starch as Hybrid London Fashion," Jones and Stallybrass observe that rough mantles and yellow starch were associated with the incivilities, crimes, and disorders held to be characteristic of the Irish — until, that is, both were adopted as fads by the Stuart court. If a pure English essence had once been identified in opposition to these foreign fashions, the accession of a Scottish king and the internationalized tastes of his court troubled the established paradigms. The court's "hybridity" (as Jones and Stallybrass term it) was responsible for changes that were not effected immediately in 1603 but that were incubated in 1603.

For Peck, Jones, and Stallybrass, the transition from Tudor to Stuart rule in 1603 was thus a watershed in elite culture. For Jane Schneider, meanwhile, 1600 is a convenient reference point for a watershed in mercantile culture. In "Fantastical Colors in Foggy London: The New Fashion Potential of the Late Sixteenth Century," Schneider demonstrates that the sober hues, sumptuary laws, and fashion proscriptions of the Tudor years were prophylactic responses to the inferiority of English cloths and dyes on the world market. Around 1600, however, the scene changed, and English goods began to dominate foreign ones. Joan Thirsk, who writes of London's commerce in provincial rather than international markets, also takes "1600" as a useful indicator for an economic divide of some significance.

For other authors in this collection, finally, "1600" assumes a more generalized meaning as a symbolic marker for the early modern era. Thus, my "Boundary Disputes in Early Modern London" assesses the impact of the population explosion of the Tudor and Stuart eras on London's "middling sort" of tradesmen and craftspersons. The mid-sixteenth-century decisions taken by a group called the London Viewers and the early seventeenth-century household surveys drawn by Ralph Treswell document a long history of neighborhood disputes over such issues as shared cesspits and blocked access. These records gain both chronological and emotional focus in the account book kept by London propertyholder Nicholas Geffe, who chronicles some of the ways in which the new urban density made itself felt in the life of an individual Londoner in the 1590s.

Even as responses to the chronological marker "1600" reveal the ways in which academic disciplines shape our assumptions, so, too, do interpretations of the second term of our project, "material." Derek Keene uses "material" in its strict sense, referring to such artifacts of culture as buildings, products, and objects in circulation. Many authors follow him: Joan Thirsk tracks the production of new consumer goods and foods; Jane Schneider outlines the history of textile manufacturing, importing, and exporting; Ann Rosalind Jones and Peter Stallybrass describe new elite fashions; and John Schofield tours the built city. David Harris Sacks takes a larger view, referring also to the material quality of "the product of people's intellects." But it remains for Alan Sinfield to voice the strongest argument for tracing "material" effects in cultural work. Briefly, he chronicles the progress of the term "material" in literary studies: first, its origin in the work of Raymond Williams; second, the development of "cultural materialism" as a critical, political practice; third, interrogations of the practice that have challenged it by privileging history; and, fourth, a strategic retreat to materialism in its narrower and more "objective" sense. Writing as a cultural materialist, Sinfield casts an ironic light on the newer preoccupations of literary historicism with objects and artifacts. In "*Poetaster*, the Author, and the Perils of Cultural Production," he argues that culture is always material (as opposed to "ideal") because it works in the networks of power that license or restrain it. The particular conditions of London around 1600 — its commercial activities, print industry, and public theater — were material to the early modern constitution of the author, which, in Ben Jonson's *Poetaster*, with its multiple models for the figure of the poet, found the critical voice of transgression.

The chapters by Linda Levy Peck, Ann Rosalind Jones and Peter Stallybrass, and Jane Schneider could be case studies of how the "material," in its narrower sense, takes on political meanings. These meanings do not all have the Marxist "edge" that Sinfield hones, but they amply demonstrate the inextricability of the mental and the material. Through both his resistance and also his eloquent insistence on larger implications, Sinfield establishes the theoretical framework that opens this collection up to subjects other than objects — to political ideology, social consciousness, gender dynamics, sexual practices, and to such work as that of Ian W. Archer, Gail Kern Paster, Jean E. Howard, and others.

Archer, for example, demonstrates that "Material Londoners" were keenly aware of their community's commercialization, as, through city pageants, civic ceremonies, and even church sermons, they found ways to celebrate trade and to incorporate it into their ethical systems. As Archer shows, the consumer culture may not have altered the prevailing tensions of age, gender, and rank, but it gave Londoners a new language for those tensions. Gail Kern Paster also looks at reinscriptions of difference in changing material conditions. She describes fashionable medical therapies as luxury commodities in "Purgation as the Allure of Mastery: Early Modern Medicine and the Technology of the Self," and she shows how London's wealthier residents flaunted their use of imported drugs and their quest for personal improvement. The purgative fads of high culture were, however, objects of satire in *The Family of Love*, a city comedy for the public theater. One aspect of London's largeness was the representational space it created for both the wealthy and the middling sorts, the landed and the mercantile classes. Their cultures survive not as text and subtext in the urban narrative, but as competing and coexistent texts.

London's commercialization introduced new meanings for gender as well as for status and taste. Again, they were mixed meanings. In "Women, Foreigners, and the Regulation of Urban Space in *Westward Ho*," Jean E. Howard demonstrates that 1599 marked the explosive emergence of city comedy as a new genre for the public stage. With their powerful female roles, these plays chronicled the high visibility of women workers and consumers in the urban environment; women contributed significantly to the polyphonic character of the city. At the same time, the plays addressed anxieties about how London's commercialization encouraged the infiltration of English culture by foreigners and their ways. The collaboratively authored city comedy *Westward Ho* depicts one adaptive strategy: male bonding, across all lines of origin, in the shared experience of misogyny. A pernicious consequence of London's material success was, thus, the new strain of gynephobia that developed from its xenophobia.

If city comedy appears as the informing genre of London in chapters by both Paster and Howard, Ben Jonson elsewhere emerges as the laureate of London. Alan Sinfield discusses a Jonson play; Ian W. Archer, a Jonson entertainment for the opening of the New Exchange; and Alice Friedman, a Jonson poem. Sinfield makes it clear how apt the emphasis is in this context. He refers to Jonson's *Poetaster* as providing "opportunities for materialists of all kinds"; the phrase could be taken to describe the entire collection.

The last term of our project, "London," also demonstrates its multiple significations. In "London's Dominion: The Metropolis, the Market Economy, and the State," David Harris Sacks outlines two ways of thinking about cities. The first model takes London as the single dominant community for the country, with supplies flowing into it from other towns and regions, with services flowing out from it, and with all England, and eventually all Britain, as its hinterland. The second model characterizes London as the "primate" or primary node in a network of urban centers. In two stories, one from high politics and one from popular culture, Sacks demonstrates that both urban models applied to early modern London. While the earl of Essex failed in his bid to seize the English throne because he did not understand the organizing terms of the new commercial culture, he was right to believe that to raise London was to effect a major rebellion; London was the dominant center for the kingdom. The report of Will Kemp's nine-day dance from London to Norwich, meanwhile, placed London as primate in a network of cities, with Norwich standing in for all the rival urban areas. In fact, the "Table of the cheiffest Cities, and Townes in England" (see fig. 1.1) perfectly anticipates Sacks's conclusion. In the "Table," London is positioned as the dominant center, with all other towns and cities as its hinterland. But it is also primate in the network of cities featured in the outer rim of the table's circle.

In Sacks's recounting, the earl of Essex and Will Kemp were unable to make their individual accommodations to the changing nature and character of the early modern city. As other authors in the collection make clear, there were also institutional battles for the constitution of London, in the differing concerns of the civic administration, the church hierarchy, the royal court, and the market. Andrew Gurr's "Authority of the Globe and the Fortune" presents a revisionist history of the enterprise of public theater within the framework of London's unique jurisdictional circumstances. City officials would have preferred to close the open-air gathering places, but their authority did not extend to the "liberties" outside the city's bounds, where these outdoor arenas were located. Meanwhile, long before 1600, the players themselves had recognized the advantages of indoor stages. But the interests of the Crown's agents, who relied on the public theaters as laboratories to develop plays that would eventually be brought to court, prevailed over the City's concerns and the players' desires. Thus, when such theaters as the Globe and the Fortune survived beyond what might have been their "natural" commercial or artistic lives, it was for political reasons. In "John Day and the Bookshop That Never Was," Peter W. M. Blayney tells another story from London's history of competing authorities. The description of Day's proposed bookshop is well known to historians of the book trade, who have extrapolated from it that "stalls" in St. Paul's Churchyard were temporary, even transportable structures. Blayney reveals that this description was deliberately misleading, part of a jurisdictional war between the Church, which aligned itself with the Crown, and the City. In this instance the City won, and Day's bookshop was never built.

Sacks is not alone in reminding us that the character of London cannot be considered independently of its relationship to the rest of the country. Joan Thirsk and Alice T. Friedman bring the provinces center stage, Thirsk unexpectedly suggesting that the provinces incited the appetites of London and Friedman oxymoronically characterizing country houses as London institutions. In "England's Provinces: Did They Serve or Drive Material London?" Thirsk recognizes the role of foreign goods, peoples, and influences in stimulating the English economy and raising its commercial standards. Still, she finds that while London's hinterlands strove to satisfy the new tastes, they also worked their own innovations on them. Thirsk thus revolutionizes our understanding of the relationship between center and "periphery" by showing how the established provincial infrastructures and regional specializations played important roles in the creation of a nationalized market. In "Inside/Out: Women, Domesticity, and the Pleasures of the City," Alice T. Friedman makes the case that the great Elizabethan country houses were thoroughgoing products of London in their design, building, furnishing, and culture. She also suggests that London's amusements lured some elite women out from behind these country-house walls, working against the cultural mandate for female seclusion and thus straining marital relations. The more that country houses were isolated from their rural surroundings, the more "London" they were in nature; the more "London" they were, the more the city itself exerted its pull on country-house occupants.

The porousness of London's borders for those at the opposite extreme of the social scale is explored by Patricia Fumerton. In "London's Vagrant Economy: Making Space for 'Low' Subjectivity," Fumerton argues that the city needed a vagrant class to move its goods into the countryside. The state of vagrancy also intersected with the character of London in the city's distinctive anonymity, transience, and alienation. In the multiple occupations that vagrants and others of the lower orders adopted and abandoned, Fumerton locates a process of sequential role speculations to which London apprentices, too, were susceptible, so that, as she posits, to be a Londoner was to experience a vagrancy of place, of status, or of identity. Through such analyses as those of Fumerton, Thirsk, Friedman, and others, it is apparent that "London" cannot be defined solely as a bounded area with a self-referencing population and autonomous interests. If London was a matter for all England, every English man and woman had a different "London." The city's definition incorporated multiple individual fantasies for betterment, splendor, and diversion; it also incorporated multiple individual disappointments and failures.

Fumerton is not the only one of our authors who expresses regret for the human costs of what she terms "the London economy and its far-reaching tentacles." In Jean E. Howard's analysis of the cultural coping strategies that developed in London's altered commercial climate, there are terrible implications for the history of gender politics and cross-cultural relations. Demonstrating how London's domination of Britain worked toward the nation's economic, political, and cultural integration, David Harris Sacks, like Fumerton, chooses a fairly ominous metaphor for the process, referring to London ideas, values, habits, and practices as "drawing more and more of England into its web." Joan Thirsk, similarly, laments the suppression of provincial character that was to result from a nationalized market and from what in other respects represented unargued material success: "the demands of material London were weaving a veritable spider's web, linking to itself and to each other scattered centers of production."

To look back to the illustration with which this chapter began is to be struck by how well Sacks's and Thirsk's arachnoid metaphor fits its dominant visual effect (see fig. 1.1). Once we might have been content with an astronomical metaphor for the "Table of the cheiffest Citties, and Townes in England" and might have accepted at face value the broadside's apparent positioning of the city as a nurturant sun. Now, however, we see also that the broadside shows us London in the character of an assiduous spinner, secreting its silk busily enough to send out snares for all of England. If we recognize that the consequences of "material London ca. 1600" were not matters only for celebration, that there were also costs to be reckoned, this is a sign of the kind of questions we have come to ask of our research subjects. As the earlier analogy to *Jeopardy* implied, much interest is in the questions.

Notes

1. I am grateful to Patricia Fumerton for calling my attention to this broadside.
2. A. L. Beier and Roger Finlay, eds., *London, 1500–1700: The Making of the Metropolis* (London: Longman, 1986).
3. Thomas Trevelyon, "Epitome of ancient and modern history" (ca. 1606), Folger Library MS. V.b.232, fol. 35v. Trevelyon also includes an illustrated London chronicle for the Elizabethan years, with an entry for each year and a brief biography of each (annually elected) mayor; his printed source was "A View of all the Right Honourable the Lord Mayors of London" (1601; STC no. 14343).
4. Excerpted in *Thomas Platter's Travels in England, 1599*, tr. and ed. Clare Williams (London: Jonathan Cape, 1937), p. 153.
5. For regional studies, see especially Peter Clark, *English Provincial Society from the Reformation to the Revolution: Religion, Politics, and Society in Kent, 1500–1640* (Sussex: Harvester Press, 1977); Anthony Fletcher, *A County Community in Peace and War: Sussex, 1600–1660* (London: Longman, 1975); Marjorie Keniston McIntosh, *Autonomy and Community: The Royal Manor of Havering, 1200–1500* (Cambridge: Cambridge University Press, 1986), *A Community Transformed: The Manor and Liberty of Havering, 1500–1620* (Cambridge: Cambridge University Press, 1991), and *Controlling Misbehavior*

in England, 1370–1600 (Cambridge: Cambridge University Press, 1998); Margaret Spufford, *Contrasting Communities: English Villagers in the Sixteenth and Seventeenth Centuries* (Cambridge: Cambridge University Press, 1974); Keith Wrightson and David Levine, *Poverty and Piety in an English Village: Terling, 1525–1700* (Oxford: Clarendon Press, 1995) and *The Making of an Industrial Society: Whickham, 1560–1765* (Oxford: Clarendon Press, 1991).

For town studies, see especially Peter Clark and Paul Slack, *English Towns in Transition, 1500–1700* (London: Oxford University Press, 1976); Alan David Dyer, *The City of Worcester in the Sixteenth Century* (Leicester: Leicester University Press, 1973) and *Decline and Growth in English Towns, 1400–1600* (Cambridge: Cambridge University Press, 1995); Sybil M. Jack, *Towns in Tudor and Stuart Britain* (New York: St. Martin's Press, 1996); Wallace T. MacCaffrey, *Exeter, 1540–1640: The Growth of an English County Town,* 2nd ed. (Cambridge: Harvard University Press, 1975); D. M. Palliser, *Tudor York* (Oxford: Oxford University Press, 1979); John Patten, *English Towns, 1500–1700* (Folkestone: Archon Books, 1978); David Harris Sacks, *Trade, Society, and Politics in Bristol, 1500–1640* (New York: Garland, 1985) and *The Widening Gate: Bristol and the Atlantic Economy, 1450–1700* (Berkeley: University of California Press, 1991).

6. It is impossible to give an exhaustive list, but books to which I am particularly indebted include Ian W. Archer, *The Pursuit of Stability: Social Relations in Elizabethan London* (Cambridge: Cambridge University Press, 1991); C. G. A. Clay, *Economic Expansion and Social Change: England, 1500–1700,* 2 vols. (Cambridge: Cambridge University Press, 1984); Lawrence Manley, ed., *London in the Age of Shakespeare: An Anthology* (University Park: Pennsylvania State University Press, 1986); Steven Rappaport, *Worlds Within Worlds: Structures of Life in Sixteenth-Century London* (Cambridge: Cambridge University Press, 1989); John Schofield, *Medieval London Houses* (New Haven: Yale University Press, 1995); and the titles mentioned below.

7. Beier and Finlay, *London, 1500–1700;* Lawrence Manley, *Literature and Culture in Early Modern London* (Cambridge: Cambridge University Press, 1995).

8. Linda Levy Peck, ed., *The Mental World of the Jacobean Court* (Cambridge: Cambridge University Press, 1991); David L. Smith, Richard Strier, and David Bevington, eds., *The Theatrical City: Culture, Theater, and Politics in London, 1576–1649* (Cambridge: Cambridge University Press, 1995).

PART I

MEANINGS OF MATERIAL LONDON

In 1599, visitor Thomas Platter wrote: "London is the capital of England and so superior to other English towns that London is not said to be in England, but rather England to be in London, for England's most resplendent objects may be seen in and around London." Platter pays tribute to one of London's identities as the kingdom's political center. With reference to London's "resplendent objects," he both alludes to another identity — the city's role as a commercial center — and implicates it in a strict interpretation of material culture as preoccupied with physical artifacts. But material London had many more meanings, meanings contested at the time and meanings contested in our time, as the essays in this section suggest.

In "London's Dominion: The Metropolis, the Market Economy, and the State," David Harris Sacks defines material culture as "things" — commodities, artifacts, people, and the products of people's intellects — "in motion." Early modern London, he asserts, was supremely a center of things in motion, in ways that made it both the engine and the product of change. With its astonishing population growth, sixteenth-century London became a city of newcomers as well as of new values. Launching his ill-fated rebellion, Essex believed that his dealings with Londoners followed the old rules of patron-client relations, and he counted on London to rise with him. But these understandings had been undone by the new relationship between city and Crown, with the Queen a greater benefactor than the earl could ever have been, and royal claims of authority more compelling than his call upon personal allegiance. While Essex misjudged his influence, he was probably right to think that to take London was to effect a major rebellion in England; it would seem from subsequent proclamations and sermons that the government suspected so, too. Meanwhile, Will Kemp depicted England's second largest city, Norwich, as *un*changing, a city that honored ancient traditions and social relations, maintained civic virtue, and welcomed his dance, a folk art form that had become outmoded in the London of the Globe theater. Kemp's pamphlet report demonstrates that London traded ideas, values, habits, and practices (as well as goods) with its hinterland. If Essex did not keep pace with the new urban reality, Kemp's nostalgia was a form of resistance to it. While Essex's story shows London as a dominant national center and Kemp's tale shows it as the primate in a network of cities, both demonstrate its new role in the political, economic, cultural, and material definition of Britain.

Derek Keene takes a longer view and adopts a more stringent definition of the "material." In "Material London in Time and Space," he argues that in 1600 London was "a city of the past and of the European periphery." The population explosion of the sixteenth century is a misleading indicator of change, he maintains. London had been as powerful a draw for migrants in 1300 as in 1600, but that earlier period of expansion was artificially terminated with high mortality rates from plague. Admittedly, there were new tastes and new commodities in 1600, but these had origins external to London and to the sixteenth century. First, the expanded consumer culture of London was thoroughly dependent on the Low Countries, where England's unfinished woolen cloth was marketed and through which the products of other countries were funneled. This was true for both high and low goods; European products were cheaper because of their systems of specialization and distribution. Second, the infrastructure of English markets and systems of transportation had been established long before the sixteenth century. Third, it was not until the religious crises of Europe that London became an attractive destination for substantial numbers of highly skilled Dutch craftsmen, who immigrated with their tools and new ideas. Even so, London did not displace the Netherlands as a dominant center of exchange and material culture until about 1700. That which came to account for London's real material revolution, Keene suggests, was its access to coal for fuel. Needing less firewood, the city developed more densely, and density facilitated the exchange of information and ideas. By 1700, London was engaged in traffic with the New World, had rebuilt to European standards following the Great Fire, and was producing higher quality goods. Owing much to external factors, these phenomena did not necessarily follow from the material state of London around 1600.

In "*Poetaster*, the Author, and the Perils of Cultural Production," Alan Sinfield takes back the meaning of "the material" for literary studies. He and other cultural materialists introduced the term in demonstrating that culture cannot transcend the material nature of its production, the power relations within which it is framed. In his analysis of Ben Jonson's *Poetaster*, Sinfield identifies the role London played (ca. 1600) in the constitution of its authors, through its several identities as the capital of the kingdom, center for printing, and permanent home for commercial theater. Jonson imagines the author in four possible positions: state servant, court or gentry amateur, writer under patronal protection, and writer in the market. Inhabiting three of these locations — and, for all his disapproval of the market, betraying the "excitement" of writing for London's public theater — Jonson acquired the "distanciation" required for a critical authorial function. *Poetaster* does not, as has been said, endorse the universality of art or condone a politically convenient ideology.

Instead, Horace's suspicion of the tyrannical Caesar represents a key point at which the possibility and desirability of a critical intelligentsia is announced in early modern England. Jonson thus does more than document the author function; he helps to constitute it. In this, *Poetaster* illustrates Foucault's thesis that the author emerges "to the extent that his discourse was considered transgressive." In a coda, Sinfield traces in *Poetaster* a discourse of *sexual* transgression, suggesting that illicit cross-sex relations, which bore serious consequences for property distribution and social order, were far more culturally disruptive than same-sex relations.

If, topically, the essays in this section seem disparate, they share space because, procedurally, they are so forthcoming. Each author is explicit in declaring his frame of reference, stating his assumptions, and arguing his premise. It can appear that three Londons come into focus here — the political capital best referenced by Sacks, the center of trade measured critically by Keene, and the cultural capital politically theorized by Sinfield. But this is to put matters in the crudest terms. As is made clear by each author in turn, London's other meanings were implicated in any one of its roles. Taken together, these essays illustrate the principle of inclusion that governs the volume, and they indicate the many meanings of the "material" that are in play for the chapters that follow.

2

London's Dominion

The Metropolis, the Market Economy, and the State

David Harris Sacks

Sociologists and urban historians normally study urban development according to one of two paradigms. One school thinks of cities as densely settled and complexly organized communities situated at the center of a well-defined rural hinterland on which they each depend for supplies and to which they provide services. A second school views them as nodal points in an organized urban system — a network of urban centers in a web of relations with the others, each providing specialized functions for the system as a whole.[1] For most cities, these two approaches normally represent analytical alternatives. However, early modern London is different. It was not just the dominant — the primate — city in England's, and later in Britain's, developing urban system, but, since it drew its supplies, new inhabitants, and markets from the four corners of the land, it also had most of England, and later much of Britain, as its hinterland.[2]

In this chapter, I consider London from this double perspective — as primate city and as dominant central place, stressing London's role in the economic, political, and cultural integration of the English, and then the British, state and nation. I begin with a discussion of the concept of the "material" as it applies to early modern London.

Materialism and the Market Economy

London loomed large in the imagination of late Elizabethan and early Stuart England. For John Davies of Hereford, it was "the Faire" that "lasts all year," a perpetual market, in contrast to the traditions prevailing elsewhere according to which fairs and markets occurred only at specific times and in specific places.[3] By Elizabeth's reign, London had long been deemed the proverbial measure for wealth, against which the riches of other English places were compared. With equal point, it was viewed as a proverbial site of dissension, where not even the tolling bells could agree on the hour; a crowded place, full of jostling bodies on the streets and the sound of angry words; and a community of "lickpennies," peopled by men and women who would lick up all the treasure of the kingdom if allowed. It is noteworthy that the last of these maxims is the earliest and also the most enduring.[4]

What, then, of the city's role in the realm of the "material"? Archaeologists and anthropologists often use the term "material culture" to identify the physical objects or artifacts — the tools, the dwellings, and the articles of domestic and religious use — that mark a particular society's or social group's way of life. This definition focuses attention primarily on the way physical objects fit into the daily routines and the life cycles of people living within a self-contained community or society viewed synchronically.[5] Lisa Jardine has characterized European society in the Renaissance in light of a similar conception, as dominated by what she calls "worldly goods" and the corresponding emergence in the period of a "culture of commodities." This material Renaissance was a world that gave primacy to places like London whose very life turned on the provision of material things, necessities as well as luxuries, to customers far and wide. But its culture is understood mainly as one of consumption and display rather than of production and exchange.[6]

However, no city's history, let alone that of a large and growing one such as early modern London, can be understood exclusively in such terms. As Fernand Braudel has observed, towns "were born of the oldest and most revolutionary division of labour: between work in the fields on the one hand and the activities described as urban on the other. . . . Where there is a town, there will be a division of labour, and where there is any division of labour there will be a town."[7] Since "even the humblest town-dweller must of necessity obtain his food-supply" from the town market,[8] no town could ever possess its own autonomous, unique, and fixed material culture, or be fully self-sufficient, however autonomous it might be in its governance. Too many of the objects that defined its way of life came from its hinterlands or beyond the seas.[9]

Braudel's analysis distinguishes between what he calls "economic civilization," dependent on market exchange, and "material civilization," that " 'other half' of production which refuses to enter fully into the movement of exchange," and changes, if at all, only at a glacial pace.[10] Early modern cities, London no less than others, depended in some measure on traditional practices typically associated with this second side of civilized life, particularly in the formation of business connections, apprenticeship ties, and neighborhood associations.[11] But what created their distinctively urban character was market exchange which facilitated the necessary movement of goods to and from cities. On this understanding, cities epitomize the exchange element in the economy, and represent, to use Braudel's terminology, the paradigm of economic life in contrast to material civilization.[12]

How then should we conceptualize the "material" dimension in early modern London's urban way of life? An analogy, derived from an early modern tradition of philosophical "materialism," draws attention to the vital role of motion and change in the material world. For Thomas Hobbes anything evidencing change was by definition a material object, since change could be imagined only as motion, and motion only as an alteration in spatial location, and any change in location necessarily requires the action of another material object upon it.[13] This form of "materialism" evokes a world of things in motion. The material life of early modern London can be conceived in much the same fashion; its life depended upon its participation in a world of things in motion — commodities, artifacts, people, and the products of people's intellects; a world whose success was evidenced by the fact of change. Indeed, Hobbes, who found those dwelling in "populous Cities" full of "insincerenesse, inconstancy, and troublesome humor," himself equated city life with the "mobility . . . of the Aire."[14]

The Calculus of Urban Growth

In the history of London, the most evident signs of movement and change appear in the records of early modern demographic growth. London's population stood at perhaps 40,000–50,000 in 1500, 200,000 in 1600, and 500,000–575,000 in 1700. In 1500, ten European cities, excluding Constantinople, had more inhabitants than London and six others had roughly the same population; in 1600, only two European urban places — Naples and Paris — exceeded the English capital in size, and neither by a very large margin. In 1700, London probably stood alone as the largest urban place in Europe with only Paris as a near rival. To look at this growth from a domestic perspective, in 1500 London was four times larger than the next most populous cities in England and Wales, more than fifteen times larger in 1600, and perhaps twenty times larger in 1700.[15]

Several features stand out in these statistics. First, and most evident, is London's exceedingly rapid growth — a 1,000 to 1,500 percent increase in two hundred years. During the same interval, Paris, London's nearest Continental rival, had grown only about fivefold. Second, London seems to have led the way in the relatively rapid urbanization of England and Wales as a whole. In 1500, perhaps 3 percent of the English and Welsh lived in significant-sized cities of 5,000 or more; of these, about half resided in London. In 1700, the proportion of urban residents in England and Wales stood at 17 percent; about three quarters of whom lived in London.[16] Although other English and Welsh towns expanded in the period, their growth was just a fraction of what London experienced. In 1500, for example, the population of Norwich — England's second largest city — stood at 10,000; in 1700, it was about 29,000 — less than a threefold increase. In 1500, Bristol — England's second port — was perhaps a shade smaller than Norwich, with, say, 9,500 inhabitants; in 1700, it had something in excess of 20,000 — representing a rise in population of perhaps 200 or 250 percent. None of the other major towns of the realm grew by as much. Nevertheless, in the course of this period England, starting from its low base and building on London's accelerating expansion, was becoming the most rapidly urbanizing region in the world. In 1700, when the proportion of its urban residents stood at 17 percent, it was the third most urbanized region in the world, after the Low Countries and northern Italy.[17]

A third feature — even more striking — is London's dominating role in the demography of England and Wales. While London's population soared between 1500 and 1700, the total number of the English and Welsh had only a little more than doubled from 2.4 to 5.06 million. To put this point in simple statistical terms, in 1500 London's inhabitants accounted for only about 1.5 percent of the English and Welsh population; in 1700, they represented around 11.5 percent. This means that over time the metropolis's own growth not only represented an increasingly large percentage of the population as a whole, but absorbed an increasingly large share of the growth. In consequence, around 1700, as E. A. Wrigley has observed, "a sixth or even higher fraction" of "the total population of England . . . at some stage" would have had "direct experience of life in the great city."[18]

This fact meant that London was very much a city of newcomers, increasingly so as the era wore on. In the decades either side of 1600, 2 percent or more of the population in any given year would have been immigrants, mostly single men and women in their late teens and early twenties.[19] Many of those who came were subsistence migrants and vagrants, whom the city authorities and Crown officials viewed with increasing alarm as their numbers grew after 1580. In this respect, London's extraordinary growth was accompanied by a significant increase in poverty and its problems.[20] But at least a third, and perhaps half, of London's newcomers in this period came to the city as apprentices, seeking opportunities to start careers. Those who stayed to take the freedom of the city enjoyed reasonably good chances for social mobility, although meteoric rises were quite rare. They also entered a sociopolitical world which depended to a striking degree on high levels of popular participation in local office and on cooperation among people of disparate social backgrounds in a variety of private and public tasks.[21]

Finally, the breakthrough period for this growth was the sixteenth century. During this hundred-year interval, the urbanization of England is accounted for mainly by the extraordinary increase in the size of London itself. Between 1500 and 1600 there had been a tripling or quadrupling of the city's total population, with much of the increase occurring without the walls and in the suburbs.[22] It was in this era that England's trade began its turn away from its concentration in the Low Countries toward ventures in wider European, Atlantic, and Asian markets, focusing on the luxury wares these regions produced. In the same period, domestic production took its first important moves toward the so-called "new draperies" to supply these foreign markets and toward new items of food and drink to meet the increasingly varied tastes of London's wealthier residents and its provincial customers.[23]

London's *material* preeminence in English society around 1600 was above all a dominion in demography, the consequence of the accumulated movements of people into the city over the previous century. Was it anything more?

The Metropolis and the Archipelago

Charles Tilly, arguing for a sharp distinction between regimes based on coercive state power and regimes based on market exchange, has proposed that "very different sorts of states" evolve "in densely urban regions and in regions with few cities," largely because of the differential presence of merchants and financiers. Nevertheless, he has singled out England along with France as representing the middle ground between a "coercion-intensive" mode of state formation in which "rulers squeezed the means of war from their own populations and others they conquered, building massive structures of extraction in the process" and a "capital-intensive" mode in which "rulers relied on compacts with capitalists—whose interests they served with care—to rent or purchase military force, and thereby warred without building vast permanent state structures." England and France represent a third paradigm, where "rulers did some of each" and "holders of capital and coercion interacted on terms of relative equality." Tilly calls this paradigm the "capitalized coercion mode."[24]

But there is an obvious difference between the British case and the French or other Continental monarchies. State formation in the latter occurred on contiguous land masses, bounded by neighboring territorial states. Hence political integration required the exact definition of land borders and their maintenance against potential and actual enemies as well as the establishment of internal dominion and order throughout the state's territory.[25] The British Isles, however, constitute an archipelago stretching across hundreds of miles of water from the English Channel into the North Atlantic and North Sea. A problem of internal order remains, of course, nowhere more so than in the Welsh and Scottish borderlands.[26] But after the dynastic union in 1603, the most important boundaries of the emerging British state were formed by water, giving special emphasis to its port towns and making direct comparison to France somewhat problematic.[27]

In the British Isles, urban-based mechanisms of market exchange, and the stabilizing structures and networks they created, balanced reliance on military force in bringing about stable internal order. On this score it is significant that as England, and then Britain, rose in the ranks of urbanized regions between 1500 and 1700 with the percentage of its urban population increasing three or perhaps even fourfold, French urban growth did not keep pace. In the same period, the percentage of its urban population grew by less than 15 percent. It is equally telling that while France is ruled from Paris, a centrally located inland city and river port, England, and later the British Isles as a whole, is ruled from London, the kingdom's greatest seaport, whose revenues, directly and indirectly, were a principal source of fiscal support to the monarchy, albeit often at the price of concessions to particular interests. For these reasons, it was frequently called the "Kinges chamber."[28]

Led by London's soaring growth, this phenomenon of urbanization was archipelagian, affecting Scotland and Ireland as well as England. In 1500, the most populous urban centers in the British Isles after London had been Norwich, Bristol, York, Salisbury, and Exeter, each no more than a quarter of London's size; in all, there were only eleven English towns with populations of 5,000 or more. Edinburgh's population probably did not and Dublin's certainly did not exceed 5,000. In 1600, there were twenty English towns, headed by Norwich, with 5,000 or more inhabitants, but the second-ranked city was Edinburgh with 30,000 inhabitants. Dublin had reached 5,000, Galway about 4,000, Limerick about 3,000, and Waterford about 2,000. By 1700, Dublin, with 60,000 inhabitants, was the second largest city in Britain, and Edinburgh, at 40,000, was the third. At this time, there were thirty-two English towns with populations of 5,000 or more, with Norwich, at 30,000, as the metropolis's nearest English rival. In Scotland, Glasgow, which had had a population of about 2,000 in 1600, expanded more than sixfold to 13,000 by 1700, and Aberdeen reached about 6,000 inhabitants. In Ireland, Cork, Limerick, Waterford, and Galway also grew rapidly, with Cork increasing in size by 1250 percent, Limerick by 367 percent, Waterford by 150 percent, and Galway by 25 percent in the course of the seventeenth century. A crude estimate would put the urban population of the British Isles as a whole in 1700 at perhaps 12 percent.[29]

London's extraordinary early modern expansion was a principal force driving these trends. By the end of the seventeenth century the booming ports in Ireland, all located in the south and west, had already joined the southern European and Atlantic trading networks dominated by London, while in Scotland the desire to gain access to this same network of commerce and finance was driving the move for political union with England.[30] Through the command that Londoners had over credit, and through their demand for goods of all sorts and their aggressive engagement in the trade of every region, London was turning England, and later the British Isles as a whole, into a single integrated national market, with a systematically organized urban hierarchy, composed of distinct tiers of urban centers, each economically commanding its own immediate hinterland as well as performing specific functions for the urban system as a whole. As London exploded in size and importance, it came to dominate the entire urban network while lesser cities and towns consolidated their range of connections nearer to home and took on specialized roles peculiar to their geography and conditions. Goods and people passed along the roads, the navigable rivers, and sea lanes that held this network together — so did ideas, styles of life, and power. These developments gave the English, and then the emerging British, state a strong urban base and system of market exchange on which to build its organization.[31]

The Earl's Folly

Material London, in the sense of which we have been speaking — the burgeoning metropolis that was simultaneously the engine and the product of change in society and the state — found a place in the history of the early modern period not merely as a social fact, operating below the level of everyday awareness, but also as a social force discernible at the time.[32] To grasp the significance of its contribution to the considered choices and purposive actions of the English around the year 1600, I want to turn to two circumstantial narratives — tales of metropolitan dominion — each well known in its own right. The earlier concerns Will Kemp's famous nine days' wonder, his Morris dance from London to Norwich, during Lent 1600; in 1600, Ash Wednesday fell on 11 February. The second narrative centers on the earl of Essex's "rebellion" — his abortive coup d'état — which occurred on 9 February 1601, almost exactly a year later.

The earl's story is certainly the more important in conventional historical terms, but in many respects it is also the less unusual — the earl hardly being the first Englishman, even in Elizabeth's reign, to have failed in an attempted rising against the monarch or the royal counselors. While Kemp's long-distance dancing was not entirely unique — Kemp himself mentions a man named Foskew who covered part of the same route — the number of his predecessors was exceedingly small.[33] His tale is also, in some respects at least, the more revealing for our purposes. But its significance will be clearer if we take up Essex's comedy of errors before we turn to Kemp's carnival in Lent.

The story of Essex's rebellion, often retold, still awaits its definitive history.[34] I propose to provide only its bare outline here, emphasizing the role of London in it. Robert Devereux, the second earl of Essex, was Queen Elizabeth's cousin on his mother's side, the stepson of Robert Dudley, earl of Leicester (who was a particular favorite of Elizabeth's), and the husband to Frances, the daughter of Sir Francis Walsingham, principal secretary to Elizabeth's privy council between 1573 and 1590; Frances, his wife, was the widow of Sir Philip Sidney, who in his own right had been Leicester's nephew. From Essex's first arrival at court in the mid-1580s, when he was in his late teens, he had risen quickly to become another favored figure of the Queen; after his stepfather's death in 1588, he succeeded to the leadership of the coterie of friends and clients that Leicester had cultivated and that had looked to Sir Philip Sidney as his political heir. By the mid-1590s Essex was engaged in a pointed rivalry with the Cecils, father and son, for the domination of patronage and policy, a rivalry which only became the more heated with the death of Lord Burghley in 1598.[35]

The earl's career took its dramatic turn for the worse at an ill-fated meeting with the Queen soon after Burghley's death. The matter under discussion concerned who to send as military commander in Ireland, where troubles with the O'Neils in the north were already underway and about to get much worse. William Camden, to whom we owe this story, says that Essex had picked out Sir George Carew, a court rival, for this unwanted task, "that so he might ridde him from the Court." But despite his best efforts, the earl could "not by perswasions draw" Elizabeth "unto it." According to Camden, Essex "forgetting himselfe, and neglecting his dutie, uncivily turneth his backe, as it were in contempt, with a scornfull looke. She waxing impatient, gave him a cuffe on the eare, and bade him be gone with a vengeance. He layd his hand upon his sword, the Lord Admirall interposing himselfe, hee sware a great oath, that he neither could nor would swallow so great an indignitie, nor would have borne it at King *Henry* the 8. his hands; and in great discontentment hasted from the Court."[36] Eventually, through the intercession of Thomas Egerton, the lord keeper of the Great Seal, the matter was patched up between the Queen and her once-favorite, but not before Essex himself had to take on the thankless assignment of command in Ireland to quell the earl of Tyrone's rebellion.

The earl's disastrous expedition, and his even more disastrous, unauthorized return from thence to Nonsuch in late September 1599, led quickly to his arrest and a trial in the Star Chamber by a commission of counselors meeting in the presence of two hundred distinguished onlookers. The humiliation of the occasion was more than matched by the punishment the commission laid down. He was placed under house arrest at the Queen's discretion and stripped of his membership in the Privy Council and of his offices of earl marshall and master of the ordnance, leaving him with just the mastership of the horse, his earliest honor. Only in late August was he finally freed from house arrest but warned to keep himself from the court.[37]

These events bring us to September 1600, when the earl's patent for sweet wines, his principal source of income, came due. Never well endowed with landed revenues and already fending off his numerous creditors, Essex was now in dire financial straits, perhaps £25,000 in debt, with interest payments amounting to about £1,500 a year, and an annual income reduced to less than £4,500, only a little over half of what it had been when he had the sweet wines.[38] Toward the end of September, Essex wrote Elizabeth a letter begging for the renewal of his patent, speaking of how in the absence of the Queen's favor his "poor estate" and his inability "of satisfying a great number of hungry and annoying creditors" robbed him of any "hope of ability to do your Majesty future service." "If my creditors will take for payment many ounces of my blood," he says, "or the taking away of this farm would only for want finish my body, your Majesty would never hear of this suit."[39] In October four more letters followed, asking the Queen "for access and an end of this exile."[40] This string of correspondence ended on the Queen's accession day, 17 November, with a truly plaintive letter in which he speaks of himself as "a man . . . dead to the world . . . exercised with continued torments of mind and body . . . full of pain, full of sickness, full of sorrow, languishing in repentance for his offenses past, hateful to himself that he is yet alive, and importunate on death, if your sentence not be revocable." All he wants, he says, is to join those who "feel the comfortable influence of your Majesty's favor, or stand in the bright beams of your presence [and] rejoice partly for your Majesty's, but chiefly for their own, happiness."[41] Even this descent into abject obsequiousness failed.

According to Sir John Harington, it was at about this moment that Essex "shifteth from sorrow and repentance to rage and rebellion" and that "strange words, bordering on strange designs" began to flow openly from him.[42] In disgrace and barred from court for the past year, he threw open the gates of his house to discontented noblemen and soldiers, a string of out-of-favor Puritan preachers, and even some Catholics—people on the margins of public affairs—hoping, it appears, to have his "popularity" produce for him the political leverage that his personal appeals could not.[43]

With his colleagues, Southampton, Rutland, and the others, he began plotting to arrest his political enemies at court and to force his way into the Queen's presence. In the midst of this fantasizing, however, Essex, believing that "the citie of london stood" for him, abruptly changed course. Telling his co-conspirators that Thomas Smythe, one of London's two sheriffs, "had giuen hym intelligence that he would make as many menne to assyst him as he could," he now declared he was determined "to possesse . . . himselfe of the citie" the "better to enable himselfe to revenge himselfe of his enemyes."[44] "Whilst disputation was holden about the love of the *Londoners*, and the uncertaine disposition of the vulgar," Camden tells us, "behold one came in of set purpose, as if he had beene sent from the Citizens, making most large promises of aide from them against all his adversaries. Here the Earle being cheered, began to discourse how much he was favoured throughout the City, and perswaded himself by the former acclamations of the people, and their hateful murmurrings against his adversaries, that very many were most devoted to his fame and fortune."[45] This belief was widespread among the conspirators. Henry Cuffe, one of Essex's confidants, in trying to recruit Sir Henry Neville into the conspiracy, "made account that the affection of the Citty was sure" to the earl, "and that of 24 Aldermen" Essex and his supporters "held them selves assured of xx or xxi."[46] These wishful thoughts predisposed Essex to look to Smythe and the "thousand trained souldiers" he commanded to "assist him on all occasions."[47] According to Camden, he resolved to ride into the city on the next day, a Sunday, and approach the aldermen and others gathered for the sermon at St. Paul's to ask their aid against his enemies. The surviving evidence supports the existence of this bizarre plan.[48]

Just how the earl came to his misapprehensions about London is uncertain—he may well have been the victim of an *agent provocateur.*[49] At about the same moment the leading Crown officials, apprised of the meetings at Essex's house, precipitated the earl into rebellion by summoning him to the council board. When four senior counselors appeared at his house—including the controller of the Queen's household, Sir William Knollys, his own uncle, and Thomas Egerton, his greatest supporter at court—Essex had them locked in his study and with two hundred followers started off on horseback for Sheriff Smythe's house near the Exchange, seeking the expected help from the London Trained Bands. Although crowds formed along the streets, only a handful of onlookers were prepared to join the lightly armed troop of colleagues, friends, and hangers-on who had entered London with the earl.[50]

At Smythe's house, the earl discovered the depth of his error. Smythe denied any willingness to aid him, and instead urged that if he felt himself in danger from his enemies, he place himself under the protection of the lord mayor to await the Queen's command. In the meantime, the mayor and aldermen, acting on orders from the Crown, began securing the city against the earl. The gates were closed and guarded, and the principal streets chained. For his part the earl was now at a complete loss what to do. He took a few halberds from Smythe's house and headed through Cheapside to St. Paul's churchyard, apparently waiting for a rising of the populace on his behalf. But nothing happened. The rest of the day's events, including a brief but bloody battle at Ludgate with some of the London Trained Bands, resulted from Essex's efforts to extricate himself from the city and return to his house on the Strand. By the time he did so—it required an exit by water—the house was surrounded. Finally, long after dark, the earl surrendered to face the now inevitable outcome: trial, conviction, last-minute repentance, and execution.[51]

The interest of these events concerns not just the earl's instinct to look to London for support, but the city's role in thwarting him. Thomas Smythe is the key to understanding both. The connections between him and the earl were quite deep. Smythe, a London Haberdasher, born about 1558, was the second surviving son of Thomas Smythe, also a London Haberdasher, who in 1557 became a collector of customs in the port of London, a position which yielded him important connections as well as vast wealth. By the time Essex met with him on Fenchurch Street, Sheriff Smythe had been a prominent figure in the Merchant Adventurers Company, the Russia Company, and the Levant Company, and was simultaneously Governor of the Levant Company and of the newly founded East India Company. These positions put him in the forefront of developments in English commercial society that went hand-in-hand with the emergence of London's new consumer economy in the Elizabethan era. He had been selected as alderman for the ward of Fenchurch Street Without in November 1599 and as sheriff the following year.[52]

Facing Crown officials eager to get to the bottom of the Essex conspiracy, Smythe was careful to distance himself from the earl. According to the testimony of his brother, Sir John Smith, of Westenhanger, Kent, who himself was sheriff of Kent in 1600, Thomas, returning home on the evening of 8 February for a brief respite from the day's turmoil, had insisted that he could not fathom what had caused the earl to come to his house: "He did protest before god," Sir John testified, "that could not imagine any cause and did very constantly afferme that he never in his lyffe speake wth hym but once and that ix yeares past and he then desired hyme to be bound for hym as my father formerly had bine but he desired his L. to pardon hyme and did it not, and since that tyme he never speake wth hyme nor never receaved meassage nor letter but one letter lattly wrightine touching some matter of the India company."[53] But the story is more complex than Sir John and his brother Thomas would have their interrogators believe. From what we are able to piece together, there was good reason for the earl to think he could count on the sheriff.[54]

One reason had to do with the intimate ties that the elder Thomas Smythe ("Mr. Customer Smythe" as he was known throughout his later life) had maintained with the earl of Leicester, Essex's uncle, and later with Essex himself. Customer Smythe was married to the daughter of Sir Andrew Judd, a prominent London skinner, sometime Lord Mayor of London and mayor of the Merchants of the Staple, and a founding assistant of the Muscovy Company. Smythe, the father, was also a charter member of the Muscovy Company and later of the Levant Company. In the 1560s, he became a principal investor and licensee and then a shareholder of the Company of Mines Royal, and in 1570 he began an eighteen-year stint as farmer of the customs inward of London, and subsequently of Chichester, Sandwich, Southampton, Ipswich, and the creek of Woodbridge. Significantly, these connections brought the father into the circle of the earl of Leicester, who was also a founding investor in the Company of Mines Royal and a member of the Russia Company of 1580. The two men were quite close. During Customer Smythe's life he acquired substantial landed estates from Leicester and on at least one occasion had the earl to dine privately at his house along with the Spanish ambassador.[55]

It was Leicester who had initially held the farm of the sweet wines and who had consigned it to Customer Smythe in return for payment of £3,500 a year. When Leicester died in 1588, and the farm of the sweet wines passed to Essex, Customer Smythe continued to handle collections, maintaining the same relationship he had previously enjoyed with the uncle. And when Smythe himself died in 1591, his obligations to Essex seem to have passed to his son Thomas, at least for the remaining term of Essex's existing lease, which did not expire until September 1593. It was apparently this relationship that the younger Smythe declined to continue.[56] Essex himself was not a heavy investor in commercial and mining enterprises, no doubt because his capital resources were habitually so strained. But others in his following — Southampton, Sir Ferdinando Gorges, and Sir Edward Michelbourne to name several — had interests quite similar to those maintained in the previous generation by Leicester and Sir Henry Sydney, and by Sir Francis Walsingham, Essex's father-in-law; Michelbourne was a charter member of the East India Company.[57]

Essex also had a few clients in the city, notably Giles Fletcher the elder, the city remembrancer, whom he had been able to use on previous occasions to engage the aldermen in favor of his aggressive foreign and military policy. Fletcher's presence itself shows the continued importance of the old Russia Company connection that had started under Leicester. In addition, the earl had sufficient influence to win the freedom of the city for some of his servants, including one granted to Arthur Strangeways in April 1600, while the earl was still under house arrest.[58] Finally, the lavish credit that his sweet wine patent had permitted him was largely owed in London as well; for example, in October 1600 he was indebted to the Chamber of the City to the tune of £2,100, to Alderman William Craven for £1,000, and to John Swynnerton, in his capacity as the farmer of wine imposts, for another £1,315; Swynnerton's son, John junior, was another charter member of the East India Company. Several other creditors were also among the company's founding investors: Sir John Harte, John Robinson, Ury Babbington, and Nicholas Crispe; significantly, Crispe was "partener with Thomas Smithe in his trade of merchandise." In total, Londoners or the city of London itself were creditors for at least half of the £16,000 the earl owed at the time.[59]

On these grounds, Essex could easily have convinced himself of the strong bonds London and the Londoners had with him. This view would only have been reinforced at the end of September 1600, a few short weeks after he was finally released from house arrest, when the members of the newly formed East India company approached him to use his influence with the Queen and her counselors to assist with the earliest of their enterprises, a voyage to the East Indies under the command of Captain John Davies, identified by the company members as Essex's "servant." The letter, "humbly presuminge vppon yo[r] L: rediness to further anie enterprise w[ch] may bring hono[r] to o[r] country or benefit to the comonwealth" asks Essex's "favo[rs] to be . . . added to this busines and to give your L: Consent for his imployment in the same." It concludes by saying that should Essex grant this request the Company "shall accompte yo[r] L: an honorable patron therof." The earl seems to have willingly obliged.[60]

Nevertheless, Essex had misjudged his relations with the city and his power within it. He viewed his dealings with the Londoners in light of the rules governing ordinary patron-client relations, according to which a good turn once given bound the recipient for the long term in loyalty and good will to his benefactor.[61] In this, the earl's "rebellion" arguably represents something new, since unlike his rebel predecessors, such as Wat Tyler or Jack Cade, he was not aiming to conqueror the city against resistance, but calling on its debt of honor to him and the putative alliance the earl and the city had with each other for their mutual benefit and advantage.[62]

But as efficacious as patron-client relationships could be in holding social relations together, they were insufficient to the earl's problem. It is not just that aristocratic patronage focused on the patron's ability to assist his clients in gaining royal favor, and that with Essex's precipitous fall from grace, his utility to his clients was at a stay, if not an end. Although he may still have had a personal hold on servants such as Captain Davies, he could do little good at court, or elsewhere, for them. Nor is it simply that London's leading citizens also had the Queen as a benefactor and that their new commercial enterprises to Muscovy, the Levant, the East Indies, and so on depended on royal charters of incorporation and patents of monopoly for their very existence. In effect, the very monopolies that Leicester and Essex and other noble patrons had helped secure for these powerful Londoners were vehicles in transferring from themselves to the monarch and the monarchy the loyalty that arose in patron-client relations. Equally important was the protection these same figures received from the law for their property rights, their contracts, and their credit, as well as the stability that came to social relations and market exchange from their relationship to the emerging urban network and to the developing English state.

The model of patron-client relations could not stand up to these more powerful claims of authority and obedience. This point was confirmed by Henry Cuffe in his declaration from the scaffold. When asked to explain his remarks to Sir Henry Neville about the loyalties of the London aldermen, he insisted that "he ment that of the 24 Aldermen, 21 were assured vnto the Earle in loue, & . . . I am sure they were. but not that he meant that they were assured vnto him to take Armes for him, to stand in his defence. he took god & his conscience to witnes that it was farr from his thoughtes."[63]

Giles Fletcher made the same point in his own confession: "For the Aldermens disposition to the Earle," he said, "though I knew that many of them wear well affected towards him (as my self & many others wear whiles hee beehaved himself duetifully towardes hir Matie) yet beeing honest & discreet men & faithfull suiects to hir Matie & carefull of their private estates I could . . . have tould him (if hee had asked my opinion of them touching such a wicked enterprize) that it had been a foolish conceipt & mad presumption in the Earle to suppose that they would allow & much more have ioigned with him in so vngodly & desperate an attempt."[64] He was right. Forewarned by the Queen and her counselors of the earl's designs, the London authorities performed loyally and effectively as the Queen's good subjects on the day of the abortive coup—showing not a moment's hesitation in defending the city and the kingdom with their arms and their blood, as Camden's account and the supporting evidence amply demonstrate. Once the moment of crisis had passed, they continued in their steadfast support of the regime in the face of further possible dangers.[65]

But if Essex was wrong in assessing his influence in London, he was not wrong in his judgment of the city's relationship to the realm as a whole. Had he been able to win the day in Cheapside or St. Paul's churchyard with his two hundred followers—had he been able to raise the Trained Bands or to arouse the apprentices and shopkeepers to his defense—what had amounted to little more than an aristocratic riot would have become a major rebellion. For this reason, the Queen and her officials were well aware of the intrinsic danger to political stability and the maintenance of public order aroused by Essex and took pains to secure the city as soon as the earl was in custody. Within hours of his arrest, a proclamation was issued by the Queen not only advertising his capture and imprisonment and denouncing him and his main associates, the earls of Southampton and Rutland, for exposing "our city and people with their goods to the spoil of a number of needy and desperate persons their adherents," but also singling out the citizens of London, "our good subjects of our city," for having "showed themselves so constant and unmoveable from their duties toward us, as not any one of them of any note . . . did offer to assist the Earl and his associates."[66]

Nonetheless, there were also sincere doubts and considerable fears about the extent of the conspiracy, and the Queen and her counselors took great pains to secure the city against further threat. Smythe, the sheriff, under suspicion because Essex had clearly singled him out as a supporter, was removed from office, incarcerated in the Tower, and closely interrogated until long after Essex's execution.[67] At the same time the citizens were called upon "to give diligent heed in all places to the conversation of persons not well known for their good behavior, and to the speeches of any that shall give out slanderous and undutiful words or rumors against us and our government . . . that by the apprehension of such dangerous instruments, both the drift and the purposes of evil-minded persons may be discovered, their designs prevented. and our people conserved in such peace and tranquility as heretofore, by God's favor, we have maintained and do hope still to continue amongst them."[68] Less than a week later, a proclamation appeared warning against the presence of "a great multitude of base and loose people" in the city and suburbs, "such as neither have any certain place of abode nor any good or lawful cause of business, but lie privily in corners and bad houses, listening after news and stirs, and spreading rumors and tales, being of likelihood ready to lay hold of any occasion to enter into any tumult or disorder, thereby to seek rapine and pillage; and likewise that further numbers of such sort of vagabound people do continually flock and gather to our city and the places confining about the same." Referring directly to the "most dangerous and desperate action of rebellion" lately experienced in the city, it ordered that all such people refrain from coming to the city, and that those found there "presently avoid and get them into the country; upon pain of death by martial law to be executed upon them."[69]

In the face of Essex's popularity and a campaign of lamentation and maudlin balladeering on his behalf that persisted for many months after his execution, the government took special care not just to suppress dissent, but to contest for the hearts of the Londoners. "We have been contented," Elizabeth says in the proclamation issued on the day after Essex's capture, "in regard of the comfort that we take to know by so notorious evidence the loyal disposition of our people (whereof we never doubted), not only to make known to all our said subjects of our city . . . in how thankful part we do accept both their loyal persisting in their duty and stay from following the false persuasions of the traitors, but to promise on our part that whensoever we shall have cause to show it they shall find us more careful over them than for ourselves."[70] Of equal importance was assuring that he would accept his condign punishment with the required dutiful expressions of contrition as he met his end—no mean feat considering his deep, almost pathological sense of personal honor, but accomplished nonetheless with aid of his own chaplain and duly recorded in numerous accounts of the moment.[71]

But even this was not enough. About the same time as the government was declaring all vagabonds lurking in London subject to the penalty of death under martial law, it was sending forth a team of preachers to undermine Essex's reputation. Their instructions were not only to point out his ingratitude to the Queen in the face of the favor he had received from her hands and his "dissimulation and hypocrisy" in matters of religion (particularly as regards his keeping company with Papists) but particularly to emphasize that in attempting to draw "the Citie after him . . . there was never rebellion in England since Richard the 2d tyme by domesticall traitors, not any atteempt against this kingdom by forraigne enemyes more desperate or dangerous. The rebellion in the North was far of, and thereby not so perilous. The great Armada of Spayne was but a thunderclap, the noise being greater then the danger, and her Ma[tes] subiectes faithfullie vnited to haue encountered it. But in this attempt; so many noble men and gentlemen of good sorte are combyned, as the event must needes haue ben most fearefull to the State if it had not ben prevented."[72] The need for the sermons was great. Even as late as April, libels in favor of Essex and against the Queen were still appearing, and the Crown felt it necessary to offer a £100 reward for information about the perpetrators.[73]

The Essex affair demonstrates the potential power of London in the state and the capacity it had to sustain its organization and shape its political agenda. In the words of the "Apologie of the Cittie of London," with which John Stow concludes his *Survey of London,* the early modern city was "a mighty arme and instrument to bring any great desire to effect, if it may be woon to a mans deuotion . . . But forasmuch as the same is by the like reason seruiceable and meete to impeach any disloyall attempt."[74] In the circumstances, the monarchy's ability to control the city and to keep the loyalty and obedience of its authorities and leading citizens, despite occasional irritants in their relations with the Crown, itself gives evidence of the significance of the city to the state, as well as of the state to the city.[75] These facts belie the stark opposition drawn by Tilly and his colleagues between the city and the state and suggest the shortcomings even of his model of "capitalized coercion" as it might apply to England. They made the city of London, by far the greatest storehouse of commercial wealth in England, a partner rather than a rival of the state, despite occasions in which there might have been tension between the Crown and the London Corporation or its leading citizens.[76]

Essex had recognized through his fog of rage in February 1601 that the kingdom could be controlled from London with the aid of the Londoners. Nothing new in that; the monarchy had long since concluded the same. What made this power overwhelming in the sixteenth century was the city's rise as a great commercial center—dominated by great London lickpennies like Customer Smythe and his son Thomas, who so profited from the trading monopolies granted by the Crown. However, the earl failed to understand that this elementary fact of London life had also weakened the hold that purely personal ties of patronage and popularity could have on its institutions or inhabitants. The alliance forged between political and economic power was a union between the developing market economy centered on the metropolis and the institutions of the state that secured, channeled, and governed it. As Stow emphasized, "the city being the hart of the Realme, the Kinges chamber, and princes seate," its fate was tied directly to the established governing regime of the kingdom and vice versa.[77] In 1600, these bonds, sealed with the Great Seal of England on patents of monopoly and London's royal charters, attached the city to the monarchy in substantive, material ways that Essex's influence alone could never have hoped to undo.

The Dancer and the Dance

We can now turn to the revealing narrative of Will Kemp's nine days' wonder, his Morris dance from London to Norwich—another story of matter in motion. It too is a tale of the market.

Kemp began his career of "mad Igges and merry jestes" about 1586 with the company of actors in the service of the earl of Leicester. On his return to England, he joined Lord Strange's Men, with which Shakespeare also performed.[78] Kemp's connection with Shakespeare persisted through most of the

1590s. When the Chamberlain's Men were formed in 1594, Kemp was among their number; by 1596 he was ranked, along with Burbage, Shakespeare, and the other principals, among the "sharers" in the company's proceeds. In 1598, he also became one of the investors in the building of the Globe, putting up, like Shakespeare himself, a tenth of the required funds, which made him a "housekeeper" entitled not only to his portion of the proceeds from each performance of the Chamberlain's Men, but to a tenth of the theater owners' take — traditionally one half of the gate receipts. But a year or so later Kemp sold out his share and left the Chamberlain's Men. It is in the context of these events that he made his nine days' wonder.[79]

Kemp himself gives us a hint of what he was about in the dedicatory letter to his pamphlet describing his journey to Norwich: "Some swear," he says, that "I have trode a good way to winne the world: others that guess righter, affirm, I haue without good help daunst my selfe out of the world."[80] As the punning reference to the Globe theater suggests, Kemp's earlier successes on the stage had resulted primarily from his dancing in performances accompanying the plays, not his character-acting in them. But about the time the Globe was built, broad shifts affecting the aesthetic and commercial economy of the London theater meant that there was less call for his skills and less time for his clowning on stage. If he stayed in "this sad world," as he called it,[81] he would earn his living primarily as an investor, not a performer, even though Kemp regularly had parts, albeit lesser ones, in the plays. In this sense, he had indeed danced himself out of the Globe, more or less in pace with the Globe's authors' writing dance out of their plays.[82]

From this perspective it looks like Kemp's nine days' wonder was an attempt to dance himself, and then in his pamphlet to write himself, back into the cultural horizons of London and the Londoners. What is of interest for present purposes, however, is that he chose to do it by "frolickly" footing it "from the right Honorable the Lord Mayors of London, towards the right worshipfull (and truely bountifull) Master Mayors of Norwich,"[83] a journey which took him through Stratford Langton, Romford, Brentwood, Inglestone, Chelmsford, Witford Bridge, Braintree, Sudbury, Melford, Clare, Bury St. Edmunds, Thetford, Rockland, Hingham, and Barford Bridge — a dance, in other words, over one of the richest and most productive regions of England, the great agricultural and clothmaking district that supplied the metropolis with a good deal of its food, a goodly number of its apprentices and laborers, many of its most valuable export items, and a solid market for its imports and its own manufactures.[84]

Kemp's reference to the two mayors represents these cities as independent corporate communities, each a separate world capable of giving Kemp his due.

One, London, is exposed as a morally suspect place; the other, Norwich, as partaking of ancient civic virtues. The mayor of London — Sir Nicholas Mosley, a Merchant Taylor and East India Company investor[85] — appears, as much by what is not said as by what is, as an aloof figure, distant from the tastes and customs of his fellow citizens. In contrast, Kemp mentions the "many good olde people, and diuers others of yonger yeeres," who lined the streets to Whitechapel and "of meere kindnes, gaue me . . . sixpences and grotes, blessing with their harty prayers and God-speedes." Nevertheless, Kemp also professed uncertainty about the "multitudes" that had accompanied him beyond Mile-End to the Bridge at Bow, since in urging him to dine and drink with them as they picnicked, they threatened his capacity for dancing. Politely refusing, "with Gentlemanly protestations," he says, he had danced "ouer the Bridge" at Bow, where he had heard "honest Conscience was once drownd," apparently on its way *into* town. "Its a pittye if it were so," he adds, "but thats no matter belonging to our Morrice." The same point is emphasized in a brief tale he tells about the capture and punishment in Brentwood of London cutpurses, who had been preying on the crowds attracted by Kemp's dancing.[86] Kemp was dancing, he seems to say, away from a corrupted and decayed world. We are meant to see the metropolis as a world deprived of its ancient virtues, and the Morris dance as its antithesis.

Here Kemp parallels John Stow, who also saw London in his day drifting away from its established customs, traditions and pastimes, its "amity" and "charity," as its "men of trades and sellers of wares" changed their neighborhoods "as they haue found their best aduantage." Stow particularly lamented the abandonment of the great midsummer vigils, which not only once had allowed Londoners to "inuite their neighbours and passengers . . . to sit, and be merrie with them in great familiaritie, praysing God for his benefits bestowed on them," but also had helped men who were "bitter enemies" to become "louinge friendes" by the light of the "Bonefires . . . of good amitie." He also bemoaned the breaking off "of the ancient dayly exercises in the long bow by Citizens," and their consequent creeping "into bowling Allies, and ordinarie dicing houses, nearer home . . . to take their pleasures." And he was especially troubled by the distance he saw growing between the Londoners and the "great Lordes of the land" and the gentry, who in "olde time" had lived in the city "together in good amity with the citizens, euery man obseruing the customes & orders of the Citty."[87] Kemp treats the Lord Mayor's aloofness in a similar light, as representing the remoteness of an elite from the popular traditions of London life. He casts the city as a whole as corrupted in its capacity for charity and good fellowship.

At the other end, in Norwich, we are given a very different picture.

Coming within sight of the city, Kemp was again thronged by well-wishers to the extent of making it difficult, if not impossible, to proceed further. Retiring to an inn in town to await "better opportunitie," he was approached by the Mayor, Master Roger Weld, whom he calls a merchant venturer, and other members of the corporation who asked him to delay his dance for several days "to the end that diuers knights and Gentlemen, together with their wiues and Children" from the surrounding region "might haue sufficient warning" to attend. During the interval, he tells us, he was handsomely entertained by the Mayor and aldermen in "theyr seuerall houses."[88] The honor and recognition thus granted, cutting across boundaries between city and country and the high and the low, seem especially important to Kemp.

On the appointed Saturday (having duly ridden out of town in order to dance his way back in), Kemp was formally greeted at his triumphal entry with an official poem of welcome composed and delivered by a civic official in the name of all the citizens and was escorted the rest of the way by officers appointed by the Mayor. At the market cross, the City Waits refreshed them with their instruments and voices. Finally, after working through the crowded lanes, he completed his journey at the Mayor's house, where he received "plenty of good cheere . . . bounty, and kind usage, together with the general welcomes of his worshipful brethren, and many other knights, Ladies, Gentlemen & Gentlewomen" and was given by the mayor "fiue pound in *Elsabeth* angels." To make a permanent record of his achievement, the very "buskins" that he "wore and daunst in from London thither" were duly nailed to the wall of the guildhall. Later, the mayor awarded him, out of the city chamber, an annuity of forty shillings yearly, and made him "a free man" of the city.[89]

Here, then, was a town which knew how to honor Kemp — to make him part of its world. It was headed, as Kemp stressed, by an exemplary figure "worthy of a singuler and impartiall admiration . . . for his chast life, liberality, & temperance in possessing worldly benefits." "If our marchants & gentlemen wold take example by this man," Kemp says, "Gentlemen would not sell their lands, to become bankrout Marchants, nor Marchants liue in the possessions of youth-beguiled gentlemen: who cast themselues out of their parents heritages for a few out-cast commodities."[90] Kemp evokes Norwich as a harmonious domain of civic virtue, of due deference and proper honor in social relations, and of festive amity, neighborliness, and good cheer. Like most urban centers in the sixteenth century, Norwich had experienced its own troubles in adjusting to religious and ecclesiastical reform, the expansion of its population, and a growing problem of poverty.[91] But Kemp saw only its bright side as a home for ancient traditions, a place that welcomed his Morris dancing and his jigs, a world that had been lost in the London of the Globe.

Kemp's journey itself reminds us of London's links to a network of small and not so small towns.[92] But almost nothing in Kemp's treatment of these places gives us a hint of the economic basis for this connection, which his hero, Mayor Weld of Norwich, must surely have understood. What is important to Kemp is not how the many notable, well-to-do local people he encountered along the way had earned their fortunes, but the fact that they gave his enterprise their wholehearted interest. He was especially concerned to note the attention paid him not just by the "country people," but the "Gentlemen and Gentlewomen" who "gathered together to see" him and to honor him with their gifts and entertainment.[93]

Outside of London, Kemp stresses, it was the people who vied for his presence, rather than he for theirs: "For euen as our Shop-keepers will hayle, and pull a man with Lack ye: what do you lack Gentlemen: My ware is best cryes one: mine best in England sayes an other . . . so was the dyuers voyces of the young men and Maydens, which should meete at euerie myles ende, thronging by twentie, and sometimes fortie, yea hundreths in companie: One crying the faryst way was thorow their Uillage: another, this is the nearest and fayrst way."[94] Kemp may have been pushed to the margins of the stage before the audiences in London, but not out here among the prosperous people and comfortable dwellings of the East Anglian towns and countryside.

Kemp also tells us that he was driven to publish his story because the ballad singers "seeing me merrily dispos'd in a Morrice, haue so be-painted mee in print since my gambols began from London to Norwich, that (hauing but an ill face before) I shall appear without a face" if the "foule colours" are not wiped away. What troubled him was not just the falsehoods that were being spread, but the fact that others were trafficking in his story—men who write "onely by report, partially, and scoffingly, of such whose pages shooes" they were "unworthy to wipe."[95] The balladeers, in effect, were stealing Kemp's own wares. Kemp was attempting to use the old festive world of places like Norwich to redress the balance of power in the new world of the metropolis.

Critical to his plan of recuperation seems to have been his capacity not just to author his own story, but to control its distribution. What occurred in his nine days' wonder was intended for his profit, which in part came from the material rewards he received along the way: a "threefold gaine" he says, on the moneys he put out. More important was the pamphlet, "the first that euer Will Kemp offered to the Presse."[96] It not only allowed him to answer his critics and thank his benefactors, but to tell the story of his countryman's dance, his Morris, to the metropolis, and then, perhaps, to have his printed image dance its own way along the very roads he himself had traversed, and along others to the remaining quadrants of the compass, to the local fairs that abounded in England or to stationers' shops and bookstalls in the provincial towns. The fact that his pamphlet had but one printing suggests that he was not entirely successful in fulfilling his aspiration, but, as with Essex, it was not for want of trying.[97]

In contrast to Essex's tale, which focused on the element of London's power in the maintenance of dominion within England, Kemp's stresses the element of communication, of network. His journey depended upon, and exploited, the prosperity of places which would hardly have been as populous or significant without their linkage to the metropolis. It was London's enormous demand for material things — and its equally great need for an outlet for what it produced or imported — that made this East Anglia region what it was at the end of Elizabeth's reign, that helped support not only Mayor Weld's distinctly urban fortune, but also the "riches and plentie, that abounded in euery corner of the house" of the "very bountiful widdow Eueret," wife of a "rich Yeoman," and that assured the generous innkeeper at Rockland, who danced part way to Hingham with Kemp, a steady stream of customers at his establishment.[98]

But Kemp's Morris dance also demonstrates that the connection between London and the provincial towns and countryside was as much cultural as economic. We know from Marjorie McIntosh's work on the breakdown of communal cooperation in the royal manor and liberty of Havering during the sixteenth century that the area around Romford (where Kemp had arrived at the end of his first day of dancing) was itself significantly transformed by its own "integration into a broader world," generated in large measure by the growth of nearby London. Havering's, and especially Romford's, history in this period seems very much the history of a local community caught up in the vortex of large-scale socioeconomic and cultural processes centered on the metropolis.[99] But Kemp's story also suggests that London itself was similarly caught up in this same vortex — that its increasing integration with the wider world was the dynamo that moved its inhabitants from membership in a medieval body politic with its emphasis on social cooperation and unity (as Stow reminisced) to participation in a community characterized by much more diverse views, a more stratified social structure, and a self-regarding focus on worldly advantage.

In using London's trade connections and its publishing industry to advertise his theatrical talents, spread his name, and attempt to recuperate his popularity, Kemp reveals that it was not merely trading commodities that spread along the highways to and from London but ideas, values, habits, and practices — the elements of a way of life centered on exchange and consumption

which drew more and more of England into its web. Neither of Kemp's preferred mediums, the theater or publishing, was an intellectual or ideological
monolith. Both were market-oriented industries, highly capitalized ones at
that, and the businessmen who ran them were concerned above all to recover
their investments and turn profits. They thrived on finding the means to attract
paying customers.[100] In consequence, the cultural production of these industries taken together stands for no single viewpoint. Instead it represents a
competition of outlooks and their material manifestations. But that in itself
contains a message, one rather different from the message that the earl of Essex,
a year later, thought he heard coming from his friends and clients in London. In
place of a world held together by "the dooing, receyuing, and requytng of good
Turnes,"[101] we have entered into the quite different world of market capitalism
where the doctrine of "creative destruction" prevails and it is necessary for
products to win sufficient favor from buyers to cover their costs if their trade is
to persist.[102] Its very growth habituated consumers, as well as producers, to a
world dependent on the open clash of doctrines or of styles, each exposing itself
to attack from potential competitors, challengers, or enemies.

Conclusion: London's Dominion

Ancient moral thinkers drew a sharp distinction between two paradigms of
exchange: gifts and contracts. The giving of gifts, they stressed, involves the
voluntary exchange of good will and has the power to hold society together by
the bonds of affection, loyalty, and friendship.[103] Yet, this mode, with its
competition for honor, glory, and deference, carries its own potential for social
violence and political chaos, as the earl of Essex's folly reveals. The making of
contracts depends on the division of labor and the exchange of goods and
services, which generates mutual dependencies and binds people together
with neither fear nor love, but quid pro quo. It creates the market, which
traditionally was viewed as a danger to stable relations within communities.[104]
But markets are themselves complex social institutions within which the exercise of power and the creation of allegiances takes place. As Will Kemp's
dance shows, they bring a structure with them that can promote the further
development of both state and nation.

    In the case of early modern England, this structure pivoted on London,
from whence flowed to other towns and the countryside not only bundles of
merchandise, but styles of life — manners of diet, dress, home furnishing, and
cultural preferences — accompanied by the habit of relying upon the market
not only for supplying necessities but for satisfying personal desires and con-

veying social identities. The resulting spread of the market economy conditioned growing numbers of the English, and somewhat later of the Welsh, the Scots, and the Irish as well, to a common set of behaviors in pursuing their livelihoods.

This development shared something with the outcome that Gnaeus Julius Agricola, imperial governor in Roman Britain, had desired to effect in pacifying its barbarous inhabitants. According to Tacitus, Agricola, faced "with people living in isolation and ignorance," sought to "accustom" his charges "to a life of peace through the provision of amenities," assisting them in "the building of temples, public squares, and good houses" and the acquisition of the accouterments of the Roman way of life. In this manner, Tacitus argues, "the population was gradually led into the demoralizing temptations of arcades, baths, and sumptuous banquets. The unsuspecting Britons spoke of such novelties as 'civilization,' when in fact they were only a feature of their enslavement."[105]

We need not conclude, with Tacitus, that the deepening attachment to the material objects of a culture of consumption, becoming evident around 1600, necessarily brought thralldom with it, any more than we must accept that freedom is the inevitable outgrowth of market development. Market exchange promotes disciplines and creates opportunities. Nevertheless, in a world in motion, where persons frequently changed places and things regularly changed hands, the developing market economy and urban network, centered on London, created an anchor for society against the forces of creative destruction that worked against stability and structured order. Urban growth alone could never sustain either state or nation. But in helping to transform the Atlantic archipelago into a single market, it also helped to create binding ties to promote the extension of political authority from the center to the peripheries, and to introduce elements of a common culture to all of England and gradually to all of the British Isles as well.

Notes

1. See Paul M. Hohenberg and Lynn Hollen Lees, *The Making of Urban Europe, 1000–1950* (Cambridge, Mass.: Harvard University Press, 1985), pp. 1–13.

2. See Michael Reed, "London and Its Hinterland, 1600–1800: The View from the Provinces," in *Capital Cities and Their Hinterlands in Early Modern Europe,* ed. Peter Clark and Bernard Lepetit (Aldershot: Scolar Press, 1996), pp. 51–83; see also Clark and Lepetit's Introduction in *Capital Cities,* pp. 1–25; and Paul M. Hohenberg and Lynn Hollen Lees, "Urban Systems and Economic Growth: Town Populations and Metropolitan Hinterlands, 1600–1850," in *Capital Cities,* pp. 26–50.

3. John Davies of Hereford, "Vpon English Prouerbes," in *The Scourge of Folly Consisting of satyricall Epigramms and others in honor of many noble and worthy Persons of our Land. Together With a pleasant (though discordant) Descant vpon most English Prouerbes and others* (1611), p. 42; reprinted in vol. 2 of *The Complete Works of John Davies of Hereford* (15..–1618), 2 vols., ed. Alexander B. Grosart (Edinburgh: T. and A. Constable, 1878).

4. Morris Palmer Tilley, *A Dictionary of the Proverbs in England in the Sixteenth and Seventeenth Centuries: A Collection of the Proverbs Found in English Literature and the Dictionaries of the Period* (Ann Arbor: University of Michigan Press, 1950), pp. 102–3 (C426), 308 (H430), 378 (L228), 705 (W69), 752 (W771); for an overview, see Lawrence Manley, *Literature and Culture in Early Modern London* (Cambridge: Cambridge University Press, 1995), pp. 409–30.

5. See, for example, Daniel Miller, "Artefacts and the Meaning of Things," in *Companion Encyclopedia of Anthropology: Humanity, Culture, and Social Life,* ed. Tim Ingold (London: Routledge, 1994), pp. 396–419.

6. Lisa Jardine, *Worldly Goods: A New History of the Renaissance* (New York: Nan A. Talese, 1996), pp. 33–34, 37–90, 277–330, 377–424, 436; see also Mary Douglas and Baron Isherwood, *The World of Goods: Towards an Anthropology of Consumption,* 2nd ed. (London: Routledge, 1996); *Consumption and the World of Goods,* ed. John Brewer and Roy Porter (London: Routledge, 1993); Joan Thirsk, *Economic Policy and Projects: The Development of a Consumer Society in Early Modern England* (Oxford: Clarendon Press, 1978); Lorna Weatherill, *Consumer Behaviour and Material Culture in Britain, 1660–1760* (London: Routledge, 1988).

7. Fernand Braudel, *The Structures of Everyday Life: The Limits of the Possible,* trans. Siân Reynolds [Civilization and Capitalism, 15th–18th Century, vol. 1] (New York: Harper and Row, 1981), p. 479; cf. Fernand Braudel, *Capitalism and Material Life, 1400–1800,* trans. Miriam Kochan (New York: Harper and Row, 1973), pp. 373–74.

8. Braudel, *Structures of Everyday Life,* pp. 479–81.

9. See David Harris Sacks, *The Widening Gate: Bristol and the Atlantic Economy, 1450–1700* (Berkeley and Los Angeles: University of California Press, 1991), pp. 1–15, 331–62.

10. Braudel, *Structures of Everyday Life,* pp. 24, 28–29; cf. Braudel, *Capitalism and Material Life,* pp. ix–xiii.

11. See, for example, Ian Archer, *The Pursuit of Stability: Social Relations in Elizabethan London* (Cambridge: Cambridge University Press, 1991), pp. 39–99, 111–24; Steve Rappaport, *Worlds Within Worlds: Structures of Life in Sixteenth-Century London* (Cambridge: Cambridge University Press, 1989), pp. 201–14; Jeremy Boulton, *Neighbourhood and Society: A London Suburb in the Seventeenth Century* (Cambridge: Cambridge University Press, 1987), pp. 206–61, 289–95; Richard Grassby, *The Business Community of Seventeenth-Century England* (Cambridge: Cambridge University Press, 1995), pp. 60–65, 84–91, 139–70, 401–7; Robert Brenner, *Merchants and Revolution: Commercial Change, Political Conflict, and London's Overseas Traders, 1550–1653* (Princeton: Princeton University Press, 1993), pp. 51–195; and Sacks, *Widening Gate,* pp. 62–73, 105–27.

12. Braudel, *Structures of Everyday Life,* pp. 484–89, 512–14, 556–58; cf. Braudel, *Capitalism and Material Life,* pp. 376–80, 398–401; Fernand Braudel, *The Wheels of Commerce,* trans. Siân Reynolds [Civilization and Capitalism, 15th–18th Century, vol.

2] (New York: Harper and Row, 1982), pp. 297–349; see also Paul Bairoch, *Cities and Economic Development: From the Dawn of History to the Present,* trans. Christopher Braider (Chicago: University of Chicago Press, 1988), pp. 93–106, 142–52, 175–88.

13. Thomas Hobbes, *The Elements of Law, Natural and Politic,* ed. Ferdinand Tönnies (Cambridge: Cambridge University Press, 1928), pp. 4–6; Richard Tuck, *Philosophy and Government, 1572–1651* (Cambridge: Cambridge University Press, 1993), pp. 299–300; see also Thomas Hobbes, *Leviathan,* ed. Richard Tuck (Cambridge: Cambridge University Press, 1991), pp. 13–14.

14. Thomas Hobbes, "The Answer of Mr. Hobbes to Sir Will. D'Avenant's Preface Before Gondibert," in Sir William Davenant, *Sir William Davenant's Gondibert,* ed. David F. Gladish (Oxford: Clarendon Press, 1971), p. 45.

15. For these statistics, see Jan de Vries, *European Urbanization, 1500–1800* (Cambridge, Mass.: Harvard University Press, 1984), appendix 1, pp. 269–87; E. A. Wrigley, "Urban Growth and Agricultural Change: England and the Continent in the Early Modern Period," in E. A. Wrigley, *People, Cities, and Wealth: The Transformation of Traditional Society* (Oxford: Blackwell, 1987), pp. 158–67; E. A. Wrigley, "A Simple Model of London's Importance in Changing English Society and Economy, 1650–1750," ibid., pp. 133–56; see also Roger Finlay and Beatrice Shearer, "Population Growth and Suburban Expansion," in *London, 1500–1700: The Making of the Metropolis,* ed. A. L. Beier and Roger Finlay (London: Longman, 1986), pp. 42, 49; Vanessa Harding, "The Population of London, 1500–1700, a Review of the Published Evidence," *London Journal,* 15 (1990): 111–28.

16. These estimates are based on Wrigley, "Urban Growth and Agricultural Change," table 7.3, p. 162; see also Penelope J. Corfield, "Economic Growth and Change in Seventeenth-Century English Towns," in *The Traditional Community under Stress,* ed. Peter Clark (Milton Keynes: Open University Press, 1977), table 1, p. 40; and Penelope J. Corfield, *The Impact of English Towns, 1700–1800* (Oxford: Oxford University Press, 1982), table 1, p. 8.

17. Wrigley, "Urban Growth and Agricultural Change," table 7.1, pp. 160–61, 176–77; De Vries, *European Urbanization,* pp. 118–19, 154, 171–72, and appendix 1, pp. 270–71.

18. E. A. Wrigley, "A Simple Model of London's Importance," in *People, Cities, and Wealth,* pp. 134–37; E. A. Wrigley and Roger S. Schofield, *Population History of England, 1541–1871: A Reconstruction* (Cambridge, Mass.: Harvard University Press, 1981), appendix 3, tables 3.1, 3.3, pp. 528–29, 531–35, appendix 5, pp. 563–87; see also Wrigley, "Urban Growth and Agricultural Change," table 7.2, p. 162; Rappaport, *Worlds Within Worlds,* pp. 61–86; A. L. Beier and Roger Finlay, "Introduction: The Significance of the Metropolis," in *London, 1500–1700,* ed. Beier and Finlay, pp. 8–10, 16; Finlay and Shearer, "Population Growth and Suburban Expansion," ibid., pp. 50–53; and Roger Finlay, *Population and Metropolis: The Demography of London, 1580–1650* (Cambridge: Cambridge University Press, 1981), pp. 51–69, 48–51.

19. The percentage of newcomers in London around 1600 was calculated using a technique derived from Wrigley, "Simple Model of London's Importance," pp. 134–135; see also Rappaport, *Worlds Within Worlds,* pp. 64, 76–77.

20. A. L. Beier, "Social Problems in Elizabethan London," *Journal of Interdisciplinary History,* 9 (1978): 203–21; Beier and Finlay, "Introduction: The Significance of the Metropolis," pp. 4–5, 17–19; A. L. Beier, *Masterless Men: The Vagrancy Problem in*

England, 1560–1640 (London: Methuen, 1985), pp. 39–47, 84–85; Paul Slack, *Poverty and Policy in Tudor and Stuart England* (London: Longman, 1988), pp. 69–72, 85, 94–97, 105, 118, 167, 189; Archer, *Pursuit of Stability,* pp. 9–10, 67–68, 96–98, 150–54, 190–97, 254–59; Rappaport, *Worlds Within Worlds,* pp. 3–5, 13–14, 43–44, 54–60, 118–22, 150–53, 157–72, 282–84, 323–36; Boulton, *Neighbourhood and Society,* pp. 92–97, 104–5, 110–15, 124–26, 160–65, 221, 224–27.

21. Steve Rappaport, "Social Structure and Mobility in Sixteenth-Century London, Part I," *London Journal,* 9 (1983): 107–35; Steve Rappaport, "Social Structure and Mobility in Sixteenth-Century London, Part II," ibid., 10 (1984): 107–34; Steve Rappaport, *Worlds Within Worlds,* pp. 176–376; Archer, *Pursuit of Stability,* pp. 39–148.

22. Wrigley, "Urban Growth and Agricultural Change," tables 7.3 and 7.4, pp. 166, 170; Finlay and Shearer, "Population Growth and Suburban Expansion," in *London, 1500–1700,* table 2, p. 42.

23. See F. J. Fisher, "Commercial Trends and Policy in Sixteenth-Century England," in F. J. Fisher, *London and the English Economy, 1500–1700,* ed. P. J. Corfield and N. B. Harte (London and Ronceverte: Hambledon Press, 1990) pp. 81–104; G. D. Ramsay, *The City of London in International Politics at the Accession of Elizabeth Tudor* (Manchester: Manchester University Press, 1975), pp. 1–80; G. D. Ramsay, *English Overseas Trade in the Centuries of Emergence* (London: Macmillan, 1957), pp. 1–33, 132–65; Ralph Davis, "England and the Mediterranean, 1570–1670," in *Essays in the Economic and Social History of Tudor and Stuart England in Honour of R. H. Tawney,* ed. F. J. Fisher (Cambridge: Cambridge University Press, 1961), pp. 117–37; Robert Brenner, *Merchants and Revolution: Commercial Change, Political Conflict, and London's Overseas Traders, 1550–1653* (Princeton: Princeton University Press, 1993), pp. 3–50; K. R. Andrews, *Elizabethan Privateering: English Privateering during the Spanish War, 1585–1603* (Cambridge: Cambridge University Press, 1964), pp. 159–238; K. R. Andrews, *Trade, Plunder, and Settlement: Maritime Enterprise and the Genesis of the British Empire, 1480–1630* (Cambridge: Cambridge University Press, 1984), pp. 1–40, 356–64; Sacks, *Widening Gate,* pp. 19–53.

24. Charles Tilly, "Entanglements of European Cities and States," in *Cities and the Rise of States in Europe, A.D. 1000 to 1800,* ed. Charles Tilly and Wim P. Blockmans (Boulder: Westview Press, 1989), pp. 6, 8–17, 22–27; see also Charles Tilly, *Coercion, Capital, and European States, A.D. 990–1990* (Oxford: Blackwell, 1990), pp. 17, 22–27, 30.

25. Peter Sahlins, *Boundaries: The Making of France and Spain in the Pyrenees* (Berkeley and Los Angeles: University of California Press, 1989); Tilly, *Coercion, Capital, and European States,* pp. 67–95; and Tilly, "Entanglements of European Cities and States," in *Cities and the Rise of States,* pp. 4–5.

26. See J. G. A. Pocock, "British History: A Plea for a New Subject," *Journal of Modern History* 47 (1975): 601–21, with comments by A. J. P. Taylor, Gordon Donaldson, and Michael Hechter and a reply by the author, pp. 622–28; J. G. A. Pocock, "The Limits and Divisions of British History: In Search of an Unknown Subject," *American Historical Review* 87 (1982): 311–36; Richard S. Thompson, *The Atlantic Archipelago: A Political History of the British Isles* (Lewiston, N.Y.: E. Mellen Press, 1986).

27. See John Patten, *English Towns, 1500–1700* (Folkestone: Dawson 1978), pp. 197–243; Edward Whiting Fox, *History in Geographic Perspective: The Other France*

(New York: Norton, 1971); Edward Whiting Fox, *The Emergence of the Modern European World: From the Seventeenth to the Twentieth Century* (Cambridge, Mass.: Blackwell, 1991). The maritime character of England's island way of life has important consequence for the character of the state; see John Brewer, *The Sinews of Power: War, Money, and the English State, 1688–1783* (New York: Knopf, 1989), pp. 34–37, esp. p. 36, and p. 255 n. 21.

28. Wrigley, "Urban Growth and Agricultural Change," pp. 180–189, esp. tables 7.8, 7.9, 7.10, pp. 182, 184–85, 187; De Vries, *European Urbanization,* table 3.7, p. 39; Bairoch, *Cities and Economic Development,* table 11.2, p. 179; table 13.1, p. 215. On London as the King's Chamber and the concessionary interests that followed therefrom, see John Stow, *A Survey of London, Reprinted from the Text of 1603,* ed. C. L. Kingsford, 2 vols. (Oxford: Clarendon Press, 1908), 85.

29. Wrigley, "Urban Growth and Agricultural Change," table 7.1, pp. 160–61; de Vries, *European Urbanization,* appendix 1, pp. 270–71. The literature on Scottish and Irish urban history is extensive and growing; for introductions see *The Early Modern Town in Scotland,* ed. Michael Lynch (London: Croom Helm, 1987), pp. 1–36; Raymond Gillespie, *The Transformation of the Irish Economy, 1550–1700* ([Dublin]: Dundalgan Press, 1991).

30. Nicholas Canny, *Kingdom and Colony: Ireland in the Atlantic World, 1560–1800* (Baltimore: Johns Hopkins University Press, 1988), pp. 69–102; L. M. Cullen, *Anglo-Irish Trade, 1660–1800* (Manchester: Manchester University Press, 1968), pp. 12, 18–21, 33, 53–54, 91, 161–64; Gillespie, *Transformation of the Irish Economy,* pp. 30–50; Brian Levack, *The Formation of the British State: England, Scotland, and the Union* (Oxford: Clarendon Press, 1987), pp. 138–67; Ian D. Whyte, *Scotland's Society and Economy in Transition,* c. 1500–c. 1700 (Basingstoke: Macmillan, 1997), pp. 154–60.

31. See Wrigley, "A Simple Model of London's Importance," pp. 142–56; Wrigley, "Urban Growth and Agricultural Change," pp. 174–93; de Vries, *European Urbanization,* pp. 118–19, 154; Fisher, *London and the English Economy,* pp. 81–130, 173–98.

32. See Sacks, *Widening Gate,* pp. 225–26; Bernard Bailyn, "The Challenge of Modern Historiography," *American Historical Review* 87 (1982): 1–24.

33. William Kemp, *Kemps nine daies vvonder. Performed in a daunce from London to Norwich. Containing the pleasure, paines and kinde entertainement of William Kemp betweene London and that Citty in his late Morrice. Wherein is somewhat set downe worth note; to reproue the slaunders of him: many things merry, nothing hurtfull* (London, 1600, STC 14923), sig. B3[a]r.

34. The starting place remains William Camden, *ANNALES, OR, THE HISTORY of the Most RENOWNED AND VICTORIOUS PRINCESSE ELIZABETH, Late Queen of England,* trans. R. N[orton], 3rd ed. (London, 1635, STC 4501).

35. Wallace T. MacCaffrey, *Elizabeth I: War and Politics, 1588–1603* (Princeton: Princeton University Press, 1992), pp. 453–94; Paul E. J. Hammer, "Patronage at Court, Faction and the Earl of Essex," in *The Reign of Elizabeth I: Court and Culture in the Last Decade,* ed. John Guy (Cambridge: Cambridge University Press, 1995), pp. 65–86.

36. Camden, *ANNALES,* p. 493.

37. Camden, *ANNALES,* pp. 493–94, 503–13, 529–35; Public Record Office [hereafter, PRO], SP12/273/35, 36, 37, 38; E. P. Cheyney, *A History of England from the Defeat of the Armada to the Death of Elizabeth, with an Account of English Institutions*

During the Later Sixteenth and Early Seventeenth Centuries, 2 vols. (London: Longman, 1914–1926), 2:503–15.

38. Calendar of the Manuscripts of the . . . Marquis of Salisbury . . . Preserved at Hatfield House [hereafter, HMC, *Salisbury*], 24 vols. (London: HMSO, 1883–1976), 10:348; Lawrence Stone, *Crisis of the Aristocracy, 1558–1641* (Oxford: Clarendon Press, 1965), pp. 426–27, 483; MacCaffrey, *Elizabeth I: War and Politics,* pp. 464–65, 505–6, 529; Frederick C. Dietz, *English Public Finance, 1558–1641,* 2nd ed. (New York: Barnes and Noble, 1964), pp. 154 n, 315–16; Paul E. J. Hammer, "'The Bright Shininge Sparke': The Political Career of Robert Devereux, 2nd Earl of Essex, c. 1585–1597," Ph.D. diss., Cambridge University, 1991, pp. 176–78.

39. Essex to Queen Elizabeth, 22 September 1600, in William Bourchier Devereux, *Lives and Letters of the Devereux, Earls of Essex in the Reigns of Elizabeth, James I, and Charles I, 1540–1646,* 2 vols. (London: J. Murray, 1853) 1:125–26.

40. Essex to Queen Elizabeth, 18 October 1600, ibid., 1:126–27.

41. Essex to Queen Elizabeth, 17 November 1600, ibid., 1:128.

42. John Harington, *Nugae Antiquae, Being a Miscellaneous Collection of Original Papers in Prose and Verse,* ed. Henry Harington, 2 vols. (London: Verner and Hood, 1804), 1:179.

43. Mervyn James, "At a Crossroads of the Political Culture: The Essex Revolt, 1601," in Mervyn James, *Society, Politics, and Culture: Studies in Early Modern England* (Cambridge: Cambridge University Press, 1986), pp. 430–38; Lacey Baldwin Smith, *Treason in Tudor England: Politics and Paranoia* (Princeton: Princeton University Press, 1986), pp. 211–12, 215; Hammer, "'Bright Shininge Sparke,'" pp. 45–46, 237; Hammer, "Patronage at Court," pp. 65–86.

44. Examination of Roger Manners, earl of Rutland, 12 February 1601, PRO, SP12/278/51, 52; see also Report of Valentine Thomas, 15 February 1601, PRO, SP12/278/64, describing a conference, after the "rebellion," with Thomas Wright, a seminary priest: "Wright reported . . . That Essex did thincke the Cittye of London would haue assisted him" (Camden, *ANNALES,* pp. 538–39).

45. Camden, *ANNALES,* p. 538.

46. Sir Henry Neville to Lords Egerton, Buckhurst, Nottingham, and Secretary Cecil, 2 March 1601, PRO, SP12/279/11.

47. Camden, *ANNALES,* p. 538.

48. Camden, *ANNALES,* p. 538; "D. Ffletcher's confession," 3 March 1601, PRO, SP12/279/12; see also examination of Sir Ferdinando Gorges, 18 February 1601, PRO, SP12/278/84; examination of William Gresham, 22 October 1601, PRO, SP12/282/17.

49. An early seventeenth-century document purporting to provide Smythe's own testimony has it that Smythe sent word to the earl "that after the Queene, both hee and the Cittye would be sure to him; ffor the suppression of those that should oppose against the Rightfull Successor," but denied having promised him anything touching his recent "unduetifull Attempt." According to this document, Smythe attributed rumors to the contrary to those in Essex's entourage "that Added to the Text, or invented out their owne Brayne" (Folger Shakespeare Library MS V.b. 50, p. 218). Given the fact that the source is not contemporary with the events and that it also reports several portents of the earl's fall, this evidence is probably equally spurious.

50. Examination of Francis Smith, gent., 10 February 1601, PRO, SP12/278/47;

confession of John Barger, [13 February 1601], PRO, SP12/278/60; examination of Thomas Ratclyffe, citizen and scrivener of London, 18 February 1601, PRO, SP12/278/91; examinations of Thomas Curson, citizen and armourer of London, and of Patrick Brewe, citizen of London and warden of the Company of Goldsmiths, 18 February 1601, PRO, SP12/278/92; "An Abstract out of the examinations of those persons that were in the late action of rebellion with the earl of Essex on Feb. 8, 1600/. Abstracted March 18, 1600/1," Folger Shakespeare Library MS V.b. 187, ff. 7r–v, 8r. A possible ancient historical model for Essex's appeal to the Londoners may be found in Herodotus's *Histories* 1:59 where the historian describes the strategem employed by Pisastratus in Athens in his rivalry with Megacles and Lycurgus, Herodotus, *The Histories,* trans. Robin Waterfield, ed. Carolyn Dewald (Oxford: Oxford University Press, 1998), p. 25.

51. Camden,*ANNALES,* pp. 536–58; Cheyney, *History of England,* 2:519–34. The events can also be followed coherently in the large body of examinations, trial records, and related documents collected in PRO, SP12/278, SP12/279, "An Abstract out of the examinations of those persons that were in the late action of rebellion with the earl of Essex on Feb. 8, 1600/1. Abstracted March 18, 1600/1," Folger Shakespeare Library MS V.b. 187, and in *Acts of the Privy Council of England,* new ser., vol. 31 (1600–1601), ed. J. R. Dasent, pp. 147–90; see also *Cobbett's Complete Collection of State Trials and Proceedings for High Crimes and Misdemeanors from the Earliest Period to the Present Time,* ed. T. B. Howell, 33 vols. (London: R. Bagshaw, 1826), 1:1333–60, 1403–51.

52. See PRO, SP12/268/5 (14 July 1598); City of London Record Office (hereafter CLRO), *Repertories of the Court of Aldermen,* Repertory 25, fol. 1v (6 November 1599); Brenner, *Merchants and Revolution,* pp. 21, 63, 63 n, 96, 98; T. S. Willan, *The Early History of the Russia Company, 1553–1603* (Manchester: Manchester University Press, 1956), p. 286; Alfred C. Wood, *A History of the Levant Company* ([London]: Oxford University Press, 1935), pp. 31, 205; East India Company, *The Dawn of British Trade to the East Indies as Recorded in the Court Minutes of the East India Company, 1599–1603; Containing an Account of the Formation of the Company, the First Adventure and Waymouth's Voyage in Search of the North-West Passage,* ed. Henry Stevens, intro. George Birdwood (London: H. Stevens and Son, 1886), pp. 3, 62, 275, 281; East India Company, *The Register of Letters &c. of the Governour and Company of Merchants of London Trading into the East Indies,* ed. George Birdwood and William Foster (London: Quaritch, 1893), pp. 9, 10, 169; K. N. Chaudhuri, *The English East India Company: A Study of an Early Joint-Stock Company* (London: Frank Cass, 1965), p. 36; "Sir Thomas Smith or Smythe," *Dictionary of National Biography* [hereafter, *DNB*], 18:536–37. One reason for thinking Smythe might be of help was because Essex had reason to believe, or rather to hope, that the sheriff had aroused the enmity of the archbishop of Canterbury by seemingly questioning the orthodoxy of raising of a cross in Cheapside. Apparently Archbishop Bancroft was "offended wth Mr Smythe . . . for writing to Oxford for the opinion of soom learned men touching the Cross wth the Crucifixe"; "D. Ffletchers confession," 3 March 1601, PRO, SP12/279/12.

53. Report of Sir John Smythe, 13 (?) February 1601, PRO, SP12/278/57.

54. See, for example, "D. Ffletchers confession," 3 March 1601, PRO, SP12/279/12.

55. J. F. Wadmore, "Thomas Smyth, of Westenhanger, Commonly Called Customer Smythe," *Archaeologia Cantiana,* 17 (1887): 193–208; "Sir Thomas Smith or

Smythe," *DNB*, 18:536; "Thomas Smythe II," in *The House of Commons, 1509–1558*, ed. S. T. Bindoff, 3 vols. (London: History of Parliament Trust, 1982), 3:340–41; "Thomas Smythe I," and "Thomas Smythe II," in *The House of Commons, 1558–1603*, ed. P. W. Hasler, 3 vols. (London: History of Parliament Trust, 1981), 3:405–7; A. B. Beaven, *The Aldermen of the City of London, Temp. Henry III.–1908*, 2 vols. (London: The Corporation of the City of London, 1908–13), 1:159; *Select Charters of the Trading Companies, A.D. 1530–1707*, ed. Cecil T. Carr (Selden Soc., 28, 1913), pp. 4–20, 30–43; W. R. Scott, *The Constitution and Finance of English, Scottish, and Irish Joint-Stock Companies to 1720*, 3 vols. (Cambridge: The University Press, 1910–12), 1:47–128; 2:36–52, 83–98, 383–405, 413–24; T. S. Willan, *The Muscovy Merchants of 1555* (Manchester: Manchester University Press, 1953), pp. 105–6, 122; Willan, *Early History of the Russia Company*, pp. 58, 156, 201–2; T. K. Rabb, *Enterprise and Empire: Merchant and Gentry Investment in the Expansion of England, 1575–1630* (Cambridge, Mass.: Harvard University Press, 1967), pp. 283, 378; Wood, *History of the Levant Company*, p. 11; M. B. Donald, *Elizabethan Copper: The History of the Company of Mines Royal, 1568–1605* (London: Pergamon Press, 1955), pp. 66–72, 77–78, 241–42; William Rees, *Industry before the Industrial Revolution, Incorporating a Study of the Chartered Companies of the Society of Mines Royal and of Mineral and Battery Works*, 2 vols. (Cardiff: University of Wales Press, 1968), 2:367–461.

56. Dietz, *English Public Finance*, p. 316 and 316 nn. 26–28.

57. See Rabb, *Enterprise and Empire*, pp. 300, 341, 376, 396, 409; *Register of Letters*, ed. Birdwood and Foster, p. 134 n. For Michelbourne's involvement in the Essex rebellion, see PRO, SP12/276/46; SP12/279/24.

58. Thomas Birch, *Memoirs of the Reign of Elizabeth from the Year 1581 till her Death*, 2 vols. (London: n.p. 1754), 2:77, 100–101; Archer, *Pursuit of Stability*, pp. 42–44; CLRO, *Repertories of the Court of Aldermen*, Rep. 21, fol. 536r (19 March 1588); Rep. 23. fol. 265r (1 August 1594), fol. 510r (21 June 1595), fol. 593v (19 October 1596); Rep. 24, fol. 223v (4 May 1598), fol. 302v (10 October 1598); Rep. 25, fol. 66v (3 April 1600), fol. 156v (7 October 1600); see also CLRO, *Remembrancia* II, nos. 7 (9 February 1593), 8 (16 June 1594), 24 (12 July 1594), 147 (2 March 1595); Corporation of London, *Analytical Index to the Series of Records Known As the Remembrancia Preserved among the Archives of the City of London, A.D. 1579–1664*, ed. W. H. Overall and H. C. Overall (London: Pardon and Son, 1878), pp. 156–158, 367, 408; Willan, *Early History of the Russia Company*, pp. 172–9, 195, 199, 205–9, 211, 218, 220, 245, 282; "Giles Fletcher, LL. D.," *DNB*, 7:299–301.

59. HMC, *Salisbury MSS*, 10:348; *Dawn of British Trade*, ed. Stevens, pp. 1–4; Rabb, *Enterprise and Empire*, pp. 238, 273, 308, 367; HMC, *Salisbury MSS*, 7:283, 375. For Crispe's connection to Smythe, see *Acts of the Privy Council*, new. ser., 31:267–68; for Sir John Harte, see *House of Commons*, 2:264–651; for John Swynnerton, the younger, see ibid., 3:469.

60. "A coppy of a *lett*re written in the behalfe of Captein Davis to the right ho: the Erle of Essex," 30 September 1600, in East India Company, *Dawn of British Trade*, ed. Stevens, p. 25; for Davies' venture see ibid. pp. 13, 14, 21, 22, 24, 26, 27, 31, 37, 47, 51, 52, 54, 55, 66, 68, 72, 74, 100, 127, 143, 152; East India Company, *Register of Letters*, pp. 11–12.

61. David Harris Sacks, "The Countervailing of Benefits: Monopoly, Liberty, and

Benevolence in Elizabethan England," in *Tudor Political Culture,* ed. Dale Hoak (Cambridge: Cambridge University Press, 1995), pp. 272–91; Linda Levy Peck, *Court Patronage and Corruption in Early Stuart England* (Boston: Unwin Hyman, 1990), pp. 1–74.

62. The earl was explicitly identified with Wat Tyler in the Peasants' Revolt of 1381 and Jack Cade in 1450; see "A Memorial about the Insurrection of the Earl of Essex," 19 (?) February 1601, PRO, SP12/278/127. Sir Thomas Wyatt in 1554 was the leader of a more recent rebellion with similar aspirations to seize London; see D. M. Loades, *Two Tudor Conspiracies* (Cambridge: Cambridge University Press, 1965), pp. 12–127.

63. "The speach of Mr Cuffe at his death," [13 March 1601], PRO, SP12/279/25.

64. "D. Ffletchers confession," 3 March 1601, PRO, SP12/279/12.

65. Camden, *ANNALES,* pp. 539–42; CLRO, *Repertories of the Court of Aldermen,* Rep. 25, ff. 197r (10 February 1601) see also 198v (14 February 1601), 201r (3 March 1601).

66. Proclamation, 9 February 1601, 43 Eliz. I, in *Tudor Royal Proclamations,* ed. Paul L. Hughes and James F. Larkin, 3 vols. (New Haven: Yale University Press, 1964–69), 3:230–32 (no. 808).

67. PRO, SP12/278/57, 58, 59, 60, 91, 92; SP12/279/6, 7, 8, 9, 10, 12, 29, 30, 58, 76; SP12/281/1, 67, 68; *Acts of the Privy Council,* new ser., 31 (1600–1601): 157–58; CLRO, *Repertories of the Court of Aldermen,* Repertory 25, fol. 198v (14 February 1601); fol. 201r (3 March 1601); East India Company, *Dawn of British Trade,* ed. Stevens, p. 166.

68. Proclamation, 9 February 1601, 43 Eliz. I, in *Tudor Royal Proclamations,* 3:232 (no. 808); *Acts of the Privy Council,* new ser., 31 (1600–1601): 147, 148, 152–53, 154–58, 162–63, 164–65, 170–71, 173, 187–88, 196–97, 224–25, 245–48, 267–68; CLRO, *Repertories of the Court of Aldermen,* Rep. 25, fol. 206v (10 March 1601), fol. 210v (19 March 1601), fol. 213r (24 March 1601).

69. Proclamation, 15 February 1601, 43 Eliz. I, in *Tudor Royal Proclamations,* 3:232–33 (no. 809); *Acts of the Privy Council,* new ser., 31 (1600–1601): 164–65.

70. Proclamation, 9 February 1601, 43 Eliz. I, in *Tudor Royal Proclamations,* 3:231 (no. 808).

71. See PRO, SP12/278/112, 113, 114, 115, 116, 117, 118, 119, 129, 121, 122, 126.

72. "A direction for the preachers," 14 (?) February 1601, PRO, SP12/278/63; this line seems to have been taken by Sir Robert Cecil. See the rough notes of the meeting of the Council in the Star Chamber on 13 February 1601, PRO, SP12/278/54; "The Substance of the Speeches spoken the 13th of this present Februarye 1600 by the right ho: the Lord Keeper and other the Lordes and others of hir Mas most honorable Priuye Counsell In Starre chamber," 13 February 1601, PRO, SP12/278/55; "A memorial about the insurrection of the Earl of Essex," 19 (?) February 1601, PRO, SP12/278/127, 128, in Cecil's hand; see also [Vincent Hussey] to ___, 18 February 1601, written on the backs of PRO, SP12/278/48, 49, 53. Cecil also seems to have provided instruction for the sermon about the earl that Dr. William Barlow preached at Paul's Cross on 1 March 1601; see [Robert Cecil to Dr. William Barlow], 26 (?) February 1601, PRO, SP12/278/126; William Barlow, *A Sermon preached at Paules Cross, on the first Sunday in Lent; Martii I. 1600. With a short discourse of the late Earle of Essex his*

confession, and penitence, before and at the time of his death . . . Whereunto is annexed a true copie, in substance, of the behaviour, speache, and prayer of the said Earle at the time of his execution (London, 1601; STC 1454).

73. Proclamation, 5 April 1601, 43 Eliz. I, in *Tudor Royal Proclamations,* 3:233–34 (no. 810); see PRO, SP12/281/67; HMC, *Salisbury MSS,* 11:132, 156; Cheyney, *History of England,* 2:538.

74. "A Discourse of the names and first causes of the institution of Cities and peopled towns. And of the commodities that doe growe by the same: and namely of the Cittie of London," in Stow, *Survey of London,* ed. Kingsford, ii, p. 206. The author of this apology for London was almost certainly James Dalton, one of London's official legal Counselors and undersheriff from March 1594; see ibid., ii, pp. 186, 386, 387. Kingsford suggests that the "Discourse" may have been written about 1580.

75. See Archer, *Pursuit of Stability,* pp. 10–11, 12, 17, 20, 25–27, 32–39, 41, 44, 50–51, 140; Brenner, *Merchants and Revolution,* pp. 688–716 and passim.

76. Ian Archer, "The London Lobbies in the Later Sixteenth Century," *Historical Journal,* 31 (1988), 17–44.

77. Stow, *Survey of London,* ed. Kingsford, 1:85.

78. For Kemp's career see E. K. Chambers, *The Elizabethan Stage,* 4 vols. (Oxford: Clarendon Press, 1923), 2:325–26; "William Kemp," *DNB,* 10:390–94; David Wiles, *Shakespeare's Clown: Actor and Text in the Elizabethan Playhouse* (Cambridge: Cambridge University Press, 1987), pp. 24–60, 73–82, 99–115; Chris Harris, *Will Kemp: Shakespeare's Forgotten Clown* (Waddeson, Bucks., Kylin Press, 1983).

79. See Andrew Gurr, *The Shakespearean Stage, 1574–1642,* 3rd ed. (Cambridge: Cambridge University Press, 1992), pp. 34, 41–42, 44–49, 86, 88–89; Andrew Gurr, *Playgoing in Shakespeare's London,* 2nd ed. (Cambridge: Cambridge University Press, 1996), pp. 157–58; Richard Helgerson, *Forms of Nationhood: The Elizabethan Writing of England* (Chicago: University of Chicago Press, 1992), p. 223; Max W. Taylor, "*Kemps Nine Daies Wonder:* Dancing Carnival into Market," *PMLA,* 107 (1992): 511, 515.

80. Kemp, *Kemps nine daies vvonder,* sig. A[2]r.

81. Ibid., sig. A[2]v.

82. See Helgerson, *Forms of Nationhood,* pp. 193–245, esp. 222–31 and 241; Gurr, *Shakespearean Stage,* pp. 173–76; Wiles, *Shakespeare's Clowns,* pp. 136–40; Taylor, *Kemps Nine Daies Wonder,* pp. 511, 515–22.

83. Kemp, *Kemps nine daies vvonder,* sig. A3[a]r.

84. See E. J. Buckatsch, "The Geographical Distribution of Wealth in England, 1086–1843," *Economic History Review,* 2nd ser., 3 (1950): 180–202; R. S. Schofield, "The Geographical Distribution of Wealth in England, 1334–1649," *Economic History Review,* 2nd ser., 18 (1965): 483–510; Fisher, *London and the English Economy,* pp. 61–80, 119–30; Reed, "London and Its Hinterland," in *Capital Cities and Their Hinterlands,* pp. 57–73; J. A. Chartres, "Food Consumption and Internal Trade," in *London, 1500–1700,* pp. 168–96; F. V. Emery, "England *circa* 1600," in *A New Historical Geography of England,* ed. H. C. Darby (Cambridge: Cambridge University Press, 1973), pp. 267–70, 279–80; H. C. Darby, "Some Early Ideas on the Agricultural Regions of England," *Agricultural History Review,* 2 (1954): 30–47; *The Agrarian History of England and Wales: Volume IV, 1500–1640,* ed. Joan Thirsk (Cambridge: Cambridge University Press, 1967), pp. 40–50, 53–55, 58, 173, 175–77, 196–97, 507–16, 546–47, 575, 644–45; Eric Kerridge, *The Agricultural Revolution* (London: Allen and Unwin, 1967), pp. 56–60,

72–80, 83–113, 136–44; see also *The Agrarian History of England and Wales: Volume V, 1640–1750; I. Regional Farming Systems,* ed. Joan Thirsk (Cambridge: Cambridge University Press, 1984), pp. 197–238; Patten, *English Towns,* pp. 244–96.

85. Stow, *Survey of London,* ed. Kingsford, 2:186; Rabb, *Enterprise and Empire,* p. 346.

86. Kemp, *Kemps nine daies vvonder,* sig. A3[a]v, sig. B[1]r.

87. Stow, *Survey of London,* ed. Kingsford, 1:81, 84–85, 89, 101–4; Archer, *Pursuit of Stability,* pp. 16, 94; Ian Archer, "The Nostalgia of John Stow," in *The Theatrical City: Culture, Theatre, and Politics in London, 1576–1649,* eds. David Smith, Richard Strier, and David Bevington (Cambridge: Cambridge University Press, 1995), pp. 17–34; see also Lawrence Manley, "Of Sites and Rites," ibid., pp. 35–54; Manley, *Literature and Culture in Early Modern London,* p. 130.

88. Kemp, *Kemps nine daies vvonder,* sig. C3[a]v–C3[b]r; Francis Blomefield, *An Essay towards a Topographical History of the County of Norfolk,* 2nd ed., 11 vols. (London: W. Miller, 1805–10), 3:359; Basil Cozens-Hardy and Ernest A. Kent, *The Mayors of Norwich, 1403 to 1835; Being Biographical Notes on the Mayors of the Old Corporation* (Norwich: Jarrold and Sons, 1938), p. 61; *An Index to Norwich City Officers, 1453–1835,* ed. Timothy Hawes (Norfolk Rec. Soc., 52, 1986), pp. xxiii, xxiv, xxix, 163; *Records of Early English Drama: Norwich, 1540–1642,* ed. David Galloway (Toronto: University of Toronto Press, 1984), pp. xliii, 114–15.

89. Kemp, *Kemps nine daies vvonder,* sig. C3[b]r–sig. D2[a]r.

90. Kemp, *Kemps nine daies vvonder,* sig. D[1]v.

91. Blomefield, *Topographical History of the County of Norfolk,* 3:182–360; John Pound, *Tudor and Stuart Norwich* (Chichester: Phillimore, 1988); J. F. Pound, "The Social and Trade Structure of Norwich, 1525–1575," *Past and Present,* 34 (July 1966): 49–69; J. F. Pound, "An Elizabethan Census of the Poor," *University of Birmingham Historical Journal,* 8:2 (1962): 135–61; *The Norwich Census of the Poor, 1570,* ed. J. F. Pound (Norfolk Rec. Soc. 40, 1971); Muriel C. McLendon, "'Against God's Word': Government, Religion, and the Crisis of Authority in Early Reformation Norwich," *Sixteenth Century Journal,* 25 (1994): 353–69.

92. Patten, *English Towns,* pp. 244–96; *Small Towns in Early Modern Europe,* ed. Peter Clark (Cambridge: Cambridge University Press, 1995), pp. 1–21, 90–147.

93. Kemp, *Kemps nine daies vvonder,* sig. B[1]v, sig. C[1]r–v; see also, Kemp's dedicatory letter to Anne Fitton, "Mayde of Honour to the most sacred Mayde Royall Queen Elizabeth," ibid., sig. A[2]r–v.

94. Kemp, *Kemps nine daies vvonder,* sig. C3[a]r.

95. Ibid., sig. A[2]r, sig. D2[b]r–v.

96. Ibid., sig. D2[a]r–v.

97. See Tessa Watt, *Cheap Print and Popular Piety, 1550–1640* (Cambridge: Cambridge University Press, 1991), pp. 16–18, 24–29, 195, 257–95; Margaret Spufford, *Small Books and Pleasant Histories: Popular Fiction and Its Readership in Seventeenth-Century England* (London: Metheun, 1981), pp. 111–28; Margaret Spufford, *The Great Reclothing of Rural England: Petty Chapmen and Their Wares in the Seventeenth Century* (London: Hambledon Press, 1984), pp. 5–6, 9, 43, 54, 56, 57, 62, 66, 80, 85–86, 88, 89, 145, 154, 163, 204, 226; see also Peter Blayney, "The Publication of Playbooks," in *A New History of Early English Drama,* ed. John D. Cox and David Scott Kastan (New York: Columbia University Press, 1997), pp. 384–89, 405–15.

98. Kemp, *Kemps nine daies vvonder,* sig. B3[b]v, sig. C[1]v–C2[a]r.

99. Marjorie Keniston McIntosh, *A Community Transformed: The Manor and Liberty of Havering, 1500–1620* (Cambridge: Cambridge University Press, 1991), pp. 1–2, 130–75, 402–11.

100. Chambers, *Elizabethan Stage,* 1:348–88; 2:353–517; Glynne Wickham, *Early English Stages, 1300–1660,* reprint 3 vols. in 4, 2nd ed. (London, Routledge & K. Paul, 1971), 2:153–205; Gurr, *Shakespearean Stage,* pp. 27–79; Andrew Gurr, *The Shakespearian Playing Companies* (Oxford: Clarendon Press, 1996), pp. 19–54; William Ingram, *The Business of Playing: The Beginnings of the Adult Professional Theater in Elizabethan London* (Ithaca: Cornell University Press, 1992); William Ingram, "The Costs of Touring," *Medieval and Renaissance Drama in England,* 6 (1993): 57–62; Kathleen E. McLuskie and Felicity Dunsworth, "Patronage and the Economics of Theater," in *A New History of Early English Drama,* pp. 423–40; Blayney, "The Publication of Playbooks," ibid., pp. 383–422; Jean-Christophe Agnew, *Worlds Apart: The Market and the Theater in Anglo-American Thought, 1550–1750* (Cambridge: Cambridge University Press, 1986), pp. 17–56; Lucien Febvre and Henri-Jean Martin, *The Coming of the Book: The Impact of Printing, 1450–1800,* trans. David Gerard, ed. Geoffrey Nowell-Smith and David Wootton (London: N.L.B., 1976), pp. 29–44, 109–42, 216–38; Elizabeth L. Eisenstein, *The Printing Press As an Agent of Change: Communications and Cultural Transformations in Early-Modern Europe,* 2 vols. (Cambridge: Cambridge University Press, 1979), 3–88.

101. On "good Turnes," see Lucius Annaeus Seneca, *The woorke of the excellent Philosopher Lucius Annaeus Seneca concerning Benefyting, that is too say the dooing, receyving and requyting of good Turnes,* trans. Arthur Golding (London, 1578, STC 22215).

102. On "creative destruction," see Joseph A. Schumpeter, *Capitalism, Socialism, and Democracy* (London: G. Allen and Unwin, Ltd., 1943), pp. 81–86.

103. See Seneca, *Woorke,* trans. Golding; Peck, *Court Patronage,* pp. 12–29; Sacks, "The Countervailing of Benefits," in *Tudor Political Culture,* pp. 282–91.

104. David Harris Sacks, "The Greed of Judas: Avarice, Monopoly, and the Moral Economy, c. 1350–1600," *Journal of Medieval and Early Modern Studies,* 28:2 (Spring 1998): 263–307.

105. Publius Cornelius Tacitus, *Agricola,* 21, in Tacitus, *Dialogus, Agricola, Germania* (Cambridge, Mass.: Harvard University Press, 1939), p. 21. The translation is from Tacitus, *The Agricola and the Germania,* trans. H. Mattingly, rev. trans. S. A. Handford (Harmondsworth: Penguin Books, 1970), pp. 72–73.

3

Material London in Time and Space

Derek Keene

Cities are as much material as social constructs. They are places where commodities are manipulated and exchanged. Their physical structures incorporate masses of stuff brought from elsewhere. Their cultural identities find vital expression in the forms those materials take. All this is brought about by the expenditure of vast quantities of energy: the source of that energy — human, animal, organic, or mineral — and the ways in which it is used shape the identity of the city. These processes of accumulation and manipulation extend over long periods, as the necessary infrastructures, both physical and social, are built up. Moreover, cities do not stand in isolation. They are shaped by, and themselves shape, wider demographic trends, political structures, accumulations of knowledge and credit, and, above all, the balance of comparative advantage between cities, regions, and states. In any one city each of these forces can follow different trajectories in time and space, although often the trajectories are linked.

This essay attempts a simple assessment of London in 1600 as a material organism in these terms, and with regard to its spatial and chronological context. To view the city in a broader context than that in which it is normally placed provides significant insights into its character and into the processes which made it what it was. The principal topics are the pattern of the city's growth over five hundred years; its standing within the networks which sustained it; and the distinctive material expressions of the city's culture of manufacture and consumption, especially as they changed during the sixteenth century.[1] Underlying the issues is the difficult, and perhaps emotive, question of where London in 1600 stood in relation to its long-term trajectory. Did Elizabethan London, and perhaps especially the foundation in 1566 of the Royal Exchange which was later such a powerful expression of the city's commercial force and pride, pave the way for metropolitan, national, and imperial

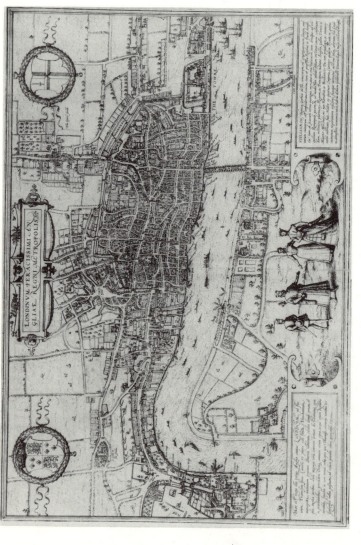

3.1. London, Westminster, and Southwark in the mid-sixteenth century, from G. Braun and F. Hogenberg's atlas *Civitates Orbis Terrarum*, first published in 1572. This reproduction is of the second state of the map, which appears in editions of the atlas published in 1574 and later, and which shows the Royal Exchange, built 1566–70. The map, however, shows the spire of St. Paul's Cathedral, which was destroyed in 1561, and appears to be derived from an earlier, more detailed survey of between 1547 and 1559. By 1600 the extent and, in particular, the density of building outside the city walls and in Southwark, on the south bank of the river, were significantly greater, although the overall pattern was still that of the Middle Ages. Copyright Guildhall Library, Corporation of London.

growth, as seems so often to be assumed?[2] Or did London's essential discontinuity with its past occur at an earlier or a later date, especially when seen from a
material point of view? And did that discontinuity reflect a dynamic which was
essentially internal, national, or insular in character? Or was it a result of wider
European forces?

During the sixteenth century London grew rapidly to become, with
about 200,000 inhabitants, one of Europe's largest cities. In 1600, one in
twenty of the inhabitants of England and Wales lived in the metropolis, by
comparison with perhaps one in fifty a hundred years before and an even
smaller proportion in earlier centuries. Over the century the total population
of London probably increased more than fourfold; the greatest rate of increase
most likely occurred during the last three to four decades. Other European
cities grew at greater rates for parts of this period, but none of them experienced the impact of such a massive total of immigrants from their hinterlands.[3]
The dominance of London, in both population and wealth, had for centuries
been an established feature of the English scene. London's primary role has
always been as a center of trade; as such, between the seventh and the thirteenth century, it gave shape to the English state by drawing in the institutions
of authority and causing them to settle in its vicinity.[4] London also contained
the largest and most diversified concentration of manufactures in the kingdom: this was as true in 1300 as in 1600, 1700, or the 1860s.[5] The sheer scale of
the city and its needs supported many artisans and a high degree of craft
specialization, but its position as a trading and political center also created a
distinctive demand for elite, high-quality goods and gave it an important role
as a center of innovation and in the organization of markets and production
elsewhere in the kingdom. In 1600 England as a whole was no more urbanized
than it had been in 1300, but the share of its urban population which resided in
London had more than doubled.[6] This shift of resources to London continued
despite the lack of demographic growth between the time of the Black Death
and about 1500, and was apparent in the flow of trade and in the further
concentration of royal interests in the city and its vicinity.[7] It had a profound
influence on the material systems upon which the city drew and was associated
with a tightening of commercial as well as social linkages between the metropolis and provincial districts, thereby accelerating the emergence of a national
market within which the "metropolitan economy" supplied entrepreneurship,
credit, and imported goods to the regions, where it fostered specialization in
both agrarian and industrial production.[8] Moreover, the period between 1300
and 1600 witnessed not simply a geographical shift in the pattern of commerce, but also a continuing process of commercialization and a significant

general improvement in the conditions of trade, changes which were themselves part of wider European developments.[9]

The great growth of London in the sixteenth century is often explained in terms internal to England and to the period. F. J. Fisher, for example, drew attention to the three factors identified by Botero as underlying the greatness of cities — princely residence, resort to courts of justice, and expenditure by noble residents and visitors — and stressed the significance for London's growth during the sixteenth and seventeenth centuries of the presence of the Crown, court, government, and law, and the great flow of business and people to the capital that they encouraged.[10] Such ideas are linked to a broader perception that the emergence of the great metropolises of the early modern period was associated with the consolidation of state power and with their particular role as capitals.[11] Yet there are some obvious exceptions to that generalization, and in the case of London it is at least arguable that the decisive stage in the development of the city as the focus of national power and expenditure was in the late thirteenth century rather than in the sixteenth. Moreover, although the rapid increase in resort to the capital was certainly associated with a growing propensity to do legal business there, it is far from clear which was cause and which effect. Furthermore, the physical bulk of the sixteenth-century central court records (to which Fisher draws attention) tends to overshadow the degree to which the more compact documents of the fourteenth and fifteenth centuries indicate that the pursuit of legal business in London was already an important feature of English society. Certainly by 1300 London (having by far the greatest concentration of wealth, trade, aristocratic residence, and spending)[12] was a powerful magnet for migrants drawn by opportunities for work and, increasingly in a period when the real value of wages was diminishing, seeking the charitable relief and marginal employment which were always more freely available in the capital than elsewhere.

It is by no means certain that this process of growth was inherently unlikely to continue. Indeed, both agrarian production and marketing and the striking response to the process of commercialization which is evident in the intellectual culture of the time suggest that the opposite was true.[13] In any event, the demographic catastrophe of the fourteenth century brought to an end this phase of London's growth, although the sharp rise in the real value of wages which followed stimulated new patterns of consumption, manufacturing, and commercial growth. By the sixteenth century this trend had been reversed, and over the century as a whole the fall in the standard of living for the mass of English people, while not so severe as once proposed, was nevertheless sharp; the 1590s were especially difficult.[14] In these circumstances, as in the thirteenth century, "subsistence migration" by the economically weak made a substantial contribution to the population growth of London, which, so far as we can tell, was probably greatest from about 1570 onward when the downward trend in the standard of living resumed after a respite of some two decades. At this time the concentration of mercantile and landed wealth and expenditure in London was much greater than in former centuries. Landlords and farmers enjoyed rising incomes as the price of food rose, while the price of manufactured products increased at a lower rate. The dissolution of the religious houses had put much agricultural land on the market, a process which itself stimulated business in London. The transfer of landed income into the hands of nobles, gentry, and merchants was even more significant, however, for the new owners were more inclined than their predecessors to spend it on consumer goods and services, of which the best were to be obtained in London, and where, through residence and fashionable display, they could express their identity and standing. This was in some ways a return to the conditions of the late thirteenth-century city, but on a greater scale since a larger group of individuals was in a position to consume a wider range of material goods. This was despite the undoubted mass of poor in London, whose living conditions may have been no better than those of their counterparts three hundred years before. We should take care not to exaggerate the novelty of sixteenth-century patterns of material consumption, however, for there are clear indications that something like a mass market in cheap manufactured goods had already come into existence in London by 1300.[15]

Contemporaries noted the improvements in housing and material possessions enjoyed by many in later sixteenth-century England.[16] In the case of London, observers particularly remarked on the fine clothing of the citizens and their wives; the ostentation, extravagance, and rapidly changing fashions in the dress of the gentry (who more frequently resorted to London for both business and pleasure); and the wide range of novelties from overseas available in the city's shops and exchanges, supplying both consumers based in the capital and those in the country; John Stow associated these developments with a court which was "greater and more gallant" than before.[17] This intensification of consumption was as impressive as the sprawling growth of the city. Both, however, had roots as much in the steady accumulation of physical, social, and commercial infrastructure, and in London's consolidation of its position as the political and administrative capital, both under way long before 1300, as in the particular developments of the sixteenth century.

Equally important was London's role as the prime link between English commerce and extended Continental routes of trade, where the city stood at the end of the line. From its origin London owed its position to its participation within networks of intensive commercial exchange which focused on the southern part of the North Sea, and especially on the territory around the mouths of the Rhine and the Scheldt. In the earlier Middle Ages, London had stood especially high as a European city on that account, but by 1200 it was being overtaken by Paris and by the dense cluster of commercial and manufacturing towns in Flanders. In 1300 the city was still outstanding as a site for material production and consumption by comparison with its immediate Continental neighbors but was clearly on the margin between an intensive zone of production to the east and one of more extensive production to the west. Like Britain as a whole, it occupied a peripheral position within the European economy and still did so in the early seventeenth century. Between 1300 and 1500, however, London fell sharply back in relation to Continental neighbors. In 1500 London was widely recognized as containing great wealth, above all visible in the windows of its goldsmiths' shops,[18] but it was not commensurate in the making of goods. The city's wealth was derived from its distributive trade and from its engrossing of the export of English woolen cloths (woven in provincial districts), which it transmitted in unfinished form to the expanding and sophisticated markets of the Low Countries, whence it received luxury commodities and an increasingly wide range of humbler manufactured goods.[19] London's wealth rested on a narrow base, which was almost certainly narrower than in earlier centuries. The imports of manufactures were perceived as undermining native industry,[20] although from the fourteenth century onward, they seem to have made available to English consumers a wider range of personal and household items, and at lower prices, than could be achieved by English workshops. This arose from the greater specialization and more efficient distribution systems of the Continental markets. Even in the manufacture of fine pewter vessels—where in the fifteenth century London was a European leader on account of its ready access to raw materials and its tradition of skill—the focus of high-quality production shifted from this peripheral site to Continental ones with more varied and specialized metal-working skills.[21] The state of affairs thus became even more extreme in the later sixteenth century when large quantities of relatively cheap manufactured goods were imported to London, both for consumption there and for distribution throughout the country.[22] There is no simple way of expressing these changes in London's standing, but its population relative to those of the principal Low Countries cities provides a partial guide. Thus in 1300 London's population was almost half the total for the leading towns of the southern Netherlands—Bruges, Ghent, Antwerp, and Brussels—while by 1500 was it was no more than a quarter. By 1550 London, with a third of the population of the southern Netherlands cities, had perhaps regained the position it had enjoyed in 1400. By 1600 it had moved decisively ahead, containing more inhabitants than the towns of the southern Netherlands and as much as two-thirds of the combined total of those towns and of the growing towns farther north.[23]

For the sixteenth century, however, London's standing by these measures of population (which are themselves uncertain) was heavily influenced by the flow of subsistence migrants, by the concentration of narrowly based mercantile wealth and by the marked increase in royal residence and expenditure in and around London, especially under Henry VIII.[24] These factors were interlinked and, like the shift in the overall concentration of England's wealth toward southeastern England,[25] reflected an increasing dependence on the markets operating through the towns of the Low Countries. It is no coincidence that throughout the later Middle Ages and for much of the sixteenth century the prime aim of English foreign policy was to secure access to those markets, and, when that access was blocked, to seek alternative avenues to European networks of trade.[26] The relative strength of those markets as sites of both production and exchange is apparent from the level of real wages. In the mid-fifteenth century, for example, the purchasing power of a craftsman's wages in Bruges was about a third as much again as that of his counterpart in London, which in turn exceeded that of craftsmen in English provincial towns by a similar degree.[27] Bruges was at that time the principal emporium of northern Europe, and in the towns of its immediate hinterland in Flanders and Brabant, the value of wages likewise fell away sharply. In the late fifteenth century, Antwerp succeeded Bruges and until the troubles of the 1560s and later, enjoyed even greater success as a commercial metropolis. During the sixteenth century the purchasing power of the London craftsman fell while that of his Antwerp counterpart was sustained.[28] Interest rates, too, reveal the relative weakness of London's economy, for in 1600, continuing the established medieval pattern, English rates were markedly higher than those in Italy, in the commercially prosperous parts of Germany, and in the northern Netherlands, which were then assuming the former role of Antwerp and the south.[29] There was no significant convergence between English and the lower Continental rates until the late seventeenth century.

Patterns of migration indicate the relative attractions of these areas. For centuries, relations between London and Flanders had been close and people from the Low Countries and the Rhineland had formed the largest element in the city's population of immigrants from overseas. In the fifteenth century, however, immigrants from the southern Netherlands were not conspicuous in that group which was dominated by people from less prosperous, and more disordered, regions to the north and east.[30] Antwerp, by contrast, was a magnet for Englishmen, French, Portuguese, Italians, and Germans.[31] It was not until the Antwerp troubles of the 1560s and the successive phases of warfare which followed that significant numbers of immigrants from the southern Netherlands arrived in London as part of a wider Protestant diaspora from that region. Many of these chose London because of existing trade and family connections, but it is clear that London was not necessarily a prime draw on its own account. After the sack of Antwerp in 1585, Amsterdam attracted many immigrants and a great deal of capital from the troubled south, thereby establishing itself as the new commercial metropolis;[32] in the difficult 1590s, immigrants returned from London to the Netherlands and there was a surge in the migration of English to Amsterdam.[33] In other European commercial centers it was not until the late seventeenth century that the English, rather than the Dutch, became prominent among foreign merchants.[34]

London's participation in this European nexus was a major influence on its material life. Crucial and immediate factors in the fifteenth century were the development of large-scale, integrated speculative markets in basic commodities (such as grain along the northern and western coasts of Europe), the growth of light textile manufactures in the lesser towns of the Low Countries, and the formation of the Burgundian state with its economic and cultural focus on the towns of Flanders and Brabant.[35] This was the context out of which the Antwerp emporium grew.[36] This intensified existing systems of exchange, drew in silver and manufactured products from far afield, redistributed them widely, and created a new focus for European markets and urban growth.[37] Just as London acted as an interchange and promoted specialized production across a large part of England, so the towns of the Low Countries performed a similar role within a larger and wealthier European hinterland. Sixteenth-century London received its goods from Antwerp, not their places of origin. Antwerp became the dominant site for cultural production and distribution in northern Europe and persisted as a cultural influence well into the seventeenth century, despite its political and military misfortunes and its eclipse by Amsterdam as a center of international trade.[38] Like the cities of northern Italy, with which they were in ever closer contact and which their cultures tended to replicate, Bruges and then Antwerp, and their immediate hinterlands, rapidly became notable as sites for the production of music, literature, architecture, painting, printing, sculpture, fine metalwork, tapestries, furnishings, scientific instruments, and ingenious machines. A pump, described as a "vyce of bras bought in the countrey of Flaunders conteyning theryn right connyng and crafty conseit of Ghematrye," evidently made a strong impression on Londoners in 1497.[39] Many of the artistic products reached a wide market among the mercantile and shopkeeping classes as well as among the landowning aristocracy, and in both towns, specialized art markets emerged on Italian lines, of a type which was not to appear in London before the late seventeenth century.[40] Burgundian magnificence, in due course mediated through Hapsburg and Spanish imperial frameworks, was a powerful influence on English court and aristocratic culture, but the impact of the more everyday life and goods of the Low Countries towns was just as important for Londoners.

London paid for its imports with exports of white, unfinished woolen cloths, a trade which expanded rapidly during the first half of the sixteenth century and, despite fluctuations, remained at a high level throughout the second half of the century and continued to serve as the backbone of the city's overseas trade.[41] The cloths were purchased in Antwerp, or other Continental marts along the coast of the North Sea, by south German traders who distributed them widely in central Europe. This *Lundisch Gewandt* or *Lunski,* not made in London but coming from there, was perhaps the most distinctive material expression of London's identity in fifteenth- and sixteenth-century Europe and the near East. The very fact that some of the *Londra* cloths mentioned in Ottoman registers of the period were perhaps a southern French imitation of the English product, and that *Lunski* could denote Dutch as well as English cloth demonstrates the strength of this element in London's identity and the city's dependence on handling a single product.[42] That the cloth was exported unfinished demonstrates not the inherent technological backwardness of London, but rather the complementary relationship which it had developed with Antwerp. The latter could add 30 percent to the value of the cloth by dyeing and other finishing processes only because it lay at the hub of a market for a high-quality product whose color and finish had continually to be adapted to the rapidly changing demands of fashion.[43] Antwerp's strength as a market for other finished goods doubtless had a similar basis. London was as yet too remote from the prime centers of demand to compete on those terms: its remoteness was to be measured less in physical distance than in its access to information flows and networks of exchange.

At the level of the social elite, the dominant cultural exemplar in sixteenth-century England was Italy. Englishmen visited Italy and adopted Italian styles of dress. In grand architecture Italian models were also influential, principally through the medium of buildings in France. Moreover, projects such as the classical facade of Somerset House in London (1547–52) were associated with a small group of wealthy aristocratic patrons.[44] The Low Countries, however, served as a more influential link between north and south. Their commerce in effect brought the Mediterranean closer to the North Sea. Italian was the language of the Antwerp Bourse, Italian merchants supplied the luxury textiles which dominated its commodity market, and Italian commercial techniques set the pace for the north.[45] Antwerp adopted features of

Italian architecture and design, albeit in a "mannered" and "provincial" form. In that way Renaissance styles came to have a more penetrating and widespread influence in London and England as a whole. As Summerson put it, "whereas the art of Italians and Frenchmen had to be fetched, the art of Antwerp flowed of its own accord."[46] For good commercial as well as artistic reasons, London's new Royal Exchange was an import from Antwerp in its purpose, design, and, to a significant extent, its materials.[47] The citizens' houses incorporated brackets and strapwork carved or modeled in the Antwerp manner, and Netherlandish carvers working in London produced high-quality work for tombs, fireplaces, and other features, which were supplied to both London and country clients.[48] In the early seventeenth century London houses with fronts in brick or stone were erected for gentry clients in the distinctive style of the southern Netherlands.[49] Royal building proclamations of the same period concerning the desirable type of mercantile house for London seem to envisage a similar style of building or, perhaps, the variant of Serlio's *casa per un vico artefice o buon mercante* recently developed in Paris.[50] Antwerp's influence similarly persisted in other forms of craft and artistic production in London. English silver, for example, underwent a dramatic change in appearance from the late 1540s under the impact of designs from Antwerp (whose goldsmiths were the leading producers of the time) and experienced no further major change of design before the seventeenth century.[51]

Through their close links to the Low Countries, Londoners of the fifteenth and sixteenth centuries steadily became more directly exposed to, and thereby acquired more of a taste for, Italian silks, lace, glassware, and paper; German and Low Countries metal goods, including blades, armor, brassware, and engraved instruments for measurement and navigation; the decorated leather of Spain and Brussels; the textiles of southern Germany; the furniture, furnishings, and miscellaneous consumer goods made in and around Antwerp; and a host of other goods.[52] Londoners were also drawn into a world of print culture where knowledge was more effectively stored and distributed than before in the form of geographies and descriptions, atlases, maps, and handbooks. For Londoners, Antwerp and then Amsterdam served as successive gateways to new worlds. In 1567 an Antwerp printer published in English a handbook on keeping mercantile accounts, whose intended readers were evidently the Merchant Adventurers of London.[53] Ideas concerning architecture and design were also transmitted to London by means of books printed in Antwerp. Serlio's "Fourth Book of Architecture" appeared in Dutch in Antwerp only two years after its first publication in Italian in Venice in 1537. The *Architectura* of Hans Vredeman de Vries, printed in Antwerp in 1577, 1581, 1597, and 1601, was until well into the seventeenth century the principal means by which Englishmen became acquainted with the writings of Vitruvius and Serlio.[54] Through such products as the tin-glazed ceramic vessels being brought, probably via Antwerp, from kilns in Spain and Italy, Londoners came into contact, if only at second and third hand, with the styles of the vastly wealthier and the materially more advanced civilizations of the Ottoman Empire, Persia, and China.[55] By the mid-sixteenth century the "Turkey carpet" was probably a common feature in wealthier English households, having often arrived via Venice, Antwerp, and London.[56] This sort of exposure generated new ideas about consumption and the possibilities of direct English involvement in distant trade, especially after access to the Antwerp market was blocked.[57]

One outcome of the flow of new and luxury products into the Netherlands was the establishment locally of the manufacture of similar items, continuing a process, extending over many centuries, of technical diffusion from the Far East and the Islamic world, at first into southern Europe and much later to the north. Foreign craftsmen and merchants were often associated with such enterprises, whose purpose was to provide a product which would undercut that brought from a distance. Initially such locally made goods seem to have aimed at the lower end of the market, while the elite sector continued to demand the higher-quality imported product. The manufacture of the cheaper types of silken cloths, previously obtained from Italy or Cologne (a major source of supply for both England and the Netherlands), was established in Bruges in the fifteenth century and transferred to Antwerp soon after 1500 when Antwerp equaled and then overtook Venice as the most dynamic European center of trade. By 1550 Antwerp-made silks were moving sharply up market, and by 1580 the industry employed many hundreds of people.[58] Tin-glazed ceramics of Spanish and Islamic type were being made in Italy from about 1440 and in Flanders by the later fifteenth century. Italians used a similar technology to make their own products in Antwerp from 1508 onward; by the 1530s, output was large and the products difficult to distinguish from those of Italy; soon afterward, natives took over the business.[59] In this way specialized crafts which had once been practiced at a great distance from London were brought closer to the city and entered a commercial environment where trade and migration across the North Sea had been commonplace for centuries.

This was the context in which beer-brewing came to be established in London during the fifteenth century. Initially, London appears to have been attractive to beer-brewers as a cheap site of production, where the product would appeal to the sizeable alien population, and whence it could be exported to substantial urban markets overseas. The taste for beer seems to have spread slowly among English drinkers and the craft of beer-brewing in London remained predominantly in the hands of Dutchmen and Germans until the later sixteenth century.[60] It seems that it was critical to the successful transfer of new types of material production to London, and indeed to the other cities, that they should become established in the native culture and that the products should suit a broad-based local market. The silk industry provides a good example of this. In the fifteenth century the simple ribbon-weaving undertaken by London's silkwomen was undermined, probably by imports from Cologne. A royal attempt at that time to establish in London the manufacture of broad silk textiles by importing a small number of highly skilled Italian craftsmen came to little or nothing, as did a similar attempt in the 1550s. Presumably they could not compete with what was available in the Netherlands. By contrast, in the 1560s and later, the larger-scale forced migration to London from the southern Netherlands of less-skilled makers of the cheaper silken and mixed light textiles associated with their towns led to the successful establishment of the industry. It seems that the traumatic nature of their expulsion from the Netherlands was important, for the arrival of the proportionally much larger alien population in London twenty years earlier had no equivalent effect. The new arrivals, cut off from their homelands, chose to adapt their skills — which in some cases seem not to have included a specialist knowledge of silk-weaving — in order to survive in a city to which they would not otherwise have chosen to migrate. Their product presumably could not compete with the best from Italy or Antwerp but met a distinctive local need, perhaps in the form of a growing, but relatively undiscriminating demand for silks or mixed fabrics of middling quality. The growth of manufacture is indicated by a sharp increase in the import of raw silk and by the fairly rapid transfer of skills to native workers. It is noteworthy that most of the immigrants with, or capable of developing, silk-weaving skills gravitated toward, or were directed to, London, where the demand for the product was most intense, while others made their way to provincial centers. There are even signs that by 1600 London was beginning to develop the high-quality dyeing and finishing skills which it had lacked for two centuries or more.[61] Similarly, Flemings from Antwerp and Bruges were involved in the successful transfer of tin-glazed ceramic manufacture to London from about 1570 onward.[62]

Italians introduced the manufacture of crystal glass to Antwerp, and in the 1540s the industry became very successful although the trade remained in Italian hands.[63] In 1567 a French-speaking refugee from Antwerp, where he had long been resident and had probably been engaged in the glass trade, arrived in London and obtained permission to set up furnaces for producing window glass in the Weald and Venetian-type furnaces for producing crystal glass in London. Within five years the crystal glasshouse in London was being run by a Murano glassworker who had worked in Antwerp for two decades. He prospered until 1592, when his monopoly was given to an Englishman. Ownership of the business thus passed into native hands, but until well into the seventeenth century, successful production of high-quality glass in London depended upon importing skilled workers from Murano, workers who proved difficult to retain. Glassmaking was one of a number of industries where the government pursued a policy of import-substitution by granting monopolies, with some success in this case. As with textiles, the location of the luxury sector of the trade in the capital was significant, and it is clear that the crystal glass was intended for the nobility who were free to import glass if the London product was not sold at a reasonable rate.[64]

London's increasing engagement with, and dependence upon, the markets of the Low Countries over the two centuries up to 1600 thus had a profound effect upon its material culture. As those markets brought distant parts of Europe and the Mediterranean world closer together, Londoners experienced a wider variety of imported goods and were brought closer to the sites of innovative manufacture of luxury goods. In due course, those new manufactures might have transferred to London of their own accord, but the process was accelerated by government policy, the traumatic disturbances in the southern Netherlands, and by an awareness, not entirely translated into policy, that "Antwerp and Venice could never have been so rich and famous but by the entertaining of strangers."[65] With the exception of beer-brewing and silk manufacture, the new manufactures established in London, of which only a small sample has been discussed here, remained small in scale, crucially dependent upon alien skills, and primarily aimed at wealthy consumers. Attempts to establish manufactures which would meet something like a mass market, such as that supplied by German stoneware, continued through the seventeenth century,[66] and attainment of the ideal represented by Venice and Antwerp (and later by Amsterdam) lay far in the future. Nevertheless, about 1600 there was an acute consciousness that recently "the people mightily increased both in number of people and in all good skill, and skilful of all kinde and manner of trades."[67] In his enlarged edition of John Stow's *Annales* published in 1615, Edmond Howes included an account of "the first knowledge and coming of divers things into England" and "the invention of divers things in this latter age, together, with the great increace of general commerce, and the unimaginable enlarging of London, and the suburbs, within the space of fiftie years."[68]

The physical growth of London was itself responsible for the greatest changes in the material condition of the metropolis, not only in the increasing density and extent of building and the sprawling shantytowns on its margins, but also in the very atmosphere and appearance of the place. In the second half of the sixteenth century London witnessed a material revolution in energy consumption. Since the eleventh century there had been a steady increase in the quantity of energy that the city consumed per capita on account of rising industrial production and the increasing durability of the fabric, but over half the demand for fuel was for domestic needs and so the impact of sixteenth-century growth was dramatic. The increase in the consumption and production of ale and beer since the mid-fourteenth century also increased fuel consumption, as did the growing use of locally produced bricks in building, which was in part stimulated by Burgundian fashion. From the earlier episode in London's growth, up to 1300, it is apparent that the capacity of its hinterland to supply food was more elastic than its capacity to supply fuel from carefully managed, renewable woodland. Thus from 1550 onward there was a rapid increase in the shipment of mineral fuel, "sea coal," from Newcastle to London; by 1600 it had become the "general fuel." This necessitated innovations which would enable coal to be used in industrial processes such as brewing and glassmaking, but above all inaugurated the period (extending up to the Clean Air Act of 1956) when one overwhelming impression of London was its sulfurous, polluted atmosphere and its ubiquitous deposits of soot. The economic arithmetic which led to London's extensive use of sea coal may have contributed to its longer-term success and given it advantages over some other European cities. It freed the territory in the vicinity of the metropolis of the necessity to produce wood fuel, allowing other productive uses of the land; it endowed London with a virtually unlimited source of energy to support its physical growth and continued industrial production; and it facilitated the reconstruction of London's fabric in brick.[69]

Just where, in relation to these longer trajectories, did material London stand in 1600? There was a strong sense of new commodities, changing fashions, new manufactures, and of reaching out to new worlds where Englishmen had hardly penetrated before. Yet to a very large extent these changes owed more to developments outside the kingdom, to structural features established in the distant past, and to the recent crises in the southern Netherlands, than to the inherent dynamism of the sixteenth-century metropolis. The cultural, material, and commercial achievements which eventually enabled London to overtake Amsterdam and at least to equal Paris, were not to be apparent until the late seventeenth century or later, and it is by no means certain that they were the inevitable outcome of conditions in 1600. The great mass of Londoners who had so recently assembled in one place undoubtedly provided a growing market for new cultural production and had great capacity for such production themselves, but as yet the tangible expression of such forces did not equal that in Antwerp or Venice. To contemporaries, as to later observers, however, the creative potential of those crowds of new Londoners was doubtless as impenetrable as that of the marginal cultures of the late twentieth-century metropolis or the thronging shantytowns of modern "third world" cities. In some obvious material ways London in 1600 was still a city of the past and of the European periphery, presenting a striking contrast to Antwerp, Venice, or even Paris. Its typical houses were of timber, clay, and plaster, as they had been in 1500.[70] Brick, although widely used for chimneys and party walls, did not become the predominant building material until well into the seventeenth century. In other ways, too, the city presented a dowdy and outdated appearance. Its parish churches were outdated and in disrepair, St. Paul's steeple, destroyed in 1561, had not been rebuilt, many of the principal streets were narrow and dangerous, the entries to the city lacked magnificence, its defensive ditches were foul, and handsome vistas or public squares, such as had recently been created in Antwerp, Rome or Paris, were strikingly absent.[71] By 1700, as London took over the role which in 1600 was being transferred from Antwerp to Amsterdam, the situation looked very different. London was now well on the way to establishing a commanding position in the new "Atlantic economy" in which it enjoyed strategic advantages over other European cities; it presented a new appearance of modernity following the rebuilding after the Great Fire; and its products were beginning to command worldwide markets. The *Londrins* which French producers in the eighteenth century exported to the Levant were now highly finished textiles, undercutting the price of English cloth but almost matching it in quality.[72] This was a clear tribute to the capacity of London dyers and finishers to attain standards in response to changing markets and fashions, in a way which formerly had been characteristic only of the Low Countries towns. That was a real material revolution, but whether it was the inevitable outcome of the condition of London in 1600 it would be dangerous to say.

Notes

1. I am grateful to Lien Bich Luu for many discussions relevant to themes in this essay, and for permission to cite her unpublished 1997 University of London Ph.D. thesis: "Skills and Innovations: A Study of the Stranger Working Community in London, 1550–1600." Michael Berlin, Rob Iliffe, and David Mitchell of the "Skilled Workforce" project, funded by the Renaissance Trust at the Centre for Metropolitan History, University of London, have also contributed many stimulating ideas.

2. R. Porter, *London: A Social History* (London: Hamish Hamilton, 1994) rehearses this view and is followed in S. Inwood, *A History of London* (London: Mac-

millan, 1998). Regarding the Royal Exchange, see A. Saunders, ed., *The Royal Exchange* (London Topographical Society, no. 152, 1997).

3. J. de Vries, *European Urbanization, 1500–1800* (London: Methuen, 1984); V. Harding, "The Population of Early Modern London: A Review of the Published Evidence," *The London Journal* 15 (1990): 111–28; D. Keene, "Medieval London and Its Region," *The London Journal* 14 (1989): 99–111.

4. Keene, "Medieval London and Its Region"; D. Keene, "London, 600–1300" and "Regional Survey: The South East of England, A.D. 600–1540," in *The Cambridge Urban History of Britain,* vol. 1, *The Middle Ages,* ed. D. Palliser (Cambridge: Cambridge University Press, forthcoming).

5. D. Keene, "Continuity and Development in Urban Trades: Problems of Concepts and Evidence," in *Work in Towns, 850–1850,* ed. P. J. Corfield and D. Keene (Leicester: Leicester University Press, 1990), pp. 1–16; A. L. Beier, "Engine of Manufacture: The Trades of London," in *London 1500–1700: The Making of the Metropolis,* ed. A. L. Beier and R. Finlay (Harlow: Longman, 1986), pp. 141–67; P. G. Hall, *The Industries of London Since 1861* (London: Hutchinson, 1962).

6. B. M. S. Campbell, J. A. Galloway, D. Keene, and M. Murphy, *A Medieval Capital and Its Grain Supply: Agrarian Production and Distribution in the London Region, c. 1300* (Cheltenham: Historical Geography Research Series, no. 30, 1993), pp. 10–11.

7. C. Dyer, "The Consumer and the Market in the Later Middle Ages," *Economic History Review,* 2nd series, 42 (1989): 305–27; Keene, "Medieval London and Its Region" and "Regional Survey."

8. For these issues, which are relevant to both earlier and later periods, see E. A. Wrigley, "A Simple Model of London's Importance in Changing English Society and Economy, 1650–1750," *Past and Present* 37 (1967): 44–70; D. Keene, "Small Towns and the Metropolis: The Experience of Medieval England," in *Peasants and Townsmen in Medieval Europe: Studia in Honorem Adriaan Verhulst,* ed. J. M. Duvosquel and E. Thoen (Ghent: Snoek-Ducaju and Zoon, 1995), pp. 223–38.

9. These changes constituted a reduction in "transaction costs" which is also reflected in the fall of interest rates, as indicated by the number of years rental income required to buy property. In London, the rate in 1300 was about 10 percent (ten years purchase) and in the mid-sixteenth century about 7 percent (thirteen to fifteen years purchase): D. Keene and V. Harding, *Historical Gazetteer of London Before the Great Fire, I, Cheapside* (Cambridge: Chadwyck-Healey, 1987). An English statutory maximum interest rate of 10 percent was established for the first time in 1545; it was not reduced to 8 percent until 1624: S. Homer, *A History of Interest Rates* (New Brunswick: Rutgers University Press, 2nd ed. 1977), pp. 121, 131. Cf. S. R. Epstein, "Regional Fairs, Institutional Innovation, and Economic Growth in Late Medieval Europe," *Economic History Review* 47 (1994): 459–82.

10. F. J. Fisher, "The Development of London as a Centre of Conspicuous Consumption in the Sixteenth and Seventeenth Centuries," in F. J. Fisher, *London and the English Economy, 1500–1700,* ed. P. J. Corfield and N. B. Harte (London and Ronceverte: Hambledon Press, 1990), pp. 105–18.

11. de Vries, *Urbanization,* pp. 141–42; Corfield and Harte, *London and the English Economy,* p. 16.

12. D. Keene, "Shops and Shopping in Medieval London," in *Medieval Art, Archi-*

tecture, and Archaeology in London, ed. L. Grant (British Archaeological Association, 1990), pp. 29–40; D. Keene, "Wardrobes in the City: Houses of Consumption, Finance, and Power," in *Thirteenth-Century England,* ed. M. Prestwich, R. Britnell, and R. Frame (Woodbridge: Boydell and Brewer, 1999), pp. 61–79.

13. Campbell et al., *Medieval Capital;* J. Kaye, *Economy and Nature in the Fourteenth Century: Money, Market Exchange, and the Emergence of Scientific Thought* (Cambridge: Cambridge University Press, 1998).

14. S. Rappaport, *Worlds Within Worlds: Structures of Life in Sixteenth-Century London* (Cambridge: Cambridge University Press, 1989), pp. 148–50; M. J. Power, "London and the Control of the 'Crisis' of the 1590s," *History* 70 (1985): 371–85 and M. J. Power, "A 'Crisis' Reconsidered: Social and Economic Dislocation in London in the 1590s," *London Journal* 12 (1986): 134–45.

15. D. Keene, "London in the Early Middle Ages, 600–1300," *London Journal* 20 (1995): 9–21, esp. p. 16.

16. W. Harrison, *The Description of England,* ed. G. Edelen (Washington and New York: The Folger Shakespeare Library and Dover Publications, 1994), pp. 128, 201–2.

17. C. M. Barron, C. Coleman, and C. Gobbi, "The London Journal of Alessandro Magno, 1562," *London Journal* 9 (1983): 136–52; W. Robson-Scott, *German Travellers in England, 1400–1800* (Oxford: Blackwell, 1953), pp. 47–48, 64; K. Newman, *Fashioning Femininity and English Renaissance Drama* (Chicago: University of Chicago Press, 1991), pp. 111–27, 131–43; A. Friedman, *House and Household in Elizabethan England: Wollaton Hall and the Willoughby Family* (Chicago: University of Chicago Press, 1989), pp. 27–30; John Stow, *A Survey of London,* ed. C. L. Kingsford (Oxford: Oxford University Press, 1908, reprint 1968), 2:211–12.

18. Robson-Scott, *German Travellers,* pp. 7, 17; C. A. Sneyd, ed., *A Relation or rather a true account, of the Island of England . . . about the Year 1500* (London: Camden Society, 1847), pp. 42–43.

19. S. Thrupp, "The Grocers of London: A Study of Distributive Trade," in *Studies in English Trade in the Fifteenth Century,* ed. E. Power and M. Postan (London: Routledge, 1933), pp. 247–92; J. L. Bolton, *The Medieval English Economy, 1150–1500* (London: Dent, 1980), pp. 254–55; H. Cobb, ed., *The Overseas Trade of London: Exchequer Customs Accounts, 1480–1481* (London Record Society, no. 27, 1990); P. Nightingale, *A Medieval Mercantile Community: The Grocers' Company and the Politics and Trade of London, 1000–1485* (New Haven: Yale University Press, 1995), pp. 448–51; P. Nightingale, "The Growth of London in the Medieval English Economy," in *Progress and Problems in Medieval England: Essays in Honour of Edward Miller,* ed. R. Britnell and J. Hatcher (Cambridge: Cambridge University Press, 1996), pp. 89–106; V. Harding, "Cross-Channel Trade and Cultural Contacts: London and the Low Countries in the Later Fourteenth Century," in *England and the Low Countries in the Late Middle Ages,* ed. C. Barron and N. Saul (Stroud: Alan Sutton, 1995), pp. 153–68.

20. For example, see Statutes 3 Edward IV c.3 and c.4, 1 Richard III c.12; *Hall's Chronicle . . . carefully collated with the editions of 1548 and 1550,* ed. H. Ellis (London: J. Johnson, 1809), pp. 586–87.

21. J. Hatcher and T. Barker, *A History of British Pewter* (London: Longman, 1974), pp. 72–80; D. Keene, "Metalworking in Medieval London: An Historical Survey," *Journal of the Historical Metallurgy Society* 30 (1996): 95–101.

22. B. Dietz, ed., *The Port and Trade of Early Elizabethan London: Documents* (London Record Society no. 8, 1972); D. Gaimster, *German Stoneware, 1200–1900: Archaeology and Cultural History* (London: British Museum Press, 1997), pp. 78–82.

23. Population totals derived or estimated from de Vries, *European Urbanization*, and W. Prevenier, "La demographie des villes du comté de Flandre aux XIIIe et XIVe siècles. Etat de la question," *Revue du Nord* 65 (1983): 255–75. The northern Netherlands towns counted in 1600 are Amsterdam, Rotterdam, Utrecht, Leiden, and Haarlem.

24. Cf. S. Thurley, *The Royal Palaces of Tudor England: Architecture and Court Life, 1460–1547* (New Haven: Yale University Press, 1993), pp. 11–65.

25. R. S. Schofield, "The Geographical Distribution of Wealth in England, 1334–1649," *Economic History Review*, 2nd series, 18 (1965): 483–510; Bolton, *English Economy*, p. 29; Keene, "Medieval London and Its Region," p. 100.

26. Bolton, *English Economy*, pp. 287–320; G. D. Ramsay, *The City of London in International Politics at the Accession of Elizabeth Tudor* (Manchester: Manchester University Press, 1975); G. D. Ramsay, *The Queen's Merchants and the Revolt of the Netherlands* (Manchester: Manchester University Press, 1986).

27. J. H. Munro, "Industrial Transformations in the North-West European Textile Trades, *c.*1290–*c.*1300: Economic Progress or Economic Crisis?" in *Before the Black Death: Studies in the "Crisis" of the Early Fourteenth Century*, ed. B. M. S. Campbell (Manchester: Manchester University Press, 1991), pp. 110–48, esp. p. 142.

28. H. Van der Wee, "Prices and Wages as Development Variables," *Acta Historica Neerlandicae* 10 (1978): 58–78.

29. Homer, *Interest Rates*, pp. 121, 131. I am grateful to Larry Epstein for discussing these matters.

30. J. L. Bolton, *The Alien Communities of London in the Fifteenth Century: The Subsidy Rolls of 1440 and 1483–4* (Stamford: Paul Watkins, 1998), pp. 29–34.

31. For a useful overview, see P. Subacchi, "Italians in Antwerp in the Second Half of the Sixteenth Century," in *Minderheden in Westeuropese steden (16de-20ste eeuw)*, ed. H. Soly and A. K. L. Thijs (Brussels: Brepols, 1995), pp. 73–90. I owe this reference to Lien Luu.

32. L. Voet, *Antwerp, the Golden Age: The Rise and Glory of the Metropolis in the Sixteenth Century* (Antwerp: Mercatorfonds, 1973).

33. Luu, "Skills and Innovations," pp. 84–95, 133–34; J. G. van Dillen, *Bronnen tot de Geschiedenis van het Bedrijfsleven en het Gildewezen van Amsterdam* I (The Hague: Martinus Nijhoff, 1929), pp. xxxiii, xxxiv.

34. For example, K. Samuelsson, *De stora köpmanshusen i Stockholm, 1730–1815* (Stockholm, 1951), pp. 38–45.

35. See, in general, W. Prevenier and W. Blockmans, *The Burgundian Netherlands* (Cambridge: Cambridge University Press, 1986).

36. H. Van der Wee, *The Growth of the Antwerp Market and the European Economy Fourteenth–Sixteenth Centuries* (The Hague: Martinus Nijhoff, 1963).

37. de Vries, *European Urbanization*, pp. 151–72.

38. For good overviews, see L. Voet, *Antwerp* and the exhibition catalogue, J. Van der Stock, *Antwerp: Story of a Metropolis, Sixteenth–Seventeenth Century* (Ghent: Snoek-Ducaju & Zoon, 1993).

39. L. Wright, *Sources of London English: Medieval Thames Vocabulary* (Oxford: Clarendon Press, 1996), p. 137.

40. Prevenier and Blockmans, *Burgundian Netherlands,* p. 313; D. Ewing, "Marketing Art in Antwerp, 1460–1560: Our Lady's *Pand,*" *Art Bulletin* 72 (1990): 558–84; R. A. Goldthwaite, *Wealth and the Demand for Art in Italy, 1300–1600* (Baltimore: Johns Hopkins University Press, 1993).

41. F. J. Fisher, "Commercial Trends and Policy in Sixteenth-Century England" and "London's Export Trade in the Early Seventeenth Century," in *London and the English Economy,* pp. 81–103, 117–29.

42. Voet, *Antwerp,* p. 147; H. Zins, *England and the Baltic in the Elizabethan Era* (Manchester: Manchester University Press, 1972), pp. 180–86; H. Inalcik and D. Quataert, eds., *An Economic and Social History of the Ottoman Empire, 1300–1914* (Cambridge: Cambridge University Press, 1994), p. 309.

43. Voet, *Antwerp,* p. 158.

44. J. Summerson, *Architecture in Britain, 1530–1830* (Harmondsworth: Penguin Books, 5th ed., revised, 1969), pp. 42–47, 53; Barron et al., "The London Journal of Alessandro Magno."

45. Subacchi, "Italians in Antwerp," p. 74.

46. Summerson, *Architecture,* pp. 53–55.

47. Saunders, *Royal Exchange,* pp. 36–49.

48. Friedman, *House and Household,* pp. 108–23.

49. Summerson, *Architecture,* pp. 99–101; H. J. Louw, "Anglo-Netherlandish Architectural Exchange, *c.*1600–*c.*1660," *Architectural History* 24 (1981): 1–23.

50. J. F. Larkin and P. L. Hughes, eds., *Stuart Royal Proclamations,* vol. 1, *James I, 1603–1625* (Oxford: Clarendon Press, 1973), nos. 120, 175, 186; H. Ballon, *The Paris of Henri IV: Architecture and Urbanism* (Cambridge, Mass.: MIT Press, 1991), pp. 84–86.

51. P. Glanville, in *The Cambridge Guide to the Arts in England,* vol. 3, *Renaissance and Reformation* ed. B. Ford (Cambridge: Cambridge University Press, 1989), pp. 286–88.

52. Voet, *Antwerp,* pp. 302–12; Dietz, *Port and Trade.*

53. Voet, *Antwerp,* pp. 44–46, 291.

54. Summerson, *Architecture,* pp. 55–56; I have also benefited from a forthcoming paper by Piet Lombaerde on this topic.

55. J. M. Baart, "Ceramic Consumption and Supply in Early Modern Amsterdam: Local Production and Long-Distance Trade," in *Work in Towns, 850–1850,* ed. P. J. Corfield and D. Keene (Leicester: Leicester University Press, 1990), pp. 74–85.

56. O. Impey, "Eastern Trade and the Furnishing of the British Country House," in *The Fashioning and Functioning of the British Country House,* ed. G. Jackson-Stops, G. J. Schochet, L. C. Orlin, and E. B. MacDougall (Hanover and London: National Gallery of Art, Washington, 1989), pp. 117–92; cf. Dietz, *Port and Trade,* no. 46.

57. Cf. D. Morgan, *Medieval Persia, 1040–1797* (London and New York: Longman, 1988), pp. 132–42; Inalcik and Quataert, *Ottoman Empire,* pp. 364–72; D. Palliser, *The Age of Elizabeth: England Under the Later Tudors, 1547–1603* (London and New York: Longman, 1983), pp. 285–91.

58. Prevenier and Blockmans, *Netherlands,* p. 88; Voet, *Antwerp,* pp. 308–9; Luu, "Skills and Innovations," pp. 154–58, 310–11.

59. Prevenier and Blockmans, *Netherlands,* p. 149; Voet, *Antwerp,* pp. 67, 137, 387–88; F. Britton, *London Delftware* (London: Jonathan Horne, 1987), pp. 18–22.

60. Luu, "Skills and Innovations," pp. 229–58.

61. Luu, "Skills and Innovations," pp. 74–75, 192–28; S. M. Jack, *Trade and Industry in Tudor and Stuart England* (London: Allen and Unwin, 1977), p. 106.

62. Britton, *Delftware,* pp. 18–22, 26–29, 34–36, 39–40, 44.

63. Voet, *Antwerp,* pp. 384–87.

64. E. S. Godfrey, *The Development of English Glassmaking, 1560–1640* (Oxford: Clarendon Press, 1975), pp. 17–47, 82, 215–22; Palliser, *Age of Elizabeth,* pp. 257–58, 284, 322.

65. Luu, "Skills and Innovations," pp. 130–31, citing S. D'Ewes, *The Journals of all Parliaments during the Reign of Queen Elizabeth* (London, 1682), p. 505.

66. See, for example, Gaimster, *German Stoneware,* pp. 82–83, 96–97.

67. Luu, "Skills and Innovations," p. 187, citing MS Lansdowne 152/64/237 (London, British Library).

68. J. Stow, *The Annales, or, General Chronicle of England, begun first by maister John Stow and after him continued or augmented . . . by Edmond Howes* (London: Thomas Adams, 1615), pp. 866–70.

69. J. A. Galloway, D. Keene, and M. Murphy, "Fuelling the City: Production and Distribution of Firewood and Fuel in London's Region, 1290–1400," *Economic History Review* 49 (1996): 447–72; J. Hatcher, *Before 1700, Towards the Age of Coal,* vol. 1 in *The History of the British Coal Industry* (Oxford: Clarendon Press, 1993), pp. 31–42, 548–50; P. Brimblecombe, *The Big Smoke: A History of Air Pollution in London Since Medieval Times* (London and New York: Routledge, 1987); M. Jenner, "The Politics of London Air, John Evelyn's *Fumifugium* and the Restoration," *Historical Journal* 38 (1995): 535–51.

70. J. Dover Wilson, *Life in Shakespeare's England: A Book of Elizabethan Prose,* 2nd ed. (Cambridge: Cambridge University Press, 1926), p. 116; Sneyd, *Relation,* p. 42.

71. G. Buck, *The Third Universitie of England* (dated 1612; printed in the 1615 edition of Stow, *Annales,* pp. 958–88), pp. 980–81, expresses these views, but does not draw the comparison with the other cities.

72. E. Frangakis-Syrett, *The Commerce of Smyrna in the Eighteenth Century (1700–1820)* (Athens: Centre for Asia Minor Studies, 1992), pp. 133–34, 191–92.

4

Poetaster, the Author, and the Perils of Cultural Production

Alan Sinfield

The term "materialism" entered English studies from Marxism. It was invoked in opposition to "idealism," which supposed that literary writing might transcend its conditions of production. However, the abbreviation to an epithet — "material London" — seems to be developing another nuance of the word, focusing on the thinginess of the city. That shift is surely producing valuable results, but some of the Marxian political edge may be slipping away. By disputing a reactionary view of Ben Jonson and crediting him with a critical stance toward authority, ideology, and the functions of the author at the metropolitan center of power, this chapter aims to reassert that materialist edge.

I discern an evolution in four stages. (1) Raymond Williams in the 1970s says "culture is material," thus locating his kind of work in the region of expressions such as "historical materialism," that is, as a kind of Marxism. (2) Some of us build on this, producing cultural materialism and, in some measure, cultural studies and new historicism. (3) That work is then open to two serious questions. (It is also open to non-serious questions, such as: Hey, is someone doubting the truth and wisdom of Shakespeare?) The first serious question is: Is this cultural work really political, in the sense that historical materialism aspires to be political? Lately, people are less interested in this question, mainly because they do not accept that political debate is part of the responsibility of the salaried intellectual. The other serious question is: Is this work really material, in the sense of getting properly into the historical actuality? — these new historicists and cultural materialists don't really know any history; they've just picked up bits and bobs from Natalie Zemon Davis and Christopher Hill. Now, this is quite a clever charge because, in a concurrent movement, history gets to be recognized as infinitely elusive anyway, receding as we approach it. So we could *never* do enough history. Hence (4), the fourth stage of the sequence: attention to clothes, pots and pans, needles and pins, and to books and manuscripts *as objects*. They are, after all, *stuff*, they are *made of* material, let's *touch* them, you can't get more material than that.

* * *

Ben Jonson's *Poetaster* (performed by the Children of Queen Elizabeth's Chapel at Blackfriars in 1601) promises rewarding opportunities for materialists of all kinds in its barbed exploration of current cultural preoccupations through the literary scene of Augustan Rome. At its notorious climax, Crispinus, a writer who has offended the establishment, is made to vomit into a bowl his fustian words — "turgidous," "oblatrant," "furibund," "prorumped" — culminating in "Snarling gusts," "quaking custard," and "obstupefact."[1] Language here — the ultimate raw material of culture — seems material enough. But what happens to Crispinus is relevant also in a cultural materialist sense: this purgation is proposed by Horace, urged by Virgil, and enforced by Caesar:

> O be his Aesculapius, gentle Horace;
> You shall have leave, and he shall be your patient.
> Virgil, use your authority, command him forth.
>   (5.3.390–92)

Cultural and state authority link arms; culture is material because it is determined in the networks of power that license and restrain ideological production.

Crispinus is by no means the only writer to face punishment, or the threat of it, in *Poetaster*. Initially, when the scene opens to discover Ovid in his study, speaking in lofty terms of poetry, it is reasonable to suppose that he is a figure for the proper poet — as against the "petty poet" of the title. Swinburne complained that this was the obvious reading; the old Mermaid edition of the text actually supplies "Ben Jonson" in editorial parentheses after Ovid's name in the Dramatis Personae.[2] Ovid is criticized by his father, first on the grounds that stage plays corrupt young gentry (he replies that he does not write for the theater), then because poetry is an unprofitable occupation — even Homer was poor. But none of this seems to constitute a strong case against Ovid, and his father's gulling by the flamboyant Captain Tucca doesn't seem calculated to increase our respect for Ovid Senior. When Ovid reveals to Tibullus that his "Corinna" is in fact the emperor's daughter Julia this may seem dangerous, but hardly disgraceful.

In act 2, Crispinus appears, among what David Riggs terms "a circle of sleazy urban social climbers"; plainly, he *is* a petty poet.[3] In act 3, Crispinus pesters Horace, who evidently is the figure closest to Jonson, and a plot is laid — a play maligning Horace.

In act 4, Ovid runs into trouble. Together with Julia, the poets Tibullus and Gallus, Tucca, Crispinus, and the middle-class people they have picked up, Ovid stages an irreverent banquet of the gods with the goal of enacting comprehensive adultery. The banquet is reported to Caesar by the magistrate Lupus, who hears of it from the players. Caesar is so enraged that he offers to kill his daughter; Maecenas and Horace intervene. However, they cannot dissuade Caesar from banishing Ovid from the court. Without goodness, Caesar says, bounty would be wasted. Poets are not privileged:

> This shows their knowledge is mere ignorance,
> Their far-fetched dignity of soul a fancy,
> And all their square pretext of gravity
> A mere vainglory.
>
> (4.6.69–72)

For modern critics, this is the crux of the play: to us, Ovid is undoubtedly a true poet; how far may his banishment be justified?

Commentators have wanted to suppose that Caesar is right. After all, in the last part of the play he endorses Horace, and especially Virgil, so perhaps he is the wise "Augustan" ruler who (like us) appreciates poetry. Anne Barton takes this line. Ovid, she claims, defiles his poetry by failing as a man: "In the end he must be exiled from the court while Horace and Virgil take their places on either side of Caesar as counsellors and friends. . . . Ovid's clandestine passion for Caesar's daughter Julia annihilates him both personally and as a poet. Moreover, it leads him to defile his own high calling. . . . Ovid distorts the proper function of art when he devises a blasphemous banquet of the gods."[4] This seems a bit austere. But the big problem with such a reading is that Horace says Ovid's offense is trivial. "Was this the treason, this the dangerous plot[?]" Horace demands of Lupus —

> Hadst thou no other project to increase
> Thy grace with Caesar, but this wolfish train,
> To prey upon the life of innocent mirth
> And harmless pleasures, bred of noble wit?
>
> (4.8.8–13)

Caesar and Horace are at odds — and the issue is not incidental. It is focused, specifically, on the relations between poetry and state power.

Howard Erskine-Hill's attempt to confront this difficulty is not very convincing: "Horace may be right to defend his friends in this way, but Augustus may at the same time be right to punish Ovid and Julia."[5] Such a compromise may be all right for most of us, but Erskine-Hill raises the stakes. He wants to attribute to Jonson "Augustinianism," which he glosses as "the Christian Humanist view" of Caesar. It is a view "which is prepared to accept the evidence of the Augustan poets and to identify the rule of Augustus with a flourishing of the arts" (109). For this elevated project, it doesn't seem good enough to dismiss Horace's judgment—on the proper scope for poetry—as biased by friendship.

This "Augustinian" combining of imperial and cultural authority evidently constitutes an ideal condition for Erskine-Hill; Augustus "would not be content with easy propaganda alone, but with that most effective of propaganda: the vision that is instinct in deeply felt, carefully worked and lasting art," he declares (16). From a cultural materialist perspective, however, an ideal unity of ideology and the state is hardly to be desired or attained. First, the goal, surely, is not to have tyrants getting authoritative advice—improbably enough, from poets—on whether to kill or banish people, but to develop in any community fair and reasonable political structures for dealing with attempts to change its cultural boundaries. Second, ideal unities can only be ideological manipulations; as I argue elsewhere, a dominant formation, inevitably, produces conflicts and contradictions—"faultlines"—within itself, even in the processes through which it strives to sustain itself.[6]

Erskine-Hill says he believes in "the principle of truth as the end of scholarship"; he has "no interest in the production of subjective myth in the guise of criticism"—unlike some unspecified others—cultural materialists, perhaps (xiii). Erskine-Hill does have a position, though. He attributes a modern belief in the universality of art both to the Roman emperor and to early modern representations of him, and allows that to legitimate an undemocratic political structure. He is drawing Jonson into a stance that is surprisingly consonant with the late-lamented Elizabethan World Picture: an ideology convenient to state power is credited to the writer, admired as the wisdom of the ages, and confirmed as the voice of humanity.

So we have this interesting situation: while cultural materialists are anxious about whether cultural producers can ever escape ideological complicity with the state, colleagues in English are looking for an ideal collusion of writer and ruler.

*   *   *

In my view, Norbert H. Platz was on the right track in his 1973 article on *Poetaster:* "Ovid is not banished because he is a bad man," Platz says, "but because he has fallen victim to an informant who seeks advancement at Court."[7] Malignant informing is signaled as a preoccupation at the start of the play, when Envy threatens to blast the audience's pleasures

With wrestings, comments, applications,
Spy-like suggestions, privy whisperings,
And thousand such promoting sleights as these.
(Induction, 24–26)

The Prologue enters armed, for

'tis a dangerous age,
Wherein who writes had need present his scenes
Forty-fold proof against the conjuring means
Of base detractors and illiterate apes.
(Induction, 67–70)

Ovid is banished because the emperor is influenced by these people. However, Platz believes that the second part of *Poetaster* presents a different, more "Augustinian" idea of Caesar: "Whereas in the earlier part of the play the Prince is the type of monarch whom Jonson as a poet actually had to cope with, at the end he becomes the ideal center of a utopian realm, a kind of wishful projection into the future." Platz does not try to fix up this split; he says Caesar exhibits a "break in characterization" (19–20). That is not intrinsically unlikely — and not expecting texts to manifest an essential continuity is a key step in a cultural materialist analysis.[8] However, I think the emperor's tyrannical tendencies are apparent throughout.

Informers were crucial to the regime in Jonson's England; he knew well several who had contributed to the suppression of the recent Essex rebellion.[9] We should envision Jonson working over a complexly challenging body of historical material, only too aware that it was highly pertinent to his circumstances and that, in the hothouse of the London political elite, a step too far would incur the wrath of the state. Even if he did mean, in some measure, to celebrate state power, the material he was re-presenting *could not but* yield more complex readings. However, I think we may go further and attribute to *Poetaster* a project more demanding than Augustinianism. By establishing Virgil as the writer who figures the unity of the state and cultural production, Jonson gains space to suggest a different, emergent possibility: Horace as the voice of a critical authorial function.

*   *   *

Caesar's view, propounded at the start of act 5, is that poesy is justified when it contributes to the legitimation of the state:

She can so mould Rome and her monuments
Within the liquid marble of her lines
That they shall stand fresh and miraculous,
Even when they mix with innovating dust.
In her sweet streams shall our brave Roman spirits
Chase and swim after death with their choice deeds
Shining on their white shoulders; and therein
Shall Tiber and our famous rivers fall
With such attraction, that th' ambitious line
Of the round world shall to her centre shrink
To hear their music. And for these high parts
Caesar shall reverence the Pierian arts.

(5.1.21–32)

Cultural achievement is inseparable, for Caesar, from the state and imperial domination.

In fact, Caesar is interested in only one poem, Virgil's *Aeneid*. In a scene which anticipates Lear's demand for his daughters' love, Horace, Gallus, and Tibullus are required by Caesar to say what they think of Virgil. In this instance, no one is so foolish as to step out of line. Caesar is pleased:

This one consent, in all your dooms of him,
And mutual loves of all your several merits,
Argues a truth of merit in you all.

(5.1.139–41)

They have merit when they agree with Caesar. Caesar honors Virgil by making him take a higher chair, but Virgil does not imagine that Caesar loses any authority thereby: "Great Caesar hath his will: I will ascend" (5.2.48).

By just so much as this oppressive imperial program tries to squeeze out the critical authorial voice, by just that much such a voice is needed. Horace is actually seen to correct Caesar on one matter: he repudiates the emperor's supposition that as the poorest he is "likeliest to envy or to detract" (5.1.78). In response, Caesar thanks him for his "free and wholesome sharpness, / Which pleaseth Caesar more than servile fawns" (5.1.94–95). However, Horace was hardly confronting imperial power, and the perils of "free and wholesome sharpness" are quickly indicated. Virgil's reading from the *Aeneid* is interrupted by another intrusion from Lupus and his friends; Horace has to defend himself against a charge that he has authored a lampoon hostile to Caesar. Fortunately, there is an explanation: the emblem which Lupus says is an eagle, signifying Augustinian rapacity, lacks its interpretive verse. When Horace supplies the verse, the eagle may be seen as a vulture — *"Thus oft the base and ravenous multitude / Survive to share the spoils of fortitude"* (5.3.76–77). This leads to the punishment of those who brought the charge, culminating in Crispinus's vomiting of words.

Virgil declares that Caesar's punishments are right, and takes opportunity to justify the Horatian critical voice:

> 'Tis not the wholesome sharp morality
> Or modest anger of a satiric spirit
> That hurts or wounds the body of a state,
> But the sinister application
> Of the malicious ignorant and base
> Interpreter, who will distort and strain
> The general scope and purpose of an author
> To his particular and private spleen.
>
> (5.3.132–39)

This politic speech effaces what actually makes malicious interpretations so crucial: the regime of state terror that depends upon a system of informers and arbitrary penalties. Horace's self-defense allows us to see this:

> A just man cannot fear, thou foolish tribune,
> Not though the malice of traducing tongues,
> The open vastness of a tyrant's ear,
> The senseless rigour of the wrested laws,
> Or the red eyes of strained authority,
> Should, in a point, meet all to take his life.
> His innocence is armour 'gainst all these.
>
> (5.3.57–63)

According to this speech, the life of the satirist is threatened when several things "in a point, meet all," and only one of them is to do with his fellow citizens — "the malice of traducing tongues." The others are to do with the state — "The open vastness of a tyrant's ear," "The senseless rigour of the wrested laws," "the red eyes of strained authority." It is tyrannical state power that sustains the system — "worldly tyranny," Julia calls it (4.10.58); this insight informs also *Sejanus* (1603). And punishing the little men only extends the terror. That is why it was important for Horace to deny that as the poorest he is "likeliest to envy or to detract" (5.1.78); he cannot afford to become linked in the imperial mind with the lower orders upon whom blame is displaced and punishment heaped.

*   *   *

Poetaster seems thoroughly to illustrate Foucault's analysis in "What Is an Author?" where he suggests that the author emerged as a distinct role when he "became subject to punishment and to the extent that his discourse was considered transgressive."[10] Foucault is still sometimes accused of proclaiming "the death of the author" — for instance, by Harold Bloom in *The Western Canon* (1995).[11] Foucault's argument, however, is that the figure of the author is very much alive and performing a range of material functions within our culture, particularly in respect of the (perceived) ownership of writing.

Chaucer, Langland, Gower, and Skelton manifest aspects of the author function as we recognize it today. Clearly, however, printing, the development of London, and the commercial organization of theater, occurring together, made early modern England one place where modern ideas of the relations between writers and texts were constituted. Jonson's publication of his collected works is generally acknowledged to be a landmark; Jonathan Haynes adduces also the War of the Theaters, of which *Poetaster* was a part. By its end, "the contemporary London setting, the audience, and the figure of the playwright had all been newly defined and were newly visible to one another."[12]

Brian Vickers believes he counters Foucault's analysis of the modern roles of the author by pointing out that writers in ancient Rome demanded and were credited with author-type attributes.[13] To be sure they were, but that doesn't mean that we should expect not to discover distinct developments in early modern England; Foucault's main argument is that we should not suppose our own notion of the relations between a text and its production to be natural, transhistorical. Of course, as Helgerson notes, Roman ideas and Jonson's were by no means the same.[14] The usefulness of classical models resided, precisely, in the interpretive gap that challenged Jonson and his audience to make sense of their own developing reality in newly emergent material conditions. *Poetaster* is not documenting the author function, it is helping to constitute it.

For the emergence of the author should not be supposed to occur without conflict or contradiction; in fact, *Poetaster* should be read as a complex intervention in a confused situation. Most recent studies of Jonson's authorship dwell upon his self-validation, his dependence on social hierarchy and the state, his ultimate complicity in the system (this is almost the Jonson of Barton and Erskine-Hill, in less favorable phraseology). I am thinking of important work by Don Wayne, Richard Helgerson, Jonathan Goldberg, Peter Stallybrass, and Allon White.[15] I began looking at *Poetaster* in this frame of mind. However, the play is dedicated to the man who interceded on its behalf with "the greatest Justice of this kingdom," so evidently it was not received as altogether complicit with the state; its concluding Apologetical Dialogue was banned; and, as Richard Burt points out, it quotes courageously from work by Marlowe and Marston that had been called in and burned in 1599.[16] Some time after the 1602 quarto, Jonson strengthened the concept of the satirist in the text by adding act 3, scene 5, which translates Horace's Book 2, Satire 1. What I now see is Jonson taking up the challenge, in his context, of authorizing the Horatian writer as a critical voice.

As Jonson's play shows very well, the concept of the writer is not just an idea. Its emergence supposes an opportunity in the prevailing institutional structure. As Stallybrass and White say, the idea of the author "was only locatable, groundable, through its symbolic relation to existing hierarchies, existing languages, symbols and practices of high and low."[17] In fact we may distinguish four *locations:* state servant, court or gentry amateur, writer under patronal protection, and writer in the market. The pattern would look rather different if it were elaborated to include the scope for women writers, but since Jonson doesn't broach that topic I don't attempt it here.

Poetaster, in effect, assesses these four locations. I have dwelt upon Jonson's wariness about the writer in the service of the state. The court or gentry amateur is represented by Ovid, a younger son who disdains "gold or titles" and proclaims "the high raptures of a happy Muse, / Born on the wings of her immortal thought" (1.2.252, 244–45). Also there are Gallus and Tibullus, but the play shows little interest in them. Horace is not of this provenance; he is the poorest of the writers, he says. In "To Penhurst," what is striking is how little Jonson's poem says about that most famous amateur, Sir Philip Sidney; he is mentioned only by way of a catalogue of trees in the park — "That taller tree, which of a nut was set, / At his great birth, where all the Muses met."[18] Jonson cannot *be* the Sidneys because he wants to be *paid by* them.

For while Horace is seen, uneasily, in the service of the state, his preferred location is the writer under patronal protection. He declares the house of Maecenas, his patron, a detraction-free zone:

> That place is not in Rome, I dare affirm,
> More pure, or free from such low, common evils.
> There's no man grieved, that this is thought more rich,
> Or this more learned; each man hath his place,
> And to his merit, his reward of grace,
> Which with a mutual love they all embrace.
>
>   (3.1.250–55)

In Rome as Jonson represents it, this is a magical space. What is perhaps disappointing is that, probably because the topic was so sensitive, no gap is allowed to appear between Horace and Maecenas. This lack of friction, indeed of event, weakens the patron as a presence in the play. It is implausible as well; Helgerson and Tom Cain remark the importance of patrons to Jonson, and how systematically he fell out with them.[19]

The market, here as elsewhere, is rejected by Jonson insofar as it supports what he regards as the trivializing pressures of the public playhouses. He distinguishes between Histrio's theater company, which is amply responsive to vulgar taste (they "have as much ribaldry in our plays as can be, as you would wish, captain"), and theaters where they do "humours, revels and satires that gird and fart at the time" — in other words, Jonson's more elevated and critical type of theater. "They are on the other side of Tiber" (3.4.194–98). Yet *Poetaster* is itself a market product; like many of Jonson's plays, it communicates the excitement of writing for the popular London theater. Jonson's pitch is that he transcends its intrigues — "His mind it is above their injuries," the Prologue says (Induction, 89). But it is not so. As much as any of Jonson's work, *Poetaster* keeps falling back — vividly and intriguingly — into the market vulgarity from which it purports to separate itself. As Riggs puts it, Jonson's version of himself as the English Horace, with Dekker and Marston as mere hacks, "was so successful that one tends to overlook the basic similarities between the poet and the poetasters."[20] If Crispinus's language is crude, so is Jonson's device of making him vomit it up on stage; or looking at it the other way round, Jonson's device shows as much inventive exuberance as the marvelous verbal excesses of Crispinus.

While these four locations offer material groundings for an author function, none of them, of itself, quite specifies a space for a critical stance. That would require not only location, but distanciation; not only identification, but a perspective upon that identification. For, as Louis Montrose observes, "The possibility of social and political agency cannot be based upon the illusion that consciousness is a condition somehow beyond ideology. However, the very process of subjectively *living* the confrontations or contradictions *within* or *among* ideological formations may make it possible for us to experience facets of our own subjection at shifting internal distances — to read, as in a refracted light, one fragment of our ideological inscription by means of another."[21] Distanciation comes with liminality; if Philip Sidney, say, achieved a critical perspective upon aspects of his society, it was at the junctures between his (likely) allegiances to the throne, the administration, the higher gentry, militant protestantism.[22] Yet these liminal locations would still not produce the critical stance as an authorial function — that would come with an awareness of the writer as writer.

At this point Pierre Bourdieu's analysis of ideological production as *doubly determined* is valuable. It suggests that we should expect texts to be responsive not only to the interests they (ostensibly) serve, but also to the interests of those who produce them.[23] Sidney, therefore, would manifest the concerns not only of his diverse sociopolitical allegiances, but also of *the writer as such,* as a distinct social category. This is likely to occur when, as in early modern England, the idea of the writer is, itself, provisional and riven by unstable boundaries. As the different concepts of the author jostle together (and Jonson, like Shakespeare, occupied three of the four locations), the writer as such is able to emerge. And as this figure produces a distance between the writer and the circumstance of writing, a critical authorial function becomes locatable.

In a complementary movement, writing comes under pressure: it is promoted and restrained by the state, solicited and rejected in the market, a sign of accomplishment but also of triviality for the courtier, a chance of fame or poverty for the writer under patronage. Above all, writing becomes subject to state vigilance. The accusation founded on Horace's unfinished emblem is a close call. An eagle (Caesar) might look like a vulture (the multitude), and either might plausibly be represented as feeding on the carcass of an ass. And which did Horace mean? It is entirely plausible that he designed a satire on imperial exploitation and saves himself with a quick-witted reinterpretation. In support of the latter view, we may notice that his claim that the ass represents "the spoils of fortitude" (5.3.76) seems strained; it would be more sensible if it were the people, preyed upon by the emperor. Nor is there any suggestion that Maecenas can protect Horace, any more than he could protect Ovid.

Under such pressures, early modern writers were well placed to apprehend power relations, and the precariousness of that apprehension, in turn, reinscribes the distance that produces a critical authorial function. The Horatian critique of Augustan tyranny is developed not out of Erskine-Hill's "vision that is instinct in deeply felt, carefully worked and lasting art" (16), but from Horace's material experience of the perils of the critical writer's location.

Two further considerations. First, none of this means that writers were prevented from aligning their ideological concerns with, or submerging them in, those of a social grouping (though a cultural materialist would expect to find faultlines in any such project). As Jonson's anatomy suggests, diverse kinds of relation were possible. But the conditions were there for writers to find themselves at points of relative, writerly, autonomy. Second, it must be said that there is no disrespect in *Poetaster* toward the writer of the *Aeneid;* on the contrary, Virgil is made to endorse the Horatian stance, perhaps recognizing it as the necessary complement to his own. But what should we expect? Today a writer can live in London and be only occasionally aware of the system and panoply of government. Jonson's London was not only smaller and its elite more integrated, there was also less reticence about surveillance, conspicuous consumption, and other mechanisms of power. There were all those people staggering around branded and flogged, with their noses slit, joints wracked, hands, tongues, and ears cut off. Of course it was sensible to align yourself as a writer in the service of the state if you got the chance.

*   *   *

I have chosen to discuss *Poetaster* because it enables me to reinflect some important discussions about the material role of the author. By way of conclusion, let me show how it opens up another topic: sexuality. As I have observed elsewhere, prestigious classical writing was planting non-Christian models of same-sex passion in early modern Europe. Virgil's second *Eclogue* is about the love of Corydon for Alexis, and Augustus was accused of prostituting himself to Julius Caesar and to the Governor-General of Spain. Horace, Bruce R. Smith remarks, "writes about sexual desire between males with a matter-of-factness that avoids romanticizing that desire no less than it refuses to be embarrassed by it."[24] The only trouble, Horace says, is that love gets in the way of writing: "O Pettius, no more do I delight as formerly to write my verses, for I am stricken with the heavy dart of Love, yea of Love who seeks to kindle me beyond all others with passion for tender boys and maids." Here, in Epode 11, it is passion for a boy: "Affection for Lyciscus now enthrals me, for Lyciscus, who claims in tenderness to outdo any woman, and from whom no friends' frank counsels or stern reproaches have power to set me free, but only another flame, either for some fair maid or slender youth, with long hair gathered in a knot."[25] Eva Cantarella terms this "a recurrent theme in the output of this poet, who likes to present himself as easy meat for *mille puellarum mille puerorum:* a thousand tormented loves both for young girls and for young boys."[26]

To be sure, neither Horace nor the other reputable characters in *Poetaster* talk about same-sex relations; indeed, in contradistinction to the low-life characters, Horace and Virgil should perhaps be seen as exercising a wise discretion. My point is not that Jonson has specifically chosen a bisexual to represent his preferred poetic voice, but that invoking the classical world brings sexuality closer to the top of the agenda. Even so, we should remark that the Roman poet who carried a torch, quite distinctively, for cross-sex passion was Ovid. The *Amores* focus on relations between the lover and his mistress, with scarcely an aside about same-sex relations. The speaker in the *Ars Amatoria* declares: "I hate a union that exhausts not both: / To fondle boys it's this that makes me loth."[27] This is remarkable because it is Ovid who is banished in *Poetaster.*

Have not Jonson, then, and the emperor, banished the "wrong" poet—the heterosexual?

The treatment of same-sex passion in this play is notably casual. Ovid Senior expostulates: "What! Shall I have my son a stager now? An engle for players? A gull, a rook, a shot-clog to make suppers, and be laughed at?" (1.2.15–17). It is taken for granted that boys have sexual relations with players; it is only one of the degrading futures that await his son. In similar vein, Crispinus is required to swear at the end that he will not again malign Horace, "thereby to endear yourself the more to any player, engle, or guilty gull in your company" (5.3.580–81). Again, when Tucca's pages perform well, Histrio offers to hire them: "No, you mangonising slave, I will not part from 'em. You'll sell 'em for engles, you" (3.4.277–78). However, Tucca wants a convincing performance from his page at the banquet of the gods: "Sirrah, boy; catamite! Look you play Ganymede well now, you slave. Do not spill your nectar; carry your cup even: so. You should have rubbed your face with whites of eggs, you rascal, . . . or ha' steeped your lips in wine, till you made 'em so plump, that Juno might have been jealous of 'em. [*To Chloe*] Punk, kiss me punk!" (4.5.65–72). Cain, editing the Revels edition, inserts "[*To Chloe*]" before the last sentence (before "Punk, kiss me punk!") so that Tucca will be kissing Chloe, not the page. It hardly matters which gets the kiss though, since the juxtaposition is likely anyway to enhance awareness that Chloe also is a boy actor and hence subject (in the terms proposed by the play) to treatment as an engle.

I am persuaded, again, to entertain the thought, broached by Stephen Orgel and Bruce Smith, that the early modern English did not treat same-sex passion as the ultimate taboo.[28] Instead, the main faultlines ran through cross-sex relations. Because women may bear children, relations between women and men affected the regulation of lineage, alliance, and property, and hence offered profound potential disruptions to the social order and the male psyche. Same-sex passion was dangerous if, as in the instance of Marlowe's *Edward II,* it was allowed to interfere with other responsibilities. Otherwise, it was thought compatible with marriage and perhaps preferable to cross-sex infidelity. The preoccupation, in writing of this period, is with women disturbing the system—resisting arranged marriages, running off with the wrong man, not bearing (male) children, committing adultery, producing illegitimate offspring, becoming widows and exercising the power of that position.

Ovid has to be banished because he is the poet who advocates unlicensed cross-sex relations. When he consorts with Augustus's daughter in the banquet of the gods, he challenges the material power of fathers and husbands at its ultimate reference point, Caesar. That is the unpardonable offense.

Notes

This chapter appeared in slightly different form in *Renaissance Drama* 27 (1996).

1. Ben Jonson, *Poetaster,* Revels edition, ed. Tom Cain (Manchester: Manchester University Press, 1995), 5.3.488, 492, 502, 513, 515.

2. *Ben Jonson,* ed. Brinsley Nicholson and C. H. Herford, 3 vols. (London: Fisher Unwin, n.d.), 1:264. On Swinburne, see Katharine Eisaman Maus, *Ben Jonson and the Roman Frame of Mind* (Princeton: Princeton University Press, 1984), p. 91.

3. David Riggs, *Ben Jonson* (Cambridge, Mass.: Harvard University Press, 1989), p. 75.

4. Anne Barton, *Ben Jonson, Dramatist* (Cambridge: Cambridge University Press, 1984), p. 82.

5. Howard Erskine-Hill, *The Augustan Idea in English Literature* (London: Arnold, 1983), p. 114. Barton and Erskine-Hill are not idiosyncratic in their attempts to justify Caesar. See Maus, *Ben Jonson and the Roman Frame of Mind,* p. 91, and Cain, ed., *Poetaster,* pp. 17–23.

6. See Alan Sinfield, *Faultlines* (Berkeley: University of California Press, and Oxford: Oxford University Press, 1992), pp. 41–42.

7. Norbert H. Platz, "Ben Jonson's *Ars Poetica:* An Interpretation of *Poetaster* in Its Historical Context," *Salzburg Studies in English Literature,* 12 (1973): 1–42, esp. p. 17.

8. See Sinfield, *Faultlines,* chapter 3.

9. See Cain, ed., *Poetaster,* pp. 40–44.

10. Michel Foucault, *Language, Counter-Memory, Practice* (Oxford: Blackwell, 1977), p. 124.

11. See Harold Bloom, *The Western Canon* (London: Macmillan, 1995), pp. 39, 60.

12. Jonathan Haynes, *The Social Relations of Jonson's Theater* (Cambridge: Cambridge University Press, 1992), p. 89. For a powerful account of these changes, see Louis Montrose, *The Purpose of Playing* (Chicago: University of Chicago Press, 1996).

13. Brian Vickers, *Appropriating Shakespeare* (New Haven and London: Yale University Press, 1993), pp. 105–6.

14. Richard Helgerson, *Self-Crowned Laureates* (Berkeley: University of California Press, 1983), pp. 2–3.

15. See Don E. Wayne, "Drama and Society in the Age of Jonson: Shifting Ground of Authority and Judgment in Three Major Comedies," in *Renaissance Drama,* ed. Mary Beth Rose (Evanston: Northwestern University Press and Newberry Library Center, 1990); Helgerson, *Self-Crowned Laureates*; Jonathan Goldberg, *James I and the Politics of Literature* (Stanford: Stanford University Press, 1983); Peter Stallybrass and Allon White, *The Politics and Poetics of Transgression* (London: Methuen, 1986). But cf. Richard Burt, *Licensed by Authority* (Ithaca: Cornell University Press, 1993).

16. Burt, *Licensed by Authority,* p. 6.

17. Stallybrass and White, *Politics and Poetics,* pp. 74–75.

18. *Poems of Ben Jonson,* ed. George Burke Johnston (London: Routledge, 1954), p. 77. On this, I offer a different emphasis from Helgerson, *Self-Crowned Laureates,* pp. 104–6, 115; Riggs, *Ben Jonson,* pp. 76, 80; and David Norbrook, *Poetry and Politics in the English Renaissance* (London: Routledge, 1984), p. 184.

19. Helgerson, *Self-Crowned Laureates,* pp. 165–66; Cain, ed., *Poetaster,* pp. 283–84.

20. Riggs, *Ben Jonson,* p. 78.

21. Montrose, *The Purpose of Playing,* p. 16.

22. See Sinfield, *Faultlines,* chapter 4.

23. Pierre Bourdieu, "Symbolic Power," in *Identity and Structure,* ed. Denis Gleeson (Driffield: Nafferton Books, 1977), p. 116.

24. Bruce R. Smith, *Homosexual Desire in Shakespeare's England* (Chicago: University of Chicago Press, 1991), p. 228.

25. Horace, *The Odes and Epodes,* trans. C. E. Bennett, Loeb edition (London: Heinemann, 1934), Epode 11.

26. Eva Cantarella, *Bisexuality in the Ancient World* (New Haven: Yale University Press, 1992), p. 140.

27. *Ars Amatoria,* 2.683–84, in Ovid, *The Love Poems,* trans. A. D. Melville (Oxford: Oxford University Press, 1989).

28. See Stephen Orgel, "Nobody's Perfect: Or Why Did the English Stage Take Boys for Women?" *South Atlantic Quarterly* 88 (1989): 7–29; Smith, *Homosexual Desire in Shakespeare's England;* Alan Sinfield, "How to Read *The Merchant of Venice* without Being Heterosexist," in *Alternative Shakespeares 2,* ed. Terence Hawkes (London: Routledge, 1996).

II

CONSUMER CULTURE: DOMESTICATING FOREIGN FASHION

As Thomas Platter expanded on his impressions of London, he emphasized the size of the city, its apparent prosperity, its vast capacity as a port, and the fact that "most of the inhabitants are employed in commerce: they buy, sell and trade in all the corners of the globe, for which purpose the water serves them well." Cheapside, he wrote, displayed "great treasures."

Joan Thirsk, too, credits foreign imports and foreign influences for transforming London into a "glittering center for consumer goods." But international trade was not the only engine of London's commercial expansion, as she demonstrates in "England's Provinces: Did They Serve or Drive Material London?" Thirsk finds that the global market developed new tastes that rural England then strove to satisfy domestically. In this way, the provinces *served* the capital city. She also argues, however, that the provinces *drove* material London by supplying it with their own innovations on foreign products. She identifies three strands in the commercial interactions of city and country. First, while rural landowners developed their advanced tastes in the urban center, country folk were surprisingly quick to cater to those tastes. They created "islands of consumerism" around country houses, planting fruit orchards, growing new vegetables, and contributing to the nationalization of London's commercial standards. Second, the provinces' embedded local traditions and skills provided the bases for innovation inspired by changing fashions. Peasant textile production came to embrace new threads and colors; established market gardens added the novel greenstuffs; a home industry like stocking-knitting incorporated fine wools developed in Italy; an imported skill like lacemaking was grafted onto native handicrafts. The exploitation of local skills and resources resulted in centers of specialization which then served the national market, like East Anglia for rush mat making, Witney for blanket making, and Sheffield for knife making. Third, the social mandate for universal employment inspired a number of educational projects, with wealthy patrons providing training for fustian making, woad growing, and pin making, for example. These local industries may have been inspired by men with London contacts, but they, in turn, stimulated the London market.

In "Fantastical Colors in Foggy London: The New Fashion Potential of the Late Sixteenth Century," Jane Schneider also traces domestic responses to an internationalized market, that of textile production. Before 1600, she shows, English fashion and sumptuary laws made a virtue of limited native resources and abilities. Other countries controlled the trade in various dyes: purple, which came from a mollusk near Tyre; red, from Asian brazilwood; scarlet, from a Mediterranean louse or a New World insect; and mauve, from a shellfish on the Pacific coast of Central America. English access to alum (a fixative mined near Rome) and to silk (the fabric which achieved the highest color saturation) was also limited. Even when exotic dyestuffs were imported, English workmen were not skilled in their use. Sixteenth-century English fashion thus limited the palette to black and white and focused on products achievable with domestic labor: elaborate ruffs, lace, embroidery, and fantastic shapes. A compensatory ideology held that bright colors masked stinking smells, blurred gender distinctions, and siphoned off national resources "in the pursuit of fantasy." But this situation changed, Schneider states, around 1600. First, the "new draperies," soft and versatile woolens introduced in Flanders, achieved production in England. Second, the religious wars on the Continent brought highly skilled dyers from Flanders, Germany, Portugal, and France into England. Third, with new trade patterns that circumvented the old Italian monopolies on dyestuffs, English woolens were dyed and finished to international standards. Fourth, Englishmen launched projects to mine for alum and to cultivate woad (for blue), saffron (for yellow), and madder (for red). In the seventeenth century, English merchants flooded the Italian markets with cheaper wares—and the Italians, in turn, enacted protectionist sumptuary laws and dressed in black.

Ann Rosalind Jones and Peter Stallybrass similarly focus on the market, the nation, and the clothing industry in " 'Rugges of London and the Diuell's Band': Irish Mantles and Yellow Starch as Hybrid London Fashion." Like Schneider, they outline some political implications of the newly internationalized market. But where Schneider identifies a pre-1600 instance of real English inferiority, Jones and Stallybrass discuss two sites for presumed English superiority post-1600. In nationalist discourse, both the mantle and yellow starch were censoriously identified with Irishness and incivility. The rough woolen mantle of Irish "rebels" was believed to enable thieves, criminals, and prostitutes to cloak their faces, weapons, stolen goods, illicit pregnancies, and bastard infants; it also elided distinctions of class and gender. The Irish fashion of yellow starch was associated with uncleanness, lousiness, and the urine used to intensify its color; it was also linked to treason and murder when Anne Turner was said to have worn a yellow band and yellow cuffs at her execution. But these dominant meanings eventually gave way to competing ones. Translated into fine fabrics, the mantle became an aristocratic fashion, displayed by Elizabeth herself in the Rainbow Portrait. And because yellow was an expensive dye, it, too, accumulated significations of luxury which help account for its adoption by the London nobility. The old prejudices did not fade away, and their uneasy coexistence with the new fads was a marker of London's simultaneous roles as national capital, trade center, style setter, and home of the court. Early representations of the Irish mantle had incorporated the Scots in developing a notion of unEnglish incivility, but by 1603 Scotsmen ruled England. Social prohibitions against Irish mantles and yellow starch may have reflected attempts to define a pure English essence, but it was an essence with which material London, the home of the newly hybridized court, was, as Jones and Stallybrass say, "at odds."

The process of national self-definition which was incited by London's influx of foreign people, foreign goods, and foreign customs is also Jean E. Howard's subject in "Women, Foreigners, and the Regulation of Urban Space in *Westward Ho.*" She demonstrates that English culture had a sensitive register for social change in that peculiarly London institution, the commercial theater, and she shows that in this space, too, multiple meanings coexisted. Arguing that theatrical vogues, like other fads, address cultural needs, Howard looks to the early seventeenth-century genre of city comedy as a rich site for contemporary discourses of foreignness. Because "foreignness" could be created on stage by "wigs, skin dyes, costume," and "exaggerated accents," it was revealed to be fungible — as was gender for the all-male acting companies of the time. Drama thus played to fears that foreigners who did not "perform their difference" could all too easily penetrate and corrupt English culture. But while an early comedy like *Englishmen for My Money* was transparently jingoistic, a later play like *Westward Ho* depicted local strategies for managing the new cultural anxieties, and it modeled a competing ethic of assimilation. This city comedy established an alternative notion of Englishness as a matter of adherence to certain codes and values, principal among them the ethic of female chastity. Howard suggests that female consumers who bought foreign fashions were themselves stigmatized as "foreigners" for importing the products of the international market into their homes, and she shows that for the male characters of *Westward Ho,* national differences became less important than their shared experience of misogyny. Analyzing the seepage of xenophobia into gender relations and marital ideology, Howard suggests how wide-ranging and long-lived were the social and political consequences of the new consumer culture.

In large part through the competitive drive of material London, England would come to play starring roles on the world stage. From its "peripheral" position in the world textile market, the country would eventually nurture the industrialization of the clothmaking industry, as Jane Schneider reminds us.

And the seeds of the British empire were sown in the attempted conquest of Ireland and the union with Scotland chronicled by Ann Rosalind Jones and Peter Stallybrass. But they, along with Jean E. Howard and Joan Thirsk, recognize some of the immediate costs of the new fashions, commercial success, international expansion, and nationalized consumer standards. These included the anxieties that were generated by change and shifting ideologies, the ugly ways in which those anxieties were displaced onto women and foreigners, and the suppression of regional difference and provincial character. "The demands of material London," Thirsk concludes, wove a "spider's web" across the nation.

5

England's Provinces

Did They Serve or Drive Material London?

Joan Thirsk

In explaining the process by which London by 1600 came to be a relatively glittering center of consumer goods, I put at the head of my list of causes foreign influences. Foreign imports, foreign visitors, foreign immigrants settling in England, English merchants trading overseas and bringing back novel wares, and Englishmen traveling abroad with a curiosity for all things foreign — these were the leading agents of the transformation.[1]

But when once those influences and the newfangled goods had settled themselves firmly into London life, when the shops routinely displayed the goods and people bought them, the situation changed. Many other agencies were at work, qualitatively altering the relative importance of foreigners and natives in carrying on and expanding the consumer market. As a historian of the agrarian economy and rural society, I then try to understand the next phase — how, quite speedily, people living in rural areas far away from London became involved in the consumer revolution and made a contribution to the market in goods on sale in London. Somehow, people in the provinces were made aware of new needs and met them effectively — in other words, they *served* material London. But they were not simply obedient servants, they also stirred the pot and stimulated consumerist urges, by supplying to London ever more varied goods, and in a widening range of qualities — in other words, they also *drove* material London.

These two processes, of serving and driving London consumerism, are explored in this essay through three themes in provincial development. They are put forward as the most significant influences, but they are so entangled that one can never be quite sure in individual places which one was more influential than the others. So, all three have to be taken together. The conclusion of this chapter considers the general role played by people who live on the fringes of things, on margins of any kind, making creative contributions to the central core of an economy or society. In 1500, the largest part of the kingdom outside London was on the margin, whereas at the present day only islands off the coast still maintain a position of some independence on the margin. It is instructive to observe their life today, detached, yet contributing culturally to the mainland. Some of the insights here are drawn from experience. The rest come from research on sixteenth-century history, especially England's rural industries and its farming for food.

It goes without saying that the first people to indulge in consumer spending in the latest modish fashion were rich people — gentry and the still wealthier nobility. At court they had a golden opportunity to show off their taste and their possessions. But documents which shed light on the countryside show the repercussions there also, and reveal how quickly the expensive or exotic tastes of London were satisfied in manor houses and shops in scattered parts of England.

Take, for example, the developing taste for new vegetables and fruits in the sixteenth century. Once upon a time, such items had been dismissed as the food of peasants, an attitude neatly summed up by William Forrest in 1548: "Our English nature cannot live by roots. By waters, herbs, or such beggary baggage. That may well serve for vile outlandish coats."[2] In fact, by 1548 that dismissive view sounded more than somewhat out of date, at least as far as courtiers were concerned. Henry VIII had made new vegetables and fruits the highest food fashion. In renovating a building which he had bought as a modest moated manor house in Surrey in 1537 and turning it into Oatlands Palace, Henry VIII invested much effort and money in the kitchen garden and orchards (1538–1547). He did not scruple to filch six loads of fruit trees from the dissolved monastic house of Chertsey abbey nearby in order to stock them.[3] By 1600, in some places distant from London, fashionable foodstuffs of this kind were actually being tithed, the tithe customs yielding evidence that such garden produce was already deemed commonplace in that parish. Thus in Great Driffield in Yorkshire in 1595, apples, pears, walnuts, filberts, warden pears, plums, damsons, onions, garlic, and red roses were all tithed, as were parsnips, onions, artichokes, carrots, and turnips at Kirby Malzeard, near Ripon in North Yorkshire in 1614.[4] The artichokes may be assumed to have been globe artichokes, for Jerusalem artichokes were very new indeed at that date, whereas globe artichokes had been made highly desirable by Henry VIII in the early sixteenth century, copying tastes which he encountered at the French court, and which, we may guess, were also urged on him, by his queen, Catherine of Aragon. Whenever the growing of these newfangled foods is found in country areas far from London, it can be taken for granted that a rich gentleman lived in the vicinity. Thus islands of consumerism are found in scattered places wherever tenants and neighbors set themselves to satisfy the advanced consumer tastes of a local family. The individual circles exerting that influence were small, but the circles were many, and they were steadily increasing in number as counties found themselves with more and more resident gentry, moving into villages and even hamlets, sometimes for the first time. Thus each circle had at its center a gentleman, or occasionally several, who were liable to absorb strong influences from London, and who then made demands on the local community which it was profitable for neighbors to satisfy.[5] If other circumstances were also favorable, provincial producers then had the chance to exploit the market further afield, even as far away as London.

The account books of gentle households graphically show the influences at work in the local setting. Lord William Howard of Naworth Castle in Cumberland paid out in 1612 for cherries brought by local women to the kitchen door in June and early July, for plums brought by boys and men in July and September, pompions (i.e., pumpkins) in September, pears in October, and apples in November. The local people, it seems, did not yet grow asparagus (though one would have found plenty in London market gardens at this time), but Lady Wintour's man brought asparagus to the door from somewhere not far away in 1629, almost certainly from her own manorial vegetable garden. In 1620, pears were brought "from the abbey"; this was Lanercost priory, which had been dissolved long since, but evidently the orchard had survived, and thus we glimpse here the horticultural traditions of a monastic house living on, perpetuated by a layman-gardener getting his living by serving the local nobleman.[6]

In other examples, gentlemen deliberately introduced high-grade horticulture into villages for the first time in the sixteenth century. Take, for example, Sir Arthur Throckmorton, brother-in-law of Sir Walter Raleigh, building a new house in Paulerspury, in Northamptonshire. He wanted his own country seat and chose a site that lay in good hunting country in the Whittlewood forest. But it was not socially a fitting place for gentry to reside in all the year round. So he was colonizing and taming a wild landscape, introducing a gentlemanly lifestyle into a district which had previously known different ways. The inhabitants would have been more familiar with forest animals like deer, hares, falcons, and wild birds. Throckmorton, in short, was creating an island of fastidious tastes, planting vines, fruit trees, and artichokes.[7] The local people responded, and his diary shows supplies of fine foods arriving at the door (for example, 2s. 6d. given for melons on August 21, 1593); he tasted a ripe apricot from his own trees in July 1611.[8]

Many more examples could be cited of gentry moving into new areas, and, through the very presence of their demanding households, familiarizing the local people with consumerism at a higher social level than they would otherwise have encountered. In such circumstances, many humble neighbors will have looked upon such scenes with some wonder, but then turned away, virtually unaffected by the sight of something which so obviously had no practical relevance for them. But another stream of influences was always at work at the same time, stimulating the imagination and encouraging inventiveness among local people. The way of life of a manorial household was seeping out all the time, and it did not seep out into a barren place, where the local people showed no originality of their own.[9]

Every local community had its own lifestyle. Many of them had never had a gentleman in residence, but they had used the local resources to the best of their ability, and that usage was sometimes original in some way and might prove in the end to be eminently marketable. The success of the lightweight textiles (called the "new draperies") in Europe, as described and analyzed by Donald Coleman, is a compelling illustration of the inventiveness and ingenuity of peasants, demonstrated, in this case, in their weaving of homemade cloths to please themselves. Some had originated in Italy, some in Flanders; they mixed threads, colors, and finishes. But one day the moment arrived when they were *discovered* and were drawn into the commercial market. Fashion relished their infinite variety; everyday speech slurred the local names into a fantastic jumble of strange words. Undoubtedly, the very success of the new draperies encouraged more and more outlandish experiments so that the frenzy was fed by success. But, at the outset, the new draperies were commercialized peasant cloths — traditional local products from different places, highly differentiated one from another, which subsequently found favor in wider markets.[10]

When consumer goods arrived in London from the English and Welsh provinces in 1600, instead of being imported from abroad, they did not appear out of nowhere. They too often represented the commercialization of a traditional local product which had hitherto served the locality without attracting any wider notice. Changing fashion is a satisfactory explanation for their lucky chance at this period when seen from a Londoner's perspective, but the phenomenon deserves a closer look from the provincial viewpoint.

Vegetables, herbs, and fruit offer a first example. They were the frugal food and medicinal cures of the poor and the meek, as well as of monks and nuns. Country people followed ancient gardening traditions in cultivating these simpler foods — mainly onions, leeks, and colewort — while monastic houses grew more numerous and some finer varieties, which they had culled sometimes from far afield. When the gardening interests of the well-to-do contributed greenstuff that was more highly esteemed than hitherto, horticultural

activity took on a new lease of life in many country places. It was most responsive, and is conspicuous in the records, in places where the gardeners were able
to exploit the London market. But Todd Gray, who works on the history of
Devon and Cornwall, finds there, too, an impressive tradition among ordinary
villagers in the sixteenth century for growing vegetables, herbs, and fruit; and
since the climate is especially favorable, we should not be surprised. But the
commercial potential of market gardening in those two counties, far away
at the tip of southwest England, was not, in fact, realized until the 1880s,
when the railways reduced the travelling time to London from days to hours.
Around London, on the other hand, market gardening already flourished in
1600, along Thames-side (in places like Fulham and Hackney) and in sandy,
gravelly areas not too far away (for example, in Surrey, on the Bagshot heaths,
and on the sandy lands of Sandwich, on the northeast coast of Kent). From
Surrey, women walked to London with their fresh produce daily, and from
Sandwich a remarkably efficient service of coastal hoys took garden produce
along the Thames. In short, the consumer market in greenstuff built on, and
exploited, an existing tradition. That observation is not intended to detract in
any way from the importance of the Flemish and Dutch gardeners in the
second half of the sixteenth century who upgraded the standard of local gardening. It simply sets in place the foundation already laid; gardening was
already embedded in the routines of resourceful, local people.[11]

Embedded traditions are also dimly seen in the case of some rural industries which developed rapidly in the sixteenth century to serve the consumer
market. The stocking-knitting industry is the supreme example. It grew from
nothing and spread in many geographically scattered places. How could it expand so quickly? Knitted stockings were imported from Spain. Thirty or forty
years later, fine woolen stockings were seen in London, brought from Italy.
Forty years later still, in 1600, thousands upon thousands of pairs of stockings
were being exported from London, not to mention those that were sold at
home. The noted centers for collecting the stockings for market were named in
1595 as Norwich, in eastern England; Doncaster, in south Yorkshire; Richmond, in north Yorkshire; and sixteen towns and villages round about Richmond, including two in Wensleydale, and Barnard Castle, further north still in
Teesdale. In other words, the industry had been stimulated in specific, but
geographically scattered centers, and some were quite remote from London.[12]

The spread of this development is only explicable if we assume the existence of some local knitting traditions, however rudimentary, before the commercial network drew on them. People had been knitting caps for two hundred years, though *commercial* cap making was a distinctive occupation found
only in certain widely separated places. We may reasonably guess that more

knitting was done in some districts than in others, but at least the craft existed. Exceedingly rarely, an early document will refer to knitted children's socks. It is likely, therefore, that knitting was a humble, domestic occupation, more practiced in some places than in others, but as commonplace and unremarked as cooking, cleaning, and spinning. Once the stocking fashion took hold, however, the market opportunities embedded in different local cultures could be seized. Only against that background can the enormous variety be explained of styles, patterns, colors, and threads that came so swiftly onto the market, in a matter of forty years or less. Scattered provincial centers offered diversity, which is the very lifeblood of consumerism.[13]

Another new consumer good for Londoners, inviting reflection from the same viewpoint, is lace. Why did lacemaking thrive in Honiton, Devon, and, on the other side of the country, in Buckinghamshire and Bedfordshire? In Bedfordshire it is associated with the presence of Queen Catherine of Aragon at Ampthill, a legend which has claims to substance because of the known excellence of Spanish lace and the Queen's interest and skill in needlework. She allegedly once came forward to greet Cardinal Wolsey (when he visited to discuss the question of her divorce) with a skein of silk around her neck; the needlewomen among us will recognize that scene.[14]

This legend might be thought to illustrate the kind of stimulus, discussed earlier, coming from a high-ranking personage who, for her own delectation, demanded newfangled consumer goods from the local inhabitants. In this case, however, it may not be the correct answer. Lacemaking does not seem to be explained as an indigenous activity, bursting forth when prodded by commercial ventures emanating from elsewhere. Rather, it appears to be a new skill brought in from the Continent. (The third of my themes will offer a better explanation, to be discussed below.) In Honiton, Devon, however, a mixture of two influences may well be present, excluding the notion of a powerful gentle family living at hand, but embracing the proposition that certain embedded traditions favored the growth of lacemaking skills, possibly strengthened by some knowledge of foreign craftsmanship. It is, in the first place, possible that a related handicraft was already practiced in and around Honiton, which suggested to outsiders that a congenial home for lacemaking was at hand. Lacemaking has its origins in what is called cutwork, a process in which threads are drawn out of linen fabric and the remaining threads are twisted and sewn into elaborate shapes. The flax produced around Axminster was remarked upon by Westcote in 1630 as being among the finest available.[15] Pride in the fine spinning of the local thread for linen, and even some interest in working cutwork patterns onto the fabric, may have given Honiton people modest local renown. A further possible ingredient in the story is the immigration of Flemish lacemakers, an event firmly put into the story by Mrs. Bury Palliser when writing her richly documented *History of Lace* in 1865. The local influence of Flemish immigrants would accord with other examples of foreigners entering upon new ventures in England and moving sure-footedly to centers already known to offer a congenial habitat. Immigrants assembled considerable prior knowledge of the most favorable locations for developing their skills, and so, if any did come to Honiton, it is certain that they knew something about it that made it seem a congenial place. H. J. Yallop's study of Honiton lace, on the other hand, emphatically insists that no trace of foreign immigrants could be found, and so he envisages a project set up in the area without preliminaries. Honiton, he notes, was a thoroughfare town between Cornwall and London. True enough; but the notion of an enterprising merchant arriving out of the blue fails to convince in the circumstances of the time. It leaves the lurking doubt that foreigners arrived in Honiton who have passed unrecognized; they so readily changed their surnames to something that was pronounceable in English.[16]

A third influence, however, was at work at this time, which forged strong links between the provinces and consumerist London and which has to be twisted into our skein of explanation in Honiton. This was the rising tide of opinion in favor of finding work for the unemployed and the vagrant poor. Idle, workless people threatened social peace and demanded positive action by local people to reduce that threat. Providing work for the poor was finally incorporated in a statute in 1576, ordering local authorities in cities and corporate towns to provide workstocks for the poor.[17] Both before and long after that date, benevolent individuals, including many Puritans, saw the sense of teaching more skills to the unemployed and took initiatives of their own.[18] The evidence of teachers being brought into large towns is impressive in the 1580s and 1590s, and sometimes earlier still.[19] It is less easy to find in small towns and country areas, but it does appear, for local gentlemen often showed care, and took practical action, to provide work for their neighbors and tenants. In the early years of the seventeenth century, for example, Lord Salisbury enlisted a teacher of fustian making in Hatfield; Lord Willoughby set up woad growing and knitting at Wollaton, in Nottinghamshire. It is possible, though unproven, that John Smith had a say in the setting up of pin making by John Tilsley in his Gloucestershire village of Berkeley.[20]

In Honiton, a small market town which became the celebrated center for bobbin lace makers, and in many villages nearby, lacemaking was taught, and the goods were marketed around 1600 by one James Rodge. Rodge was gratefully remembered in the church, when he died in 1617, for giving £100 to the poor. The inscription to his memory points to the inspiration which drove his life: "remember the poor." He looks like the teacher/dealer who successfully launched an industry which served London—perhaps, as already suggested, building on some existing skills in promising local circumstances.[21] In the case of Bedfordshire lace, all that is known about Catherine of Aragon suggests that, if she was indeed the prime mover in bringing lacemaking to that county, she, too, was governed by the same strong motives, to employ the poor.

Three streams of influence, then, converge around 1600, tying some places in the provinces into the network of commercial links with London. Gentlemen, moving back and forth to Westminster, introduced some elements of a London lifestyle to the villages where they resided and drew a positive response from their tenants. Provincial places had their own indigenous cultures, everywhere different in some way or other, but offering skills that might one day be appreciated and exploited when the time was ripe. In 1600 that moment ripened under the influence of changing fashions and benefited those places with a tradition of gardening, knitting, and lacemaking. More such occupations are waiting to be identified and added to the list. In the space available here, two more may be briefly and tentatively adduced; they call for further research but they strengthen the argument that more are waiting to be uncovered.

One local skill which became a local industry was the making of rush mats in the fenlands of East Anglia;[22] rush-matting became a modish floor covering in manor houses at this period. That fact is made evident in the household accounts of the Howard family at Naworth Castle, Cumberland. In 1624 they procured the matting for flooring from Norfolk; it was sent from King's Lynn, near the Norfolk fenlands, and was used to cover the floor of "Sir Francis, his chamber," and "Lady Phillip's chamber." The blankets of Witney, Oxfordshire, were another fashionable consumer good in larger houses. Witney had become known for its special blanket cloth, shaggy and unshorn, as the rhyme tells us ("with its shag unshorn . . . in the lashing tempest worn"), which made a cozy, warm bed covering. William Harrison remarked on the greater comfort which people were enjoying on softer beds by Elizabeth's reign; the well-to-do plainly chose the comfort of blankets. The fact is made crystal clear in the purchase by Robert Dudley, Earl of Leicester, in 1584, of thirty blankets from John Collier of Witney for use in Kenilworth Castle, Warwickshire. The same indulgence was evidently enjoyed at Paulerspury, Northamptonshire, for Arthur Throckmorton's diary for 28 August 1594 records the payment of thirty-eight shillings "for a pair of the best sort of woollen blankets," while, "for blankets of another sort," he paid only eleven shillings.[23]

More indigenous industries, supplying domestic wares, blossomed around 1600, such as the knife making of Sheffield, and, among more utilitarian wares still, the iron cooking pots of the Weald of Sussex and the weeding hoes from the Forest of Dean, bought by those who organized the loading of cargoes for Virginia.[24] If, on the other hand, we had been visualizing material London in 1700, the list of currently fashionable goods from the provinces would have been different, including cheeses from many different districts of origin, nuts from Croydon, potted meats, potted fish, and cider, and, among industrial goods, local soaps, small metal wares including toys, gloves, and the fabrics that were by then deemed necessary to serve a newfangled purpose as curtains for windows.[25]

The third stream of influence converging with the others in 1600 was a drive to set up schools and teach skills more widely, which surged strongly between about 1580 and 1630, accelerating the engines of production in local places where they had often turned over quietly, and without urgency, before that date. After 1630 enthusiasm for setting up schools seems to have faded, partly because other developments like overseas colonization alleviated the problems of unemployment and the vagrant poor, but also because the earlier initiatives had been successful enough to establish many rural industries and relieve the unemployed.

This view of three strands in the skein of provincial activity, serving but also driving consumerist desires in London, prompts further reflections on variety which is such a necessary characteristic of consumer goods if they are to enjoy a long life in the market. Provincial cultures left to themselves nurture and preserve their own individuality. When we look at English knitware today, for example, the strongest individuality survives on the islands around the coast, in the knitting of the isles of Aran, Shetland, Fairisle, and Guernsey, not on the mainland, where knitting was standardized long ago. We still, of course, see individuals emerging from that sea of standardization, but they no longer recognize their roots in a local culture, whereas in 1600 local cultures on the mainland were numerous.

When the tide of consumerism swells, it also unfortunately fosters the urge to standardize. Its purpose is quite reasonable, to raise standards, as we see in the sealing of textiles; we see it also described in remarkable detail in the making of sailcloth in Ipswich in Elizabeth's reign, when the finished canvas was examined by the experts, who pointed out the faults to the makers and indicated ways of remedying matters. But it had a negative side, as the knitters of stockings bitterly complained. They stressed that when varying qualities were allowed, it permitted varying prices and every class had the chance to buy. In other words, freedom allowed more experimentation, out of which more variety could emerge.[26]

A continual tension exists between the drive to standardize, which irons out diversity, and the drive to innovate. In an occupation serving wide national, even international demands, the constraints imposed by the need for uniform production does not, of course, suppress all originality; they must not do so if the occupation is to continue to flourish. But undoubtedly they curb innovation in many directions. Pools of originality lie outside every arena of recognized skill and market success, and many of these existed in rudimentary form in 1500, totally unnoticed. Then they were drawn into the consumerist vortex, and by 1600 they had been tied to London, as well as being tied to one another. The demands of material London were weaving a veritable spider's web, linking to itself and to each other scattered centers of production. Nevertheless, large areas of country were left as yet untouched by London's tentacles, allowing them to harbor their distinctive skills and special cultural attributes for some time yet. They would serve their turn at another time in the future, sometimes two centuries hence. But the ingredients in the situation would be recognizably similar, as, for example, when fine knitted shawls were drawn into London's maw in the 1880s from Shetland, and at the same period fine Donegal tweed and stockings were drawn from Ireland.[27]

Notes

1. A good example of a traveler urged to travel with curiosity is contained in William Higford's advice in the early seventeenth century to his grandson, urging him, while traveling abroad, to study politics and administration and talk to men at the universities, "looking for what you may find rare and fit for imitation when you return into England." William Higford, "The Institution of a Gentleman," *Harleian Miscellany*, 10 vols. (London, 1808–13), 9:580–99.

2. Cited in P. Clark, *The English Alehouse: A Social History, 1200–1830* (London: Longman, 1983), p. 112.

3. H. M. Colvin, *The History of the King's Works: 1485–1660* (London: HMSO, 1982), Part II, p. 213.

4. Borthwick Institute, York, Dean and Chapter of York, Tithe Cause Papers, 1595, no. 9; 1614, no. 2. I owe these references to the kindness of John Addy. Jerusalem artichokes were a novelty in France in 1607 and are first clearly referred to in England in 1622. Redcliffe N. Salaman, "Why 'Jerusalem' Artichoke?" *Journal of the Royal Horticultural Society* 55 (1940):340–42.

5. Driffield, for example, was the site of a royal residence of some importance in the thirteenth century, which then reverted to the house of Aumale. R. Allen Brown, H. M. Colvin, and A. J. Taylor, *The History of the King's Works*, vol. 2 (London: HMSO, 1963), p. 924. On rising numbers of gentry resident in counties, see M. Havinden, "The Increase and Distribution of the Resident Gentry of Somerset, 1500–1623," *Southern History* 20–21 (1998–99):68–107.

6. Reverend George Ornsby, ed., *Selections from the Household Books of the Lord William Howard of Naworth Castle*, Surtees Society 68 (1877):29–32, 129, 263.

7. A. L. Rowse, *Ralegh and the Throckmortons,* rev. ed. (London: Macmillan/Reprint Society, 1962), pp. 190–91, 14, 275, 281–83.

8. Canterbury Cathedral Archives, Sir Arthur Throckmorton's Diary, vol. 2, fol. 117; Rowse, pp. 281–83.

9. Such reflections are prompted by Arthur Throckmorton's luring away the gardener, Thomas Shipton, who had been employed by Sir Christopher Hatton when he built his grand house at Holdenby, Northamptonshire. Throckmorton obliged him by contract to produce herbs, sallets, artichokes, and fruit trees, and we may readily imagine his impact on the young gardeners working under him at Paulerspury. Canterbury Cathedral Archives, Sir Arthur Throckmorton's Diary, vol. 2, fol. 117; Rowse, p. 283.

10. D. C. Coleman, "An Innovation and Its Diffusion: The 'New Draperies,'" *Economic History Review,* 2nd ser., 22, no. 3 (1969): 417–29. For a comparable example in linen goods, see the eight different kinds of Holland linen, named after separate places in the Low Countries, in "A Book of Values of Merchandize imported, according to which excise is to be paid by the first buyer," British Library, London, Thomason Tracts, E 1065 (21), 1657, p. 48. See also N. B. Harte, ed., *The New Draperies in the Low Countries and England* (Oxford: Pasold Research Fund and Oxford University Press, 1997), passim.

11. Malcolm Thick, "Market Gardening in England and Wales," in *The Agrarian History of England and Wales,* V, ii, ed. Joan Thirsk (Cambridge: Cambridge University Press, 1985), pp. 503–7.

12. Joan Thirsk, "'The Fantastical Folly of Fashion': The English Stocking Knitting Industry, 1500–1700," in Thirsk, *The Rural Economy of England: Collected Essays* (London: Hambledon Press, 1984), pp. 235–57, esp. p. 245.

13. Ibid., pp. 242–44.

14. Fanny Bury Palliser, *History of Lace* (London, 1865), p. 7.

15. H. J. Yallop, *The History of the Honiton Lace Industry* (Exeter: Exeter University Press, 1992), pp. 19–20.

16. See Palliser, *History of Lace,* revised and enlarged by M. Jourdain and Alice Dryden (London: Sampson Low, 1902), pp. 399ff; Emily Nevill Jackson, *A History of Hand-Made Lace . . .* (London: L. U. Gill, 1900), p. 167 claims that Honiton's lacemakers were "reinforced" by Flemish refugees. The presence of foreign immigrants in Honiton is put in doubt, but not entirely discredited, by Yallop. It is not necessary to envisage a large number of immigrants; one family would have been sufficient to exert significant influence. Yallop, *History of Honiton Lace Industry,* pp. 12–20.

17. R. H. Tawney and Eileen Power, eds., *Tudor Economic Documents* (London: Longmans, Green 1924), 2:331–34.

18. For example, Paul Slack, ed., *Poverty in Early Stuart Salisbury, Wiltshire Record Society* 31 (Devizes, 1975), pp. 9–12, 83–86.

19. W. K. Jordan, *The Charities of London* (London: Allen & Unwin, 1960), pp. 177–78; E. M. Hampson, *The Treatment of Poverty in Cambridgeshire, 1597–1834* (Cambridge: Cambridge University Press, 1934), pp. 31–34; *Victoria County History, Yorkshire,* vol. 3, pp. 466–69; *Victoria County History, City of York,* p. 134; Mary Bateson, ed., *Records of the Borough of Leicester, 1509–1603* (London: C. J. Clay, 1905), pp. 232–34.

20. *Calendar of State Papers Domestic, 1603–10,* p. 478; PRO C2, Jas. 1, M12/41; R. S. Smith, "A Woad-growing Project at Wollaton in the 1580s," *Transactions of the*

Thoroton Society of Nottinghamshire 65 (1961): 27–46; Gloucester City Museum and Art Gallery, unpublished MS by R. A. Lewis on the pin industry.

21. Yallop, *History of Honiton Lace Industry,* p. 1.

22. I am grateful to Peter Thornton for drawing my attention to the rush matting industry.

23. Alfred Plummer, ed., *The Witney Blanket Industry* (London: George Routledge, 1934), pp. 8–9; *Victoria County History, Oxfordshire,* vol. 2, pp. 247–48; Canterbury Cathedral Archives, Arthur Throckmorton's Diary, vol. 2, fol. 130.

24. David Hey, "The Origins and Early Growth of the Hallamhire Cutlery and Allied Trades," in *English Rural Society, 1500–1800,* ed. John Chartres and David Hey (Cambridge: Cambridge University Press, 1990), pp. 346–48; Susan Myra Kingsbury, *Records of the Virginia Company* (Washington, D.C.: Government Printing Office, 1906–35), 3:186.

25. Some examples include the cheese reputation of Leicestershire; see Earl of Cardigan, "Domestic Expenses of a Nobleman's Household, 1678," *Bedfordshire Historic Record Society* 32 (1951): 119, showing the earl bringing in a dairywoman and maids out of Leicestershire; for metal toys, see Marie Rowlands, *Masters and Men in the West Midland Metalware Trades before the Industrial Revolution* (Manchester: Manchester University Press, 1975), p. 128; for curtains, see Margaret Spufford, *The Great Reclothing of Rural England, Petty Chapmen, and their Wares in the Seventeenth Century* (London: Hambledon Press, 1984), pp. 108–9. Spufford concentrates on the imported textiles, used for curtains, but she also shows how cheaper, substitute cloth, "scotch cloth," was used, which plainly stimulated commercial production somewhere in Scotland or England. The documents, unfortunately, do not indicate exact places of manufacture.

26. Joan Thirsk, *Economic Policy and Projects: The Development of a Consumer Society in Early Modern England* (Oxford: Oxford University Press, 1978), pp. 41, 116.

27. Lerwick Museum and Library, Shetland, E. S. Reid Tait Collection, MSS 17/26 and 18/1. Number 17/26 contains publications by Jessie M. Saxby, including a threepenny pamphlet on *Shetland Knitting;* number 18/1 contains an anonymous article on "A Shetland Cottage Industry" from *Chamber's Journal,* 31 July 1897, pp. 487–88, probably by Jessie Saxby. Saxby's mother fostered the development of, and commercial market for, the laceknitting of Shetland shawls. See also Helen Bennett, "The Shetland Handknitting Industry" in *Scottish Textile History,* ed. John Butt and Kenneth Ponting (Aberdeen: Aberdeen University Press, 1987), pp. 57–60. On Donegal tweed and stockings, see D. M. Mulock, *Concerning Men and Other Papers, by the Author of "John Halifax, Gentleman"* (London: Macmillan, 1888), pp. 128–38.

6

Fantastical Colors in Foggy London

The New Fashion Potential of the Late Sixteenth Century

Jane Schneider

Ensembles of fashion and their respective elements — shapes, colors, and textures — are often laden with historical significance. Among their most interesting meanings are those that speak to the drama of great nations building up their cloth-manufacturing capability, an act of necessity in a highly competitive field. For history is replete with, and has even been partly propelled by, intense rivalries among centers of cloth manufacture, each striving to turn out fabrics more attractive, or valuable, and possibly less costly, than the rest.

All over the world and throughout history, state-makers have understood that to pay for imported cloth they would have to disburse critical resources such as food and bullion. (Earlier on, slaves were also traded for cloth, spelling an obvious weakness of position.) As a prophylactic against resource depletion, and against domestic crises of unemployment, the builders of states typically encourage the home manufacture of textiles, their export, and the management of the export trade by native merchants. They also welcome, and often manipulate, the moral and religious revulsion that fashion tends to provoke, recognizing in the boycott of foreign luxuries a reinforcement for policies of "import substitution." The sumptuary laws and practices of any number of historical polities, not least those of Elizabethan England, conveyed the idea that fashion mocked sobriety, was an affront to God, and should be restrained for all but the highest classes of society. In addition, and most important, these laws and practices charted the uneasy and shifting relationship of foreign and domestic, exotic and home grown, contributions to the fashion swirl.

The late years of Elizabeth's reign were a special instance of this general process; England, with London as its foremost center of cloth exchange, was poised to shift from an insecure and peripheral position in the world of textile rivalries to a position of considerable prominence that would, as we know, eventually nurture the industrialization of cloth making. This essay focuses on one aspect of the bridging moment: the play of colors. If the year 1600 can serve as a metaphorical divide, it separated a time in which garments of "sad" or dark hue predominated among trend-setting elites (punctuated by dazzling chromatic displays only on ceremonial occasions) from a time when peacock splendor had its coming out (if suppressed for awhile by the Puritan backlash). Regarding London, the transformation applied to both of its poles of power: the circle of merchants, drapers, and aldermen who ran the city's economy and government; and the royal court, busy constructing a nation through a combination of military and textile strategy. Elizabeth's death in 1603 may be taken to have crystalized the shift. In Martin Holmes words, "The new king saw no reason to wear, or even to suggest, mourning for his predecessor. The black, white, or black-and-white attire that had been the regular wear at Elizabeth's court gave place to light colours such as red and yellow . . . [a] new age . . . was felt to be beginning."[1]

The black and white coloration of the Elizabethan court has been much remarked upon by scholars of ceremony and costume. Analyses of the two colors — Elizabeth's favorites — generally fasten on their users' semiotic intent: black is thought to represent constancy and white to represent purity, above all the purity of the "Virgin Queen." Roy Strong's analysis is a good example. His studies show how Elizabethan pageantry transformed the banished Catholic liturgy into not only a secular entertainment but a "dynastic apotheosis," in which the values of constancy and purity found expression in images of black and white.[2]

As has often been remarked, the trappings of feudalism, reinvented for the purpose, contributed to the cult of the Virgin Queen, among them jousting tournaments that enlivened state spectacles such as the magnificent anniversaries of Elizabeth's accession. Period artists captured the romantic chivalry of the resurrected knights who longed for their beloved monarch. In a detailed exegesis of one of the most famous portraits, *Young Man Amongst the Roses,* Strong notes the elegance of the youth's black and white hose, cape, and doublet. "Virgin white" and "constant black," the latter a "sable sad" color, are argued to convey this ideal courtier's lovesickness for the Queen.[3]

Assigning the same valences of constancy and purity to black and white, Valerie Cumming comments that these "preferred colours" of Elizabeth "provided subtle messages for those educated to understand such matters."[4] The messages are decoded in Grant McCracken's structural analysis of 101 male courtiers as depicted in Elizabethan paintings. Seventy-three percent of the youthful figures are in white or light colors; 70 percent of the older figures are in black. The young men, he proposes, reflect the light of the monarch, who, as a metaphorical sun, illuminates the world around her. The black of their elders evokes not so much sadness, or the humoral state of melancholy, as stability — steadfast constancy and solemn depth.[5]

Analyses of this kind are not contradicted or precluded by the following attempt to look at color symbolism in the wider context of the textile rivalries that served the formation of great states. The two approaches are complementary. I will suggest, in conclusion, however, that it is through textile history that we can better appreciate the turnaround in costume colors of "circa 1600."[6] What follows is in three parts: a discussion of the special status of dyestuffs and dyers in textile rivalries, of Londoners' suspicions of color before the watershed of "circa 1600," and of the political-economic shifts that enabled a much richer palette for clothes on the seventeenth-century side of the divide.

Dyestuffs and Dyers

My foray into textile history some twenty years ago led me to propose that conservative, often black dress was, historically, a key symbol around which Europeans rallied as they warded off, defended against, and ultimately reversed the hegemony of manufacturing centers more developed than their own that exported an array of brightly colored textiles.[7] Black cloth, even of very high quality, was relatively easy to produce under the local conditions that prevailed in Europe from the eleventh century. But polychrome cloth was not, for its manufacture depended upon access to quality dyestuffs whose distribution was, like the distribution of silks and spices, concentrated in Asia and the Near East but poorly represented in Europe. Until the invention of aniline (coal-tar) dyes and other chemical substitutes in the nineteenth century, this highly uneven presence of reputable dyes and of craftsmen skilled in dyeing led to monopolistic conditions in textile industries with dyeing and finishing capabilities. In the Middle Ages, these industries flourished in the eastern Mediterranean, from which they diffused to the wool and silk towns of northern Italy. Northern Europe remained sartorially "backward" until, in the early modern period, England and Holland raced each other to catch up.

Unlike staining cloth, dyeing is a chemical process that alters the structure of the fibers so that the color will not wash out or fade from exposure. Pre-aniline substances were prepared through lengthy, difficult, and polluting operations. I touch on the primary colors as examples. One could get a good yellow from saffron, as we know from Buddhist monks, but to obtain a small vial of this ingredient, it was necessary to collect the stamens from hundreds of crocuses.[8] The sources of blue — plants of the indigo family — were widely cultivated and their application not overly demanding of technical skill, yet processing them was obnoxious. Dyers first obtained a precipitant from the soaked leaves of the plant, then mixed it with an alkaline solution to create a bath. Cloth dipped in the bath emerged greenish or white but oxidized to blue upon drying, the depth of the blue depending on the number of baths and the quality of the dye.[9]

A world survey would show that the most ready-to-hand alkaline was household urine. While the best blues came from the tropical indigos, other variants would do. Hand-kneaded balls of woad, the English "indigo," took nine weeks to ferment and gave off a smell so disgusting that Queen Elizabeth would not allow woad processing within a five-mile radius of her residences.[10] (The polluting smoke of sea coals, burned in place of more costly firewood by an increasing number of artisans, including dyers, also bothered the Queen.)[11]

Good reds and purples were the hardest of all to obtain. In the classical and Byzantine empires of the Mediterranean, purple was derived from a glandular secretion of the whelk mollusk (the murex or purpura) that was fished and sun-dried near Tyre. It took 1,200 murexes to obtain 1.4 grams of dye, while a pound of murex-dyed wool equaled a stone mason's daily wage. So exotic an origin guaranteed exclusive use to those who were "born to the purple," even in the absence of royal restrictions.[12] Another renowned source of Old World red was brazilwood, which yielded orange to red shades. Made from ground, fermented, and boiled wood that was Asian in origin, it was imported into Europe by Venetian merchants from the old ports of Gujarat, Cambay, Ceylon, and the East Indies. (Brazil, the country, was so named when Europeans discovered brazilwood on its soil.)

Clear, brilliant scarlets came from kermes, the shield lice of the Coccus family. Parasitic on evergreen oaks in the Mediterranean, this insect was harvested while pregnant with eggs, killed with vinegar, and dried in the sun, its worm-like larvae then rolled into little balls called "grains." These yielded a clear, bright red upon soaking in water and were the source of the word "ingrained" and, as in wormlike, the word "vermilion." Although accounting for as much as 60 percent of the cost factors in some textiles, kermes could be transported to distant centers of dyeing and did not give rise to state monopolies in the manner of murex purple, usable only when fresh.[13]

New World sources of red show a similar duality. A murex-like shellfish harvested on the Pacific coast of Central America constituted the source of a rare purple (*purpura patula*) that was traded to the Guatemalan highlands and as far north as Oaxaca. To this day, mauve — the New World's murex purple —

is the most prestigious color in the brocaded and embroidered *huipils* or blouses of these regions. Meanwhile, the Mediterranean kermes had a parallel in cochineal, produced from an insect parasitic on the nopal cactus, native to Mexico, Central America, and Peru. This dyestuff attracted the attention of the Spanish colonists, who organized nopal plantations on which Indian laborers harvested up to 225 pounds of insects per acre three times a year, the exported surplus competing with Europen kermes.[14] Madder, a root, provided less costly and less thrilling reds in both the New and Old Worlds.

It is no accident that a discussion of textile dyeing should highlight red, by all accounts the most challenging color to achieve before synthetic dyes and, among colors, the most noticed and desired. That red has long been special and hard to come by can be seen from the eagerness with which the cloth artisans of colonial Africa and native North America — areas on the margins of the Coccus reds — avidly unraveled cochineal and kermes-dyed commercial cloth for yarn. With the exception of gold threads and a native silk called "sunyan," magenta ravelings from the silk industries of Lyons and the Middle East, traded through the trans-Saharan caravans, were the most prestigious elements in the weft blocks of many West African men's cloth.[15] In the American southwest, cochineal-dyed European cloth provided ravelings for Pueblo and Navajo weavers from the 1600s until the American Civil War, after which, machine-woven and synthetically-dyed American flannels became the source, followed by industrial yarns.[16] Throughout, the ravelings and yarns that mattered were red.

Dyeing cloth required other ingredients besides dyestuffs. To facilitate the chemical reaction that fixed color in fibers, mordants were necessary. The excellent mordant, aluminum sulphate or alum, was mined in the Papal state at Tolfa, near Rome, which is why one found it in the holds of the ships of Italian merchants in sixteenth-century London.[17] Stale urine, rancid oils, lye, or the brine of pickled fish were used to remove iron salts from alum, which otherwise darkened the cloth. Such processing is one of the earliest examples of chemical purification.[18] To vat-dye a length of cloth, craftworkers would immerse it in successive solutions, usually over several months, combining dyes, mordants, and other ingredients according to custom or recipe. All over the world dyers, including women in some places, possessed unique skills and closely guarded secrets. Many were only wage-earners, but in renowned centers of dyeing and finishing, they often acquired economic muscle, trading in dyestuffs and other ingredients, maintaining high cost inventories, loaning money at interest, and investing in specialized craft installations and other projects as well. It was a dyer and moneylender, Philip Henslowe, who built the Rose Theatre in Southwark in 1586.[19]

Not all yarns and cloth take well to dyeing. Speaking again of the time before the coal-tar dyes, craftsmen knew that cellulose fibers (linen and cotton) stubbornly repelled colors while protein fibers (silk and wool) absorbed them with relative ease. A secondary hierarchy differentiated the two color-friendly fibers. Even the most supple wools fell short of the coarsest silks in fineness, luster, and color saturation. It is no accident, therefore, that the geographical distribution of skilled and well-capitalized dyers roughly matched the distribution of silks as well as dyestuffs — these commodities shared overlapping trajectories of trade. England was blessed with wool — very fine wools by the sixteenth century. Its landscape yielded woad and madder, not to mention a host of roots and barks that could be used in dyeing. Short-distance trade augmented these benefits, for example, when woad arrived from Toulouse. But England was several steps removed from the luxury fiber silk; from the most finely and exquisitely woven silks, brocades, and damasks; and from the dyestuffs with the best reputations for beauty, versatility, and fastness — namely, tropical brazilwood, indigo, kermes, and murex purple.

Color in Late Sixteenth-Century London

Something can be learned about colors in London's distant past from the sources that John Stow interrogated for his 1598 *Survey*. From late medieval times when kings, lords, and municipal officers chartered companies and doled out privileges, their proclamations were accompanied by grants of cloth (called "liveries," after the word "delivery"), from which the recipients made robes or cloaks for themselves.[20] One year, during the reign of Edward II, the household of Thomas, earl of Lancaster, disbursed the following, obviously ranked fabrics: scarlet for himself, russet for the bishop, blue for the knights, medley for the clerks, and pieces of unspecified color for the esquires, officers, grooms, archers, minstrels and carpenters. Linen cloth, possibly bleached, went to both the earl and his chaplains. Within the lesser ranks, barons, knights, and clerks received hoods of purple and saffron-colored cloths in summer. "Mixed" reds and rays, which are cloths of many colors, and some green silk went to these levels as well.[21]

In the late Middle Ages, according to Stow, ray gowns, differentiated according to status, were worn by the mayor and sheriffs, while officers of the city wore "party colours" — that is, different colors on their right and left sides. Mustard, blue, red, medley, and purple were among the colors in use. By the reign of Henry VIII, however, neither ray cloths nor party cloths were popular, and grants of cloth consisted of solid colors. Mustard was by then out of use.

Especially interesting for our purposes are the *Survey*'s descriptions of the ceremonial presence of red. Henry V, arriving from Dover in 1415 with his prisoners from France, was greeted by London's mayor, aldermen, and crafts-men "riding in red, with hoods red and white." The mayor on horseback who greeted Henry VI in 1432 was dressed in "crimson velvet," followed by hench-men in suits of red and by aldermen in "gowns of scarlet, with sanguine hoods." All of the "commonality of the city" was, on this occasion, "clothed in white gowns, and scarlet hoods." Somewhat later in 1458, Henry VII was greeted by "the mayor, aldermen, sheriffs, and commonality, all clothed in violet." Later, hats replaced hoods. Henry VIII already had a round flat cap of scarlet.[22]

At the time of Elizabeth, the color red, above all the resonant scarlets and crimsons, continued to announce both rank and ceremony. Descriptions of the Queen entering London for her accession and subsequent anniversaries, of the annual celebration of the Lord Mayor's Day, and of the processions of companies that honored visiting dignitaries suggest that pomp, whether civic or royal, was utterly dependent on this fiery color. Even canopies — those "rich and very spacious pavilion(s)" — were crimson red.[23] Yet silk cloth, bril-liant reds, and bright colors in general, were not yet under English control; in Stow's account, faraway India was responsible for "purple garments," as France was responsible for wine.[24] Ambassadors from the Spanish court of Philip II flaunted silk, albeit in black, while Italian merchants displayed this luxury fabric in an array of beautiful colors.[25] Londoners possessed such finery as gifts from ingratiating foreigners or at a debilitating cost to themselves.

It is against this background that we might reconsider Elizabeth's favorite colors, white and black. For although her gowns, and her courtiers' attire, were often of imported silk and satin, the court as a whole seemed to shun the competitive display of variegated colors as a route to prestige or status. Drawn to this court as if by a magnet and forced to maintain expensive residences and rounds of hospitality in London, members of the aristocracy and gentry cer-tainly spent prodigious amounts of their family fortunes on clothing.[26] But the most invidious displays of fashion had little or no chromatic resonance: starched ruffs, lace or pearled embroidery, and fantastic shapes. Compared with color, each of these elements depended heavily, if not utterly, on native, as opposed to foreign, craft production. For example, the ample cartwheel ruffs which many would consider a leitmotif of both men's and women's dress in late sixteenth-century London did not require exotic materials or technologies. Made of linen produced in the British Isles or nearby Low Countries and trimmed with lace, they achieved their brilliant whiteness through repeated bleaching. The Low Countries were also the source of the starching methods that made the ruffs as stiff as boards; migrant Flemish starchers transmitted this craft to England.[27]

Lacemaking and embroidery are crafts whose perfection depends more heavily on skilled labor than on particular materials.[28] And the laborers in question learned quickly from each other, even across national boundaries. Nothing stood in the way of the development of lacemaking and embroidery within England's borders, or of the intensification of these industries as Elizabeth's courtiers rivaled each other in the size of their ruffs and the density of decoration on their bodices, sleeves, and doublets. As Lawrence Stone wrote in his classic study of the "crisis of the aristocracy," it was embroidery "which really ran away with the money." The materials could be expensive — gold and silver threads, for example — and "the labour involved [was] prodigious."[29]

Stone also describes London tailors "crouched anxiously behind the pillars in old St. Paul's watching for a new cut of doublet or a novel pair of hose displayed upon the gallants exhibiting themselves in the aisles."[30] Claims to social status were closely linked to the "extraordinary shapes that elegance demanded."[31] Women, in particular, used "canvas and stuffing to puff out [their] gown[s], whalebone to compress the bodice, buckram and whalebone to support the wings, and pasteboard and wire to hold up the collar."[32] All the wiring and padding severely distorted their shapes.[33] Shakespeare, in *The Taming of the Shrew*, offers a husband's perspective on these practices, likening a woman's sleeve to a "demi-cannon . . . up and down, carv'd like an apple-tart. Here's snip and nip and up and cut and slish and slash, like to a censer in a barber's shop. Why, what, i' devil's name, tailor, call'st thou this?"[34] Again, the tailor would be local, if skilled at following foreign pattern books. Although in 1567 the Queen tried surreptitiously to recruit a tailor from Paris (without the French queen finding out), two English tailors, Walter Fyske and William Jones, constructed most of her wardrobe until her death in 1603.[35]

Overall, as Valerie Cumming argues, Tudor grandeur consisted of bulky, swaggering, and highly decorated clothes in which imported luxuries, although present, did not swamp or undermine a strong sense of national identity.[36] Elizabeth was sometimes caricatured as a "strutting bird of fantastic plumage,"[37] yet it was not color that defined the image, but rather, huge ruffs, bodices stretched to exaggerated lengths permitting bigger fields for bejeweled embroidery, and enormous farthingales, as if each gown were a black or white cage or fortress.[38] Starched and stiffened shapes, and the heavy weight of ornament, were what counted. Meanwhile, the city's richest citizens, its merchants and drapers, were abstemious in appearance, their gowns being, in Stow's word, of the "saddest" color.[39]

London's leading citizens were, as a rule, closely associated with one or another branch of the woolen textile industry. Some of them, along with their apprentices, wove woolen cloth out of yarns brought in from the countryside; others dyed and finished whole cloths or cut and sewed them into clothes. There were, as well, competing coalitions of merchants, the most powerful of whom, the Merchant Adventures, mediated the export of undyed woolens, manufactured in the rural districts, to nearby Antwerp, returning home with silks and spices acquired from Italian and other merchants in this important center of "world trade."[40]

Most of these citizens, above all the merchants, knew that, as Sylvia Thrupp has argued, English producers did poorly with color.[41] Each piece of finished cloth sent to Antwerp was said to lose from ten to twenty shillings because it had to be redyed. Perhaps the water of the Thames was totally inferior to the water of the Elbe and Scheldt. Certainly, "English workmanship was inferior to the foreign."[42] "At this daye," said the designer of a late sixteenth-century project for dyeing cloth in England, "any-one who can afford it wyll not meddle with any cloth that is dyed within this realm—Our ignorant dyers . . . washe awaye and poure downe the gutters well most as much [dye] as they cast awaye upon the cloth." Yet, he continued, colors were "necessary to the English nation"—without them, "we enrich strangers and impoverish our countrymen."[43]

A royal statute of 1552 enumerated as true, rather than false and deceivable, the following hues: scarlet, red, and crimson, and then a host of nondescript shades including brown-blue, orange-tawny, russet, marble, sheep's color, lion's color, motley or iron gray, something called "new sad color" and something called "puke."[44] The latter, unrelated to present usage, was an inky blue-black, made from boiling wool with oak galls and then copperas (copper sulphate). The criticism of English dyers extended to their use of rynes, barks, galls, and copperas "afterwarde floryshed up with a shewe of disceptfull brasell. . . . Thereby they take great hyre for slender coste."[45] Not mentioned by the statute, but produced at the time, were other miserable shades: rat's color (a dull gray), horse flesh (bronze, like the hide of bay horses), and gooseturd, a yellowish green.[46] One quickly grasps the state of dyeing from William Harrison's list of colors, claimed by his 1587 *Description of England* to have been devised "to please fantastical heads"; this list included "devil in the hedge" (an off-shade of red) and "pease porridge tawny" as well as gooseturd green.[47]

Protestant rhetoric offered a way around this dull array by condemning colors outright. Bright ones, especially, were labeled offensive to God for diverting attention from the "true colors" of virtue — colors that could not be judged by appearances or "works." One 1603 text complained that "every man has fallen in love with himself . . . his mind is set on fashions, fangles and garish clothes . . . in the judgement of wise men, such [people] are but a blowne bladder, painted over with so many colours, stuft full of pride and envy . . . in whomsoever such [outward] badges of vanitie appears, it is a sure token there is a stinking puddle of vainglory within."[48]

The idea that bright colors masked stinking smells was an old one in England and had often been given a political-economic twist. In the fifteenth century, for example, Edward IV declared that "as well men as women wear excessive and inordinate apparel to the great displeasure of God, the enriching of strange realms, and the destruction of this realm."[49] His contemporaries who visited Italy were said to return either horrified or contaminated, and the Italianized Englishman was nicknamed "devil incarnato" — a play on words because red solutions, like flesh and meat, were "carnate."[50]

A hundred years later, an Englishman could still protest the "number of trifles [that] come hither from beyond the seas, that we might clean spare, or else make them within our Realm. For the which we . . . pay inestimable treasure every year."[51] William Harrison agreed, claiming that things were never merrier with England than when "an Englishman was known abroad by his own cloth and contented himself at home with . . . coat, gown, and cloak of brown-blue or puke."[52] Harrison worried that, their clothes full of jags and cuts and garish colors, "women are become men and men transformed into monsters."[53] Driving home the same point, Phillip Stubbes wrote in his Puritan tract of 1583, *The Anatomie of Abuses,* that clothes of "dyverse and sundry colours" in "silk, velvet, taffetie and such like," were a colossal waste: "the day hath bene, when one might have brought two clothes for lesse than now he can have one."[54]

Late sixteenth-century England was noted among textile rivals not for color, but for the export of uniformly undyed or "sadly" dyed cloth of wool. The main foreign markets for this cloth were in the Baltic and Eastern Europe. Merchants who carried it to India feared their ships would "rot in the river" if they persisted in the trade. In India great men used English broadcloth to cover their elephants and horses.[55] For the citizens of London and the royal court to indulge in variegated displays of color would have signaled the sacrifice of national resources in the pursuit of fantasy. Conversely, their essential chromatic conservatism communicated to others, and to themselves, a commitment to their own identity and industry — a refusal to become addicted on others' terms, above all the terms of Italian artisans and merchants.

Into the Seventeenth Century

And yet, by the late 1500s, the ground was shifting, with northern Italy soon to lose its preeminence in textile manufacture to Holland, the north of France, and England. The story of this process is complex and can only be highlighted here. One element was the so-called "new draperies" — soft, versatile worsted cloths of long staple wool which could be combed — it did not have to be carded and fulled. Weighing much less than the heavy, fulled fabrics of the past, this revolutionary textile was originally developed in Flemish villages but greatly advanced in England by Flemish migrants, the more so as the enclosure movement of the late fifteenth and sixteenth centuries improved the quality of midlands pastures, permitting grangers to breed larger sheep whose wool had a longer staple.[56] Of special interest were the peacock hues of the new draperies, for unlike medieval broadcloth, they were dyed and finished at home. Sometimes "dyed in the wool" (that is, before weaving) to produce several colors in the same piece of cloth, they accelerated the pace of fashion change. Manufacturers of the draperies were well aware that the decreased outlay for wool was balanced by an increase in the value of dyeing and finishing.[57]

Worsted wool lay behind the most important fashion innovation of the Elizabethan era — knitted stockings — which, by 1600, were displacing imported silk and woolen hose. Manufactured in several of England's wool-producing districts, they dared to come in multiple colors, some "striped with a fiery red."[58] Phillip Stubbes, the above-noted Puritan, railed that even children "are not ashamed to weare hose of . . . greene, red, white, russet, tawny and els what, whiche wanton light colors, any sober chaste Christian . . . can hardly without any suspicion of lightnesse at any time weare."[59]

Two fundamental changes associated with dyestuffs and dyeing contributed to the polychrome features of the new draperies (and stockings). The first was transoceanic shipping that brought tropical dyestuffs to northern ports via the Atlantic coast, circumventing the Levantine bottleneck and undermining Italian monopolies in the luxury trade. Javanese indigo, for example, was unloaded in Antwerp from Portuguese ships in such quantities as to cause English woad producers to organize against this "deceitful, devouring, and corrosive devil's dye"; newly available brazilwood was similarly stigmatized as having been "invented by aliens to the great hurt and slander of woolen cloths."[60] Perhaps because such resistance ran counter to economic realities, however, it paled before the welcome given to cochineal, which pirates from Holland and England, with the backing of their respective governments, seized from the holds of Spanish ships.[61] Dressed in scarlet attire to celebrate the defeat of the Spanish Armada in 1588, London's splendid elites were no doubt aware that cochineal was about to become more accessible to their city's dyers. Thanks to the defeat, moreover, English shippers found it less and less dangerous to enter the Mediterranean, circumventing the overland routes of Italy's merchant elite, earlier the main exporters of English cloth. Among the items picked up on the return voyage was alum which, no longer carried on the ships of Lucca, declined considerably in price.

The second change of significance to the repositioning of England in the wider sphere of textile rivalries was the religious wars, which in the 1570s and 80s knocked out Antwerp as the main entrepot for the North Atlantic region. Until then, Antwerp had been the first destination for England's undyed woolens; Flemish artisans dyed and finished these "semi-manufactures," reaping the rewards of the added value at the expense of London's dyers and finishers.[62] In the "days of its greatness," moreover, Antwerp was "bound . . . to things Italian [which] made it virtually an outpost of the cities of Italy on the northern coast of Europe."[63] Italian merchants, courted and patronized by the Antwerp authorities, handled the further export of English cloth, London's Merchant Adventurers losing out. The repression of Antwerp's freedoms by the Counter-Reformation armies enlarged the possibility for London to shed its satellite status vis-à-vis this important port city, above all in the textile field.[64]

The religious wars also produced the "celebrated diaspora of Protestants."[65] Counter-Reformation violence in south Germany, France, and the Low Countries turned many thousands of Protestants into migrants and refugees. Among them not a few were craftsmen in the textile trades, the most highly skilled being dyers. Both England and Holland, competing to develop viable textile exports, offered protection and exemptions to Flemish, German, Portuguese (Jewish), and Huguenot dyers and weavers, especially of silk.[66] Early in her reign, Elizabeth had welcomed returning Protestant exiles from England, as well as some 18,000–20,000 Flemish heretics. As Ramsay notes, "The immigrants paid for their shelter by the transplantation of new varieties of the textile industry. To them was due the establishment of the 'new draperies.'"[67]

Meanwhile, in late Elizabethan England, landowners and merchants launched projects to cultivate more woad, saffron, and madder at home, to open up alum mines, and to supplant olive oil, imported from Spain for use in dyeing, with home-grown rape seed oil.[68] A famous experiment provoked a trade war with Holland. In the early years of James I, a London alderman, William Cockayne, convinced the royal authority to block the export of undyed cloth. Holland, by then a center of dyeing and finishing, retaliated by increasing its own production of woolens, provoking England to interdict the export of raw wool.[69] Although the Cockayne Project failed, causing rising unemployment in the English textile industry,[70] dyers gravitated in increasing numbers to England. One, in particular, Bauer, is reported by Roger Coke to have brought "fifty Walloons with him who instructed the English how to 'make and dye fine woolen cloths cheaper by forty percent than they could before.'"[71] Most significant, the Flemish chemists, Cornelius Drebbel and his sons-in-law, the Kufflers, experimented in England with a pewter mordant for cochineal, inventing the bow-dye process that considerably reduced the cost of making good reds.[72]

The manufacture of new draperies (and knitted stockings) picked up modestly after the first migrations of 1560 and the fall of Antwerp. By the early seventeenth century, they were taking over, underwriting a complementary shift of English trade. As substitutes for imported "light cloths"—above all colorful silks—they "stimulated economic energies that filtered through to the very heart of the national economy (and) heralded the development of a consumer society that embraced not only the nobility and gentry."[73] As exports, they multiplied five times between 1600 and 1640, by which time they equaled the value of the exported semi-manufactures, "profoundly alter[ing] the nature of the English textile industry and the geographical pattern of English trade."[74] By 1616 worsted yarn absorbed a third of all the wool produced in England, while the new draperies, not even taxed in 1595, were deemed "more vendible than any cloth we make."[75]

The fact that the new draperies were dyed and finished in England gave a particular boost to London's long-distance merchants. No longer subordinated to the great Italian houses, these adventurers were off to distant places like India and Turkey, the old Byzantine "Mecca," not to mention such Mediterranean destinations as Spain, Portugal, North Africa, the Levant, and Italy itself. Meanwhile, the Italian mercantile colony of London declined. In Ramsay's words, "At this point we cross a watershed, and the weight of interest moves from the history of the Italians in England to that of the English in the Mediterranean."[76]

Conclusion

The early pages of this essay evoked the black and white hues of Queen Elizabeth's court and the "sad," dark colors of prestigious Londoners during her reign. Black was thought at the time, and by many scholars thereafter, to convey steadfast support for the monarch, and white to symbolize the Virgin

Queen's purity. This essay proposes, however, that beyond these representations, black and white were thoroughly intertwined with England's determination to hold its own in the lively textile rivalries of the time. Above all, these colors served to repel the brilliantly dyed silks and wools originating in the expansionist city-states of Italy and carried around Europe by precocious Italian merchants. As such, Elizabeth's court shared in the political economy of other renowned "black courts" — the fifteenth-century Burgundian court of Philip the Good that had so influenced her father, and the contemporary Hapsburg court of Philip II in Spain.[77] In both of these instances, care was taken to resist or refuse the colorful cloths of Italy, at the same time communicating allegiance to the wool industries of the Low Countries — industries that excelled in the production of fine black cloth, but not in polychrome fabrics.[78]

In conclusion, we might note how this interpretation enables a deeper reading of the fashion changes that occurred "circa 1600." For these changes involved much more than a shift in textures, shapes, and colors. As the intensively tailored farthingale and stomacher gave way, as a focus, to soft and richly hued silks,[79] they constituted a transformation of national mood. Valerie Cumming notes, for example, how the House of Stuart ended "the old xenophobia," its Scottish founder, always more engaged than the Tudors with the European continent, pursuing different manners, methods, and styles.[80] Clothing became, correspondingly, more cosmopolitan, its variety of cut and color ever more "indescribable."[81] Although failing to establish silk production in England, James paved the way for thinking that "a wealthy country at peace with its neighbors might use both native and foreign talent in the creation of a more civilized, pan-European state."[82] This was, in Cumming's words, a "partly developed cultural revolution."[83]

According to Richard Rapp, the English, among other northern powers, challenged Italian leadership in textiles by flooding Italy and Italy's foreign markets with cheaper imitations of its own polychrome wares.[84] Venetian senators, faced with the threat that English cloths posed to markets at home and abroad, referred to them contemptuously as gaudy and outlandish.[85] As they, the Venetians, retreated to their terra firma, they clothed themselves ever more cautiously in black, while Londoners had their colorful coming out. Italians also fought back with sumptuary laws, enacted ever more frequently after 1600 to interdict the fashions of Paris and London. Reciprocally, England, enjoying an ever more favorable balance of exchange based on textile exports, "had no formal clothing ordinances on the law books [after] 1604."[86] The year 1600, our metaphorical divide, anticipated the "London season" — the openended, ever differentiating, fashion system of capitalism.[87] Looking back to this moment, one suddenly appreciates why red became the defining color of Britain's imperial armies and, more recently, of London's tourist brochures.

Notes

1. Martin Holmes, *Elizabethan London* (New York: Praeger, 1969), p. 104.

2. Roy Strong, *Splendor at Court: Renaissance Spectacle and the Theater of Power* (Boston: Houghton Mifflin Company, 1973), pp. 22–23.

3. Roy Strong, *The Cult of Elizabeth; Elizabethan Portraiture and Pageantry* (Berkeley and Los Angeles: University of California Press, 1977), pp. 56–83.

4. Valerie Cumming, *Royal Dress, the Image and Reality 1580 to the Present Day* (London: B. T. Batsford, 1989), p. 17.

5. Grant McCracken, "Dress Colour at the Court of Elizabeth I: An Essay in Historical Anthropology," *Canadian Review of Sociology and Anthropology* 22 (1985): 515–33.

6. Frederique Lachaud also notes the narrowness of associating particular values or moral states with particular colors. See Lachaud, "Liveries of Robes in England, c. 1200–c. 1330," *English Historical Review* 111 (1996): 279–98.

7. Jane Schneider, "Peacocks and Penguins: The Political Economy of European Cloth and Colors," *American Ethnologist* 5 (1978): 413–38. In preparing the present essay, in particular its section on dyestuffs, I have borrowed from this article. See also my "Anthropology of Cloth," *Annual Review of Anthropology* 16 (1987): 409–48.

8. William F. Leggett, *Ancient and Medieval Dyes* (Brooklyn: Chemical Publishing, 1944), pp. 43–44.

9. C. Polakoff, *African Textiles and Dyeing Techniques* (London: Routledge and Kegan Paul, 1982). See also N. Stanfield, "Dyeing Methods in Western Nigeria," in *Adire Cloth in Nigeria*, ed. J. Barbour and D. Simmonds (Ibadan: University of Ibadan, Institute of African Studies, 1971), pp. 7–42.

10. Herbert C. Baker, *Plants and Civilization* (Belmont, Calif.: Wadsworth, 1965), pp. 160–64.

11. William H. Te Brake, "Air Pollution and Fuel Crises in Preindustrial London," *Technology and Culture* 16 (1975): 337–60.

12. John H. Munro, "The Medieval Scarlet and the Economics of Sartorial Splendor," in *Cloth and Clothing in Medieval Europe: Essays in Memory of Professor E. M. Carus-Wilson,* ed. N. B. Harte and K. G. Ponting (London: Heinemann, 1983), pp. 14–15, n. 6.

13. Ibid., p. 17.

14. Ibid., p. 63.

15. M. Johnson, "Technology, Competition, and African Crafts" in *The Imperial Impact: Studies in the Economic History of Africa and India,* ed. C. Dewey and A. G. Hopkins (London: Athlone, 1978), pp. 259–70. V. Lamb and A. Lamb, *The Lamb Collection of West African Narrow Strip Weaving,* ed. P. Fiske (Washington, D.C.: The Textile Museum, 1975). J. Picton and J. Mack, *African Textiles: Looms, Weaving, and Design* (London: British Museum Publications, 1979).

16. K. P. Kent, *Pueblo Indian Textiles: A Living Tradition* (Albuquerque: University of New Mexico Press, 1983), pp. 29–32.

17. G. D. Ramsay, "The Italian Mercantile Colony in London," in *Textile History and Economic History; Essays in Honour of Miss Julia de Lacy Mann,* ed. N. B. Harte and K. G. Ponting (Manchester: Manchester University Press, 1973).

18. Charles Singer, et al., eds., *The Mediterranean Civilizations and the Middle Ages,* vol. 2 of *A History of Technology* (Oxford: Clarendon Press, 1956), pp. 367–69.

19. Holmes, *Elizabethan London.*

20. See Lachaud, "Liveries of Robes," p. 279.

21. John Stow, *Survey of London* (1598; reprint, with an introduction by H. B. Wheatley, New York and London: Everyman's Library, 1956), pp. 78–80. See also Lachaud, "Liveries of Robes."

22. Stow, *Survey of London,* pp. 479–80.

23. Jennifer Harrison, "Lord Mayor's Day in the 1590s," *History Today* 42 (1992): 37–43. See also Lawrence Manley, ed., *London in the Age of Shakespeare: An Anthology* (University Park: Pennsylvania State University Press, 1986), p. 350. Henry Thew Stephenson, *Shakespeare's London* (New York: Henry Holt, 1905), p. 12.

24. Stow, *Survey of London,* p. 73.

25. Ramsay, "Italian Mercantile Economy." Stephenson, *Shakespeare's London,* p. 129.

26. Ronald M. Berger, *The Most Necessary Luxuries: The Mercer's Company of Coventry, 1550–1680* (University Park: Pennsylvania State University Press, 1993), pp. 22–23. F. J. Fisher, "The Development of London as a Centre of Conspicuous Consumption in the Sixteenth and Seventeenth Centuries," in *Essays in Economic History,* vol. 2, ed. E. M. Carus-Wilson (London: Edward Arnold, 1962), pp. 197–208. Grant McCracken, *Culture and Consumption; New Approaches to the Symbolic Character of Consumer Goods and Activities* (Bloomington: Indiana University Press, 1988), pp. 11–16. Lawrence Stone, *The Crisis of the Aristocracy, 1558–1641* (Oxford: Clarendon Press, 1965).

27. Holmes, *Elizabethan London,* pp. 24–25.

28. Jane Schneider, "Trousseau as Treasure: Some Contributions of Late Nineteenth-Century Change in Sicily," in *Beyond the Myths of Culture: Essays in Cultural Materialism,* ed. Eric B. Ross (New York: Academic Press, 1980), pp. 323–59.

29. Stone, *Crisis,* pp. 564–65. See also Jane Arnold, *Patterns of Fashion: The Cut and Construction of Clothes for Men and Women, c. 1560–1620* (London: Macmillan, 1985).

30. Stone, *Crisis,* p. 562.

31. Ibid., p. 564.

32. Ibid.

33. Arnold, *Patterns of Fashion.*

34. Quoted in Violet A. Wilson, *Society Women of Shakespeare's Time* (Port Washington, N.Y., and London: Kennikat Press, 1970), p. 7.

35. Arnold, *Patterns of Fashion,* pp. 3–8.

36. Valerie Cumming, *Exploring Costume History, 1500–1900* (London: Batsford Academic and Educational, 1981), pp. 19–30. Cumming, *Royal Dress.*

37. Stone, *Crisis,* p. 563.

38. Cumming, *Exploring Costume History;* Cumming, *Royal Dress.*

39. Stow, *Survey of London,* p. 481. See also Holmes, *Elizabethan London,* p. 4.

40. Manley, *London*, pp. 7–8 ff. G. D. Ramsay, *The City of London in International Politics at the Accession of Elizabeth Tudor* (Manchester: Manchester University Press / Rowman and Littlefield, 1975) and "Cloth Workers, Merchant Adventurers and Richard Hakluyt," *English Historical Review* 92: 504–22.

41. Sylvia Thrupp, "The Grocers of London: A Study in Distributive Trade" in *Studies in English Trade in the Fifteenth Century*, ed. Eileen Power and M. M. Postan (New York: Barnes and Noble, 1966), p. 270.

42. Ramsay, *City of London*, pp. 44–46; "Cloth Workers," p. 504.

43. Quoted in *Tudor Economic Documents, Being Select Documents Illustrating the Economic and Social History of Tudor England*, ed. R. H. Tawney and Eileen Power (London: Longman's Green, 1965), vol. 3, pp. 130–49. See also Ramsay, "Cloth Workers."

44. Marie Channing Linthicum, *Costume in the Drama of Shakespeare and His Contemporaries* (New York: Russell and Russell, 1963), p. 11.

45. Tawney and Power, *Tudor Documents*.

46. Linthicum, *Costume*, pp. 33–36.

47. William Harrison, *The Description of England*, ed. Georges Edelen (1587; reprint, Ithaca: Cornell University Press, 1961), p. 148. Published for the Folger Shakespeare Library.

48. Henry Crosse, *Vertue's Commonwealth*, ed. Alexander Grosart (1603; reprint, Manchester: C. E. Simms, 1878), pp. 74–75.

49. Quoted in Millia Davenport, *The Book of Costume* (New York: Crown Publishers, 1948), p. 190.

50. Leggett, *Ancient and Medieval Dyes*, pp. 76–77. John Addington Symonds, *The Age of Despots* (New York: G. P. Putnam's Sons, 1960), pp. 370–71. (Original text, *Renaissance in Italy*, vol. 1, 1887–88).

51. Quoted in John Southerden Burn, *The History of the French, Walloon, Dutch and other Foreign Protestant Refugees Settled in England from the Reign of Henry VIII to the Revocation of the Edict of Nantes* (London: Longman, Brown, Green and Longman, 1846), p. 252.

52. Harrison, *Description of England*, p. 148.

53. Ibid., p. 147. See also Joan Thirsk, "The Fantastical Folly of Fashion: The English Stocking Knitting Industry, 1500–1700," in *Textile History and Economic History; Essays in Honour of Miss Julia de Lacy Mann*, ed. N. B. Harte and K. G. Ponting (Manchester: Manchester University Press, 1973), pp. 50–74.

54. Quoted in Arnold, *Patterns of Fashion*, p. 35.

55. F. J. Fisher, "London's Export Trade in the Early Seventeenth Century," *Economic History Review*, 2nd series, 3 (1950): 151–61, esp. 157.

56. P. J. Bowden, "Wool Supply and the Woolen Industry," *Economic History Review*, 2nd series, 9 (1962): 44–58. D. C. Coleman, "An Innovation and Its Diffusion: the 'New Draperies,'" *Economic History Review*, 2nd series, 22 (1969): 417–29.

57. Charles Wilson, "Cloth Production and International Competition in the Seventeenth Century," *Economic History Review*, 2nd series, 13 (1960): 209–21, esp. 214–15.

58. Thirsk, "Fantastical Folly," pp. 58–59. See also E. A. Wells, *The British Hosiery and Knitwear Industry, Its History and Organization* (New York: Barnes and Noble, 1972).

59. Quoted in McCracken, "Dress Colour," p. 522.

60. Leggett, *Ancient and Medieval Dyes,* p. 22; Linthicum, *Costume,* p. 5.

61. Kenneth R. Andrews, *Elizabethan Privateering During the Spanish War, 1585–1603* (Cambridge: Cambridge University Press, 1964).

62. Ramsay, *City of London,* pp. 22–24, 44–50.

63. Ibid., pp. 9–10.

64. Ibid., pp. 33–80.

65. Coleman, "An Innovation," p. 426.

66. Helen Douglas-Irvine, *History of London* (New York: James Pott and Co., 1912), p. 186.

67. Ramsay, *City of London,* pp. 179–80.

68. Coleman, "An Innovation," p. 46. Esther Moir, "Benedict Webb Clothier," *Economic History Review,* 2nd series, 10 (1957): 256–65.

69. Astrid Friis, *Alderman Cockayne's Project and the Cloth Trade: The Commercial Policy of England in Its Main Aspects, 1603–1625* (London: Oxford University Press, 1927), p. 237. Charles Wilson, *England's Apprenticeship, 1603–1763* (London: Longman's Green, 1965), pp. 69–70.

70. See A. L. Beier, "Social Problems in Elizabethan London," *Journal of Interdisciplinary History* 9 (1978): 203–21, p. 214.

71. Quoted in Wilson, "Cloth Production," p. 215, n. 2.

72. Richard T. Rapp, "The Unmaking of the Mediterranean Trade Hegemony: International Trade Rivalry and the Commercial Revolution," *The Journal of Economic History* 35 (1975): 499–525, see esp. 517. Singer, *History of Technology,* pp. 692–95.

73. Quoted in Berger, *Necessary Luxuries,* p. 24.

74. Barry Supple, *Commercial Crisis and Change in England 1600–42: A Study in the Instability of a Mercantile Economy* (Cambridge: Cambridge University Press, 1959), pp. 103, 153–54. See also Berger, *Necessary Luxuries,* p. 149.

75. Quoted in Berger, *Necessary Luxuries,* p. 149.

76. Ramsay, "Italian Mercantile Economy," p. 47. See also Beier, "Social Problems," p. 210; Holmes, *Elizabethan London,* p. 90; D. W. Jones, "The 'Hallage' Receipts of the London Cloth Markets 1562–c. 1720," *Economic History Review,* 2nd series, 25 (1972): 567–87.

77. See Chandra Mukerji, *From Graven Images: Patterns of Modern Materialism* (New York: Columbia University Press, 1983), pp. 171–72.

78. Schneider, "Peacocks and Penguins," pp. 429–31.

79. Berger, *Necessary Luxuries,* pp. 21–22.

80. Cumming, *Royal Dress,* p. 18. For a similar characterization of the shift, see F. J. Fisher, "Commercial Trends and Policy in Sixteenth-Century England," in *Essays in Economic History,* 1:152–72. Writing in the 1950s, Fisher used the expressions "economic nationalism" and a "pattern of mercantilism" to characterize the second half of the sixteenth century, suggesting that the restrictions on foreign merchants that matured in this period, and the simultaneous support of manufacturing innovations at home, "may be said to have given a stimulus to [the] economic progress" evident after 1600, when "feelings against . . . expansion declined" and freer trade resumed (pp. 171–72).

81. Cumming, *Royal Dress,* p. 20.

82. Ibid., p. 21.

83. Ibid., p. 21.

84. Rapp, "Mediterranean Trade." See also Bowden, "Wool Supply," p. 54; Wilson, "Cloth Production."

85. Carlo Cipolla, "The Decline of Italy: The Case of a Fully Matured Economy," *Economic History Review,* 2nd series, 5 (1952): 178–88.

86. Herman Freudenberger, "Fashion, Sumptuary Laws and Business" in *Fashion Marketing: an Anthology of Viewpoints and Perspectives,* ed. Gordon Wills and David Midgley (London: George Allen and Unwin, 1973), p. 137.

87. See Douglas-Irvine, *History of London,* pp. 179–80.

7

"Rugges of London and the Diuell's Band"

Irish Mantles and Yellow Starch as Hybrid London Fashion

Ann Rosalind Jones and Peter Stallybrass

In sixteenth-century colonial tracts, the Irish mantle, a woolen cloak worn by both sexes and all classes of Irish people, was a particular target of colonial intervention.[1] Writers such as Edmund Spenser, Fynes Morrison, and Sir John Davies saw this garment as an affront to colonial rule. Earlier English officials in Ireland had agreed. In 1537, for instance, "An Act for the English Order, Habit and Language" had been published in Ireland, declaring that "no person or persons, the King's subjects within this land . . . shall use or wear any mantles, coat or hood made after the Irish fashion."[2]

But the ineffectiveness of this sort of edict is evident from later representations of the mantle. Examples include an anonymous Englishman's drawing of Irish kerns (rural foot soldiers) from about 1544, in which all six men wear cloaks, three with shaggy undersides and ragged edges;[3] Lucas de Heere's drawing, around 1575, which includes a "wild" Irishman wearing a mantle with the shaggy side turned outward around his neck;[4] and the woodcuts illustrating John Derricke's *The Image of Ireland with a Discoverie of Woodkarne*, written in 1576 and published in London in 1581. One striking woodcut of the chieftain "Macke Swine" at an outdoor banquet shows the chieftain's wife, two friars, and a harp-playing bard all wearing versions of the mantle (fig. 7.1).[5] Derricke's work is satirical and the prints in his book may exaggerate the commonality of the mantle. But the garment is also assigned a cross-class typicality in an engraving accompanying John Speed's map of Ireland in his *Theatre of the Empire of Great Britain* (1612, republished in 1616) (fig. 7.2).[6] Here men and women of high, middling, and low Irish status all wear mantles, although it should be noted that the barefoot wild Irishman wears a broadly, diagonally woven fabric different from the longer rough fleeces worn by the neighboring figures.

Curiously, however, this representation of the wild Irishman and his wife

7.1. Woodcut from John Derricke, *The Image of Ireland with a Discoverie of Woodkarne* (London, 1581). By permission of the Folger Shakespeare Library.

is based on engravings of a *Scottish* Highland chieftain and his wife printed in an early French costume book, the *Recueil de la diversité des habits* (Paris, 1562) (figs. 7.3 and 7.4).[7] "La Sauuage escossaise" wears an ankle-length mantle exactly like the one worn by Speed's "Wilde Irish Woman," and the knee-length herringbone cape worn by "Le Capitaine des Escossais sauuages" closely resembles that worn by Speed's "Wilde Irish Man." Speed, however, omits the Scottish captain's elaborate helmet, bow and arrows, sword and fringed (lamb-tailed?) shield, and, understandably, the anti-English attitude in the quatrain accompanying the French image:

> Vous pourrez voir entre les Escossoys
> Tel Capitaine faisant là leur[s] seiours,
> Qui souvent font nuysance aux Angloys,
> Peu de profit leur fait faire maintes tours.[8]

You may see among the Scots / Such a captain spending his time, / Who often do harm to the English, / Whose many trips there bring them little gain.

Within the engraving, the figures are labelled:

The Gentleman of Ireland — The Gentlewoman of Ireland

The Civill Irish Woman — The Civill Irish man

The Wilde Irish man — The Wilde Irish Woman

7.2. Engraving, detail from John Speed's map of Ireland, *The Theatre of the Empire of Great Britain* (London, 1612, reprint 1616). By permission of the Folger Shakespeare Library.

La sauuage d'Escosse.

Si tu mets l'œil dessus ceste figure
A celle fin que certain tu en soys,
C'est la sauuage au pays Escossoys,
De peaux vestue encontre la froidure.

7.3. "La Sauuage d'Escosse," from *Recueil de la diversité des habits* (Paris, 1562). Department of Printing and Graphic Arts, The Houghton Library, Harvard University.

Le capitaine Sauuage.

Vous pourrez voir entre les Escoſſoys,
Tel Capitaine faiſant là leur ſeiours,
Qui ſouuent font nuyſance aux Angloys,
Peu de profit leur fait faire maints tours.

7.4. "Le Capitaine des Escossoys sauuages," from *Recueil de la diversité des habits* (Paris, 1562). Department of Printing and Graphic Arts, The Houghton Library, Harvard University.

The English image of a quintessentially Irish mantle, then, actually derives from a hybrid importation of mixed sources. We want to trace here the ambivalent and conflicting attempts to define and impose a pure English essence against antithetically "impure" Irish customs, particularly customs of dress. Yet even as the English attempted to "civilize" the Irish at the margins of their kingdom, the migration of the mantle into the heart of the realm revealed that the fashionable Londoner of 1600 was as implicated in international trade, competing ideologies of nationality, and unstable mixtures of style as was the "uncivil" Irishman against whose supposed lack of an ordered culture one version of Englishness was constructed.

In Speed's commentary on the dress of his six Irish types clad in mantles, he elides differences that his illustration reveals. The "Gentleman of Ireland" wears a broad-brimmed hat in contrast to the "Wilde Irish man's" bare head and glib (long forelock); the "Gentleman" has ribbons on his shoes, the "Civill Irish man" has buckles, and the "Wilde Irish man" wears boots; the "Civill Irish Woman" covers her head with a linen coif, in contrast to the unbound hair of the "Wilde Irish Woman." But Speed writes that all Irish women, like the generalized category of "men," wear "shagge rugge mantles purfled [lined and bordered] with a deepe Fringe of diuers colours, both sexes accounting idlenesse their onely libertie, and ease their greatest riches."[9] The mantle becomes a sign of the "looseness" and "idlenesse" of the Irish in general, their incivility being marked by their refusal of civil fashions — that is, English fashions such as long robes and front-closing cloaks.

The incivility is embodied, as well, in the naming and materials of the Irish mantle. "Rug" is derived from the Scandinavian *rugga* (a coarse coverlet) and is etymologically and ideologically closely related to "rag." The "rug" as a garment was usually associated with poverty. In 1558, records of the church court in Chester declare that "xij peces of gray rugge" were given to the poor;[10] Richard Hakluyt describes a people "rude in conditions, apparelled in diuers coloured rugs;"[11] and Henry Peacham depicts the month of December as "clad in Irish rugge, or coorse freeze [coarse frieze]."[12] To wear "rug" was to be both ragged and rugged, the latter word originally meaning rough with hair, shaggy, or hirsute. In Jonson's *The Alchemist,* Face recalls Subtle's previous poverty by recalling how he went in rags and rug alike:

> . . . you went pinn'd vp, in the severall rags,
> Yo'had rak'd, and pick'd from dung-hills, before day,
> Your feet in mouldie slippers, for your kibes,
> A felt of rugg, and a thin thredden cloake,
> That scarce would couer your no-buttocks.[13]

Similarly, when the soldier in Henry Shirley's *Martyr'd Soldier* declares himself "Lord over these Larroones [robbers], Regent of these Rugs, Viceroy over these Vagabonds," the rug is a metonymy for villainy and vagrancy.[14]

A second term frequently associated with the Irish mantle was "shag." Speed writes of "shagge rugge mantles," and William Camden in his Latin history of Britain defines the outer garment that the Irish called a *brat* as "rugges or shagge mantles," "mantells or shagge Rugges."[15] "Shag" referred to rough hair or wool, matted or pressed rather than woven, or to a garment or rug of coarse, hairy material. Indeed, "rug" and "shag" were used interchangeably as well as simultaneously to define the Irish mantle, and both terms were extended to define the Irish themselves as "rugged" and "shaggy," the two terms being particularly used in reference to the hair of the Irish. "Shag-hayr'd" conflates the long-haired coiffure of the Irish troops with the common depiction of them wearing shag mantles over their heads. The "shag" is, thus, interchangeably mantle and hair. Hence Richard in Shakespeare's *Richard II* refers to light-armed Irish foot-soldiers as "rough rug-headed Kernes,"[16] an expression which, as Matthew Black and Michael Neill have observed, simultaneously conjures up shaggy hair and the rough head-covering mantle.[17] Paradoxically, the vagrancy of the Irish kern (a "vagrancy" intensified by colonizing forces) was located by the English in the imperviousness of kerns to the vagrancy of fashion. Indeed, Spenser claimed in his *View of the Present State of Ireland* that the mantle itself became the home of the outlaw, thus facilitating his nomadism even as it acted as a cover for his imagined iniquities: "banished from the townes and houses of honest men, and wandring in waste places, far from danger of law, [he] maketh his mantle his house, and under it covereth himselfe from the wrath of heaven, from the offence of earth, and from the sight of men."[18] Equally, the mantle was, in Spenser's account, the emblem of the geographical and sexual vagrancy of Irish women:

and surely for a bad huswife it is no lesse conuenient, for some of them that bee wandering woe men, called of them *Monashul* [the mantle] is halfe a wardrobe; for in Summer you shal find her arrayed commonly but in her smock and mantle to be more ready for her light services: in Winter, and in her travaile, it is her cloake and safeguard, and also a coverlet for her lewd exercise. And when she hath filled her vessell, under it she can hide both her burden, and her blame; yea, and when her bastard is borne, it serves insteed of swadling clouts.[19]

The Irish are here imagined as the extreme antithesis of the English.

Fynes Moryson, in his *Itinerary* (1617), claims that the Irish are unable to maintain proper social differentiations because their clothes are undifferentiated. In a passage that pinpoints why the English mistrusted the mantle—it covered over distinctions of class and sex—Moryson writes, "In the remote parts where the English Lawes and manners are unknown, the very cheefe of the Irish, as well men and women, goe naked in very Winter time, onely having their privy parts covered with a ragge of linen, and their bodies with a loose mantell."[20] Moryson, however, is not satisfied that the English demonstrate sober preciseness in dress. Echoing many other critics of the English mania for foreign fashion, he points out that his countrymen have entered with a vengeance into the carnival of international trade, through which the sheer proliferation of differentiating material forms undoes all categories. Borrowing from everybody, the English are nobody: "With singular inconstancy they have in this one age worne out all the fashions of France and all the Nations of Europe, and tired their owne inventions, which are no lesse busie in finding out new and ridiculous fashions, then in scraping up money for such idle expences."[21]

Paradoxically, one instance of this promiscuous sartorial acquisitiveness lay in the fact that English contempt for the mantle coexisted with practical acknowledgements of its usefulness—for the English. In her fine study of Irish apparel in early modern history and English fantasy, Margaret Jaster points out that "Sir Henry Wallop wrote Sir Robert Cecil on 29 July 1597 from Dublin that the English army could be better fitted with a cassock of Irish frieze, and a mantle for winter, both at little more than half the price of an English cassock; the suggestion was vehemently censured."[22] But in 1599, Thomas Lee (an English soldier-adventurer who had spent over a decade in Ireland, siding at times with Hugh O'Neill, Earl of Tyrone, against corrupt and violent English officials) recommended to Robert Cecil in a widely read pamphlet, *The Discoverye and Recoverye of Ireland,* that English soldiers wear clothes like those of the Irish, including Scottish-style caps made of water-resistant Irish frieze. Saving money on locally made shoes and headgear would mean that they could also afford good Irish mantles "for protection in all weathers and makeshift lodging at night."[23] In the same year, George Carew, Master of Ordnance in Ireland, drew up a list of supplies needed by English soldiers, including the recommendation that the queen authorize an allowance for each soldier "for an Irish mantle, which costeth but 5s," to "be his bed in the night, and a great comfort to him in sickness and in health; for the mantle, being never so wet, will presently, with a little shaking and wringing, be presently dry."[24] Thus the garment officially prohibited to the "wild" Irish was redefined as a necessity for the "civil" colonizing army.

But this rough military cloak was only one form that the Irish mantle took. It existed, as well, in expensive, even sumptuous versions, worn not only by the wealthy Irish and Anglo-Irish but also by the English within their own borders. Although Andrew Trollope in 1581 commented scornfully of the visit of the "Erle of Clancar and the Lord Morrys . . . to my Lord Deputye in Dublen" that "all their bravery, and the best robe, or garment, they wore, was a russet Irish mantle, worth about a crown a pece,"[25] elaborate Irish mantles had long been made in Ireland and trimmed with rich imported materials. Ada Longfield remarks in her study of Anglo-Irish trade in the sixteenth century that "specially fine wool for the fringes of the better quality mantles was imported from Spain and sometimes from England. We also sometimes hear of silk fringes. . . . There was really quite a variety among those in use in Ireland, as the better classes had theirs embroidered or ornamented with fringes of many-coloured silks and wools."[26] In Wenceslaus Hollar's engraving of the "Mulier Hibernica," she wears a rich, dark, velvety mantle trimmed with a thick, evenly shaggy neckpiece that looks soft and luxurious.[27] And in John Michael Wright's 1680 portrait of Sir Neil O'Neil, painted in Dublin, the chieftain wears a splendid blue antique mantle with a green lining and a gold fringe.[28]

The importation of Irish mantles, rugs, or friezes into England was mentioned as early as 1566 by the Jesuit William Good, whose remarks were incorporated into Camden's *Britannia*. The Irish, he wrote, "have many goodly flockes of sheepe, which they sheare twice a yeere, and make of their course wool rugges or shagge mantles, Caddowes also or coverlets, which are vented into foreaine countries."[29] Waterford rugs — that is, mantles woven of heavy, even shaggy wool — are recorded as Irish exports as early as 1504.[30] Richard Stanihurst tells a comic tale suggesting that such mantles were often worn in London in the late sixteenth century. A friend of his, he writes, "repaired to Paris garden clad in one of these Waterford rugs. The mastifs had no sooner espied him, but deeming he had beene a beare, would fain haue baited him. . . . wherevpon he solemnlie vowed neuer to see beare baiting in anie such weed [again]."[31] Ada Longfield points out the hybridity of mantles that were made in Ireland, sometimes of English textiles, then exported to England and worn by the English. The figures she offers for this early Irish-English trade are surprisingly high: "In three months of the year 1505–06, 96 mantles . . . were brought from Ireland in Irish vessels to Fowey, Penzance, St. Ives, and Padstow. . . . In 1504, 2,320 mantles (value £386 13s. 4d.) were sent to Bristol."[32]

By the early 1600s, English versions of the Irish mantle were being made of velvet and richly colored satin. Janet Arnold describes the rich "lap mantles" often given as gifts in London and analyzes the elaborate design and workmanship of a crimson mantle lined with silk shag and embroidered with gold and silver lace, worn by the Londoner Jane Lambarde in a portrait painted in the early 1620s; she traces the high-fashion mantle or *bernia* (originally the Hibernian, that is, Irish wool of which soldiers' cloaks were made) through its European migrations and into English aristocratic portraits and masques up to the 1640s.[33] In royal portraits and fantastic costumes, the shagged Irish mantle was hybridized with classical togas and even with images of feathered, reed-woven, and animal-skin capes and cloaks from Africa and the New World.

The power of Elizabeth I herself was also affirmed by the representation of a satin mantle that makes up part of her costume in the Rainbow portrait. Janet Arnold first suggested that the cloak might be an Irish mantle; her study of the inventories of Elizabeth's wardrobe revealed several cloaks so described, including one, a gift in 1589 from the deputy to Ireland Sir John Perrott, that was still listed in 1600: "Item one Irishe Mantle of a Murrey [mulberry-colored] networke flourished with Venice golde silver and silver plate like waves," further trimmed with a luxurious version of the characteristic Irish "deep frenge of venice golde and silver aboute the Coller and downe before."[34] Roy Strong, in an interpretation that otherwise stresses the idealism by which the iconography of the painting elevates the queen, followed Frances Yates in suggesting that the heavy orange cloak worn over Elizabeth's left shoulder, embroidered with eyes and ears, might carry a sartorial meaning similar to the skirt worn by the female figure in Ripa's icon of "La ragione di stato," symbolizing "those who watched and listened to purvey their intelligence to her" and, thereby, implying the political power her spies assured her.[35]

In a brilliant further reading of the garment, Michael Neill points out that the painting attributes a feat of political reversal to the queen: by putting on the mantle that had frustrated English attempts to survey and catalogue the Irish, Elizabeth assimilates the symbol of Irish inscrutability to her own status as the ruler who sees and hears everything throughout her empire. According to Neill, the caption painted in above her right hand, "Non sine sole iris," means not only "No rainbow without sunshine" but also "No Ireland without its radiant queen" since "Iris" was an ancient name for Ireland (used, for example, by William Camden, citing Diodorus Siculis).[36] Here, through a sleight of public-image formation and the skill of the embroiderer's and painter's hands, the Irish mantle becomes an emblem of English sovereignty over the entire nation. The gender-blurring, quintessentially Irish garment could be appropriated into the triumphant costume of a quintessentially British female ruler.

The Irish mantle, then, was a garment that shifted from Ireland to England, from the kern's "house" to aristocratic display and allegory, mixing categories and continents, complicating clear boundaries. Chameleon-like, it could be appropriated by rival groups, from military enemies to combatants in political, ideological, and cultural realms. Ironically, the aristocratic appropriation of the Irish mantle in England coexisted with its staging for London theater audiences as a mark of the poverty of English servants and the deceptions of English thieves. One of several thieves in Fletcher's *The Night-Walker* (1661) confesses to robbery and disguise both: "We have devided the Sextons houshould stuffe amongst us, one has the rugge, and hee's turn'd Irish."[37] The thief, clothed in the rug he has stolen, is "translated" from English to Irish.

The criminal associations of the rug are reaffirmed in the legend of Mary Frith, the cross-dressing woman of London nicknamed Moll Cutpurse. In Middleton and Dekker's play, *The Roaring Girl* (1610), Moll says she is going to order from a tailor a "shag ruff," interpreted by the woodcut in the 1611 quarto of the play as a thick, short cape in the Irish style.[38] Toward the end of the 1662 text purporting to be Moll's autobiography, *The Life and Death of Mrs. Mary Frith,* she confesses that her criminal career has ended in poverty and illness. Suffering from a large belly caused by dropsy, she has to stop wearing her snug man's doublet and cover herself with a loose blanket instead — a garment that she says lacks any regional character: "I was forced to leave off that upper part of my Garment, and do penance again in a Blanket; a Habit distant from the Irish Rug, and the Scotch Pla[i]d, their National Vests for Women of Quality, whom my Scoffing Neighbours said I did very much resemble."[39] Paradoxically, while her neighbors scoff at her, presumably for the poverty of her blanket, she herself emphasizes her garment as a form of humility, in contrast to the Irish and Scottish "Vests" worn by "Women of Quality." She manages to assert her own "penance" while simultaneously mocking her mockers, who do not recognize that this "foreign" vest can also be a badge of status.

Moll's mockery of those who deride the mantle can be read as a belated echo of the garment's contested status in the late sixteenth century. As we have argued, it could be either aristocratic finery or the emblem of incivility. But a third possible reading of the mantle emerged in antithesis to the extravagances of London fashion — the Irish mantle being made to figure ancient "English" virtues. In Holinshed's 1577 *Chronicles,* he celebrates the early queen Boadicea's leadership of English tribes against the invading Romans: "Her mighty tall personage, comely shape, severe countenance and sharp voice, her brave and gorgeous apparel, caused the people to have her in great reverence. She wore a chain of gold . . . and was clad in a loose kirtle of sundry colors; and thereupon she had a thick Irish mantle."[40] Boadicea's power and virtue are given material affirmation in the Irish mantle, contrasting in its simple form to her "brave and gorgeous" gold chain and multicolored kirtle.

Boadicea seems to stand in stark opposition to the colonial policy that was increasingly being advocated by men like Sir John Davies. Davies saw the mantle as the indelible mark of Irish incivility. Only if the Irish could "conform themselues to the maner of England in al their behauiour and outward formes," he argued, would English rule succeed. It was thus crucial that the Irish should "conuert their mantles into Cloaks."[41] Yet, perhaps surprisingly, Boadicea's mantle came to have its supporters among English writers on Ireland precisely because it was "unEnglish." Barnabe Rich, for instance, although he violently attacked the Irish for their customs, their religion and their language in his colonizing tracts, praised the Irish mantle in *The Irish Hubbub, or the English Hue and Cry* (London, 1619). Presenting the Irish mantle as form of virtuous resistance to the excesses of London fashion, he even assumes it for himself as author: "For want of a better cloake, whereby to shelter these endeauors of my untutored pen, I have borrowed an Irish mantle. I might have clad them in a more glorious garment, I confesse that would have made them more acceptable to the world, which graceth men now adayes more for their outward shew, then for their inward vertue; but this habit wherein I have now suted them, carrieth no shew of pride, and is fittest for them to trauell in."[42] Rich goes on to denounce the ways that London fashions have been carried to Ireland. By contrast, the mantle, so often seen by English writers as a form of Irish subterfuge, assumes positive moral qualities against which decadent English extravagance can be critically measured.

In *The Irish Hubbub,* Rich paradoxically turns to the Irish mantle to figure early English purity because his new concern is to revile London fashion for turning the body of the Irishman as well as the Englishman into the body of a traitor. And here Rich makes a second extraordinary reversal of earlier accounts of Irish fashion. In the sixteenth century, while the mantle had been depicted as the Irish habitat *par excellence,* it was frequently associated with a second sartorial marker: linen dyed yellow. The yellow coloring came from saffron, derived from the dried stigmas at the top of the pistils of crocus flowers. In the sixteenth century, the use of saffron was associated above all with the Irish. Saffron had in fact been imported to Ireland, possibly as early as the tenth century, either from Spain or the Middle East. The dyestuff was expensive because it took so long to pick the thousands of stamens necessary to produce it, but the Irish were dyeing linen with saffron in considerable quantities by the early sixteenth century.[43] Saffron-dyed linen was, indeed, targeted as a form of excessive luxury in the early Tudor attempts to control the country. In 1536, Henry VIII, in an effort to suppress what was seen as Anglo-Irish as well as native extravagance, forbade his subjects in Galway to wear saffron in their "shirts, smocks or any other garments," and he extended the prohibition to the rest of the country the next year.[44]

Yet saffron was also seen as a sign of poverty, of the uncouth roughness of people who owned too few clothes and harbored vermin as a result. Edmund Spenser thought the Irish had adopted the dye from Spain because it was used there "for avoyding that evill which commeth of much sweating, and long wearing of linnen."[45] Moryson, reporting on his Irish travels, was more specific: because the "wild Irish," a very "lowsie people," wore their shirts constantly, never removing them until they fell apart, their shirts were "coloured with saffron to avoid lowsieness, incident to the wearing of foule linnen."[46] Several English commentators also remarked on the fact that the Irish used urine to intensify the dye. William Camden in his history of Britain quotes William Good, a priest and schoolmaster of Limerick, on the technique: "Their way is not to boil the thing long, but to let it soak for some days in urine that the colour may be deeper and more durable." Camden himself remarks that when Shane O'Neill visited Queen Elizabeth, his bodyguards wore shirts that had been dyed with saffron or "infected with human urine."[47] As a culturally freighted color, saffron-yellow linked luxury and contaminating waste; at the same time, it was seen as originating with England's traditional enemies, Spain and France.[48]

But by the early seventeenth century, both at court and in the city of London, saffron was becoming a popular dye with which to starch bands, cuffs, and ruffs. No fashion troubled Barnabe Rich more than the use of yellow starch. Indeed, he represents this new style as having already unmanned London: "Our mindes are effeminated, our martiall exercises and disciplines of warre are turned into womanish pleasures and delights: our Gallants thinke it better to spend their lands and liuings in a whores lap, then their liues in a martiall field for the honour of their Countrey. Wee haue conuerted the coller of steele to a yellow-starched band."[49] Like tobacco, Rich writes, yellow starch "was first brought into England by some man of little vertue." But although a foreign import, the dye is now the mark of English corruption. And it is the English who are in turn, he claims, corrupting Ireland. Base women, "proud and new upstart changelings," "haue filled *Ireland* so full of new fashions, by their strange alterations in their Ruffes, in their Cuffs, in their huffes, in their puffes, in their muffes, and in many other vanities, that *Ireland* was neuer acquainted withall, till these women brought them vp."[50] In other words, rebellion is located by Rich not in the wild Irish but in London fashions. But if yellow starch is now infecting Ireland, it has first transformed London itself into the seat of treason.

The connection between treason and yellow starch had been literalized in the social imaginary through a recent crisis: the execution of Anne Turner, found guilty of the poisoning of Sir Thomas Overbury and hanged in 1615 in a collar and cuffs dyed with yellow starch.[51] In fact, this image is probably inaccurate. No one who actually attended Anne Turner's execution commented on her yellow starch at the time. But within three years it was difficult to find a social critic who had not commented upon it. Even more extraordinary is the fact that the list of crimes of which she was accused was condensed into the accusation that it was she who had introduced Londoners and the Court to yellow starch. While she was accused at her trial by Edward Coke, the Lord Chief Justice, of being "a whore, a bawd, a sorcerer, a witch, a papist, a felon, and a murderer," she was accused, after her death, by James Howell, by Simonds d'Ewes, by Richard Niccols, by the writer of the pamphlet *Hic Mulier*, and by Barnabe Rich of having corrupted English virtue through fashion. Sir Simonds d'Ewes, for instance, wrote: "Mrs. Turner had first brought up that vain and foolish use of yellow starch, coming herself to her trial in a yellow band and cuffs; and therefore, when she was afterwards executed at Tyburn, the hangman had his band and cuffs of the same colour, which made many after that day of either sex to forbear the use of that coloured starch, till it at last grew generally to be detested and disused."[52] D'Ewes was wrong on several points—not least in that the publicity attending Anne Turner's trial seems to have *increased* the use of yellow starch. In 1617, the painter Paul van Somer depicted Queen Anne herself in a yellow ruff and cuffs, while Rubens depicted the Duchess of Buckingham in the early 1620s in yellow-dyed lace and cuffs.[53]

In fact, in the National Portrait Gallery, directly across from the portrait of Frances Howard in yellow starch, there is a portrait of George Villiers with collar and cuffs dyed yellow.[54] Buckingham had been expressly groomed as a rival to Somerset by the Protestant faction at court, led by the Earl of Pembroke and the archbishop of Canterbury, George Abbot. The rise of George Villiers, the son of a Leicestershire gentleman, was meteoric. On 23 April 1615 (St. George's Day), he was knighted; on 4 January 1616, he was made Master of the Horse; in April 1616, he was appointed a Knight of the Garter; and in July he was given the lands of Lord Grey of Wilton, who had been found guilty of treason, and created Viscount Villiers. In early 1617, he was made Earl (later Duke) of Buckingham and appointed to the Privy Council.[55] The portrait of him in the National Portrait Gallery shows a very youthful Villiers in the full robes of a Knight of the Garter. The portrait was probably painted in 1616 to commemorate his new position. It was painted, in other words, in the same year as the conviction of Somerset and, retrospectively, can be seen as marking the displacement of the Scottish favorite, assimilated to the pro-Catholic, pro-Spanish Howards, by an English favorite, promoted by the anti-Catholic, anti-Spanish faction. Yet Buckingham is depicted, like Frances

Howard, wearing yellow starch; and he is depicted a year after the supposed "death" of the fashion with the execution of Anne Turner. The fashion was, thus, deeply embedded in the culture of the court.

How, then, are we to read Rich's violent attacks upon yellow starch as a vanity that adulterates the wearer's body, masculinizing women and effeminating men, transforming Protestant into papist, patriot into traitor, and the human into the monstrous or the demonic? Rich's focus upon yellow starch is not a displacement of the charges of witchcraft and poisoning leveled against Anne Turner. Fashion, like witchcraft, is imagined as an illicit form of *making*. As Karen Newman remarks, "In the notorious Lancashire trials of 1612, clay pictures and images were frequently adduced as evidence of *maleficium*. Witchcraft involved injury, doing harm; but my emphasis here is on the etymological force of the word, its root in the verb *facio*, to make, construct, fashion, frame, build, erect, produce, compose. The fashioning of such images at once suggests the power and danger of mimesis."[56] The accusation that Anne Turner had invented yellow starch was an accusation of evil making, *maleficium*, a making which introduced *faction* (like *fashion* derived from *facio*) into the body politic, dismembering it through the act of molding and remaking it.[57] The "Vanity" of London, then, is seen by Rich not as some marginal vice but as the process by which the kingdom is remodeled in a demonic image. It is a form of magic in which the "fashioned" person is permeated by the materials and dyes which he or she touches.

Moreover, Anne Turner's "vaine desires" were, according to Richard Niccols, the author of a poem on the trial, fed from "ouer-seas."[58] The implication that foreign fashions dismember the body politic was a commonplace. Thomas Dekker, for instance, claimed that "an English-mans suite is like a traitors bodie that hath beene hanged, drawne, and quartered, and is set up in seuerall places."[59] To fashion oneself through alien clothes was to factionalize both one's own body and the state. The materiality of the foreign cloth and dye effected a material dislocation, fracturing the wearer's body into conflicting kingdoms.

Thus yellow starch condensed into the detail of a fashion accessory a whole series of histories of the "foreign." In "inventing" yellow starch, Anne Turner was seen as instating the whore of Babylon at the heart of London and of a court which, according to its critics, was already suspiciously unEnglish, governed by a Scottish monarch who pursued a policy of peace with Spain and who patronized both Scottish favorites and the Howards, a family widely believed to be Catholic as well as pro-Spanish.

It was at the moment of greatest triumph for the Howard faction — the marriage of Frances Howard to the King's Scottish favorite Somerset in

1613 — that Ben Jonson's *Irish Masque* was performed at court. David Lindley and Margaret Jaster have written powerfully about the masque, whose central image is the displacement of Irish mantles by English clothes.[60] The masque thus acts out the demand of Sir John Davies that the Irish "convert their mantles into cloaks, [and] conform themselves to the manner of England in all their behaviour and outward form."[61] But the most striking aspect of the performance at court is that it was staged before an audience in which the opposite movement was, according to its critics, taking place. For the court, led by the Howard faction, was shedding the English cloak and replacing it with an Irish mantle.

Throughout the 1610s and the 1620s, mantles in the Irish style and yellow starch alike became high fashion in London. In a painting completed close to the date of the Howard-Somerset wedding, William Larkin's full-length portrait of Richard Sackville, third earl of Dorset, the earl wears a sumptuous mantle lined with silk shag, described in a 1617 inventory as "a Cloake of uncutt velvett blacke . . . above the borders powdred [sprinkled] with slipps [floral motifs] of sattin embroad[ered] with gold and lyned with shagg of black silver and gold"[62] (fig. 7.5). Two noblewomen allied with the Howard clan were also painted wearing fashionable mantles, not shagged like Suffolk's but worn in Irish fashion over one shoulder. A heavily embroidered velvet mantle is tied over the shoulder of Frances Howard's cousin, the duchess of Richmond (also named Frances Howard), who sat for Marcus Gheeraerts the Younger in 1611.[63] And a formal satin mantle is knotted at the shoulder of Lady Isabella Rich, painted by Larkin about 1615 (fig. 7.6). Another portrait in this group, also painted by Larkin about 1615, is of Dorothy St. John, Lady Cary, who wears a yellow-starched collar and cuffs.[64] By attacking the Irish mantle at the celebration of the Howard-Somerset wedding, Jonson was, deliberately or not, attacking the new court fashion; he was also potentially attacking both the monarch and his favorite, Somerset. Like the Irish mocked in the masque, James and Robert Carr spoke in what English critics considered barbaric accents.

In fact, there was no simple way to distinguish the Irish from the Scots who now ruled England. William Harrison argued that the Scots, like the Irish, were descended from the Scythians and that they had "passed by sea from Ireland." And Harrison's description of the Scots as "barefooted and clad in mantles over their saffron shirts after the Irish manner" corresponds exactly to sixteenth-century images of Irish kerns.[65] As we saw, the pictorial conflation of Scotland and Ireland is at its most acute in the two "wild Irish" at the bottom of the illustration from Speed's map of Ireland (see fig. 7.2), figures based upon the Scottish highlanders in a French costume book of 1562. For all

7.5. Portrait of Richard Sackville, third earl of Dorset, by William Larkin (1613). Ranger's House, Blackheath, London. © English Heritage Photo Library.

7.6. Portrait of Lady Isabella Rich, by William Larkin (ca. 1615). Ranger's House, Blackheath, London. © English Heritage Photo Library.

Jonson's attempts to construct a purified English civility in the wedding masque, it was Irish mantles and yellow starch, the hybridity of London fashions, that fashioned the English court — a court composed of Scots as well as Englishmen, Catholics as well as Protestants, a court fashioned quite literally by London's international trade in the silks, satins, velvets, gold thread, cochineal, and indigo of the high-fashion Irish mantle and in the saffron, starch, linen, and lace of ruffs and cuffs.

Notes

1. We discuss the colonizing tracts in detail in an earlier study of English texts about the Irish mantle, "Dismantling Irena: The Sexualizing of Ireland in Early Modern England," in *Nationalities and Sexualities,* ed. Andrew Parker, Mary Russo, Doris Sommer, and Patricia Yaeger (New York: Routledge, 1992).

2. "An Act for the English Order, Habit and Language," in *Irish History from Contemporary Sources (1509–1610),* ed. Constantia Maxwell (London: Allen and Unwin, 1923), p. 113.

3. "Irish kerns," anonymous drawing, ca. 1540–1547 (Ashmolean Museum), reproduced in Mairead Dunlevy, *Dress in Ireland* (New York: Holmes and Meier, 1989), p. 53.

4. Lukas de Heere, "Noblewoman, townswoman and 'Wild Irish,'" reproduced in Dunlevy, p. 52.

5. John Derricke, *The Image of Ireland with a Discoverie of Woodkarne* (London, 1581).

6. John Speed, *The Theatre of the Empire of Great Britain* (1612, 1616). Reproduced in Liz Curtis, *Nothing But the Same Old Story: The Roots of Anti-Irish Racism* (London: Information on Ireland, 1984), pp. 15–17, and in Dunlevy, with commentary, pp. 79–80.

7. H. F. McClintock identifies the French/Scottish source for Speed's print in *Old Irish and Highland Dress* (Dundalk: Dundalgan Press, 1943), p. 122.

8. *Diversi Nostrae Aetatis Habitus / Recueil de la diversité des habits de present en usage tant es pays d'Europe, Asie, Afrique et Isles sauuages, le tout fait apres le naturel* (Paris: Richard Breton, 1562), pp. 124b, 125.

9. Speed, *Theatre,* Book 4, p. 138.

10. *Lancashire and Cheshire Wills and Inventories from the Ecclesiastical Court, Chester, 1525–1807,* Chetham Society (1857–1897), 2:114.

11. Richard Hakluyt, *Diuers Voyages* (London, 1599), bk. 2, chapt. 2, p. 87.

12. Henry Peacham, *The Gentlemans Exercise* (London: John Brown, 1612; reprint 1634), bk. 2, p. 126.

13. Ben Jonson, *The Alchemist* (acted 1610, 1616 text) in *Ben Jonson,* ed. C. H. Herford, Percy and Evelyn Simpson (Oxford: Clarendon Press, 1954), vol. 5 (1937, rpt. 1965), I. 1. 33–37. In *The Divell is an Asse* (acted 1616, printed 1631), Ambler, the Gentleman Usher of Lady Taile-bush, has his clothes stolen and walks home "[i]n a

rug, . . . barefoote," a "kind of Irish penance!" according to the character Merecraft (in *Ben Jonson,* vol. 6 [1938, rpt. 1966], 5.1.47–48).

14. Henry Shirley, *The Martyr'd Soldier* (London, 1638), 2.3.

15. William Camden, *Britannia,* trans. as *Britain, or a Chorographical Description of the Most Flourishing Kingdomes, England, Scotland, and Ireland* by Philemon Holland (London, 1610), "Ireland," pp. 63, 148.

16. William Shakespeare, *Richard II,* 2.1.156; TLN 803. Quotations from Shakespeare, including act-scene-line numbers, are from *The Riverside Shakespeare,* ed. G. Blakemore Evans (Boston: Houghton Mifflin, 1974); Through Line Numbers (TLN) refer to *The Norton Facsimile: The First Folio of Shakespeare,* ed. Charlton Hinman (New York: Norton, 1968). See also *Macbeth* 4.2.82; TLN 1807, where the Folio's "thou shagge-ear'd Villaine" is emended by most editors to "thou shag-hair'd villain" (*Macbeth,* ed. Horace Howard Furness, New Variorum edition [Philadelphia: J. B. Lippincott, 1903], p. 225).

17. See *The Life and Death of King Richard the Second,* ed. Matthew Black, New Variorum edition (Philadelphia: J. B. Lippincott, 1955), p. 115 n, and Michael Neill, "Broken English and Broken Irish: Nation, Language, and the Optic of Power in Shakespeare's Histories," *Shakespeare Quarterly* 45: 1 (1994), 24–25 and 25 n.

18. Edmund Spenser, *A View of the State of Ireland,* ed. Andrew Hadfield and Willy Maley (Oxford: Blackwell, 1997), p. 57.

19. Spenser, *A View,* p. 58.

20. Fynes Moryson, *An Itinerary of His Travels* (London, 1617; reprint Glasgow: James MacLehose, 1902), vol. 2, p. 237.

21. Moryson, *Itinerary,* vol. 4, p. 231.

22. Margaret Rose Jaster, "'Out of all Frame and Fashion': The Difference in Gaelic Garb," an unpublished article derived from her "'Fashioninge the Minde and Condicions': The Uses and Abuses of Apparel in Early Modern England," Ph.D. diss., University of Maryland, College Park, 1994, p. 157 n.

23. Paraphrased by Hiram Morgan, "Tom Lee: The Posing Peacemaker," in *Representing Ireland: Literature and the Origins of Conflict, 1534–1660,* ed. Brendan Bradshaw, Andrew Hadfield, and Willy Maley (Cambridge: Cambridge University Press, 1993), p. 155.

24. "Irish Clothes Recommended for the Soldiers" (1599), in Maxwell, *Irish History,* p. 215.

25. Cited in Jaster, "'Out of all Frame and Fashion,'" p. 44.

26. Ada Kathleen Longfield, *Anglo-Irish Trade in the Sixteenth Century* (London: Routledge, 1929) p. 85.

27. Wenceslaus Hollar, *Theatrum Mulierum* (London, 1643/9), "Mulier Hibernica," n.p.

28. John Michael Wright, 1680 portrait of Sir Neil O'Neil (1680), Tate Gallery, London.

29. Camden, *Britannia,* bk. 2, p. 63.

30. Longfield, *Anglo-Irish Trade,* p. 84.

31. Richard Stanihurst, *Description of Ireland,* in Raphael Holinshed, *Chronicles of England, Scotland, and Ireland* (London: Richard Taylor, 1808), vol. 4 (*Ireland*), p. 29.

32. Longfield, *Anglo-Irish Trade,* p. 84.

33. Janet Arnold, "Jane Lambarde's Mantle," *Costume* 14 (1980): 56–72.

34. Arnold, "Jane Lambard's Mantle," p. 63; see also Arnold's *Queen Elizabeth's Wardrobe Unlock'd* (London: Maney, 1988), p. 81.

35. Roy Strong, *The Cult of Elizabeth* (London: Thames and Hudson, 1977), p. 52.

36. Neill, "Broken English and Broken Irish: Nation, Language, and the Optic of Power in Shakespeare's Histories," pp. 29–31.

37. John Fletcher, *The Night Walker,* ed. Cyrus Hoy, in *The Dramatic Works in the Beaumont and Fletcher Canon,* gen. ed. Fredson Bowers, 10 vols. (Cambridge: Cambridge University Press, 1989), 7:513–637. See 5.1.36–38.

38. Thomas Middleton and Thomas Dekker, *The Roaring Girl,* ed. Andor Gomme (London: New Mermaid edition, 1968; reprint 1976), for Moll's lines about the "shag ruff" see 2.1.184. For a detailed study of different qualities of "shag" in Irish mantles worn by Englishwomen, see Arnold, "Jane Lambarde's Mantle," pp. 58, 61–3.

39. *The Life and Death of Mrs. Mary Frith,* ed. Randall Nakayama (New York: Garland, 1993), p. 277.

40. Holinshed, *Chronicles,* vol. 1, pp. 42–43. We thank Jodi Michalachki for alerting us to this passage.

41. Sir John Davies, *A Discovery of the True Causes why Ireland was never Entirely Subdued* (London, 1612), p. 271.

42. Barnabe Rich, *The Irish Hubbub, or the English Hue and Crie* (London, 1618), prefatory letter to Sir Oliver St. John, A2.

43. Dunlevy, *Dress in Ireland,* p. 54; Longfield, *Anglo-Irish Trade,* p. 180.

44. Dunlevy, *Dress in Ireland,* p. 54.

45. Spenser, *A View,* p. 65.

46. Moryson, *An Itinerary,* 2:236.

47. McClintock, *Old Irish . . . Dress,* p. 53.

48. William Camden claimed that the fashion for yellow starch came from France and had been invented to set off sallow faces to advantage. See Joseph Allen Matter, *My Lords and Lady of Essex: Their State Trials* (Chicago: Henry Regnery, 1969), p. 160.

49. Rich, *Hubbub,* p. 8. Rich had denounced yellow starch even before the trial of Anne Turner. In *The Honestie of this Age* (London, 1614), he had written: "Amongst all the rest of these ill becomming follies, that are now newly taken vppe, (me thinkes) these yellow starcht bandes should bee euer best suited, with a yellow *Coate*" (p. 35).

50. Rich, *Hubbub,* p. 49.

51. For recent studies of the Overbury scandal, see David Lindley, *The Trials of Frances Howard: Fact and Fiction at the Court of King James* (London: Routledge, 1993); David Underdown, "Yellow Ruffs and Poisoned Possets: Placing Women in Early Stuart Political Debate," unpublished paper for the third conference, "Attending to Women," University of Maryland, 1994; Anne Somerset, *Unnatural Murder: Poison at the Court of James I* (London: Weidenfeld and Nicolson, 1997). We analyze the role of yellow starch in the scandal at length in our forthcoming book, *Renaissance Clothing and the Materials of Memory* (Cambridge: Cambridge University Press), chpt. 3.

52. *The Autobiography and Correspondence of Sir Simonds D'Ewes,* ed. James Orchard Halliwell (London: Richard Bentley, 1845), vol. 1, p. 79.

53. Paul van Somer, "Portrait of Queen Anne of Denmark" (1617), reproduced in Graham Reynolds, "Elizabethan and Jacobean," *Costume of the Western World: Fashions*

of the Renaissance, ed. James Laver (New York: Harper and Brothers, 1951), p. 146; see the analysis of the "masculine" style of this portrait by Stephen Orgel in *Impersonations: The Performance of Gender in Shakespeare's England* (Cambridge: Cambridge University Press, 1996), pp. 83–105. Peter Paul Rubens' "Catherine Manners, Duchess of Buckingham" is in the Dulwich Picture Gallery, London.

54. Attributed to William Larkin, "George Villiers, 1st Duke of Buckingham (1592–1628)," ca. 1616.

55. See Roger Lockyer, *Buckingham: The Life and Political Career of George Villiers, First Duke of Buckingham 1592–1628* (London: Longman, 1981), pp. 16–29.

56. Karen Newman, *Fashioning Femininity and English Renaissance Drama* (Chicago: University of Chicago Press, 1991), pp. 65–66.

57. We are indebted to conversations with John Guillory on the relation between fashion, faction, and fetishism.

58. Richard Niccols, *Sir Thomas Overburies Vision* (London: The Hunterian Club, 1873), p. 31. Compare Barnabe Rich, *Irish Hubbub,* where the yellow of the starch is figured as the singeing of the collars by hellfire. How, Rich inquires, can men "walke the streets with one of these base, odious, vgly, beastly bands, this new diuellish inuented fashion, looking as though they had scaped from the Diuell in hell, and there had scorched his band . . . ?" (pp. 40–41).

59. Quoted in Newman, *Fashioning Femininity,* p. 125.

60. David Lindley, "Embarrassing Ben: The Masques for Frances Howard," *English Literary Renaissance* 16 (Spring 1986): 343–59 and *The Trials of Frances Howard* (New York: Routledge, 1993), chpt. 4; Margaret Jaster, "Out of All Frame and Fashion," pp. 64–69.

61. Davies, *Discovery of the True Causes,* p. 268.

62. Inventory of 1617, quoted in Roy Strong, *Artists of the Tudor Court: The Portrait Miniature Rediscovered* (London: Victoria and Albert Museum catalogue, 1983), pp. 166–67.

63. Marcus Gheeraerts the Younger, Portrait of Frances Howard, Duchess of Richmond, 1611, reproduced in Roy Strong, *The English Icon,* p. 293. Other Gheeraerts portraits depicting Irish-style mantles include Mary Herbert, Countess of Pembroke (1615, Strong, p. 301) and Frances Knyvett, Countess of Rutland (1615, Strong, p. 302).

64. Lady Cary's portrait is also at the Ranger's House, London.

65. William Harrison, *A Historicall Description of the Iland of Britaine,* ed. Georges Edelen (Ithaca: Cornell University Press, 1968), p. 198.

8

Women, Foreigners, and the Regulation of Urban Space in *Westward Ho*

Jean E. Howard

By many accounts displays of xenophobic feeling were not uncommon in early modern London. In the sixteenth century urban riots often involved expressions of anti-immigrant sentiment, beginning with the infamous Ill May Day riots of 1517, but continuing as late as the London apprentice disturbances of the 1590s.[1] Some of this anger was directed against foreign workers, especially the French and Flemish refugees who in the latter half of the century came to London fleeing religious persecution and bringing craft skills which put them in competition with domestic workers. There was also anxiety, not only about economic competition by foreigners, but also about the insinuation of foreign ways and foreign wares into England's cultural economy. Recall, for example, Roger Ascham's castigation in *The Scholemaster,* published in 1570, of the Italianate Englishman.

If some yet do not well understand what is an Englishman Italianated, I will plainly tell him: "He that by living and travelling in Italy, bringeth home into England out of Italy, the religion, the learning, the policy, the experiences, the manners of Italy." That is to say, for religion, papistry, or worse; for learning, less commonly than they carried out with them; for policy, a factious heart, a discoursing head, a mind to meddle in all men's matters; for experience, plenty of new mischiefs never known in England before; for manners, variety of vanities, and change of filthy living.

These be the enchantments of Circes, brought out of Italy, to mar men's manners in England; much by example of ill life, but more by precepts of fond books, of late translated out of Italian into English, sold in every shop in London; commended by honest titles, the sooner to corrupt honest manners; dedicated overboldly to virtuous and honorable personages, the easilier to beguile simple and innocent wits. It is a pity, that those which have authority and charge to allow and disallow books to be printed, be no more circumspect herein than they are.[2]

Ascham worries about the adulteration of English religion, manners, and morals by things Italian, not only Italian people, but also Italian books. By the early seventeenth century, many commodities, and not just books, were accused of bringing foreign corruption into the urban space. As Robert Brenner makes clear in *Merchants and Revolution,* during the first decades of the seventeenth century there was an enormous increase in England's import trade. The Levant Company, the East India Company, the Venice Company, and the Muscovy Companies collectively were bringing to England a vast array of sought-after consumer goods from currants to Italian silks to spices to perfumes to sugar.[3] What Brenner does not fully account for is the *effect* of these goods on the social, as well as the political, relations within urban London. While many people were probably happy to eat and dress better than before, or at least eat and dress differently, there was also a sustained outcry against persons perceived to live above their stations and to be deformed by outlandish foreign fashions, foods, and manners.[4] Frequently it was the female consumer, rather than the male traveler or merchant, who through her purchase of foreign fashions bore the brunt of the preachers' and the polemicists' displeasure.[5] English by birth, such women were accused of being foreign in their dress, their cosmetics, and their morals.

I am, of course, using "foreign" here in the modern sense of what is not part of one's own nation. Technically, in the late sixteenth century, Londoners most often labeled as *foreigners* those born in England who were not Londoners or those who lived in the city but were not freemen.[6] People from beyond England's borders were most often designated as *aliens* or *strangers.* City culture was such that there were, in effect, two categories of outsiders: those from beyond the city walls and those from beyond the seas. In this essay my concern is not primarily with domestic foreigners, but with the various types of European nationals that people the London city comedies produced in the first decade of the 1600s. I will show, however, that a language of national difference could also be used to create and/or buttress a number of divisions among English men and among English men and women.

As a discursive construct, "foreignness" did not adhere in particular bodies but was created by both legal and cultural means. The stage helped in the latter process. There, "foreignness" could be produced by means of costume, skin color, speech, or conventionalized attributes. But the very technologies by which effective illusions of differences were created — wigs, skin dyes, costume, and exaggerated accents — could also reveal the inessential and fungible nature of social identities. It has now become a commonplace that in early modern plays when crossdressed women trade their men's clothes for women's weeds, the moment can reveal the performativity of gender.[7] But what of the moment in Marston's *Dutch Courtesan* when Cocledemoy assumes the accent and the stage gear of a Scottish barber in order to fool his antagonist, the vintner Mulligrub? On the stage it was as possible to reveal the performativity of national identity as it was to reveal the performativity of gender. The theater thus could both enforce and also undermine the idea of national differences; it could also play on fears that foreigners who refused to perform their difference from English people could penetrate the national body undetected. At the same time, while anxiety about foreigners and their detectability was enacted in the drama, not all discourses of "foreignness" were applied to people born outside England or were necessarily about them. Rather, as a language of difference, "foreignness" could be attributed to English men and women who for one reason or another were on the margins of, or excluded from, the group of those who had the power to claim cultural centrality and an uncontested place at the heart of the nation.

City comedy provides an especially rich site for exploring the various ways in which discourses of foreignness could function on the early modern stage. City comedies began to be written and staged in the late 1590s, and one of the first of them, William Haughton's *Englishmen for My Money* (1598), focuses precisely on the issue of national differences and hierarchies. In it, against the wishes of their father, three daughters of a usurer, Pisario, choose three Englishmen rather than three Europeans (an Italian, a Frenchman, and a Dutchman) for their husbands. The play approves the women's choices and is forthrightly chauvinistic, representing Englishness and English men as superior to the nations and the men of the rest of Europe. Haughton's play, I would argue, is not an anomaly. While much of the criticism of city comedy focuses on the genre's chorographic mapping of city space and the changes in urban life caused by commercialization and class mobility, the genre can also be read as a renegotiation, through a focus on the urban site, of England's self-definition and its position in a global arena. Europe and Europeans certainly loom large in the genre's exploration of national identity, but the world beyond Europe also enters these texts through their repeated references to the commodities being brought to London from Asia and Africa and through the discourses of racialized and exotic difference that occasionally, but insistently, emerge in these plays.

As a genre of national self-definition, city comedy is an interesting successor to the history plays that had been so much in vogue throughout the 1590s and had been a primary dramatic site where understandings of England and Englishness were negotiated.[8] City comedy continued this preoccupation with national identity, but defined Englishness differently. Especially in Shakespeare's history plays, the nation is first posited in relationship to the monarch.

By contrast, in city comedy monarchs are seldom represented at all. Instead, the focus is on the defined space of London and its environs and on the lives and values of those social groups—merchants, artisans, gallants, foreign traders and domestic consumers, both men and women—who populated the urban landscape.[9] While national identity is far from homogeneous and uncontested in this genre, it depends less on a subject's relationship to the monarch than on his or her relationship to certain places, values, customs, and institutions that could provide points of identification for London's urban dwellers and lead to new understandings of what constitutes Englishness.

Westward Ho, a city comedy written collaboratively by Dekker and Webster in 1604, shows how complex the process of defining national identities could be. The play has most often been discussed in relation to *Eastward Ho*, a riposte penned by Jonson, Marston, and Chapman, which in turn prompted Dekker and Webster's *Northward Ho*. But *Westward Ho* is interesting on its own, as well as when considered in relation to these other plays, and this is particularly true of its handling of "foreignness." As A. J. Hoensenlaars has argued, by the turn of the century there was a well-established stage language of ethnic and religious and national "types," the most common being the bloody Turk, the lascivious and devilish Moor, the foppish Frenchman, the boorish Dutchman, and the guileful Italian. But after 1600—and this is apparent in *Westward Ho*—it is increasingly inadequate to speak of these figures exclusively as sources of anxiety or sites of otherness.[10] City comedy, in short, did not simply reproduce xenophobic feeling or endlessly replay the binary difference between England and various "others." Rather, it could use the language of national difference to map distinctions among and between groups of Englishmen or to acknowledge, and often simultaneously resist, the hybridity of urban culture. In the largest sense, discourses of foreignness became part of the stage's resources for posing and for providing imaginary solutions to the problems of its urban site of production. These problems could include the way the import of foreign goods was changing the tenor of urban life; the way new modes of acquiring wealth pressured the traditional status system; or the way urban practices created specific kinds of sexual or gender anxieties.

In *Westward Ho* a language of national differences becomes deeply woven into the heart of a comedy that on the surface seems simply to be about jealous husbands and wandering wives. At every turn, the idea of "foreignness" intrudes itself into the many strands of the dramatic narrative, revealing how the problems of the play's urban milieu are represented in terms of encounters with imagined others and articulating a longing for urban and national purity even while acknowledging its impossibility. Unwittingly, *Westward Ho* reveals the cultural and social miscegenation of urban life and holds in tension com-

peting models of national identity, one based on essentialist fictions of exclusion and purity, the other on the cosmopolitan incorporation of difference and
awareness of its constructed nature.[11] Dramatically, these tensions are con-
cretely expressed through the play's insistent focus on the penetrability of
supposedly inpenetrable spaces. Mapping the play's urban geography, therefore, becomes one means of understanding the particular way the play's deep-
est preoccupations are given dramatic form and the way a discourse of national
difference helps to articulate and resolve the problems of urban life which the
play foregrounds.

In city comedy, as in some other genres of the period, such as domestic
tragedy, the household is foundational to social order and English national
identity, but it is also often represented as a highly fraught and endangered
space. *Westward Ho* opens with three scenes set in merchant households, and
each scene presents household space as imperiled. Fran Dolan has demonstrated that in domestic tragedy danger to the household issues from familiar
members of that household — from servants, apprentices, and above all, from
wives.[12] City comedy, however, often specifies the danger to the household
somewhat differently, as the penetration of domestic space by foreign bodies —
foreign people, foreign goods, or class enemies who function as strangers or
aliens — and by the subsequent weakening of the boundaries of the household
as a container for the people, especially the women, who dwell within it.
Perhaps even more than in most city comedies, domestic space in *Westward Ho*
is porous: open to penetration from without and to transgression of its boundaries from within. While the first three scenes focus insistently on imperiled
domestic space, the play subsequently moves to other locales: two London
taverns, a brothel, an earl's mansion, and finally an inn in Brainford. As the play
negotiates these places, its telos appears to be the recovery of impermeable
domestic space. But *Westward Ho* also resists and complicates the achievement
of this goal, in the process pressuring fictions of purity and impermeability that
traditionally undergird both domestic and national ideologies.

The play opens with a bawd, Mistress Birdlime, at the door of a merchant,
Justiniano's, house. With her is a tailor carrying a velvet gown. They offer the
gown and some jewels to the wife of the house so that she will leave her
impoverished merchant husband and become the mistress of a wealthy old
earl. Returning home to discover Birdlime and the tailor on the threshold of
his house, the jealous husband quarrels with both. The breakup of the household ensues as the merchant, accused of prodigality, declares he will leave
London and his wife. She declares that she will make her own way in the
world, presumably by accepting the old earl's proposition.

The scene suggests some of the social forces endangering the merchant household, such as the disparities of rank and wealth that make the old earl, despite his age, an attractive sexual alternative to a poor merchant. It also points to the power of commodities to create desiring subjects who find it difficult to accept limits to the play of their desires. Birdlime, part of the discursively constructed rogue underworld sometimes characterized as a nation *within* the English nation, is a master at manipulating desire.[13] She holds out to the city wife an expensive velvet gown, simultaneously reminding her of the high cost of the *other* things Mistress Justiniano values: "rich apparell, choyce dyet, excellent Physicke."[14] Later, when Birdlime wants to stoke the old earl's sexual desire, she says of Mistress Justiniano: "youl find the sweetest, sweetest bedfellow of her. Oh! She looks so sugredly, so simpringly, so gingerly, so amarously, so amiably. Such a redde lippe, such a White foreheade, such a blacke eie, such a full cheeke, and such a goodly little nose, nowe shees in that French gowne, Scotch fals, Scotch bum, and Italian head-tire you sent her, and is such an intycing shee-witch, carrying the charmes of your Jewels about her! Oh!" (2.2.31–38). Mistress Justiniano's desire for fashionable attire has turned her into a sartorial United Nations, foreign fashion thoroughly hybridizing her body and desire for those fashions pulling her out of her domestic space. At the same time Birdlime knows that these clothes and jewels will, in turn, incite desire in the earl.

The first scene, then, plays on the fear, so well explored by Karen Newman, that woman's desire, stimulated by the availability of foreign luxuries, will lead her out of her domestic space and out of her marriage into adultery.[15] Yet the issue of the foreign requires further exploration. Justiniano, the jealous husband, is himself a foreigner, an Italian, though his wife is an Englishwoman.[16] At first glance the play seems to be an object lesson in the evils of "mixed marriages." As G. D. Ramsey indicates, there were a number of Italian merchants in London in the sixteenth century.[17] As long as Antwerp remained the clearing house for English textiles, Italian merchants were active in promoting north-south commerce. English cloth moved south through Antwerp, and oil, currants, spices, and luxury fabrics such as velvets and silks moved north. With the disruption of the Antwerp trade in the 1560s, a number of Italian merchants left London, though some attempted to reroute the cloth trade through Hamburg, and some eventually became involved in new ventures such as the exporting of herring to the Mediterranean. Justiniano, then, might well be a not unfamiliar figure in early modern London, an Italian merchant who seems to be struggling financially; and when he says he will leave London, Justiniano claims to be going to Stoade, a city at the mouth of the Elbe very close to Hamburg, the site some Italian merchants actually attempted to use to reroute north-south overland trade.

Yet I do not think verisimilitude of this sort is the *real* issue. There *were* Italian merchants in London circa 1600, though probably fewer, relatively speaking, than fifty years before. But what Justiniano also embodies is something culturally constructed and partly purely fantastical: that is, the idea of the guileful, passionate, sometimes Machiavellian Italian.[18] For part but not all of the play Justiniano lives out this stereotype. He is jealous of his wife, prone to lies and disguises, and obsessive. Along with Birdlime the bawd, he represents all that is dangerous to the city's well-being. Yet Justiniano would not be interesting if he were simply a stereotypical Italian villain used to buttress the binary opposition between things Italian and things English. What is intriguing is the increasing instability of the opposition he supposedly secures. At first simply a figure through whom the play articulates anxiety about the permeability of domestic and urban spaces by foreign wares and foreign people, Justiniano eventually becomes the vehicle for exposing the hybrid nature of those spaces and the constructed and unstable nature of the categories by which the domestic is sealed off from the foreign.

Before exploring his role in depth, I think it is useful to point out that there is one other stranger in this text, a Dutch serving man named Hans, who works at the Rhenish wine house in the Steelyard. Like other plays of the period, *Westward Ho* associates Dutchmen with the sale and consumption of alcohol,[19] and in drawing their picture of Hans, Dekker and Webster assign him a broad, intentionally comic Dutch accent. If, as David Kastan has argued, real Flemish refugees were taking "English" jobs in the 1590s,[20] *Westward Ho* accepts this fact but disempowers Hans by having him "talk funny." Accepted as a part of urban life, he is nonetheless rendered comic by his accent. Most important, his speech "fixes" him in his assigned role as alien. He can't talk as he does and ever pass for English. His language functions to render him always already "different," and in this text there is no hint, as there is in *The Shoemaker's Holiday,* that the Dutch accent is just a performance. It is presented as an essential and unchanging aspect of this particular character.

Justiniano's case is very different. He does not get assigned a stage accent, and this fact makes him a more complicated and potentially more dangerous figure than Hans. At times he seems like just another London merchant, his class position and interests obscuring his foreign nationality. He, like the other merchants, finds himself threatened by a class enemy, a lecherous earl with a title and great wealth who wants to steal his wife. Moreover, the other London merchants are upset when this man whom they characterize as a friend "breaks," experiences a business failure, and has to give up his trading activities. At other times, however, Justiniano's *difference* from the other merchants is emphasized by means of his jealousy, his disguises, and, I would especially emphasize, his overt breach with his wife. Initially, at least, foreignness is associated with loveless, acrimonious marriages. But the net effect of Justiniano's representation is to depict him as both foreign and not-foreign, depending on his position at different points in the narrative. That he is not marked as foreign by his speech allows him flexibility of maneuver. For example, after he leaves his wife, he does not go to Stoade; rather he capitalizes on his ability to "pass," disguises himself as a writing master, and begins to insinuate himself into the houses of London merchants. When he is disguised, Justiniano's Italian origins seem not to be perceived by the London merchants whose households he enters, though the audience is always aware of the writing master's real identity. Unlike Hans, Justiniano in effect becomes a foreign body whose presence cannot be detected by those around him, but who in the eyes of the audience constitutes a threat to the sexual purity of English wives and the integrity of English households.

Exactly how the English household is threatened by this foreign presence becomes more clear in the play's third scene involving the London merchant, Master Honeysuckle, just after he has returned from France. The encounter underscores the degree to which commerce mandates permeable national boundaries. Not only are there Dutchmen and Italians in London, but this English merchant has just been traveling on business to France. Unfortunately, he has returned with French diseases as well as French coins. To his servant he complains of lameness, the wrinkles on his face, his too-small nightcap. Foreign travel has endangered and enfeebled him. Moreover, the first thing he does is to welcome into his house what the stage directions describe as "*Signior* Justiniano *the Merchant, like a wryting Mecanicall Pedant*" (s.d. after 2.1.21). The two of them, English merchant and disguised Italian, begin to speak in Latin, the transnational language of learning and politics, but immediately Honeysuckle protests: "No more *Plurimums* if you love me, lattin whole-meates are now minc'd, and servde in for English Gallimafries; let us therefore cut out our uplandish Neates tongues, and talke like regenerate Brittains" (2.1.24–27). Honeysuckle claims that what distinguishes a regenerate Briton is the English language and an English diet, yet at that very moment he welcomes the Latin-speaking penmaster into his house to instruct his wife, unwittingly letting a foreign and threatening figure into his domestic space.

As a writing master the disguised Justiniano figures foreign danger as sexual danger. He is both highly sexualized and a promoter of sexuality in the wives. In his new role he calls himself Parenthesis. Puttenham in *The Arte of English Poesie* lists Parenthesis among the figures of tolerable disorder and gives it the name "The Insertor."[21] Certainly this is an apt term to describe Justiniano's behavior as writing master. He inserts himself everywhere, showing off his expertise as penman, messenger, and spy. In this first scene, Honeysuckle's French-induced feebleness provides the foil to set off Justiniano's expertise with his phallic instrument. Saying he desires to "please al those that come under my fingers" (2.1.57), Justiniano earns Honeysuckle's praise: "Your hand; I am glad our Citty has so good, so necessary, and so laborious a member in it: we lacke painfull and expert penmen amongst us" (2.1.59–61). Ironically the best penman is not a regenerate Briton, but a foreigner. National difference is here implicitly figured as the opposition between sexual lack and sexual excess. All the merchants' wives love Justiniano. He is a source of pleasure and power to them, and they pass him from hand to hand, sharing the pleasure. If women stereotypically circulate between men, here a man circulates among women, teaching them a skill, writing, that enhances their power even as it sexualizes them. Justianiano's description of his wife's scribal accomplishments is one long double entendre.[22] The pen, but also a certain degree of phallic power, come into the women's possession by the incorporation of this "foreign body" into their domestic space.

Unwittingly, then, the enfeebled Honeysuckle has opened his doors to a Latin-speaking, disguised Italian who will sell as a commodity a skill once reserved for men and a select number of aristocratic women, a skill that gives to women new ways to put themselves and their words into circulation. By the middle of the play the merchants' wives are circulating madly, and the centrifugal spatial logic of the narrative becomes clear. Using Justiniano to carry messages and having at hand the all-purpose excuse that shopping must be done (2.1.214–18), the wives sally forth to meet their gallants in public places: behind the pillars in St. Paul's, in the back rooms of taverns. These places concretize the significance of this urban narrative. Once the foreigner disguised as a writing master has penetrated their household space, the empowered women become transgressive, meeting the gallants in public places, their only attendants the eavesdropping writing master and the bawd, Birdlime. The perambulations of the women eventually take them even further afield when they agree to spend a night with their gentlemen in Brainford, a village on the Thames west of London and famous in other city comedies as a rendezvous for lovers and pleasure seekers. The women not only leave their domestic spaces; they also leave the city walls.

At one level Brainford represents for the women in the play what the city whorehouse represents for the men: a place of sexual freedom outside marriage. If the period saw the household as crucial to social order and marriage as a privileged relationship, especially among the middling sort, the play clearly reveals that the foreigner, Justiniano, is not the only one with a troubled marriage and that the burdens of this institution, so crucial to a certain version of "Englishness," can be considerable. The geography of act 4 is telling. As the women transgressively wend upriver to Brainford with their gallants, their merchant husbands are straggling in, one by one, to Birdlime's London brothel, an illicit space within the city walls. In many city comedies, prostitutes are literally from other nations, Marston's "Dutch courtesan" being the most notorious of these characters. Moreover, city comedies often contain set speeches describing how the prostitute serves men of all nations, being a common road, or harbor, where all may anchor.[23] The foreign prostitute's activities thus threaten to erase differences between man and man, nation and nation, as her clients are rendered interchangeable when sexuality enters the marketplace.

Birdlime is a decidedly English prostitute, but her brothel activates *some* of the same fears as does the foreign prostitute, and her brothel serves as an alternative to the domestic life with which Englishness is associated in the play. The whorehouse places the men in unfamiliar subject positions. At one point Mr. Tenterhook comes up behind Lucy and puts his hands over her eyes, asking that she guess who he is. She names just about every man in the play's cast of characters and a host of others besides. The sequence hilariously reveals how prostitution renders men interchangeable. Birdlime and Lucy do their best to make each client feel special. But it isn't so. None of these men has a special claim on the person or emotions of the whore. She is not anyone's wife, and they are all just her clients.

The most unusual aspect of the brothel scenes in this play, however, is their playfulness. Birdlime's male customers joke and play cards with her, and she and Lucy, the chief whore, display great teamwork in hustling the men in and out of the bedroom. Moreover, when the three merchant husbands crash into one another at Birdlime's and realize their common situation, they are not upset. In fact, they praise Birdlime for her cleverness in shuffling them about (4.1.155–57). Paradoxically, the whorehouse openly allows men to bond through the sharing of a common woman, in distinction to the jealous guarding of private property that characterizes their domestic lives. Here the impure space of the brothel, dominated by unmarried and culturally disreputable women, allows one to sense, by contrast, the costs — to men and women — of domestic enclosure. The whorehouse is certainly a threat to the household; it draws husbands from home and siphons away their money, but it also unwittingly serves as a critique of the possessive paranoia that domesticity engenders in men like Justiniano. The homosociality of the whorehouse, moreover, allows Justiniano to shed his writing master's disguise and reveal to the other merchants both his own identity and the fact that their wives have gone to

Brainford. The episode transforms Justiniano from being the husbands' enemy, the foreign object in their households, to being their friend, bonded with them by the shared plight of having wives flying out of control. Homosocial bonding allows national difference first to be exposed and then elided as the three Englishmen and the Italian begin a joint pursuit of their lost female property. As Justiniano becomes one of a quartet of vengeful husbands, the English merchants begin to display his jealousy and lust for revenge. It is now quite difficult to distinguish the Italian from his English mates according to behavior. Up to this point, the disruption of domestic harmony and the unsealing of domestic spaces has been associated with Justiniano, the penetrative writing master and jealously obsessive foreigner. But the play manages, through a fantasy of homosocial bonding, to erase national distinctions among the four merchants. Their occupations and their subject positions as vulnerable husbands unite them more than nationality separates them.

This blurring and elision of national difference through homosocial bonding founded on suspicion of wives has a class component as well, and that becomes more clear when the four husbands go to the old earl's house to punish him for the attempted seduction of Justiniano's wife. The earl's mansion is a special place, one constructed by unmistakable markers of decadence, luxury, and sin. By presenting the earl's milieu in this way, the playwrights can displace onto him the burden of Italian degeneracy formerly carried by Justiniano. The earl has, for example, prepared a banquet to seduce Justiniano's wife, and woos her in extravagant Petrarchan conceits.[24] The delicious irony of the scene, however, is that Justiniano, dressed in his wife's clothes, is the actual recipient of the earl's attentions. When he unmasks, melodramatic events cascade down. Justiniano reveals the body of his dead wife, poisoned for her adultery; but then the audience learns that she did not lose her chastity and is only pretending to be dead — all of this results in the earl's repentance. The scene — with its high drama and exotic turns — seems to have fallen into this city comedy from an entirely different kind of play, an Italianate revenge tragedy.[25] The earl is connected, as much by genre as by his actions, with something foreign. And even though he repents, he does not go with the others when they head off to Brainford, and he is never depicted anywhere but in his luxurious mansion. His house, where he attempts to install a mistress, not a wife, remains sealed off from the city around him. The earl, in short, is "Italianated" and isolated from the other Englishmen by his decadence and adultery, while Justiniano is gradually "Englished" by his renewed commitment to his wife and marriage. No longer a devious writing master teaching dangerous skills to married women, Justiniano heads down the Thames with his newly reconciled wife by his side.

The markers of foreign difference, in the case of the old earl, are thus mobilized to isolate a class enemy. Yet the language of the foreign continues to disrupt the identities of even the most "English" of the characters. Looking at the fine clothes his chaste and chastened wife has borne away from the Earl, Justiniano exclaims: "Was it ever heard that such tyrings were brought away from a Lord by any wench but thee Moll, without paying, unlesse the wench coneycatched him? go thy wayes: if all the great Turks Concubins were but like thee, the ten-penny infidell should never neede keep so many geldings to ney over em" (4.2.190–94). The chaste wife remains hybridized by fashion. A merchant's wife, she wears the clothes of an earl's mistress; likened to a Turkish concubine, perhaps because of this exotic dress, she nonetheless has more regard for her chastity than the eunuchs who guard the harem. Mistress Justiniano's married chastity makes her a true English wife, even though her dress speaks otherwise. It speaks of the desire for foreign luxury and upward mobility that make her and other London women divided subjects. The play thereby reaches a fantasy resolution to a real social problem. Militant chastity is the magic charm, the innoculation, that permits innocent enjoyment of exotic foreign goods. An extra delight accrues if these are acquired through the "sharp practice" so valued by a merchant class rather than by the inherited lands and revenues that presumably mark the wealth of the old earl.

At Brainford, therefore, the other three wives must also make manifest their own commitment to chastity, but the resolution of the main plot again complicates the idea of a "pure" identity cordoned off from national and sexual difference. As in many texts of the period, Brainford is the conventional place beyond the immediate London suburbs where gallants and city wives go to outwit jealous husbands. In *Westward Ho,* these wandering wives don't actually sleep with the men who pursue them. To do so would shatter too conclusively the fiction of female chastity underpinning domestic ideologies and definitions of English womanhood. Instead, at Brainford the gentlemen self-destruct as wooers — they get drunk, wander off to smoke, and allow the women to plot an escape. More importantly, at Brainford the wives redefine for themselves what the "freedom" of the outlying regions will mean. Rather than becoming adultresses, they bond *as women* against men, gallants and husbands alike. In striving for a dramatic resolution to the problem of over-stimulated city wives, subject to foreign desires, the play entertains for a moment the possibility of a community of women who would live outside of marriage altogether.[26] Ironically, the only safely enclosed space in *Westward Ho* is the bedroom to which the women retreat after Mistress Tenterhook feigns an illness. Here the women spend the night together, and here they are found by their husbands the next morning, chastely separated from the gallants next door. This enclosed space, however, is not a domestic space, shared by a married couple and their children and servants, but an extradomestic, extra-mural space claimed by women to express their solidarity against the men who would "conycatch" them (5.1.158).

Like Birdlime's whorehouse, but for different reasons, this bedchamber, sealed against husbands as well as gallants, is a threat to domestic space. But like the whorehouse it also offers a positive alternative to vexed and troubled domesticity. Female friendship, female solidarity, and perhaps female homo-eroticism are possible there. Even Birdlime can be included in this space when she pants in, bringing to Mistress Tenterhook the jewels she had used to ransom Monopoly from the officer who arrested him. Symbols of Tenter-hook's chastity, the jewels had come into Birdlime's hands in the brothel, and Birdlime, for no apparent reason but solidarity with her sex, has journeyed upriver to return them to Mistress Tenterhook before her husband could reach Brainford. Her action gives the wives the crucial information that their hus-bands have been visiting a brothel and removes all proof of Mistress Tenter-hook's liaison with Monopoly. Just as Justiniano and the merchant husbands were homosocially bonded in Birdlime's brothel, overriding national differ-ences, so the wives and Birdlime are momentarily joined in the bedchamber at Brainford, overriding the differences that supposedly separate wife from bawd, the respectable city from its rogue underworld. I find it significant that a play whose plot centers on the endangerment and restitution of marriage and domestic spaces, twice offers an alternative to those spaces and that institution. One can explain this by the "sophisticated" tastes of a boys' company audience, but one can also see it as a perhaps unwitting recognition of the burdens and the artifice of this quintessentially English and bourgeois institution, the effort required to make it "natural" and "inevitable."

The play, moreover, does not ever actually depict the reconstitution of the merchant households within the city walls. Rather, *Westward Ho* closes with the embarkation from Brainford back to London. As everyone climbs into boats and heads home, the centrifugal forces that have threatened to destroy households and hurl people into the tavern, the whorehouse, and the subur-ban inn are seemingly reversed. It is worth considering further, however, the play's closing moments and the different ways they affect the play's male and female subjects. There is irony, of course, in the fact that the possibility of restoring domestic harmony, of reconstituting the play's fragmented house-holds, depends in large measure on the agency of Birdlime, the underworld figure who in act 1, scene 1 stood at the door of Justiniano's house enticing his wife with foreign fashions, and of Justiniano himself, the Italian merchant and disguised writing master who had once served as broker between the wives and the gallants. At first embodying impurity and the contaminations of a market economy, these illicit and/or foreign characters are eventually incorporated into the project of re-establishing English domesticity and female chastity. Yet their incorporation remains, especially in Birdlime's case, incomplete and destabilizing. Justiniano is still Italian by birth, though one who can pass as English by his return to the domestic ideal. But Birdlime remains a bawd and can't pass. For a time, at Brainford, with the other women, her sexual status did not seem to matter. In fact, the most dangerous scandal of Birdlime's representation is that it threatens to expose the whore-wife binary as a patriarchal tactic for dividing and controlling women. It is this scandal that the final moments of the narrative must handle. Consequently, once reunited with their husbands, the wives turn on Birdlime and revile her. She is forced to row home in her own boat, and the bar separating wives from disreputable women redescends. Like the old earl, Birdlime is cordoned off to re-establish the imagined purity of English wives.

But the final moments of the play also variously threaten this vision of bounded, pure spaces and social identities. The motliness of the returning crew suggests the unchangeable hybridity of that urban space. However much the respectable people want Birdlime to stay in the suburbs, she insists on returning to the walled city. London must accommodate her, as much as the chaste wives, just as it must accommodate the reformed foreigner, Justiniano, as well as the English merchants and the gallants who prey on city wives. Moreover, the very ideology of purity is complicated by what is in effect the play's coda. As the men and women launch down the river, eastward toward home, they sing a remarkable song.

> Oares, Oares, Oares, Oares:
>   To London hay, to London hay:
> Hoist up sailes, and lets away,
> For the safest bay
> For us to land is London shores.
> Oares, Oares, Oares, Oares:
> Quickly shall wee get to Land,
> If you, if you, if you,
> Lend us but halfe a hand.
> O, lend us halfe a hand.
>
>   (5.4.309–18)

For anyone attuned to the aural pun on "oars" and "whores," the song is a fitting ending to a drama that worries about the contamination of pure spaces by impurity, the domestic by the foreign. The song celebrates the return of domestic harmony and the return to the walled city from the licentious outlying regions. Yet within this song there erupts a praise of whores, whores, whores, underscoring that even in its conclusion this play cannot quite assent to the fiction that any space is impermeable to the admixture of the low, the foreign, and the illicit.

Dramatic genres have their vogue not merely, I would argue, because the marketplace always requires something new; they also arise to address social needs and anxieties. *Westward Ho* is just one of a host of Jacobean city comedies in which an urban culture uses an urban institution, the commercial theater, to negotiate its fears of foreign encroachment in the form of people, goods, and customs, as well as to negotiate the class and gender antagonisms of the urban milieu. Unwittingly or not, *Westward Ho* reveals the extraordinary instability of the Italian-English opposition upon which it is built. The only "real" Italian in this text turns out to be an English earl, indicating the way in which a discourse of national difference can be used to reinforce class difference and turn *some* Englishmen into foreigners. The second remarkable thing is the way misogyny helps to manage xenophobic impulses. There is in this play an unmistakable anxiety about the phallic prowess of the play's best penman, the foreigner, who pleasures all the ladies, either with his own instrument or the prosthetic device suggested by his writing accouterments. The English-Italian binary is thus in part constituted as an opposition between sexual lack and sexual excess. Yet in the brothel that antagonism between men of two nations is converted into a solidarity among men of the same class against gadding women and against the men of another class, the gallants who would steal the wives away and make them adulteresses. The desire to punish the wives and recapture their property, and the assumption that the women are inevitably unchaste, are what bind the men, Englishmen and Italian, together; and that homosocial bonding is not disrupted when the wives are recovered.

The last act fetishizes the chastity of the merchants' wives and makes a commitment to marriage the sign of true Englishness, but the consequences are different for men and women. Birdlime must be repudiated. While the men's homosocial bond, forged in the brothel, stands, the women's solidarity in the Brainford inn is fractured, the "wives" hived off from the "bawd." An inclusive community of women emerges as a threat that can't be tolerated. Birdlime is thus returned to her place as the outsider within the city walls, much as the old earl has been turned into the Italian stranger within his own country. The class enemy and the bawd become the play's real foreigners. In the end, *Westward Ho* reveals Englishness to be not simply a matter of place of birth, but a matter of accommodation to certain codes and values. Foreignness means living otherwise, whether you are an earl, an old bawd, or an Italian Machiavel. This is a knowledge many states and many people have repressed, so blatantly does it reveal the domestic component of what we prefer to characterize as foreign matters.

Notes

1. Steven Rappaport, *Worlds Within Worlds: Structures of Life in Sixteenth-Century London* (Cambridge: Cambridge University Press, 1989), pp. 11–17; Mark T. Burnett, "Apprentice Literature and the 'Crisis' of the 1590s," *The Yearbook of English Studies: Politics, Patronage and Literature in England 1558–1658* 21 (1991): 27–38.

2. Roger Ascham, *The Scholemaster,* ed. R. J. Schoeck (Don Mills, Ontario: J. M. Dent and Sons, 1966), bk. 1, pp. 65–66.

3. Robert Brenner, *Merchants and Revolution: Commercial Change, Political Conflict, and London's Overseas Traders, 1550–1653* (Princeton: Princeton University Press, 1993), pp. 51–91.

4. In Robert Greene's 1592 *A Quip for an Upstart Courtier,* for example, the offending courtier — born in Italy but called to England by courtiers wishing to imitate foreign fashions and manners — is first described in terms of his outlandish breeches: "At least, as it drew more nigh unto mee, I might percive that it was a very passing costly paire of Velvet-breeches, whose paines beeing made of the cheefest Neapolitane stuffe, was drawn over with the best Spanish satine, and marvellous curiously over whipt with gold twist, interseemed with knots of pearle: the netherstocke was of the purest Granado silke. No cost was spared to sett out these costly breeches, who had girt unto them a rapyer and dagger, gilt, point pendante, as quaintly as if som curious Florentine had trickte them up, to square it up and downe the streetes before his mistresse" (*Illustrations of Early English Literature,* ed. J. Payne Collier [London, 1867–70], p. 13). By contrast, the English yeoman who wears cloth breeches inveighs against "malapert upstarts" who wear apparel that does not accord with their status (p. 21). He also attacks barbers who cut hair to accord with foreign fashions (p. 33) and complains against foreign artisans such as French milliners and Dutch shoemakers who displace English craftsmen and bring newfangled products and styles into England (p. 65).

5. Karen Newman, *Fashioning Femininity* (Chicago: University of Chicago Press, 1991), esp. pp. 133–34.

6. Steven Rappaport, *Worlds Within Worlds,* p. 42; Roger Finlay, *Population and Metropolis: The Demography of London, 1580–1650* (Cambridge: Cambridge University Press, 1981), p. 68.

7. There is an enormous literature on this question. I summarize much of it in my chapter on crossdressing in *The Stage and Social Struggle in Early Modern England* (London: Routledge, 1994), pp. 93–128.

8. Jean E. Howard and Phyllis Rackin, *Engendering a Nation: A Feminist Account of Shakespeare's English Histories* (London: Routledge, 1997); Richard Helgerson, *Forms of Nationhood* (Chicago: University of Chicago Press, 1993), pp. 195–224.

9. Helgerson, in *Forms of Nationhood,* describes the way in which chorographic

descriptions of England's shires and towns enabled an identification of English people with the land, rather than with the monarch (pp. 107–47). The chorographic attention devoted to the city of London in city comedy serves the same function, allowing the audience to identify with the city and its customs and landscape and downplaying identification with the king.

10. A. J. Hoenselaars, *Images of Englishmen and Foreigners in the Drama of Shakespeare and His Contemporaries: A Study of Stage Characters and National Identity in English Renaissance Drama, 1558–1642* (Toronto: Associated University Press, 1992), pp. 108–43.

11. In "Patriarchal Territories: The Body Enclosed," Peter Stallybrass has argued that as the nation-state was forming in the early modern period, there was increased emphasis on boundaries and concepts of national purity. The bounded domestic space of the household was seen to parallel national space, and both were defined in terms of exclusion and purity. See his essay in *Rewriting the Renaissance: The Discourses of Sexual Difference in Early Modern Europe,* ed. Margaret W. Ferguson, Maureen Quilligan, and Nancy J. Vickers (Chicago: University of Chicago Press, 1986), pp. 123–42. This coincides with Benedict Anderson's view in *Imagined Communities* (London: Verso, 1983) that the nation is usually imagined as a bounded space enclosing citizens who view themselves as sharing a common origin, whatever the reality. By contrast, I would argue that there is also a discourse of cosmopolitanism permeating some city comedies that is less invested in ideas of purity and boundaries than in hybridity and accommodation of difference. Lawrence Manley in *Literature and Culture in Early Modern London* (Cambridge: Cambridge Univesity Press, 1995) touches on the cosmopolitanism of urban life, which he defines in part as a disinvestment in the local and parochial (p. 566), but which I wish to think about in terms of a particular attitude towards difference. For further discussion of this issue, see my essay, "Mastering Difference in *The Dutch Courtesan,*" *Shakespeare Studies* 24 (1996): 105–17.

12. Fran Dolan, *Dangerous Familiars: Representations of Domestic Crime in England, 1550–1700* (Ithaca: Cornell University Press, 1994), pp. 1–19.

13. As A. L. Beier explains in *Masterless Men: The Vagrancy Problem in England, 1560–1640* (London: Methuen, 1985), pp. 7–8, the fantasy of an anti-society of rogues, masterless men, and coneycatchers was widespread in sixteenth-century England. Writers such as Thomas Harmon, John Awdeley, and Robert Greene wrote books and pamphlets detailing the speech and the activities of these underworld figures. The actual evidence for an organized society of rogues, however, is slim. In *Westward Ho,* Birdlime seems like a figure from this imagined underworld, especially in the first scene when she tries to lure away Mistress Justiniano and cozen her husband.

14. All quotations from the play will be taken from the edition prepared by Fredson Bowers, *The Dramatic Works of Thomas Dekker,* vol. 2 (Cambridge: Cambridge University Press, 1955). This quotation occurs at 1.1.77 (p. 321).

15. Karen Newman, *Fashioning Femininity,* pp. 131–43.

16. A. J. Hoenselaars in *Images of Englishmen and Foreigners in the Drama of Shakespeare and His Contemporaries* notes how unusual it was in the drama of the time for a foreigner to be depicted as the successful suitor of an English woman, since, for the most part, such suitors went away empty handed or were the objects of ridicule.

17. G. D. Ramsey, "The Undoing of the Italian Mercantile Colony in Sixteenth-Century London," *Textile History and Economic History: Essays in Honour of Miss Julia de*

Lacy Mann, ed. N. B. Harte and K. G. Ponting (Manchester: Manchester University Press, 1973), pp. 22–49.

18. G. K. Hunter in "Elizabethans and Foreigners," *Shakespeare Survey* 17 (1965): 37–52, esp. 46 where Hunter discusses the animus consistently directed against Italians in early modern drama.

19. A. J. Hoenselaars, *Images of Englishmen and Foreigners in the Drama of Shakespeare and His Contemporaries,* pp. 115–17.

20. David Scott Kastan, "Workshop and/as Playhouse," *Staging the Renaissance: Reinterpretations of Elizabethan and Jacobean Drama,* ed. David Scott Kastan and Peter Stallybrass (New York: Routledge, 1991), pp. 51–63.

21. George Puttenham, *The Arte of English Poesie,* ed. Gladys Dodge Willcock and Alice Walker (Cambridge: Cambridge University Press, 1936), p. 169.

22. Charles R. Forker, "*Westward Ho* and *Northward Ho:* A Reevaluation," *Publications of the Arkansas Philological Association* 6 (1980): 1–42, at 11–12. In the period Italy and figures such as Aretino were famously associated with sexual vice. As writing master, Justiniano embodies a comic version of a dangerous Italianated sexuality.

23. In *The Dutch Courtesan,* for example, the bawd, Mary Faugh, says to the courtesan, Franceschina, that she has made her "acquainted with the Spaniard, Don Skirtoll, — with the Italian, Messer Beieroane, — with the Irish lord, S. Patrick, — with the Dutch merchant, Haunce Herkin Glukin Skellam Flapdragon, — and specially with the greatest French, and now lastly with this English" (*The Works of John Marston,* vol. 2, ed. A. H. Bullen [London: John C. Nimmo, 1887], 2.2.16–20 [p. 32]).

24. Forker, "*Westward Ho* and *Northward Ho,*" p. 26, notes how the play makes fun of the earl through the absurd exaggeration of his Petrarchanisms.

25. Alexander Leggatt, in *City Comedy in the Age of Shakespeare* (Toronto: University of Toronto Press, 1973), p. 132, says that in this part of the play the writing is "high-flown and rhetorical, and the action, with its threats of poisoning and stabbing, smacks of Italianate melodrama."

26. Simon Morgan-Russell, "Male Expectations and Female Alliances in Dekker and Webster's *Westward Ho,*" in *Women's Alliances in Early Modern England,* ed. Susan Frye and Karen Robertson (Oxford: Oxford University Press, 1999), pp. 70–84.

PART III

SUBJECTS OF THE CITY

Despite the best efforts of William Harrison and Sir Thomas Smith to make the social hierarchies of early modern England seem orderly and rational, they sometimes had difficulty reconciling two fields of difference: rank and wealth. The one seemed ancient; the other, too often new. Because the creation of wealth was largely identified with London, it might be expected that stresses upon the hierarchy would be particularly in evidence there.

Ian W. Archer's "Material Londoners?" demonstrates that residents of the early modern city were supremely conscious of their culture's commercialization. There were civic ceremonies, like the paean to international trade that Jonson wrote for the opening of the New Exchange, and annual inaugural pageants for the lord mayors. During the last half of the sixteenth century, the pageants neglected their roots in the morality tradition for frank tributes to the city's commercial success. Meanwhile, although preachers continued to inveigh against covetousness, usury, and fraud, the fissure between trade and traditional values was narrowed as notions of fair business dealings gave commerce a place in a Christian ethical system. Even the old conviction that mercantile pursuits were incompatible with gentility was rethought, as merchants were praised for contributing to national prosperity. But civic festivities could not entirely conceal the fact that some social pressures remained. As Archer indicates, consumerism seems to have been implicated in tensions between citizens and gentlemen, rich and poor, men and women, old and young. There was a gap between the newcomers who migrated to London to better themselves and the gentry who came to enjoy London's pleasures and luxury goods. The frictions of age and gender were more acute in London than elsewhere because so many young men lived restrictively, as apprentices, and so many women challenged the patriarchal order in running their own households or businesses. Still, there were sufficient ameliorating factors and collective values that Archer is not willing to say that these social tensions were acute or unprecedented. It may simply have been that they found a different vehicle of expression around 1600, in the rhetoric of the new consumer culture.

In "Purgation as the Allure of Mastery: Early Modern Medicine and the Technology of the Self," Gail Kern Paster gives a case study of the role of luxury goods in urban systems of difference. The goods at issue are medical therapies. Paster points out that when treatment was purchased from a doctor (rather than received from a mother or wetnurse), it became an object of consumption and exchange and, in the expanding medical market of early modern London, also a form of competition. Exotic imported drugs and herbs were markers of high culture and urban sophistication. Describing a New World root, for example, a physician emphasized the benefit it had conferred upon "a person of much estimation" — the use by the person of quality enhancing the root's market appeal. The disparities between kitchen physic and doctor's physic, simple and compound drugs, and herbal and chemical treatments also participated in distinctions between male and female, gentle and common. Thus, the new professionalized medical consumption "not only mimicked the structures of difference in early modern London," Paster says, "but added significantly to the symbolic exchanges by which individuals conveyed meaning to themselves and others." Catharsis, in particular, was seen as an instrument of human perfectibility. In this critical historical moment, before the physical and spiritual meanings of well being, ill health, and therapeutic purgation had become clearly differentiated, the belief was that improving the body improved the self. The stage play *The Family of Love* (another product of material London ca. 1600) satirized the quests for bodily and spiritual perfectibility represented in the fashionable urban pursuit of purgation.

With "London's Vagrant Economy: Making Space for 'Low' Subjectivity," the focus turns to a social problem that also left a substantial textual trace — in public proclamations, prohibitive statutes, and the rogue literature of Thomas Harman, Robert Greene, and Thomas Dekker. Patricia Fumerton argues that members of the displaced classes never enjoyed the subculture that was mythologized for them; instead, theirs was an experience of isolation and alienation. She finds important points of intersection between vagrancy and London. First, the new economy of London was supported by and produced a class of vagrants, pedlars, and working poor who moved the city's consumer goods within London and into the hinterlands; London, in other words, *required* a vagrant class. Second, of the immigrants who flooded into the city, even those who undertook positions of service or apprenticeships became disconnected from their households surprisingly often, swelling the ranks of those who turned vagrant or who picked up and discarded trades as encouraged by the economy. Third, argues Fumerton, the comparative anonymity, disconnection, and mobility of the urban center meant that in many ways "To be a Londoner was to be a vagrant" — not necessarily homeless, but masterless, out of service, single, unplaced, practicing a profession outside the guilds, or shifting occupations at will. The subjectivities produced by these vagrant phenomena did not leave a textual residue. But Fumerton finds analogies for them in the experience of apprenticeship, with its prolonged adolescence, estrangement from home and kin, and prohibition against marriage and attachments. Apprenticeship allowed for extended experimentation with roles and models—which was also the nature of the vagrant experience, with its serial occupations and serial selves, a multiple identity uniquely common to and uniquely visible in London.

From the overview provided by Archer, the essays that follow seem to take soundings at opposing ends of the social scale, with Paster studying elite consumers and Fumerton speaking for the marginal classes. In fact, *The Family of Love* gives evidence that the new luxury therapies were known to all who would have frequented the public theater, even if those who could not afford to practice these treatments were encouraged to view them satirically. Meanwhile, the demands of commerce produced serial or "vagrant" identities and adaptive strategies even among what has been called the "middling sort." If material London reified some social gaps, in other words, it worked to deconstruct others. As these essays make clear, social identities, social hierarchies, and social tensions were mapped in new ways in the consumer culture, and the changes did not pass unexamined by material Londoners.

9

Material Londoners?

Ian W. Archer

What doe you lacke? What is't you buy? Veary fine China stuffes, of all kindes and quallityes? China Chaynes, China Braceletts, China scarfes, China fannes, China girdles, China knives, China boxes, China Cabinetts, Casketts, Umbrellas, Sundyalls, Hower glasses, lookinge glasses, Burninge glasses, Concave glasses, Triangular glasses, Convexe glasses, Christall globes, Waxen pictures, Estrich Egges, Birds of Paradise, Muskads, Indian Mice, Indian ratts, China dogges, and China cattes? Flowrs of silke, Mosaick fishes? Waxen fruict, and Purslane dishes? Very fine cages for Birds, Billyard Balls, Purses, Pipes, rattles, Basons, Ewers, Cups, Cans, Voyders, Toothpicks, Targets, falchions, Beards of all ages, Vizards, Spectacles? See what you lack.[1]

Such was the address made to James I, his wife Queen Anne, and his heir Prince Henry on 11 April 1609 by a character representing a shop boy in the entertainment devised by Ben Jonson (and recently discovered by Dr. James Knowles) at the opening of Britain's Burse, a new retail complex in the Strand built as a speculative enterprise by the lord treasurer, Robert Cecil, earl of Salisbury. The New Exchange, as it was otherwise called, was based on the Royal Exchange built by Sir Thomas Gresham in the heart of the city. Surrounding a large courtyard were two elaborately decorated galleries in which were shops for the sale of all kinds of goods.[2] *The Entertainment for Britain's Burse* frankly acknowledged the benefits of trade, particularly the profusion of exotic goods newly available in the metropolis through the opening up of the East Indies trade. But the entertainment could not entirely conceal the tensions opened up by the culture of consumption it celebrated. Cecil's project had attracted criticism from the city fathers, fearful that it would draw off much of the lucrative west end demand from the ancient City. Cecil, denying any intention to harm Londoners, had affirmed that "when I balance London with Westminster, Middlesex, or rather with all England, then I must conclude that London might suffer some little quill of profit to pass by their main pipe."[3] The entertainment incorporated some sideswipes at city merchants. The shop master proclaimed the superiority of his shop to "divers china houses about town," indeed to "all the magazines of Europe." In an earlier version of the masque, Thomas Wilson, Cecil's agent, records an anti-masque of false wares in which two characters, presumably representing conventional city types, played "their mountebank tricks" handing out trifles, only for one to remove his vizard and "unmask as a merchant that sells not *merces adulterinas*" and hand out rich presents to the spectators.[4] Although the surviving text does not refer to this element of the entertainment, it incorporates sneering references to city types of a kind one is familiar with in Jonson's satires of London life. Among the goods offered by the shopkeeper were a set of spectacles, "an excellent payer of multiplying eyes . . . made at the request of an ould Patriarche of usurers in towne here to see his mony come home in." One of the points of the drama was to stress the distinctive aristocratic ethos of the New Exchange: "All other places give for money, here all is given for love."[5]

The celebration of the treasures newly available in the city's shops was an increasingly common trope of the turn of the century. John Stow's continuator, Edmund Howes, using a language with which his more conservatively minded mentor would probably have been uncomfortable, described the capital as a "citty filled more aboundantly with all sorts of silkes, fine linnen, oyles, wines, & spices, perfection of arts, and all costly ornaments and curious workmanship, then any other province, so as London well deserves to beare the name of the choicest storehouse in the world."[6] The city's commercial wealth received an increasingly frank acknowledgement in the pageants which formed a key element in the elaborate ceremonies accompanying the inauguration of a new lord mayor. Anthony Munday's pageants regularly included allusions to the mayor's craft demonstrating its contribution to national prosperity. In 1605 his water pageant involved the representation of a ship, the *Royal Exchange,* newly returned from the Indies loaded with spices and silks, which its captain orders to be distributed among the crew "to make this up a cheerful holiday"; his 1614 pageant *The Triumphs of Old Drapery* included a representation of English cities "whose best advantage ever ensued by making of woollen cloths for the continuance of England's drapery."[7] The shift from the morality tradition which had predominated in the early Elizabethan pageants to an increasing emphasis on commercial wealth can be paralleled by shifts in the content of the poems of praise for the city identified by Lawrence Manley: whereas in the fifteenth century they had tended to deal in chivalric abstractions, by the later sixteenth century their content had shifted to increasingly concrete images of wealth and commerce.[8]

How far this explosion in the celebration of commerce reflected the emergence of a distinctive material culture is a question which must give us pause. The growth of London fed an expansion in consumer demand in the city.

From a population of about 60,000 in 1500, London grew to be one of the front-rank European cities with a population of 200,000 in 1600. Although some of this growth was due to the subsistence migrants attracted to the city in years of economic difficulty by the capital's charitable resources and by its perceived employment opportunities, it was to a greater degree than is sometimes acknowledged fueled by "betterment" migration, as children from middling provincial backgrounds sought their fortunes in the expanding commercial and manufacturing opportunities of the metropolis. It has been estimated that in the later sixteenth century London needed about 3,750 immigrants each year to sustain its population growth; a very high proportion of these were apprentices.[9] Although by no means were all of these upwardly mobile, their presence contributed to a thickening of the middle station in the city. As the author of *The Apologie of the Citie of London* (1580) commented, "in number they of the middle place be first, and doe farre exceede both the rest; hirelyngs be next, and marchantes bee the last."[10] Wage levels in London were about 50 percent higher than in the countryside, and foreign visitors were impressed by the standard of living of the artisans, particularly their high consumption of meat.[11] William Harrison, an Essex clergyman who also held some London livings, commented on rising standards of domestic comfort among tradesmen: "in the houses . . . of merchantmen, and some other wealthy citizens, it is not geason [uncommon] to behold generally their great provision of tapestry, Turkey work, pewter, brass, fine linen, and thereto costly cupboards of plate. . . . But as herein all these sorts do far exceed their elders and predecessors, and in neatness and curiosity the merchant all other, so in time past the costly furniture stayed there, whereas now it is descended yet lower, even unto the inferior artificers . . . who . . . have for the most part learned also to garnish their cupboards with plate, their joint beds with tapestry and silk hangings, and their tables with carpets and fine napery."[12] The absence of probate inventories from the sixteenth century make it difficult to prove the truth of contemporary assessments such as these, but a survey of a national sample of probate inventories confirms the expansion in the availability of consumer goods in the Elizabethan period.[13]

Growing demand from the middling sections of the city population was one element in the explosion of consumer goods in the metropolis around 1600, but the importance of aristocratic and gentry demand should not be underestimated. The extraordinary growth in litigation in the central courts brought the gentry to London on business, pushing up the demand for grain by 13 percent during the legal terms as early as the 1570s.[14] The presence of the court in the vicinity of the capital was such an important factor in sustaining demand that whenever Elizabeth was absent from Westminster, we are told that "the poore people forthwith complain of penury and want of a hard and miserable world."[15] By 1600 with the proliferation of commercialized entertainment facilities, the London social season had emerged. Many preferred residence in the capital to the countryside holding that it was one of the advantages of metropolitan life that one could choose one's dinner guests, "men of more civilitie, wisdome and worth then your rude Country gentlemen or rusticall neighboures."[16] By 1614 there were already 71 people with claims to gentility in the parish of St. Martin in the Fields alone, by 1629 there were 118, and by 1637, 242.[17] Since F. J. Fisher's classic essay on the subject little work has been done on the precise economic impact of this aristocratic demand, but it was probably a major economic stimulus. By the 1590s individual courtiers were spending up to £1,000 per annum on clothes, as much as 25 percent of the cost of which was consumed in labor. Much of the increase in imports was in luxury commodities like wine and silks. Imports of wine doubled between the 1560s and the 1590s, and doubled again in the following twenty years. Retailing facilities like Goldsmiths' Row directed at an elite clientele consistently attracted favorable publicity.[18]

The growth in demand was reflected in changes in the extent and nature of retailing within the city. Changes were discernible as early as 1549 when Sir Thomas Smith reflected on the proliferation of haberdashers' shops: "I have sene within these xxtie yeres, when there weare not of these haberdashers that sell french or millane capes, glasses, Daggers, swerdes, girdles and such thinges, not a dossen in all London. And now from the towere to westminster alonge, everie streat is full of them; and their shoppes glisters and shine of glasses, as well lookinge as drinckinge, yea all mannor vessells of the same stuffe, painted cruses, gaye daggers, knives, swordes, and girdles, that is able to make anie temporate man to gase on them and to bie sumwhat."[19] Retail spaces by the later sixteenth century were larger than their medieval predecessors. Derek Keene has pointed out how the pressure of population in the later sixteenth century caused land values in the inner city to rise to the levels of the thirteenth century. But whereas in the thirteenth century very small shops had been normal, by 1600 retailing units were larger, reflecting changes in the organization of trade. Thus a Cheapside location formerly known as the "Broad Seld" had contained four shops and a number of small booths, but when rebuilt in 1530 as "The Key" it contained only one great shop measuring sixty feet by twenty-one feet.[20] Some businesses expanded over several tenements. Reyner Wolf had built a printing shop on the site of the former charnel house of St. Paul's and acquired leases of adjacent properties in subsequent years, so that by the time of his death in 1573 he owned 120 feet of the best bookselling frontage in England in St. Paul's churchyard.[21] The appearance of shopping malls in the Royal and New Exchanges was another manifestation of a changed retailing environment. Although the booths in the Royal Exchange were very small ($7'6''$ by $5'$) the novelty lay in the concentration of so many (150) shops under one roof.[22]

The celebration of wealth did not go unchallenged. The acquisitive drive on which the city's wealth rested sat uneasily with the dictates of Christian morality. Preachers did not pull their punches in fulminating against covetousness, identified by silver-tongued Henry Smith, lecturer at St. Clement Dane's, as "the Londoners sin." Smith could hardly have been more pointed when he warned that "the riches and lands of aldermen and merchants and other in London do not last so long nor indure so well as the riches and lands of others in the countrey," and found the explanation in the providential chastising of the elite for their usury.[23] Richard Turnbull, the minister at St. Pancras Soper Lane, a stone's throw from the bustling thoroughfare of Cheapside, held that the rich could be considered accursed because of their tyranny in oppressing the poor through usury and engrossing.[24] To the claims that usurers "doe good service in the citie, are very profitable members, and might be ill spared," William Fisher replied that "if you take him and looke in his mouth, you shall see his teeth all gore blood with eating and devouring his needy debtors."[25] Andrew Willet denounced fraudulent mercantile practices: "a trade well knowne to many merchantes in this cittie whoe what with bad and naughty wares what with excessive and unreasonable prises doo even no better than steale from their brethren."[26] Turnbull, Fisher, and Willet were among the most popular preachers of their day. How could their commercial auditory have sat through this kind of diatribe with a clear conscience? Richard Allington, afflicted with apparitions "lyke puppets" on his death-bed in 1561, undertook to repay all the money he had gained through a lifetime's usury coming to a total of £1,800, but his case was sufficiently rare to merit attention from the chroniclers![27]

But there were means by which the tensions between Christian morality and commercial acquisitiveness could be negotiated. We should be aware that the stereotypes of the avaricious and deceitful tradesmen do not capture the full range of contemporary trading practice: it was perhaps through these stereotypes that goals for appropriate behavior were set. Writers like Nicholas Breton, employing the binary systems of classification which so characterized popular thinking, distinguished between a type of the "good merchant" and a type of the "bad merchant" in his contribution to the character literature; ballads in the early 1630s set out competing versions of tradesmen's standards, *The Honest Age* answering *Knavery in All Trades,* but both works serving to underscore the same message about ideals of appropriate conduct.[28] Much more work needs to be done on the nature of business ethics in this period, and the records of the central equity courts will doubtless prove a useful resource. But there are several indications that the position is likely to be more complex than the stylized denunciations of covetousness suggest. Credit was maintained by one's ability to mobilize friends to stand surety for one's loans, and reputation seems to have depended on honesty and plain-dealing. There were strong collective pressures through the guilds for honest trading practices: not only was guild honor (a by no means negligible quality) at stake, but also guildsmen had an interest in preventing the kind of deceptions by which other traders and craftsmen might be able to undercut prices.[29] In negotiating prices, contemporaries agreed that the golden mean was the guiding principle: "you must deal by another, as you would regularly have them deal by you," but (intriguingly) when dealing with someone who was poorer, "you must endeavor that it be more to his commodity than yours."[30] The implication that one observed different standards as between one's social equals and one's inferiors is highly suggestive and in need of further investigation.

There are indications of more positive evaluations of the contribution of merchants to the commonwealth around the turn of the century. Rather than engaging in the generalized denunciations of covetousness which had characterized the mid-Tudor commonwealthmen, the arguments of the moralists become more nuanced, stressing the lawfulness and utility (even in some cases, the nobility) of the merchant's calling, while also pointing to the dangers to which it is subject. Thus Immanuel Bourne, preacher at St. Christopher le Stocks, explained to his auditory at Paul's Cross in 1619 that "buying and selling in its owne nature is a calling lawfull necessary and commendable." Not only were merchants responsible for the exchange of necessary commodities, but "by this [trade] we have gotten acquaintance with forreigne nations and the Kingdom of Christ hath beene enlarged, by this we have leagues of amitie contracted with people of divers languages, by this we have gotten knowledge and experience in severall sciences." Biblical references confirmed the lawfulness of the calling: "merchandise hath beene auncient even in the dayes of Noah"; the patriarch Jacob in his institution of the commonwealth of Israel "gave every of his sons a calling," including that of merchant to Zebulon (Gen. 49:13); St. John the Baptist did not condemn but instructed merchants in their callings (Luke 3:13); Christ had used mercantile imagery in talking about heaven (Matt. 13:45–46). Merchandise only became unlawful when its end was covetousness rather than the maintenance of the merchant's family "according to that decency which is fitting for his state and calling" (the qualifier being capable of a certain amount of subjective interpretation).[31]

Other preachers engaged with the world of commerce through the development of a commercial casuistry. To his sermon before the Grocers' Company in 1619, Thomas Cooper appended a series of cases of conscience, such as "whether we may use such meanes for the gathering of riches as mans law doth tollerate . . . as usury, monopolies, trading with infidels . . . &c." His answer was found in the law of equity: "that whatsoever is not against the law of equitie and charitie without intent to deceive as would be done unto, that may lawfully be done herein."[32] Preachers were careful to distinguish between lawful profits and lending without labor. Richard Turnbull explained that his attack on usury was "nothing preiudicial unto the dangerous adventures of lawfull marchants, neither condemneth it tollerable gaine in the retailing occupier, whereof the one fetcheth wares farre of with great danger, the other venteth them with labor and industrie: therefore in good conscience they make gaine of theyr labours."[33] "Not every loan which bringeth some gain above the stock is to be counted usury," explained Andrew Willett. With the evolution of a theology which emphasized the primacy of the individual conscience guided by God, the sin of usury became an internal matter, and lending at interest need not be counted usury if the parties were in charity with each other.[34]

If the values of the church represented one source of tension with the values of commercial acquisitiveness, the values of the gentry were another. In the mid-sixteenth century the predominant position was that mercantile pursuits were incompatible with gentility. The noted humanist pedagogue Richard Mulcaster asserted that "of all the meanes to make a gentleman, it is the most vile to be made for money"; the herald Gerard Legh claimed that the only road to gentility was service in war or in a royal or magnate's household; the man of affairs, Sir Thomas Chaloner wanted to prevent merchants from acquiring land save for suburban villas. There were dissentient voices like Sir Thomas Smith who stressed the primary role of wealth as a component of gentility in so far as it provided the means to support status, and Thomas Churchyard who numbered among the four sorts of nobility or gentlemen "merchauntes that sails forrain countreys and brynges home commodities and after great hazardes abroad do utter their ware with regard of conscience and profite to the publike estate." But the strength of the prejudice against merchants is suggested by the fact that Mulcaster was headmaster of Merchant-Taylors' School in the City, Legh the son of a draper and himself a member of the London Company of Drapers, and Chaloner the son of a London mercer. Even men as familiar as they were with the world of the city had internalized the dominant values.[35]

Over the course of the Elizabethan and Jacobean decades, more positive evaluations of the merchants emerged and the dissentient voices more frequently expressed. Laura Stevenson has shown how on the London stage the stock figure of the usurer came to be supplanted by more favorable representations of merchants as benefactors of the people and heroic defenders of the kingdom's rulers, displaying the essentially aristocratic qualities of magnanimity, courtliness, and chivalry.[36] While it is true that the plays performed in the private playhouses in the early seventeenth century presented some spectacularly rapacious city ogres, their targets are often broader, as the folly of *all* social groups is ruthlessly exposed, and their messages more ambivalent, because it was only certain forms of citizen behavior that were satirized.[37] By the 1620s comedies were appearing which suggested that merchants did not always threaten aristocratic values. Richard Helgerson, working on a different genre, that of the colonial projectors, has drawn attention to the way some were coming to recognize the contribution of the merchant to national prosperity. Whereas the Portuguese writer Camoes evaluated the imperial enterprise primarily in terms of the fame and glory that would ensue, Richard Hakluyt (intriguingly a clergyman who enjoyed the patronage of the Clothworkers' Company) thought in much more explicitly economic terms. "Commodity" and "vent" were his watchwords, and insofar as he equated wealth and honor with overseas trade, he was stressing that merchants were exceptionally important Englishmen. Helgerson concludes that Hakluyt's *Principal Navigations* "brings merchants into the nation and brings gentry into trade."[38] Although the process by which the gentry became reconciled to commercial values was protracted and always partial, by the early seventeenth century more commentators seem to have been willing to make concessions to the merchant. John Wheeler, the secretary of the Merchant Adventurers' Company, argued in 1601 that nobles could trade without derogating from their nobility.[39] Edmund Bolton denied that apprenticeship was a mark of servitude, stressing instead the relationship of teacher and pupil inscribed within it, and praising merchants and wholesalers as "most generous mysteries."[40]

There was then something schizophrenic about the attitudes of contemporaries to the wealth of the London business elite. Playwrights like Jonson and Middleton combined the writing of pageants which celebrated the benefits of the city's wealth with the writing of comedies which ruthlessly exposed the money-grubbing charlatans operating within the capital. The city's indefatigable chronicler John Stow admired the charitable endeavors of earlier generations of London merchants but felt uneasy about the social mobility released by the generation of wealth, recording with grim satisfaction the fate of Alderman Sir John Champeneys — whose presumption in building a brick tower in his house to overlook his neighbors was punished with blindness — and commenting of Thomas Cromwell's arbitrary seizure of surrounding properties to extend his garden, that "the suddaine rising of some men causeth them to forget themselves."[41] Likewise, John Taylor, the water poet, recently analyzed by Bernard Capp, combined an admiration for urban life and its amenities with an awareness that economic development and full employment were incompatible with Christian values.[42]

Crucial to the negotiation of these tensions was the notion that the rich owed obligations to the poor. "The rich are but tenants at will and stewards for others and must give up their account . . . it is not the having of aboundance but the right use thereof which is the blessing of God," declared Thomas Cooper entirely conventionally.[43] These messages were driven home repeatedly. Benefactors were commemorated through tables of charities, stained glass windows, portraits, and statues. Guilds and parishes recited the names of benefactors and sermons commemorated the works of worthy Londoners. The popular press churned out epitaphs mourning the passing of virtuous merchants like Robert Dowe, merchant tailor, who "whilst he lived was a mirror of charity, and now being dead is a true pattern of perfect Christianity."[44]

To articulate the social order in terms of the ties of reciprocity, the wealth of the rich offering benefits to the poor and creating vertically integrated communities, was to stand in the face of certain brute facts about metropolitan life in the later sixteenth and early seventeenth centuries. London offered the most startling juxtapositions of wealth and poverty. By comparison with other towns her elite was fabulously rich. Robert Lang's study of the business fortunes of the Jacobean aldermen suggests that about 40 percent of them possessed inventories of over £20,000, whereas none of the merchants of Elizabethan and Jacobean Exeter analyzed by W. G. Hoskins could muster more than £5,000.[45] Londoners, it is true, did not flaunt their wealth as conspicuously as the aristocracy. As Fynes Moryson reports of their houses, "they are stately for building, yet being built all inward, that the whole roome towards the streete may be reserved for the shops of tradesmen, makes no show outwardly, so as in truth all the magnificence of London building is hidden from strangers at the first sight."[46] But magnificent their houses often were. Sir William Craven, lord mayor in 1610–11, resided from 1607 in the former Zouche's Inn, recently fashionably rebuilt by another alderman, Sir Robert Lee. It was set back from the street, but the house's suite of rooms nevertheless advertised the claims of its owner to status: there was a great hall, a great parlor, a great dining chamber, and a gallery. The great hall's scheme of decoration incorporated a carved screen with Queen Elizabeth's arms and cupboards "all carved and garnished with imagery"; the great parlor was wainscotted and its alabaster chimney piece was surmounted by the Queen's arms and carvings of St. George, Justice, and Charity; other rooms were wainscotted and had marble hearths or painted tiles. In the garden was a paved walk leading to a banqueting house.[47] Sir John Spencer, the fabulously wealthy Turkey merchant and unpopular lord mayor of 1594–95, owned not only one of the most lavish of the older city mansions, Crosby Place in Bishopsgate Street, but also a pleasure palace at Canonbury in Islington to which he added elaborate chimney places and plaster ceilings (some still extant).[48]

The poor, by contrast, were stuffed into the rapidly proliferating alleys and subdivided tenements. In the words of the largely futile royal proclamation of 1580 prohibiting new building within a three-mile radius, "great multitudes of people [had been] brought to inhabit in small rooms whereof a great part are seen very poor, yea such as must live of begging or by worse means, and they heaped up together, and in a sort smothered with many families of children and servants in one house or small tenement."[49] Many shared cramped conditions with other families, living in single rooms just twelve foot square, and often deprived of the basic amenities like privies.[50] With residents of alleys paying as much as twenty to forty shillings per annum, the rents they paid were disproportionately high (pensions to the poor paid from the poor rate ran at sixpence per week). Those living in alleys were vulnerable to other forms of exploitation by their landlords, particularly through the operation of truck systems. John Howes, an official of Christ's Hospital, gives us a graphic picture of the alley landlords, "sytting in theire maiestie in a cheire in the chymney corner," calling the poor to them saying: "sirra, would you be our tenaunte. Yea, forsoothe saithe the poore man. Wee must have our rent wekely payde us, saie they. Ye shall, forsoothe, saith the poore man. You must fetch your bread, beeare, butter and cheese, wood and coale of us. Yea, forsooth, maysters, with many a crooked courtesie." Residential propinquity of rich and poor was no guarantee of harmonious social relations.[51]

The moralists regarded the problem of the capital's poverty as being exacerbated both by rapacious consumption and by the aggressive business practices which accompanied economic expansion. Consumption of superfluities withdrew resources from poor relief and weakened overall national resources; the poor frittered away their resources in idle pastimes, and excessive consumption impoverished citizens. Thus in the case of feasting, the authorities tried to drive home the connection between consumption by the rich and the growth of poverty by calling for fasting in times of dearth and seeking to curtail the cycle of lavish guild feasting, the monies saved to be directed to poor relief. But moralists like Richard Turnbull were skeptical as to whether their directions had been observed: "Did not they in the great famine of the land (wherwith the poore were miserably pinched) sit eating and drinking, feeding themselves and feasting, banquetting and surfetting."[52] Likewise, money spent on clothing could be better directed to poor relief: Henry Smith claimed to know people with as many as twenty coats who refused to support the poor.[53] Another common theme in contemporary economic discourse was the way in which money was being drained away from the country because of an allegedly unfavorable balance of trade resulting from English people's pursuit of imported foreign luxuries. Philip Stubbes expressed frustration with the failure of Englishmen to be content "with such attire as our owne country doeth minister unto us"; Burghley anxiously noted the "excess of silkes, . . . of wyne and spyce," regarding any measures to promote them as a means to "consent to the robbery of the realm."[54] The haunting of alehouses and taverns was seen as a factor in impoverishment as well as contributing to drunkenness, while the temptations of dicing houses brought about the decay of citizens.[55] Economic oppression, as we have already seen, was denounced in uncompromising terms, and among the regular targets of moral denunciation for their contribution to poverty were usurers and landlords of alleys.

It was not only the division between rich and poor that was focused by the increasingly conspicuous consumption of the later sixteenth and early seventeenth centuries. For consumption also contributed to the anxieties about the position of women and the young in the capital. The position of both women and the young in early modern London was at odds with elements of the prevailing patriarchal ideology, and the inevitable result was a flurry of regulative concern. London was remarkable for the extraordinary number of young males in its population, apprentices accounting for about 12 percent of London's population in the mid-sixteenth century. That such a high proportion of the population should have been subject to the kind of constraints which apprenticeship placed upon accumulation, sexual expression, and the free use of leisure time was a major source of friction in metropolitan society. The irksome nature of these constraints was underscored by the fact that many apprentices, particularly in the retailing and mercantile trades, came from gentle backgrounds, and clashed regularly with that other youth group who enjoyed much greater freedom, the gentlemen studying at the inns of court.[56] Women probably enjoyed more independence in the capital because of the nature of their work, participating at the front of the shop, running an alehouse, buying provisions in the market. But certain demographic peculiarities of the metropolitan scene help to account for the intensity of anxieties about women. High mortality in London meant that many households, no less than 16 percent in Southwark in the 1620s, were headed by women; it also meant that remarriage in the capital was common; no less than 25 percent of the marriages of London tradesmen were to widows, running counter to the recommendations of the moralists that the husband should always be older, and thereby giving women greater leverage within the household. The lack of confinement of women in the capital impressed foreign visitors who commented on their drinking in taverns and engaging in unsupervised sports with members of the opposite sex.[57]

In both cases the exploitation of the opportunities and temptations of the city's consumer culture focused anxieties because participation by apprentices and women threatened to erode social boundaries. "Of late time servants and apprentices within the city are by indulgence and lack of convenient severity grown to great disorder in excess of apparel and fashions thereof uncomely for their calling," declared the mayor's proclamation of 1572 which formed the basis for later regulative drives.[58] Groups of apprentices like those who banqueted, gambled, and whored at the Bell tavern and were brought before the Bridewell governors in December 1576 aroused particular anxiety because they had broken key elements of their covenants, cheating their masters, resorting to places of ill repute without permission, and engaging in the explicitly forbidden sexual relations.[59] In acting in this way they were probably imitating the leisure and consumption patterns of gentlemen from which social milieu they (as merchants' apprentices) probably sprang. As William Gouge put it, "clerks, prentices, waiting women and such like, being borne gentlemen and men of good degree, are for the most part guilty of this fault: the reason is because their birth and parentage maketh them forget their present place and condition; or else maketh them wilfully presume above it."[60] The status uncertainties of those apprentices who came from substantial backgrounds were vented in attacks on the peers and gentry and their servants when they ventured in to the city. In 1621 the aldermen had to issue a proclamation warning householders to instruct their apprentices "from henceforth civilly and orderly [to] behave and demean themselves without ill or unseemly gestures," and to allow the coaches of peers, nobles, and gentry to pass through the streets without bouts of name-calling.[61]

As Karen Newman has observed, consumption was seen as an activity to which women were conspicuously (and dangerously) prone.[62] Foreigners like Jacob Rathgeb, visiting London in 1592, were impressed by "the exceedingly fine clothes" of London women of relatively meagre means, for they "give all their attention to their ruffs and stuffs to such a degree indeed that . . . many a one does not hesitate to wear velvet in the streets, which is common with them, whilst perhaps at home they have not a piece of dry bread."[63] Ben Jonson gives vent to the anxieties produced by women's attractions for the city life in his play *Epicoene* (performed soon after the opening of Britain's Burse), which satirizes the rapacity of women, verbal, intellectual, and material. In the play, Truewit attempts to dissuade Morose from marriage by warning him of the

limitless desire of women for consumer goods: "She must have that rich gown
for such a great day, a new one for the next, a richer for the third; be served in
silver; have the chamber filled with a succession of grooms, footmen, ushers,
and other messengers, besides embroiderers, jewellers, tire-women, semp-
sters, feathermen, perfumers."[64] Similar themes emerge in ballads where the
hen-pecked city husband is scolded by his wife for ever more consumer goods:
"even to my disgrace/ My neighbours exceed me in dressings and lace/ I will
have a silke Gowne, a Maske, and a Fanne."[65] When a mercer went bankrupt in
1601, the city gossips drew what within this framework of prejudices was the
obvious conclusion when it became known that his wife had thirty smocks
valued at £60.[66] In 1616 in a major speech in Star Chamber, James I opined that
"one of the greatest causes of all gentlemen's desire, that have no calling or
errand, to dwell in London, is apparently the pride of women. For if they bee
wives, then their husbands, and if they be maydes, then their fathers, must
bring them up to London because the new fashion is to be had nowhere but in
London." Not only did the king engage in periodic (and largely ineffective)
campaigns to drive the gentry out of London, but he also picked specifically on
female apparel, tuning the pulpits in 1620 by instructing preachers to tackle
the problem.[67]

Consumption was a moral problem because the desire for goods was
linked with sexual desire. The Christian tradition had conflated luxuria and
lust: luxury was equated with desire, and desire with disobedience.[68] Contemporary moralists regularly drove home the parallels between prostitution and
trade: "The setting up of a whore house is now as common as the setting up of
a trade," the bawd's "shop has the best ware"; "if as their ends, their fruits were
so, the same, / Bawdry, and usury were one kind of game."[69] The drama
suggests that shopping expeditions by court gallants were as much occasions
for sexual aggression against citizens' wives as for the purchasing of goods.
There is some evidence to suggest that tradesmen placed their wives in prominent positions to entice passers-by into making purchases. From Marston's
Dutch Courtesan we learn that "in troth a fine fac'd wife in a wainscot carved
seat is a worthy ornament to a tradesman's shop, and an attractive I'll warrant;
her husband shall find it in the custom of his ware, I'll assure him."[70] In 1619 a
contemporary observed of the New Exchange that "thy shops with pretty
wenches swarm / Which for thy custom are a kind of charm to idle gallants."[71]
Thus shopping became a locus for anxieties about the gender order: the apparent availability of women in the shops and the desire of city women for consumer goods threatened the patriarchal order on which the authority of citizen
husbands rested.

It will be clear from the foregoing that the consumerism of the turn of the century focused anxieties along all the major faultlines within metropolitan society: we have seen the ways in which it fueled tensions between citizens and gentlemen, rich and poor, men and women, young and old. How far the tensions really were greater than at any other period and how far the moral anxieties merely gave new and/or intensified forms of rhetorical expression to long-standing tensions within metropolitan society remain subjects for debate. It would be wise to end the chapter, however, with a reminder of some of the ways in which the anxieties may have been exaggerated, and the tensions negotiated. For all the dramatic representation of conflict between citizens and gentlemen, there were many areas in which they cooperated. For many courtiers their ties to shopkeepers were characterized by relationships of patronage and clientage rather than strict economic exchanges; they cooperated in overseas trading ventures and in the operation of economic concessionary interests; noblemen and gentlemen were regular guests at company feasts.[72] Rather than engaging in an orgy of consumer spending, most citizens were frugal: where they did spend lavishly it was on plate and linenware, elements which stressed their hospitable role.[73] It is difficult to identify a distinctive youth culture marked out by different conceptualizations of time, leisure, and work from those of the elite when so many apprentices participated vigorously in the cycle of godly observances and enjoyed the trust of their masters. Likewise, it is difficult to see a real crisis in gender relations in this period. Given the burdens of child-rearing and the marginal nature of most of the economic activities open to them, women possessed very weak occupational identities; denied participation in guild structures, save as widows carrying on their husbands' businesses, they lacked institutional means of expression. Tensions between rich and poor were alleviated to some extent through the operation of charity. Sir William Craven, whose house we explored earlier, was one of the London godly, and a man with a consistent record of charitable involvement; he was a major benefactor to the Merchant-Taylors' Company, his birthplace of Burnsall in Yorkshire, St. John's College, Oxford, and Christ's Hospital, of which he was a most assiduous president (1611–18). Even Sir John Spencer, who enjoyed a bleak reputation because of his failure to give monies to city charities, may have been the victim of his spendthrift son-in-law, Lord Compton, who probably suppressed the will. Collective values retained a powerful hold in London (and would continue to do so), blunting the force of the individualist ethos contemporary moralists claimed had been released in the economic growth and consumerism of the capital.[74]

Notes

1. J. Knowles, "Jonson's Entertainment at Britain's Burse: Text and Context," in *Re-Presenting Ben Jonson: Text, History, Performance,* ed. M. Butler (Basingstoke and London: Macmillan, 1999), p. 133; PRO, SP14/44/62*.

2. L. Stone, *Family and Fortune: Studies in Aristocratic Finance in the Sixteenth and Seventeenth Centuries* (Oxford: Oxford University Press, 1973), pp. 95–105; J. Knowles, "Shopping with Cecil: A New Ben Jonson Masque Discovered," *Times Literary Supplement* (7 February 1997), pp. 14–15; Knowles, "Jonson's Entertainment."

3. Stone, *Family and Fortune,* pp. 96–97.

4. *Calendar of the Manuscripts of the . . . Marquis of Salisbury . . . Preserved at Hatfield House,* 24 vols. (London: HMSO, 1883–1976), 21:37.

5. Knowles, "Jonson's Entertainment," p. 136, Knowles, "Shopping with Cecil," pp. 14–15.

6. J. Stow, *Abridgement of the Chronicles of England* (London, 1611), letter dedicatory; cf. T. Johnson, *Cornucopiae, Or Divers Secrets* (London, 1596), sigs. F2r–v.

7. A. Munday, *The Triumphs of Re-United Britannia* (London, 1605); A. Munday, *Himatia-Poleos: The Triumphs of Olde Draperie* (London, 1614).

8. L. Manley, *London in the Age of Shakespeare* (London and Sydney: Croom Helm, 1986), pp. 51–52.

9. S. Rappaport, *Worlds Within Worlds: The Structures of Life in Sixteenth-Century London* (Cambridge: Cambridge University Press, 1989), pp. 76–77; *London, 1500–1700: The Making of the Metropolis,* ed. A. L. Beier and R. Finlay (Harlow: Longmans, 1986), pp. 9–10; E. A. Wrigley, "A Simple Model of London's Importance in Changing English Society and Economy, 1650–1750," in *People, Cities, and Wealth,* ed. E. A. Wrigley (Oxford: Basil Blackwell, 1989), pp. 134–37.

10. J. Stow, *A Survey of London,* ed. C. L. Kingsford, 2 vols. (Oxford: Oxford University Press, 1908), 2:208.

11. J. Chartres, "Food Consumption and Internal Trade," in *London, 1500–1700,* pp. 170–72; *Antiquarian Repertory* 4 (1809): 510; "The London Journal of Alessandro Magno 1562," ed. C. M. Barron, C. Coleman, and C. Gobbi, *London Journal* 9 (1983): 142–43.

12. W. Harrison, *The Description of England,* ed. G. Edelen (Washington, D.C.: Folger Shakespeare Library, 1968), p. 200.

13. C. Muldrew, *The Economy of Obligation: The Culture of Credit and Social Relations in Early Modern England* (Basingstoke and London: Macmillan, 1998), pp. 21–36.

14. F. J. Fisher, "The Development of London as a Centre of Conspicuous Consumption in the Sixteenth and Seventeenth Centuries," in F. J. Fisher, *London and the Economy, 1500–1700,* ed. P. J. Corfield and N. B. Harte (London and Ronceverte: Hambledon, 1990), pp. 105–18; Corporation of London Records Office (hereafter, CLRO), Repertory 18, fols. 182v–86r.

15. J. Norden, *Speculum Britanniae: The First Parte. An Historicall and Chorographicall Discription of Middlesex* (London, 1593), p. 47.

16. *Cyvile and Uncyvile Lyfe: A Discourse Very Profitable, Pleasant and Fit to be Read of all Nobilitie and Gentlemen* (London, 1579).

17. R. M. Smuts, "The Court and Its Neighbourhood: Royal Policy and Urban Growth in the Early Stuart West End," *Journal of British Studies* 30 (1991): 122.

18. Fisher, "Development of London"; L. Stone, *The Crisis of the Aristocracy, 1558–1641* (Oxford: Oxford University Press, 1965), chpt. 10; J. Arnold, *Queen Elizabeth's Wardrobe Unlock'd* (Leeds: W. S. Maney & Son, 1988); Public Record Office (hereafter, PRO), SP14/37/8; B. Dietz, "Overseas Trade and Metropolitan Growth," in *London, 1500–1700,* pp. 123–26; T. F. Reddaway, "Elizabethan London: Goldsmiths' Row in Cheapside, 1558–1645," *Guildhall Miscellany* 2 (1963): 181–206.

19. *A Discourse of the Commonweal of this Realm of England,* ed. E. Lamond (Cambridge: Cambridge University Press, 1895), p. 64; *Tudor Economic Documents,* ed. R. H. Tawney and E. Power, 3 vols. (London: Longmans, Green & Co., 1924), 3: 111.

20. D. Keene, "Shops and Shopping in Medieval London," *Medieval Art, Architecture, and Archaeology in London,* ed. L. Grant (British Archaeological Association, 1990).

21. P. W. M. Blayney, *The Bookshops in Paul's Cross Churchyard,* Occasional Papers of the Bibliographical Society, 5 (1990).

22. *The Royal Exchange,* ed. A. Saunders (London: London Topographical Society, 1997), pp. 36–49, 59–67.

23. H. Smith, *Sermons* (London, 1591), p. 231.

24. R. Turnbull, *An Exposition Upon the Canonicall Epistle of Saint James* (London, 1606), p. 104.

25. W. Fisher, *A Sermon at Paules Crosse* (London, 1580), sigs. D2r–v.

26. A. Willet, *A Fruitfull and Godly Sermon Preached at Pauls Cross 1592* (London, 1592), sig. B3v. Cf. J. Hall, *The Righteous Mammon. An Hospitall Sermon* (London, 1618), pp. 31–35; C. Richardson, *A Sermon Against Oppression and Fraudulent Dealing* (London, 1615), pp. 17–23.

27. *Three Fifteenth-Century Chronicles with Historical Memoranda,* ed. J. Gairdner (Camden Society, new series, no. 28, 1880), pp. 117–21.

28. N. Breton, *The Good and the Badde Or Descriptions of the Worthies and Unworthies of this Age* (London, 1616), pp. 18–19; T. Fuller, *The Holy State* (London, 1642), pp. 113–16, 119–23; *A Pepysian Garland: Black Letter Broadside Ballads of the Years 1595 to 1639,* ed. H. E. Rollins (Cambridge: Cambridge University Press, 1922), pp. 410–20.

29. Muldrew, *Economy of Obligation,* chpts. 5–7; J. Ward, *Metropolitan Communities: Trade Guilds, Identity, and Change in Early Modern London* (Stanford: Stanford University Press, 1997), chpt. 3.

30. Muldrew, *Economy of Obligation,* pp. 43–46.

31. I. Bourne, *The Godly Man's Guide With a Direction for All Especially Merchants and Tradesmen* . . . (London, 1619), pp. 25–39. Cf. R. Barckley, *A Discourse of the Felicitie of Man* (London, 1598), pp. 368–69; T. Holland, *A Sermon Preached at Pauls in London on 17 of November 1599* (London, 1601), sig. E1v; R. Wilkinson, *The Merchant Royall. A Sermon Preached at Whitehall* . . . (London, 1607), p. 17; D. Price, *The Marchant. A Sermon Preached at Paules Crosse* (London, 1608), p. 17.

32. N. Jones, *God and the Moneylenders: Usury and Law in Early Modern England* (Oxford: Basil Blackwell, 1989), chpt. 6; T. Cooper, *The Worldlings Adventure* (London, 1619), pp. 62ff.

33. Turnbull, *Exposition on Saint James,* sig. E4r.

34. A. Willet, *Hexapla on Exodus* (London, 1608), pp. 509–11.

35. J. P. Cooper, "Ideas of Gentility in Early Modern England," in his *Land, Men, and Beliefs* (London: Hambledon, 1983), pp. 56–59, where the quotations will be found.

36. L. C. Stevenson, *Praise and Paradox: Merchants and Craftsmen in Elizabethan Popular Literature* (Cambridge: Cambridge University Press, 1984).

37. B. Gibbons, *Jacobean City Comedy: A Study of Satirical Plays by Jonson, Marston, and Middleton* (London: Hart-Davis, 1968), pp. 118–19; L. Venuti, *Our Halcyon Dayes: English Pre-Revolutionary Texts and Post-Modern Culture* (Madison: University of Wisconsin Press, 1989), pp. 130–36; M. Butler, *Theatre and Crisis, 1632–1642* (Cambridge: Cambridge University Press, 1984), chpt. 7.

38. R. Helgerson, *Forms of Nationhood: The Elizabethan Writing of England* (Chicago and London: University of Chicago Press, 1992), chpt. 4.

39. J. Wheeler, *A Treatise of Commerce,* ed. G. B. Hotchkiss (New York: Columbia University Press, 1931), pp. 6–7.

40. E. Bolton, *The Cities Advocate* (London, 1629).

41. Stow, *Survey,* 1:104–17, 133, 151–52, 179.

42. B. Capp, *The World of John Taylor the Water Poet, 1578–1653* (Oxford: Oxford University Press, 1994), p. 108.

43. Cooper, *Worldlings Adventure,* pp. 32, 34.

44. A. Nixon, *London's Dove* (London, 1612). I hope to publish my work on "The Arts and Acts of Memorialisation in Early Modern London" shortly. In the meantime, see I. W. Archer, "The Nostalgia of John Stow," in *The Theatrical City: Culture, Theatre, and Politics in London 1576–1649,* ed. D. L. Smith, R. Strier, and D. Bevington (Cambridge: Cambridge University Press, 1995), pp. 31–32.

45. R. G. Lang, "The Greater Merchants of London in the Seventeenth Century," Ph.D. diss., University of Oxford, 1963; W. G. Hoskins, "The Elizabethan Merchants of Exeter," in *Elizabethan Government and Society: Essays Presented to Sir John Neale,* ed. S. T. Bindoff, J. Hurstfield, and C. H. Williams (London: Athlone Press, 1961), pp. 172–73.

46. F. Moryson, *An Itinerary* (London, 1617), sig. Kkk4r.

47. J. Schofield, *Medieval London Houses* (New Haven and London: Yale University Press, 1995), pp. 161–63, 194–95, 233–35.

48. H. W. Fincham, *An Historical Account of Canonbury House* (London, 1926); P. Norman, *Crosby Place* (London: Survey of London, monograph no. 9, 1908).

49. *Tudor Royal Proclamations,* ed. P. L. Hughes and J. F. Larkin, 3 vols. (New Haven and London: Yale University Press, 1964–69), 2:466.

50. *The London Surveys of Ralph Treswell,* ed. J. Schofield (London: London Topographical Society, 1987), pp. 132–33, 136–37.

51. I. W. Archer, *The Pursuit of Stability: Social Relations in Elizabethan London* (Cambridge: Cambridge University Press, 1991), p. 192; *Tudor Economic Documents,* 3:427.

52. Turnbull, *Exposition,* p. 287.

53. Smith, *The Poore Mans Teares. A Sermon* (London, 1592), pp. 19–20; cf. R. L. Greaves, *Society and Religion in Elizabethan England* (Minneapolis: University of Minnesota Press, 1981), pp. 471–83, 502–20.

54. P. Stubbes, *Anatomie of Abuses* (London, 1583), sig. C1r; *Tudor Economic Documents,* 2: 124–27.

55. Greaves, *Society and Religion,* pp. 483–90; G. Whetstone, *A Touchstone for the Time* (London, 1584).

56. Rappaport, *Worlds Within Worlds,* pp. 388–93; P. Griffiths, *Youth and Authority: Formative Experiences in England, 1560–1640* (Oxford: Oxford University Press, 1996); Archer, *Pursuit of Stability,* pp. 3–4.

57. J. P. Boulton, *Neighbourhood and Society: A London Suburb in the Seventeenth Century* (Cambridge: Cambridge University Press, 1987), pp. 127–29; V. Brodsky, "Widows in Late Elizabethan London: Remarriage, Economic Opportunity, and Family Orientations," in *The World We Have Gained,* ed. L. Bonfield, R. M. Smith, and K. Wrightson (Oxford: Basil Blackwell, 1986), pp. 122–54; L. Gowing, *Domestic Dangers: Women, Words, and Sex in Early Modern London* (Oxford: Oxford University Press, 1996); "Journal of Magno," p. 144.

58. CLRO, Journal of Common Council 20, fols. 13–14, 343v, 350v, 351; Griffiths, *Youth and Authority,* pp. 221–29.

59. Guildhall Library, Bridewell Hospital Court Book, III, fols. 113–114v, 138v–39v.

60. W. Gouge, *Works,* 2 vols. (London, 1627), 1:334–35.

61. Griffiths, *Youth and Authority,* pp. 126–7.

62. K. Newman, "City Talk: Women and Commodification," in *Staging the Renaissance: Reinterpretations of Elizabethan and Jacobean Drama,* ed. D. S. Kastan and P. Stallybrass (New York and London: Routledge, 1991), pp. 181–95.

63. W. B. Rye, *England as Seen by Foreigners in the Days of Elizabeth and James the First* (London: J. T. Smith, 1865), pp. 7–8, 13, 71–73, 89–90.

64. B. Jonson, *Epicoene,* ed. R. V. Holdsworth (London: Ernest Benn, 1979), 2.2.101–5.

65. *A Pepysian Garland,* pp. 207–11.

66. *The Letters of John Chamberlain,* ed. N. McLure, 2 vols. (Philadelphia: American Philosophical Society, 1939), 1:166.

67. *The Political Works of James I,* ed. C. H. McIlwain (New York: Russell and Russell, 1965), p. 343; *Chamberlain Letters,* 1:400; 2:286–87, 289, 294, 475, 487.

68. C. J. Berry, *The Idea of Luxury: A Conceptual and Historical Investigation* (Cambridge: Cambridge University Press, 1994), pp. 87–98; D. Bruster, *Drama and the Market in the Age of Shakespeare* (Cambridge: Cambridge University Press, 1992); J. Twyning, *London Dispossessed: Literature and Social Space in the Early Modern City* (Basingstoke and London: Macmillan, 1998), pp. 59–70.

69. T. Dekker, *The Deade Terme,* in *Non-Dramatic Works of Thomas Dekker,* ed. A. B. Grosart, 5 vols. (reprint; New York: Russell and Russell, 1963), 4:58; J. Marston, *The Dutch Courtesan,* ed. M. L. Wine (London: Edward Arnold, 1965), 1.2.29–54; B. Jonson, *The Complete Poems,* ed. G. Parfitt (London: Penguin, 1975), p. 52.

70. *Dutch Courtesan,* 3.3.10–12. Cf. T. Middleton and T. Dekker, *The Roaring Girl,* ed. E. Cook (London: A & C Black, 1997), 2.1; T. Middleton, *The Family of Love,* in *The Works of Thomas Middleton,* vol. 3, ed. A. H. Bullen (London: John C. Nimmo, 1885), 2.1.2–6.

71. *Pasquin's Palinodia* (1619), cited by Newman, "City Talk," p. 181.

72. *Household Accounts and Disbursement Books of Robert Dudley, Earl of Leicester,* ed. S. Adams (Camden Society, fifth series, no. 6, 1995); R. Ashton, *The City and the Court* (Cambridge: Cambridge University Press, 1979); Archer, *Pursuit of Stability,* p. 117.

73. F. W. Fairholt, "On An Inventory of the Household Goods of Sir Thomas

Ramsey, Lord Mayor of London 1577," *Archaeologia* 40 (1854): 311–20; Hertfordshire Record Office, MS 27423 (Sir William Garrard); PRO, PROB2/256 (Sir Ralph Warren).

74. PRO, PROB11/132, fols. 70r–73v; L. Stone, "The Peer and the Alderman's Daughter," *History Today* (1963): 48–55; J. Barry, "Bourgeois Collectivism? Urban Associations and the Middling Sort," in *The Middling Sort of People: Culture, Society, and Politics in England, 1550–1800,* ed. J. Barry and C. Brooks (London and Basingstoke: Macmillan, 1994), pp. 84–112.

10

Purgation as the Allure
of Mastery

Early Modern Medicine and the Technology of the Self

Gail Kern Paster

In the anonymous early seventeenth-century city comedy entitled *The Family of Love,* a particularly nasty but very funny variant in the conventional sexual warfare between gallants and citizens takes place. Two gallants, Lipsalve and Gudgeon, seeking to gain access to the wife of Dr. Glister, take temporary lodgings in the doctor's house and enlist his services for a course of physic. Their action — if not their motives — would not have seemed unusual, even apart from its comic context. As Margaret Pelling has demonstrated, medical consumers in early modern London sought help from a wide variety of practitioners not only for medical remedies for specific ailments but also for therapeutic counsel on a host of matters — psychological, cosmetic, and sexual. The wide availability of such help, the intense social competition of London life, and the London consumer's active role in his own health integrated the pursuit for physical well-being into the fabric of daily life.[1]

Expensive, thoroughgoing courses of physic involved considerable preparations, physical and psychological, under medical supervision. Treatment could easily extend over several days and require successive administrations of different vomits, laxatives, and clysters, all directed towards the goal of restoring or maintaining the ideal solubility synonymous with health in the world of early modern medical practice. It was considered so essential to well-being, in fact, that Samuel Pepys considered "costiveness" the first warning sign of ill health. In October 1663, after a period of intestinal pain he labeled retrospectively "My great fitt of the Collique," he resolved "To begin to suspect my health immediately when I begin to become costive and bound, and by all means to keep my body loose, and that to obtain presently after I find myself going to the contrary."[2]

In *The Family of Love,* the gallants' strategy of seeking erotic ends through cathartic means proves disastrous. Dr. Glister, discovering their intentions to cuckold him and with means almost uniquely at his disposal, is able to punish the two gallants with their own consent. He purges them wisely by purging them too well: "They are here in the house," the doctor's niece Maria reports, "so handled by mine uncle that they are the pitifullest patients that ever you beheld."[3] Their final onstage appearance, after violent offstage evacuations at the doctor's hands, motivates a series of scatological jokes linking fecal production to the judicial production of shameful knowledge. When the gallants are called on as witnesses, the doctor warns, "they will bewray all" — that is, accuse all, befoul all.[4] The gallants' mere appearance on stage memorializes their shameful subjection, initiating the first in a series of widely distributed punishments through exposure. All the erring characters of *The Family of Love* are forced to offer up not the ugly evidence of the contents of their bodies, but equally shameful evidence of the contents of their desires.

A remarkable degree of aggressiveness, scatological and otherwise, marks *The Family of Love,* beginning with the names of its characters. With regard to the two gallants, the play's onomastic explicitness encourages us to fantasize about the aggression which characterizes the somatic relations of patients and the medical professionals who would service them, about the somatic subjection which medical treatment entails. The play not only names its doctor Glister but also provides an apothecary named Master Purge, who serves as another medical professional for the gallants to cuckold. The gallants' suggestive type-names, Lipsalve and Gudgeon, conflate their oral appetitiveness and penetrability (both oral and anal) and exaggerate the efficacy of the men to whom they must turn for medical and/or erotic relief.[5] Handing themselves over to Dr. Glister, the gallants Lipsalve and Gudgeon undergo a far more violent purgation than they had anticipated as the cost of entry to the doctor's house and wife, or might even have sought as prelude to a wished-for sexual encounter.[6] "Here they come, in pain I warrant them," Glister exclaims triumphantly as the two gallants return slowly across the stage in act 5. The body of the doctor swells with laughter at the deflation of his enemies: "How works your physic, gallants? do you go well to the ground? now cuckold the doctor! . . . ha, ha, ha" (5.3.1981–84). At this pure juxtaposition of phallic triumph and phallic collapse, purgation can be seen to encode the causal relation between bodily openness and masculine injury, the exacting somatic complementarity of victory and defeat in medical agency.

In its lineaments — the sadistic anal punishment of sexual presumption meted out by an authoritative clyster-wielding figure — the denouement of this city comedy resembles comic materials I have considered elsewhere, under a scandalous rubric, as "the scatological imperatives" of Elizabethan-Jacobean comedy. That discussion speculated on possible consequences for the early modern history of the subject of a medical practice dependent on often violent evacuations. I sought to identify a memorial structure in purgative treatments akin to the earliest pleasurable bodily disciplines of the mother-child relation. The culture's semiology of the bodily sign of the open male breech was linked to child-rearing practices and the expulsive pleasures of the close stool were seen to compete in erotic appeal with the socially more demanding pleasures of sexual — especially heterosexual — intercourse.[7] As John Harington notes in *The Metamorphosis of Ajax,* "This surpassing pleasure [of sex] I have heard confessed before a most honourable person . . . to have bred no more delectation to him (after the first heate of his youthe was past) then to go to a good easie close stoole, when he had a lust thereto."[8]

Here I want to move away from my earlier focus on the history of the individual subject in order to consider purgation as early modern culture's signifying practice upon the social body as a whole. This move from the individual subject to the collective body does not, of course, mean that purgation becomes any more available to representation. Like the prohibited scene of sexual intercourse to which it is closely allied, the scene of bodily purgation remains firmly outside the limits of all dramatic, and most narrative, representation — even as the scene of psychosocial purgation or the narrative disclosure of desire's crimes and misdemeanors is foregrounded as the telos of much plotting, tragic and comic alike. In transferring the scene of physical purgation from home to the public sphere, from the domain of a clyster-bearing mother-nurse to that of a clyster-bearing doctor, the cathartic experience changes from being an involuntary, though pleasurable subjection to domestic disciplines into a freely willed act of rational consumption akin to the purchase of other goods and services. As Mary Douglas has suggested, all goods are "transitory markers of rational categories" which "make visible statements about the hierarchy of values to which their chooser subscribes."[9] The statement of values and the expression of social differences are most evident, according to Pierre Bourdieu, in the "world of luxury goods" because "the relationship of distinction is objectively inscribed within it, and is reactivated, intentionally or not, in each act of consumption."[10] What I wish to argue is that willed acts of purgative catharsis by adult men and women in early modern England were a socially visible performance which engaged the body's internal habitus, both directly and symbolically, as the subject of an emergent practice of early capitalist consumption. The specifics of cathartic practice — what drugs were administered to whom, by whom, for what physical, psychological, and social ends — became markers of status and the host body's internal habitus was enlisted experimentally as a new kind of social space for the intensification, enactment, and exhibition of desire.[11]

The range of cathartics and the commercial discourse of their use in early modern England offer a vivid demonstration of what was at stake, culturally, in the practices of purgation. The equation of domestically produced commodities with a rearguard defense of the social hierarchy, situated somatically, reveals itself in William Harrison's *Description of England* when Harrison advocates the use of homegrown herbals over imported compounds: "Our continual desire of strange drugs, whereby only the physician and apothecary hath the benefit, is no small cause that the use of our simples here at home doth go to lose and that we tread those herbs under our feet whose forces, if we knew and could apply them to our necessities, we would honor and have in reverence as to their case behooveth."[12] For Harrison, an endless centrifuge of desire for novelty is premised on a literal erasure — from knowledge and use — of native plants, treading "those herbs under our feet." Thus, on the nativist ground that English bodies require English herbal remedies, Harrison protests vigorously against snobbish preference in the choice of medicines: "Alas, what have we to do with such Arabian and Grecian stuff as is daily brought from those parties which lie in another clime."[13] A character in Greene's *Quip for an Upstart Courtier* explains his similar choice of old-fashioned simplicity and domestic self-reliance: "for my selfe if I be il at ease I take kitchin physicke, I make my wife my Doctor, and my garden my Apoticaries shop."[14]

The purchase of luxury drugs at the apothecary's shop or the purchase of the doctor's professional secrets, by contrast, worked like the direct appropriation of high cultural goods — in Bourdieu's terms, being subject to "exclusive appropriation," they "yield a profit in distinction," not of plain Englishness but of urban sophistication and economic power.[15] Furthermore, because of the reciprocal exchanges to which cultural capital is given, the remedies themselves acquired value through the visibility of their users. Indeed, one way to make sense of the expanding number of new medicinal commodities was to recognize the social attributes of those who took them. In such a rapidly expanding medical marketplace, establishing the social credentials of a drug's consumers seems to improve not just the drug's reputation but the efficacy of its workings. This saturation of medicinal plants by the social expressiveness of cultural capital is everywhere evident, as for example in the writing of Nicolás Monardes, a Spanish physician whose account of New World drugs was translated into English in 1577.[16] In Monardes' description of a New World medicine made from Mechoacan root, botanical identification and social promotion blend. Among the root's many virtues are the character, rank, and judgment of those who have been helped by it: "I knowe a person of much estimation that did use [this root] and beyng of great yeres: did looke like a young man and lived after he used it without occasion of any evill . . . some gentle women that have not brought forthe children, have used it . . . for to pourge the Mother, and it hath doen them much good."[17] In the transaction between new drugs and their takers, such language implies, the benefits are reciprocal.

In fact, among those who could choose, early seventeenth-century London had a variety of new goods and services with which consumers could express their values and enlarge their vocabularies of desire. As Sidney Mintz has pointed out, the "explanation of individual lusts for such goods" as the new drug-foods of tobacco, sugar, and tea "is to be found in a redefinition of the social context of needs and desires within which the 'individual' . . . is behaviourally visible."[18] And what is visible about individual consumers up and down the social hierarchy of seventeenth-century London is how important the lust for medical goods and services was in the expansion of choice and intensification of desires which mark the history of bourgeois economy.[19] The medical services of elite practitioners "became a major item of consumption for those classes which were becoming more prosperous by the late sixteenth century," Margaret Pelling has suggested, and "medicine of a different kind and price provided an invaluable source of consolation for those most helpless in the face of change."[20]

The taking of medicine was thus part of an expanding prospect of material agency for the desiring subject, a form of somatic and psychological intensification that mixed pain with pleasure: when early modern men and women took medicine, they desired its strongest effects, most of them noxious.[21] It was a recognizably potent means of instrumentation over one's own store of pleasure and pain, a major form of definition of one's own store of pleasure or pain. The visible instrumentality of drugs was especially true for medicines bought from an apothecary and prescribed by a physician in the circumstances represented in *The Family of Love* — choosing, as the gallants Lipsalve and Gudgeon do, to take a powerfully cathartic medicine in the absence of predisposing symptoms — we might even say, for the hell of it. Furthermore, as Pelling's differentiation between consumption habits for rich and poor implies, taking medicine may be especially revealing of the values of those leisured classes whose pleasure and pain were of most positive concern to themselves. Theirs was the horizon of desire most conspicuously capable of manipulation and expansion, most eligible for intensification. But, as the violently cathartic experience of Lipsalve and Gudgeon also attests, this material dream of desire realized could turn into seriocomic exposure if desire was judged to be presumptuous and aggressive or if it involved the theft of another's property in goods or person.

I will return at the end of this essay to the overdetermined cathartic encounter between Dr. Glister and his depleted rivals in *The Family of Love*. For the moment, it can serve as a framework for considering the scene of catharsis within an ensemble of socially charged practices and key categorical oppositions of medical-material life in seventeenth-century London. As has been suggested by the quotations above, the categories which come into play involve such terms as kitchen physic and doctor's physic, simple and compound, herbal and chemical. But at their farthest semantic reaches, such medical terms expand to include the broadest of social distinctions — say, those between male and female, or between gentleman, professional man, and citizen. Both in the taking of internal medicine and in the nature of the commodities themselves, medical consumption not only mimicked the structures of difference in early modern London but added significantly to the symbolic exchanges by which individuals conveyed meaning to themselves and others. Legible in these symbolic exchanges is the rational struggle for autonomy, both personal and social, within and against a medical orthodoxy which promised palliation, remediation, or psychological benefit through the equivocal violence of powerful purgatives.

From our perspective, the extent to which internal medicine in the early modern period relied on the use of purgatives is almost astonishing. As Roy Porter has suggested, "medical materialism conceived of the pulsating body as a through-put economy whose efficient functioning depended upon generous input and unimpeded outflow."[22] Casual perusal of the recipe books of a gentlewoman practitioner like Lady Grace Mildmay reveals ominous opening formulas: "The first day before the full or change give this glister"; "First let her take 3 days together this purge following"; "First give a vomit of antimony but no cordial upon it"; or "First purge with this drink."[23] Reliance on cathartics resulted less from a belief in the curative properties of any single cathartic remedy than from a medical paradigm which explained illness and wellness in the same terms. Disease came not from the invasion of an alien entity into a body otherwise healthy, but from a localized instance of insolubility which threatened the humoral balance of the body as a whole. This insolubility sometimes took the form of a rheum — the congestion of the common cold, for example, or sometimes the vaguer sensation of general bodily plethora. Sometimes it must have resulted from the social rhythms of a culture which, as Porter has suggested, afforded many "times and sites devoted to bingeing" and which "regarded 'high living' as a form of preventive medicine."[24] But, because humoral imbalance was thought to be caused by internal obstruction, it was often experienced as, and cannot be clearly distinguished from, a state of internal defilement requiring vigorous expulsion. As long as health was equated with a regimen of cleanly solubility and attained through the regulated promotion of physical and emotional flow, leaving well enough alone in such a body could hardly be considered, much less sanctioned. As with leaving a sewer-ditch uncleaned or a hearth unswept, allowing the body to remain insoluble, stewing unhealthily in its own juices, would soon result in a noxious, dangerous burdensomeness. This was the impetus to act, the motive to purge.

In a medical regime at once accustomed to risk but manifestly limited in long-term efficacy, the domain of rational choice in the pursuit of "unimpeded outflow" must have seemed perilously fraught though not inconsiderable. The great unregulated medical marketplace of seventeenth-century England made individuals finally responsible for knowing and manipulating the key variables of their own internal hygiene and that of their families. Since even serious illness was often treated in the home without consulting a physician, so the wellness of cleanly health was often sought inside and outside the home, for reasons we can only guess at from this distance of time and unbelief. It isn't clear why, for example, in June 1650, Jane and Ralph Josselin gave physic to their two healthy children only to watch in dismay when their bodies reacted violently: they became "sick even to death," reports the diary, "so that our hearts trembled, fearing the issue, but the lord in mercy to us quickly blew it over."[25] It seems clearer why the Hobys, Sir Thomas and Lady Margaret, traveled to a surgeon in York every spring for bloodlettings — presumably to relieve their plethoric bodies from the excess of blood and humors thought to accumulate over a winter of feasting and indoor inactivity.[26] Gentry closer to London looking for the relief of doctors' physic or surgical phlebotomy would have journeyed there, as did Master Buckland of Reading who, the surgeon William Clowes tells us, "hauing a full and plethoricke body, and thereupon inclined to sicknesse: made his iourney vnto London, only to take Physicke."[27]

In interpreting such acts of medical choice, it seems important to understand that, since taking physic and phlebotomy improved the contents of one's body, by extension it could also be thought to improve the contents of one's person, the nature of one's self.[28] In early seventeenth-century London, to place oneself voluntarily in the care of a physician was apparently to enter into a fashionable competition of conspicuous consumption for improving the contents of one's body. The nature of this competition in high living and thorough purging may be inferred from the following satiric advice to the would-be gallant: "You may rise in dinner-time," Dekker's narrator in *The Gull's Hornbook* suggests, "to ask for a close-stool, protesting to all the gentlemen that it costs you a hundred pound a year in physic besides the annual pension which your wife allows her doctor."[29] Dekker seeks to ridicule such an announcement in company, which tries to make the ordinary act of evacuation different from itself, to semiotize the bodily wastes and digestive rhythms of the would-be gallant as the product of fashion. But satire can only attack what already signifies. Hence the link between taking physic and fashions in evacuation underscores the social logic of the *Hornbook* narrator's next recommended impudency, to "sharpen the wits of all the eating gallants about you . . . to ask what pamphlets or poems a man might think fittest to wipe his tail with . . . and purchase to yourself in time the terrible name of a severe critic."[30] In the close confines of the privy, where reading matter services both mind and body, the worldly practices of taking physick and judging poems meet and become one.

The difficulty with physic, however, as a form of social competition in the consumption of luxury goods was the ceding of bodily control to the wages of strong medicine that it necessarily entailed. As we saw in the case of the Josselin children, once the cathartic was taken into a body, healthy or not, its effects could not necessarily be controlled — despite the best efforts of mother or doctor to control the dosages. The purgatives that almost invariably commenced a course of internal physic might include such gentle instruments as rhubarb and senna, the mainstays of garden physic. But settled costiveness and thorough purgations required the stronger measures of hellebore, mastic, and antimony to move the humors, expel the waste, secure solubility, and produce the physical or psychological alteration that was desired. Lady Grace Mildmay notes with a certain resignation that humors are sometimes ready to leave the body, sometimes not: "This humour of melancholy," she writes, "must not be evacuated by medicine which carrieth hastily, for it is a cold and dry humour and therefore slow and will cleave to the parts as it passeth. And medicines which carrieth hastily must take such humours as are ready to go with them." The melancholic patient might have to inure himself to a course of purging "many days together."[31] To undertake such cathartic experiments for the sake of distinction and socially meaningful acts of consumption might be costly on one's purse and one's body alike.

In the "through-put economy" of an early modern body bent on competing in perfectability and distinction, purgatives were an uncertain but necessary instrument. Thus it is no small part of Nicolás Monardes' *Joyfull Newes from the New World* to bring joyful tidings of new purgatives, including one newly discovered plant that promised complete evacuation without loss of bodily control. Monardes carefully sets the stage for the introduction of his wonderful new plant by recounting the near-disasters which the Spaniards' rash imitation of Indian pharmacology sometimes occasioned. Thus, "of necessity," Monardes relates, the Spaniards purged themselves with certain three-cornered nuts from Santo Domingo. For the Indians of the island, these were "a familiar purgation." The Spaniards, however, found "hazarde ynough . . . for with the use therof, many thought to lose their lives . . . And although that it doeth make a great excesse of stooles, yet doeth it also provoke vomitte verie strongly, and with muche violence, with greate faintnesse and heavinesse. Afterward some did rectifie [the beans] by tosting of them, and then they bee not so violent" (50). Other new drugs in Monardes' pharmacopoeia, such as piñon nuts or purgative beans from Cartagena used safely by the Indians, had similarly violent effects on the Spaniards. So it is with some due access of rhetorical flourish that Monardes introduces his best new medicinal discovery by relating the story of one Spanish friar who, falling sick, is cured by a friendly Indian lord by means of the powdered Mechoacan root, "with the whiche he did pourge so muche, and withoute paines, that the same daie he was muche lightned, and muche more from that time forward" (55). This story is followed by several similar examples of the wonderful new purgative which "thei take . . . with so much truste and easenesse, that when thei take it, thei thinke to have certainly their healthe" (56).

In certain respects, Monardes allows, the drug required the same bodily preparations as other purgatives except that it left "the interiour members strengthened, without debilitation and weakenesse, that the other purgative Medicines doeth leave them in" (60). What distinguished it from all others was that it lightened the body too full of itself without sacrificing the bodily agency and autonomy of the purger and in so doing, we may infer, affirmed the rationality and wisdom of his act. It was safe enough to be used without the advice of a physician, "whiche is that, as unto all menne geveth moste content" (58). And it worked "as the will of hym that doeth take it" (65) remaining the servant not the master of the taker. It has become, says Monardes, "Merchandise of very greate price" (56).

Monardes' interest in promoting the remarkable properties of this New World drug is less important to my concerns here than noting the widespread cultural issue which such a drug seemed to resolve: the contradiction in the project of perfectability and distinction between augmenting agency over one's inner physical and emotional being and ceding control to the means of that desired expansion. The ability of Monardes' new drug to produce bodily "lightness" without sacrificing the taker's autonomy to any external agency would have seemed especially attractive when the external agency came in the form of a physician distinctly lower in social status than one's own gentlemanly self.

It is such issues of rank, distinction, and autonomy which return with a vengeance in *The Family of Love* where Lipsalve and Gudgeon elect to purchase a course of physic, in the first place, because they have the financial ability to act on their desires and, as city-dwellers, easy access to Doctor Glister and his services. It would not have made medical or social sense for Glister to turn them away on the grounds that they were not sick and hence not in need of his services; such grounds were specious given the apparent conventionality of their course of action as men of fashion. Purgation in circumstances of their choosing, purgation in response to their innermost strivings or self-diagnosis or desire for recognition as consumers of luxury goods, was their right as medical consumers.

What is apparently not their right in this city comedy is sexual possession of city wives — the motive for Glister's purgative revenge. If city wives are bent on infidelity, this play suggests slyly, let them at least keep it within their own ranks by practicing extramarital sex only within the confines of the Family of Love. Lipsalve and Gudgeon do not cherish noble dreams of expanded personal agency which sadly go awry in their botched purgation; their desires are too specific and conventional, their characters too negligible to support such an interpretation. On the contrary, the very fact of a cultural understanding of catharsis as an instrument of perfectability is what gives their conventionality whatever satiric force it possesses and underscores the play's playful linking of the gallants' appetite for sexual pleasure with that of the Familists. From the beginning of the play, Lipsalve and Gudgeon employ the discourse of bodily solubility in order to compete with one another in the satisfaction of desire or to test the availability of city wives. Indeed the actions of Gudgeon and Lipsalve are almost an allegory of the route of purgation; they arrive at their decision to use Glister's house and purgatives to get at Mistress Glister only after an earlier failure to use the gentler remedies, specifically the sexual attractions of the apothecary's wife Mistress Purge.

It is the sexually adventurous Mistress Purge who belongs to the nonconforming sect which gives the play its title and much of its emplotment. She herself alternates between mornings spent with the Family of Love or taking visits from Doctor Glister. Her attractiveness to the cluster of men around her seems unambiguously connected to the physical "looseness" her apothecary husband's medicines promote and the moral "looseness" her husband releases in her by using her to attract his customers. Thus Gudgeon confesses to Lipsalve that "she makes civil wars and insurrections in the state of my stomach. I had thought to have bound myself from love, but her purging comfits makes me loose-bodied still" (2.3.448–51). Lipsalve argues that Mistress Purge herself is too "soluble" — that is, too healthy both spiritually and physically — to stoop to sin with gallants: "she is not troubled with carnal crudities nor the binding of the flesh" (455–56). He could hardly be more mistaken — as they discover in a pleasurable rendezvous at the Family of Love.

But the sexual appetite of courtiers and city wives is too familiar a topic to be anything other than the means to a larger satiric end. What *The Family of Love* is most engaged in deriding is not the sexual appetites of courtiers per se but the moral and physical hypocrisy of courtiers and citizens alike. Where the gallants use the cultural competition in therapeutic purgation to mask their sexual intentions towards the citizen wives of medical practitioners, the city puritans — Mistress Purge especially — use the pursuit of spiritual well-being in the form of non-conforming religion to mask their pursuit of sex. The play mocks the project of perfectability in both religion and physic by making clear that the three characters with the most avid appetites for medicine — Lipsalve, Gudgeon, and Mistress Purge herself — are also the characters with the most avid appetites for sex.

The play's great distinction, at least for my purposes here, is to mock the project of personal perfectability in a way which shows the discourse of purgation at a crucial historical moment. This was a moment before the physical and spiritual frames of reference for purgation had divided, at a moment when the borders between the physical and spiritual meanings of purgation no less than the physical and spiritual experiences of purgation were not completely differentiated. No matter how punitive the experience of purgation in *The Family of Love* may be, in early modern medical practice the instruments of purgation seemed to promise a well-being just within reach.

Notes

1. Margaret Pelling, "Appearance and Reality: Barber-Surgeons, the Body and Disease," in *London, 1500–1700: The Making of the Metropolis,* ed. A. L. Beier and Roger Finlay (London: Longman, 1985), pp. 89–105.

2. Samuel Pepys, *The Diary of Samuel Pepys,* ed. Robert Latham and William Matthews, vol. 4 (Berkeley: University of California Press, 1971), p. 324, 333; also quoted in Lucinda McCray Beier, *Sufferers and Healers: The Experience of Illness in Seventeenth-Century England* (London: Routledge & Kegan Paul, 1987), p. 165.

3. I quote throughout from Thomas Middleton, *The Family of Love,* ed. Simon Shepherd, Nottingham Drama Texts (Nottingham: Nottingham University Press, 1979) which cites act, scene, and through-line numbers. The play has usually been regarded as collaboratively authored by Middleton among others; because of the decision of the Oxford Middleton editors to exclude the play from that collected edition, I have decided not to name Middleton as the play's author here.

4. The two words, "bewray" and "beray," were often conflated, according to the *OED:* the first means to accuse, the second to defile or befoul.

5. The *OED* defines gudgeon as a small freshwater bait fish; its figurative meanings — as a gullible person who will swallow anything or as the bait itself — capture the

ambivalence of figuring the open mouth as vulnerable or aggressive, receiving or devouring. "Lipsalve" is figured as flattering speech.

6. For a discussion of the purge as preliminary to sexual experience, see Gail Kern Paster, *The Body Embarrassed: Drama and the Disciplines of Shame in Early Modern England* (Ithaca: Cornell University Press, 1993), p. 135.

7. Ibid., pp. 113–62.

8. John Harington, *A New Discourse of a Stale Subject, Called the Metamorphosis of Ajax,* ed. Elizabeth Story Donno (New York: Columbia University Press, 1962), p. 84.

9. Mary Douglas and Baron Isherwood, *The World of Goods* (New York: Basic Books, 1979), p. 5.

10. Pierre Bourdieu, *Distinction: A Social Critique of the Judgment of Taste,* trans. Richard Nice (Cambridge, Mass.: Harvard University Press, 1984), p. 226.

11. On the development of this pattern, the classic account is by F. J. Fisher, "The Development of London as a Centre of Conspicuous Consumption in the Sixteenth and Seventeenth Centuries," in F. J. Fisher, *London and the English Economy, 1500–1700,* ed. P. J. Corfield and N. B. Harte (London and Ronceverte: Hambledon Press, 1990), pp. 105–18.

12. William Harrison, *Description of England,* ed. Georges Edelen (Washington, D.C.: Folger Shakespeare Library, 1968; and New York: Dover, 1994), pp. 266–67.

13. Ibid., p. 267.

14. Greene, "A Quip for an Upstart Courtier" in *Life and Works of Robert Greene,* 12 vols., ed. Alexander B. Grosart (London, privately printed, 1849), 11:248.

15. Bourdieu, *Distinction,* p. 228.

16. Nicolás Monardes, *Joyfull Newes out of the Newe Founde Worlde,* trans. John Frampton (1577; reprint 2 vols; New York: Knopf, 1925).

17. Ibid., 1:60.

18. Sidney W. Mintz, "The Changing Roles of Food in the Study of Consumption," in *Consumption and the World of Goods,* ed. John Brewer and Roy Porter (London: Routledge, 1993), p. 267.

19. For a discussion of this history, see ibid., pp. 267–69.

20. Pelling, "Appearance and Reality: Barber-Surgeons, the Body and Disease," p. 82.

21. See Beier, *Sufferers and Healers,* p. 5.

22. Roy Porter, "Consumption: Disease of the Consumer Society?" in *Consumption and the World of Goods,* p. 60.

23. Linda Pollock, *With Faith and Physick: The Life of a Tudor Gentlewoman, Lady Grace Mildmay, 1552–1620* (London: Collins and Brown, 1993), pp. 114, 119, 120, 124.

24. Porter, "Consumption," p. 59.

25. Lucinda McCray Beier, "In Sickness and in Health," in *Patients and Practitioners: Lay Perceptions of Medicine in Pre-industrial Society* (Cambridge: Cambridge University Press, 1985), pp. 119–30.

26. Beier, *Sufferers and Healers,* p. 222.

27. See William Clowes, *Booke of Observations* (London, 1596; STC 5442; reprint Amsterdam: Da Capo Press, 1971), p. 31.

28. It is only a slight exaggeration of real practice in Rabelais' *Gargantua* when, in preparation for his introduction to humanist education, the young giant is given a

strong purgative of black hellebore in order to rid his body of the noxious residues of scholasticism; see *The Body Embarrassed,* p. 132.

29. Thomas Dekker, "The Gull's Hornbook" in *Thomas Dekker,* ed. E. D. Pendry (Cambridge, Mass.: Harvard University Press, 1968), p. 95.

30. Ibid., pp. 95–96.

31. Excerpted by Pollock, *With Faith and Physick,* p. 121.

11

London's Vagrant Economy

Making Space for "Low" Subjectivity

Patricia Fumerton

In 1594, Thomas Spickernell was listed by the town clerk of Maldon, Essex, as among those disaffected toward the Puritan magistracy and described as "somtyme apprentice to a bookebynder; after, a vagrant pedler; then, a ballet singer and seller; and now, a minister and alehouse-keeper in Maldon."[1] "Minister," taken in the religious sense (as clergyman or, more generally, agent of a faith), would seem to be the key appellation in this list of occupations — given the intent of the clerk to indicate spiritual deviance. But the title is arrived at through the loosest of temporal connections — "somtyme," "after," "then," "now" — and fails to achieve a culminating position of prominence in the list of occupations. Rather, "minister" is displaced from such a preeminent seat by the highly secular nomen, "alehouse-keeper" (with which "minister" shares syntactical as well as temporal and geographical space). One might at this point even question the spirituality of the term "minister" and conclude that it is not meant in the religious sense at all but in the secular meaning of servant, attendant, or administrator — of ale not faith.[2]

Such a deviant slippage from sacral to secular place, whether consciously made by the clerk or not, may well have been inspired by the lone descriptor in the sequence of occupations: "vagrant." No matter what the clerk's prioritizing intent, no occupation in his list can necessarily follow another and none can achieve sole preeminence because all are versions of the same lack of acceptable occupation: *a profession of vagrancy*. This is the real heresy posed by Spickernell. As "somtyme apprentice" Spickernell was "masterless," free of the binding terms and regulatory "freedom" of a company. He was unsupervised, unplaced, and hence socially vagrant. As pedlar wandering from place to place selling his wares, he was not only socially but physically and legally vagrant, hence the specific designation of such in the clerk's list (pedlar was included among the illegal occupations detailed in the vagrancy acts of 1572 and 1598).[3]

In addition to pins, lace, and other such trinkets, the "vagrant" pedlar would almost certainly carry pamphlets, chapbooks, and/or ballads for sale, perhaps singing snatches of the latter to advertise his wares. As "ballet singer and seller" alone, Spickernell would not be officially labeled vagrant but would, nevertheless, often be treated as such[4] and would have frequented the same places as the pedlar: street corners, fairs, markets, theaters, wakes, and anywhere else people congregated. In their vagrant print-trades, Spickernell's alternative occupations ("somtyme apprentice to a bookebynder," "vagrant pedler," "ballet singer and seller") are essentially interchangeable.

To be "now" an alehouse-keeper was provisionally, and thus suspiciously, to site all three of the above "professions" since vagrants (including runaway apprentices and servants), pedlars, and ballad singers would all frequent the alehouse for food, shelter, sales, and the hope of finding service. Finally, all such groups also came together under the nomen of disaffected "minister" in the term's secular sense (the alehouse-keeper "ministering" ale to his customers) as well as — at least in the minds of many authorities like Maldon's clerk — its religious meaning. On the latter score, officials often suspected vagrants of being religious dissidents — especially when gathered together at ungodly assembly points such as alehouses — because, by the very nature of their mobility, they were considered *wholly* deviant.[5] From the perspective of authority in a patriarchal and theoretically static society, the vagrant who moved from job to job and place to place was tremendously threatening and subversive, whatever his or her actual religious or political position might be.

What particularly concerns me here is how the heretical connection between vagrant "professions" (such as those undertaken by Spickernell) might inform our understanding of the lower-order subject in early modern England. Specifically, I aim to make space for a new notion of "low" subjectivity — economic, social, psychological, and metonymic — that escaped the "bound" and made a home of homelessness. An originary trace of such an unbound subject can be detected, we will see, in a newly emergent "vagrant" economy that was centered on London. Spickernell likely began his wandering there, given that most printers/bookbinders at the time were in London. Like Spickernell's shifting career, we shall find, the London economy and its far-reaching tentacles were characterized by mobility, diversity, alienation, freedom, and tactical (as opposed to strategic or *authorized*) craft.

To trace the topography of this new fluid market, as we shall do here, is to liberate the subject from the insistent critical positioning of "low versus high," "margin versus center," "subversive versus contained." This sometimes nuanced but ultimately dead-end dialectic is dependent on a *placed* universe (i.e., one in which the voices of the low must be measured relative to the

voices of those who have a "place" in society). But truly to understand the
"low," we must inhabit their own space—a spaciousness of itinerancy, fragmentation, disconnection, and multiplicity that produces a very different topographical mapping of societal relations. Traced spatially, as well as economically and socially, the largely invisible vagrant/laboring poor glimpsed in the
case of Spickernell—who were produced by, and in great part supported, the
new economy—emerge as distinctive subjects but with an expansive reach.
Indeed, they can be seen metonymically to embrace most of the lower orders,
not just the indigent and homeless, of early modern England: itinerant laborers, including servants and apprentices, as well as those poor householders
from the lowest depths of the amorphous "middling sort," who were at any
time liable to such unsettling change (indigent husbandmen and small craftsmen and petty traders in the poorer occupations, such as glovers, carpenters,
fishmongers, fruiterers, and the like).

In order to make visible such lowly lines of connectivity, however, we
need to rethink not only our traditional theories of place as hierarchical and
stable, but also our traditional notions of subjectivity as "high" or erudite and
as unitary or consistent. We must make more class-specific the totalizing language of exchange and theatricality, or self-fashioning, that Christopher Pye
rightly sees has characterized new historicist notions of early modern subjectivity.[6] This essay thus concludes by positing a theory of "low" subjectivity that
is itself vagrant: a subjectivity that could be experienced not only by a range of
lower-order subjects, but also as multiple types of "selves" (whether addi-
tionally, intermittently, or provisionally).

In the spirit of this volume, and following most vagrants and itinerant
laborers of the period, we shall pursue low subjectivity by heading straight for
London. But, as with many of the lowly who only provisionally invested in the
London economy, our path shall necessarily wander far beyond.

Provisional Investments: London and Beyond

London, it should first be observed, bore the brunt of the nation's vagrancy
problem. According to A. L. Beier and Roger Finlay, vagrancy in the city rose
twelvefold from 1560 to 1625 whereas its population only quadrupled. Many
of these vagrants came from the swell of immigrants that yearly flooded London and its suburbs (on the order of some 10,000 a year).[7] But many others
were home-grown. The latter—mostly male—derived primarily from the
ranks of servants and apprentices, who between 1597 and 1608, in Beier's
accounting, constituted almost three quarters of the vagrants of London

origin.[8] These "native" vagrants conspicuously comment on the metropolis as a whole.

For there is a sense in which vagrancy was inherent or native to early modern London. That is, for many, to be a Londoner in the sixteenth and seventeenth centuries was to experience a degree of alienation and anonymity cognate with the vagrant experience as recently documented by the work of Beier and Paul Slack, among others. What these historians of vagrancy have found is that—contrary to the myth of a vagrant subculture promulgated in contemporary rogue literature—vagrants of the period were in fact mostly solitary and anonymous wanderers, cut off from any stable community, family, or lasting affective ties.[9] Such a state of radical detachment could distemper the urban experience of housed contemporaries as well. As Beier and Finlay observe, in the city of London "almost everyone was a migrant; the operation of the labour market, together with child-care by nurses, meant that many people lacked family ties or any sense of belonging. Relatively poor communications made it very difficult to keep in touch with relatives; there was no Post Office until the later seventeenth century. In periods of peak alien immigration, language and dialect problems would also have been encountered." "All this," they conclude, "provided the conditions for a sense of isolation and insecurity with possible psychosocial effects."[10] Though we should resist exaggerating the anonymity of city life (as Ian W. Archer and others caution, noting that "the obligations of neighbourhood were taken seriously" in London),[11] the fact is that traditional ties could only be intermittent. Lawrence Stone sums up the new character of neighborhood in citing a London parson writing from 1587 to 1590: every twelve years or so, the parson noted, "the most part of the parish changeth, as I by experience know, some goinge and some comminge"—a situation, Stone observes, which resembles nothing so much as modern day Los Angeles.[12] The resulting sense of urban instability and disassociation would have been most intensely felt, I argue, by the largest socioeconomic group in London: servants and apprentices.

Of course, in many important respects servants and apprentices little resembled vagrants. After all, the former occupied sanctioned social, physical, and economic places in the city, constituting 40 to 50 percent of London's labor force in 1600.[13] This was especially true of apprentices, who belonged to an elaborate guild system aimed at disciplining and socializing such youths. Although this ordered structure placed apprentices "low" within its hierarchy, it held out the prospect of future advancement. Indeed, however "lowly" their status by virtue of being apprentices, many such youths at the time of their apprenticeships could claim "high" family connections in the middling ranks and, increasingly in the seventeenth century, in the gentry.[14] Paradoxically,

however, such elevated social ties situated some apprentices in highly problematic "nowhere" positions — simultaneously high and low — which could
destabilize any sense of secure place. Even more important, despite the trappings of "place," as noted above, servants and apprentices in London circa 1600
in fact made up the group most prone to vagrancy. Authorities especially
suspected the vagrant inclinations of our "placed" apprentices. In official documents, William C. Carroll notes, "'apprentices' was usually a term of contempt equal to, and essentially identical with, 'masterless men.'" Thus apprentice disturbances, such as those which occurred in 1595, triggered an intensive
roundup of vagrants.[15] Paul Griffiths attributes such suspicions about apprentices specifically to their "youth," which he terms a "contestatory territory"
whose dark side was envisioned by contemporary moralists to be unsettled,
licentious, irreligious, rebellious, and dominated by a "vagrant will." Griffiths
further investigates the criminalization of vagrancy and of "masterless" young
people as part of the efforts by authorities in the period to regulate youth.[16]

One of the fascinating discoveries of Griffiths' study of such youths in
early seventeenth–century Norwich is the equivalent intolerance by authorities of, on the one hand, the out-of-town homeless and vagrant and, on the
other hand, locally housed but "masterless" youths, specifically single men
who lived at home "out of service" and single women who had independently
taken lodging and were living "at their own hand." The latter were persecuted
by officials as if they were masterless vagrants: incarcerated in a bridewell, put
to supervised work, and instructed to find service, apprenticeship, or, in the
case of the women, a husband.[17] What is so intriguing about such persecutions
is that, in the minds of contemporary authorities, the vagrant experience need
not involve physical mobility or even homelessness. That is, vagrancy could be
metaphorical, or perhaps more accurately, metonymic. Such "associative vagrancy," implied in the persecutions of masterless residents, opens up our
study of housed servants and apprentices in London as well.

Even without becoming vagrants in fact, members of the huge body of servants and apprentices in London, as in other urban areas like Norwich, could
very well have experienced some of the conditions of vagrancy within their
designated social, economic, and physical positions. In the most basic sense,
such youths would have shared the sense of estrangement associated with
London life that has also been identified with vagrancy. Like many other Londoners and like vagrants, most servants and apprentices were immigrants, detached from their local communities and parental homes. They were also overwhelmingly young and single.[18] But, unlike other Londoners, yet especially
like vagrants, servants and apprentices were encouraged to remain unattached.
As Beier notes, "celibacy and sexual abstinence were written into apprentice-

ship indentures, and among servants it appears to have been exceptional, if not unheard of, for them to marry and have children while in service."[19]

Not only detached from their originary communities and homes but also barred from establishing their own families, such workers were caught in what amounted to a state of rupture. The extent to which an individual servant or apprentice might have experienced such dislocation would have depended on many other aspects of his or her position. Some apprentices, especially those from more well-to-do families placed in lucrative trades, would have probably felt less vulnerable (although status tensions could undermine such security, as discussed above). Others would have felt more vulnerable, especially parish apprentices taken from families desperately fractured by parental death, desertion, or destitution. Generally, however, the experience of service was fraught with potential fissures. To begin with, the length of service tended to be short-term and subject to layoffs if a master died or left town or suffered a financial setback. Even the contracted term of apprenticeship was no security. Violations of the seven-year apprenticeship term were so common, Beier points out, that "a contemporary singled out short apprenticeships and early marriages as causes of poverty and vagrancy."[20] We know that 60 percent of London's apprentices never completed their terms.[21] Certainly some of these workers profited from early termination, themselves breaking their indentures in order to return to their homes with their newly-acquired skills, as Steve Rappaport conjectures. But given the large numbers of apprentices among those arrested for vagrancy, a less rosy picture of broken terms colors the urban scene.[22] Furthermore, much evidence points to unsettling relations between servants/ apprentices and their masters. Theoretically, and especially in the case of apprenticeships, masters were to provide an alternative family for their dependent laborers, guiding and instructing them as father figures. Surely many masters strove to realize this ideal. But, as court records testify, mistreatment and violence as well as sexual relations were common. The end result of such mistreatment could be devastating: vagrancy, prostitution, even suicide.[23]

The master-servant bond was thus at best insecure and at worst subject to gross violation, unmooring apprentices and servants from any secure social, economic, or physical place. Dependent workers so cut loose might turn vagrant in deed. But such vagrancy most likely took the form of continuing and displaced labor. That is, the liberated apprentice or servant might take to the suburbs or the back alleys of the city proper and practice a craft illegally and surreptitiously, without the "freedom" of a company. Even more likely, he might craftily take up and cast off jobs as they came to hand: at one point practicing a trade, at the next working as a wage-laborer, at the next hawking ballads, pamphlets, or brooms, at the next shining shoes, begging, or stealing, at the next just roaming the streets, shops, and market stalls of London.[24] Nor was such shiftless trade-shifting solely a male prerogative, although the scope of female vagrant labor was more restricted. Women might also take up and cast off various crafts (spinning, stocking-knitting, lace-work), hawk sundry goods on the streets, and, of course, sell themselves as prostitutes. Any one of these nomadic laborers might actually have crossed paths with the industriously vagrant Thomas Spickernell (or his many look-alikes), who ended up wandering beyond London itself.

The case of London apprentices thus allows us to reimagine the displacement of vagrancy both metonymically and expansively. Just as actual vagrants / itinerants found themselves detached from a stable or cohesive community and family, Londoners were vulnerable to alienation, especially the huge socioeconomic group of London servants and apprentices, whose often fractured and uncertain place as dependent laborers could render them psychically — if intermittently — unmoored, even while physically housed, that is, without becoming vagrants in fact. What the special situation of London apprentices "at large" further offers us is a way of understanding such a state of alienation and instability in terms not only of community and family, or of a metonymic association of shared feelings of displacement, but also, more literally and expansively, of a new fluid economy that produced, and was reliant upon, mobile and intermittent labor. Many an apprentice who terminated his indenture or was terminated, as we have seen, joined this nomadic labor pool on the fringe of vagrancy itself. Paul Slack provides the example of Edward Yovell: "A vagrant taken in Salisbury," Yovell "had been born in London and begun wandering after ending an apprenticeship in Worcester. Twice in two years he took up casual work back in London, where he had friends, then helped with the harvest at his uncle's in Surrey, next worked at various inns in Chichester, and finally returned to Worcester via Salisbury, Bristol and Gloucester, where he might hope for casual work, or charity."[25] Ilana Krausman Ben-Amos also cites a host of other such mendicant laborers among early modern youths. One such youth worked at various times as an errand boy, a domestic servant, a gunmaker's apprentice, a pitman, a coachman, a driver, an agricultural laborer, a beggar, and a gardener.[26]

It is but a sidestep from such diversely employed youths, dispersed spatially as well as economically over the English landscape, to the pedlars and chapmen of all ages who linked town and country in a network of exchange. So necessary were these tradesmen to the dissemination of consumer goods that the new vagrancy law of 1604 omitted them from the list of the legally vagrant (though they continued to be persecuted well into the late seventeenth century).[27] Spickernell was seizing an opportunity and capitalizing on a demand when he shifted from being an apprentice for a bookbinder to becoming a pedlar. Pedlars and petty chapmen specialized in trading in the diverse cheap luxury goods of a burgeoning new domestic economy discussed at length by Joan Thirsk. The late sixteenth and early seventeenth centuries, Thirsk notes, saw the rise of new goods that capitalized on surplus labor. Lace-work, or stocking-knitting, or the making of pins and buttons, or distilling *aqua vita* were all such new trades.[28] That they were conceived of not only as requiring few start-up costs but also as occupying a space outside the traditional labor force is suggested by the setting up of vagrants to work in such trades in institutions designed during this period for employing the poor. Among the twenty-six "Artes, Occupations, Labors, and Works, to be set up in Bridewell" in London, for instance, were included such new domestic labors as the making of "nayles," "gloues," "Combes," "Inkle and Tape," "silke Lace," "Pinnes," "Pointes," "bayes," and "feltes," as well as the "knitting of hose," "spinning of Linnen yarne," and "Drawing of wier."[29]

Even outside the workhouse, much of the lower spectrum of society was engaged in by-employments of these kinds in addition to their "established" trade. Holding down more than one job was becoming the norm. As Thirsk points out, "poorer men had two and three occupations at once. Licensed alehouse keepers in Staffordshire, for example, were also tailors or weavers, shearmen or wheelwrights, husbandmen, shoe makers, dyers, or joiners."[30] Such multi-tasking was the geographically placed equivalent to the other common practice of shifting from job to job (into which simultaneous multiple employment easily converted) that especially characterized the wage-earner and other laboring poor. As Jeremy Boulton observes in his study of Boroughside, Southwark, laborers could be variously described as "porters, ostlers, tapsters, husbandmen, carmen, draymen, chamberlains and servingmen," reflecting the various kinds of employment they typically undertook.[31]

That sixteenth- and seventeenth-century authorities felt uneasiness with such diffusion of labor can be seen in the conceptual problem they faced when listing the "occupation" of those arrested for vagrancy. Typically, as with the occasionally and serially employed Wiltshire musician arrested in 1605 — "sometimes a weaver, sometimes a surgeon, sometimes a minstrel, sometimes a dyer, and now a bullard" — the vagrant laborer would be accused of having "*no trade to live by.*"[32] The notion of a new category of poor — neither deserving impotent nor undeserving sturdy rogue, but deserving, sturdy indigent who sought but could not find enough work — did slowly seep into the official consciousness. The 1572 vagrancy law, for instance, though severe against offenders, also included for the first time a proviso for itinerant harvest workers and for servants who had been turned away or whose masters had died.

And later statutes attempted to employ resident "able" poor by providing for parish apprenticeships and workhouses. For all its well-meaning efforts, however, authorities continued to have difficulty distinguishing the unemployed, the underemployed, and the multi-tasked or in-transit laboring poor from the incorrigibly idle or "sturdy beggar."[33] Such a category crisis fueled fears and hostilities on the part of authorities. Official attacks (proclamations, statutes, roundups) against "vagrancy" proliferated. And, though the vagrancy laws might appear to have softened as the sixteenth century progressed—as punishments shifted from ear-borings and death to, more typically, whippings—such "leniency" was in fact aimed at widening the punishing reach of the law.[34]

How much did the "common man" share the authorities' relentless fears and antagonisms toward the vagrant? It is hard to say. Certainly, many would have also experienced the conceptual problem and anxiety of officials over "placing" the vagrant laborer. With the rise of whipping posts all over London in the 1590s, the "man on the street," in the form of the lowly constable, took on the primary responsibility of inflicting punishment for the "crime" of vagrancy.[35] But, as Steve Hindle comments, "historians have underestimated the sheer difficulty experienced by parish constables in identifying poor migrants."[36] The common man could be not only a confused but also an unwilling participant in persecutions, as is evident in complaints by officials such as Edward Hext, a Somerset justice, about the poor rate of apprehension, conviction, and punishment for vagrancy and related crimes.[37] It would seem that contemporaries generally experienced a confusing mixture of attitudes—fear, antagonism, sympathy—in thinking of the vagrant and in their vagrant thinking.

Such conflicted feelings were no doubt further complicated by the extent to which residents profited from the migrant/laboring poor by employing them for occasional work, for example, or by taking rent money from them. And, of course, such attitudes were also inflected by the extent to which contemporaries actually saw themselves in such impoverished itinerants. A large percentage of householders did not pay poor rates but were not on poor relief (44 percent in Warwick in 1583, for instance; 43 percent in Boroughside, Southwark, in 1618; 50 percent in Aldenham, Hertfordshire, in the early seventeenth century).[38] These unrelieved householders were able—though just able—to maintain their families in "normal" years. We might designate such independent poor "middling" sorts, as does Boulton. Certainly some of them would have met one modern definition of this class: "independent trading households." As recent studies of "the middling sort" have shown, however, the category, while not invalid, is highly elusive. Ascription of "middling" status varies according to such diverse factors (locale, wealth, age, etc.) that the category, in the words of Jonathan Barry, can be separated "into a thousand different categories."[39] My concern here is not so much with sorting through such nuances in the service of class or status identification, as it is with viewing the poor householders identified above within certain shared habits or experiences of living and working, which certainly cut across class lines. Whether we call these people "the poorest of the middling sorts," "the low," or just "the poor," we can recognize that they constituted the group just above those on parish relief and the vagrant, people who were most prone to unemployment, multiple employment, desperate indigence, and mobility. One would expect that, especially for this lowest sector of housed society, uneasy identification with the "vagrant" migrant/laboring poor could have been very strong. For the middling "low," especially, then, the space of vagrancy — geographical, social, psychological, and economic — would have been variously and at times ambivalently inhabited.

To conclude, the special situation of London apprentices opens up this multiply conceived space by exposing its investment in a vagrant market. Such a market, as characterized by Jean-Christophe Agnew, took the form of a market *process* rather than a traditional market *place*.[40] Nevertheless, I would add, many of the lower orders within London and beyond experienced its workings physically and topographically, that is, in the form of formless or spacious wandering. The unbound or "freelance" apprentice can be seen as a type of this new itinerant laborer. When an apprentice's indenture was terminated and he became a wage-laborer, or when he was accepted into the freedom of a company and — as in 50 percent of the cases of those who so completed their terms — became a journeyman,[41] he entered a vagrant economy that had a wide reach. The wage-laborer and journeyman joined large numbers of other itinerant and variously employed workers, including servants, painters, seamen, soldiers, purveyors of medicine, entertainers, tinkers, masons, carpenters, carriers, hawkers, and chapmen (not to mention the multitasked but geographically "placed" workers who could at any point "move on") that formed the shifting "ground" of a strangely vagrant economy.

Finally — and here our investigative labors come full circle — the unstable and exchangeable *investment* of the vagrant/laboring poor in diverse employments within this new market allows us to revisit the psychic space of vagrancy and hypothesize more fully the character of vagrant identity. As we shall see in the next section, the vagrant subject, detached from a secure community, family, or even marketplace, takes on the contours of a truly spacious, one might even say *virtual,* subjectivity. Such an open identity could have been occasionally and provisionally shared by others, such as the "middling" poor discussed above, who might be similarly or closely, if not identically, positioned socially, economically, and/or geographically. For, as we have seen, one need not be vagrant to be treated like a vagrant or to feel vagrant. The vagrant experience was truly spacious. That said, we can begin sketching out vagrant subjectivity with the physically as well as economically itinerant poor foremost in mind.

Vagrant Subjectivity: The Virtual "I"

Before beginning it can be legitimately asked: how can we pretend to "know" the vagrant subject when such a subject is virtually invisible and incomprehensible not only to us but to many of his or her contemporaries? Certainly few vagrants left written records of their thoughts or feelings. Furthermore, authorities who "investigated" vagrants primarily gathered only bare-bones accounts: "Most records," notes Beier, "give no more than a name, place of origin, date and place of arrest."[42] Rare are fleshed-out accounts of vagrants or the itinerant/laboring poor, and even those are usually mediated by the authority doing the reporting. Given the kinds of "evidence" we are dealing with, then, one could argue that any notion of what such a subject actually experienced is largely conjectural, an imaginative creation of a virtual "I." To a certain extent this is true. In fact, one of the defining features of the vagrant subject cited in the statutes of the period was an inability to give a proper "reckoning" of his or her life. The Salisbury entries of arrested vagrants often take pains to note this failing. An entry of 8 April 1605, for instance, regarding "Dorothy Grene *alias* Percye, a wanderer" concludes "She is *not able to give account of her life*" and a 7 April 1606 record of "one naming himself Thomas Carter" declares that he is "an idle person and a vagrant *not able to yield any account of his idle course of life*" (my emphases); he was thus "punished."[43] It is as if, in the minds of early modern authorities, an account of one's life, or what we might call "autobiography," could belong only to the settled. Not to be able to give such an account labeled one as criminal.

Lacking such "legitimate," autobiographical accounts, we cannot penetrate the self-reflections of the early modern vagrant. If we cannot speak with most of these vagrant dead, however, we are not reduced to silence, nor to the simply imaginary. We can at least catch momentary voicings of them within the official mediations and — based on our mappings of their disconnected positionings within early modern society — we can begin to sketch an outline, however tentative, of what identity vagrants might have formed. With the goal of reaching such a hypothesis in mind, I propose we revisit two well-documented "groups" of the period whom we have found to be metonymically akin to vagrants: youths and apprentices.

The work of Steven R. Smith on apprentices (whom we have found to be always precariously placed, often psychically dislocated, and frequently turning vagrant in deed) is especially helpful. Drawing on Erik Erikson, Smith observes that the long and uncertain terms of apprenticeship created something of a "lifestyle" of adolescence: a "way of life between childhood and adulthood." Such an adolescent lifestyle, Smith goes on to argue, involves a period of "free role experimentation" whereby youths search for a niche or identity in adult society and in the process establish "an adolescent subculture with what looks like a final rather than a transitory or, in fact, initial identity formation." Smith finds such role experimentation in contemporary ballads and stories of apprentices, which depict a spectrum of characters from riotous youths to manly heroes, and sees it facilitated by "the vast range of opportunities in London." Out of such role experimentation, Smith argues, apprentices developed a subculture, replete with rituals, creeds, and programs, that assumed a permanent rather than transitory status.[44]

Ben-Amos and other historians have since questioned the extent to which apprentices or youths in general formed any organized subculture, countering this theory in the same way that the theory of a vagrant subculture has been undermined. Griffiths, however, has recently countered the counter by claiming that "subculture" **is too** restrictive a notion. That is, he posits, we need not argue for a youth "subculture" in order to recognize a common character to the age of youth. Such an age, he argues, amounted to a complex, ambiguous, and contested territory signposted and shaped by "shared formative experiences." Two such formative experiences that both Griffiths and Ben-Amos agree on were service or apprenticeship and mobility. Indeed, Ben-Amos (concurring with Martin Ingram as well) asserts that "the spatial mobility of young people was itself perhaps the most important feature of an adolescent culture in early modern England."[45] For Griffiths, such mobility was a significant factor allowing youths creative expression in the face of repressive households and local communities: "The high rate of migration," he contends, "was one way in which young people crossed these alleged obstacles." Griffiths further extends the notion of liberating spatial mobility to include the many "shared cultural and social moments" experienced by youths outside the constricting place of the household where they lived and served — roaming the streets, playing games on the green, indulging in alehouse pleasures, and so on — activities which adults often condoned and in which they also sometimes participated.[46]

Griffiths' flexible and open-ended characterization of the youth experience can help us further understand the vagrant experience as well. Rather than thinking of vagrants as constituting an organized subculture or specific class, we might best think of them as sharing an array of practices or habits —

foremost being social, economic, and geographical mobility—that could be experienced in some forms and on certain occasions by more than the legally vagrant: many of Griffiths's unsettled youths, for instance, as well as itinerant laborers and multi-tasked, poor householders of all ages. Thinking along these lines, we can return to Smith's notion of role experimentation. The common experience of mobility among vagrants, I would argue, would itself have allowed for, or more probably, required role experimentation—if not produced a categorical subculture—similar to the kind Smith discusses. Repeatedly moving from place to place (both geographic and socioeconomic), the mobile "vagrant" youth would most likely adopt a casual and provisional attitude to the variously undertaken jobs and relationships along the way. Furthermore, if we take away the ultimate "niche" in society that such youthful experimentation temporarily filled—which happened in over half of apprenticeship cases—we have the potential for open-ended role-playing or, perhaps more accurately, since it involved serious economic investment, role-*speculation*.

Such was the very situation, I propose, of the vagrant subject in early modern England. Traveling the byways of urban and rural England, the vagrant subject was at all times, one might say, an "apprentice" or "journeyman." As with apprentices embarked upon serial role-speculation, the vagrant subject—shifting from place to place, relationship to relationship, and job to job—apprenticed in a range of different identities without ever attaining the "freedom" of a whole and stable subject. This perpetually speculative subject would have little resembled Stephen Greenblatt's notion of self born out of masterful acts of "fashioning" or "rehearsal." Such conceived self-determination (however ultimately illusory and culturally defined, as Greenblatt shows) is grounded in a power structure by which the dominant creates himself—or in the case of a class, itself—through assertion over an imagined other.[47] The vagrant had no such empowering "place," either physical, social, or economic. This is not to say that the vagrant subject would have lacked any sense of autonomous subjectivity. Indeed, vagrancy approximated in many ways what we have come to think of as a kind of free individualism. The vagrant was detached, solitary, and independent. He was "his own man." But, at the same time, the vagrant occupied a spaciousness that was provisional (subjected to the vagaries of an unpredictable marketing network), multiple, and anonymous. He was "no man" or, perhaps more accurately, "many men." In the spirit of vagrancy, we might best characterize such a subject by a deviant coining of our own: "multi-vidualism."

The multi-vidual vagrant subject in the early modern period, then, can be seen to be composed of dispersed, serial "selves"—variously defined occupationally, relationally, or spatially—which could be taken up, adjusted, and cast off as occasion demanded. One might be tempted to equate this notion of subjectivit(ies) with theatrical role-playing, especially since unlicensed actors were included among those listed in the vagrancy acts of 1572 and 1598, and players cohabited with the vagrant/laboring poor in the suburbs and liberties of London.[48] Indeed, disguise and theatricality do figure prominently in contemporary beggar and rogue literature. However, as we try to focus on the shifting "I" of actual vagrants and their fellow itinerant laborers, I hesitate to ascribe the notion of theatricality to their activities (and even in the rogue/beggar literature, I would argue, disguisings in practice are of a more extra-theatrical or "tactical" nature). Certainly vagrants engaged in undertakings or speculations that involved changing "roles" and adopting aliases to hide their vagrant identity — ironically, at the same time thus underscoring it. But surely vagrants could not have afforded to engage in role-*playing* in any theatrical sense of the word. Too much was at stake or *invested* in their roles, however transitional or casual they might have been. We might best think of such a subject as "performative" in an intensive and extensive version of Judith Butler's sense of the term: as variably constructed in and through acts of continual displacement.[49]

It is in light of this multiply-displaced identity formation that we can further expand Christopher Hill's notion of vagrant "mobility and freedom." In a section under this heading in *The World Turned Upside Down,* Hill emphasizes the independence and liberty that characterized vagrant life. Whether squatters in woodland and pasture areas or the more typical frequenters of the suburbs of towns, Hill argues, vagrants sought out places that were free from established and coercive authority. Thus, for instance, one contemporary complained that in London's suburbs "many vicious persons get liberty to live as they please, for want of some heedful eye."[50] Other cultural critics have since further focused on the "place" of liberty, most notably Steven Mullaney in his study of the theater and London's suburbs, *The Place of the Stage.* But I would argue that it was not simply the *placement* of woodlands or suburbs — or, for that matter of the streets of London (where trading was virtually unregulated) — that bestowed liberty.[51] It was also, and perhaps even more importantly, the unattachedness and dispersal of the vagrants who frequented them. In other words, vagrant freedom is more a matter of *space* than place. Sociological and philosophical studies ranging from the geographer Yi-Fu Tuan's *Space and Place* to more postmodern works, such as Michel de Certeau's *Practice of Everyday Life* and Henri Lefebvre's *Production of Space,* help us to conceptualize this distinction.[52] Together these studies unmoor conventional place to make room for space: as a state of consciousness, as constructed, as mobile, and as free. A modern example of place, in these terms, would be one's home or workplace, where familiar and predictable activities occur. Space is more strange, shifting, and malleable, more open to being differently inhabited or used, like an airport lounge area.

The Renaissance, I would posit, also understood such distinctions between place and space — however suspiciously, cautiously, or enthusiastically — as Andrew McRae has shown in his study of changing attitudes toward travel in England from the sixteenth to the seventeenth centuries.[53] Furthermore, I would argue, the actual terms by which we are construing this distinction would not have been foreign to contemporaries of the period. Acknowledgment in the Renaissance that the term "space" meant mobility can be seen in the common use of the word to designate the passage of time: as, for example, in the phrase, "the space of two days." Such temporal usage of the term "space" appears regularly in descriptions of lengths of various punishments that should be meted out to apprehended vagrants articulated in the successive statutes against vagrancy of the sixteenth and seventeenth centuries. The term "space" in these acts is associated with transience akin to the vagrant him- or herself. In official and common contemporary parlance, that is, time is space without place; it moves.

The early modern vagrant subject, I would argue, occupied just such a transient space, especially in urban environments such as London. Tramping the streets of London (within or without the walls), speculating in a range of affective, social and economic roles, and thus continually remaking the spaces he or she inhabited, the vagrant made of the city itself, in de Certeau's words, "an immense social experience of lacking place."[54] And, of course, this unlocalized social experience, which extended to other urban and country spaces as well, was also for the vagrant a psychological one, a state of consciousness that existed from place to place and was thus everywhere and nowhere at once. The inability of vagrant subjects to name many of the towns they passed through underscores such unplaceable "nowhereness." Ann Smyth, in search of the husband who twice deserted her and stole her cloak, began her wandering relatively grounded but increasingly, as she confessed to the examiner, she knew not her place: "And when he came not to her agayne," according to the examiner's report, "she went out of Warwik to Kenelworth and lay there that night. The next night she lay at a towne twoo miles beyond coventry the name she knoweth not. And so from towne to towne in & out. And one night she lay in Noneton but where she hath bene ever sithens she knoweth not."[55] Such an expanding "nowhere experience" could finally have been at best but a "simulation" of free subjectivity, in the Baudrillardian sense: an enactment for which there was no foundational reality in the background.[56] The contemporary John Taylor, in his ambivalent paean to beggary, *The Praise, Antiquity, and*

Commoditie of Beggerie, Beggars, and Begging (1621), momentarily captures just such an ungrounded simulation of vagrant "freedom":

> A begger liues here in this vale of sorrow,
> And trauels here to day, and there to morrow.
> The next day being neither here, nor there;
> But almost no where, and yet euery where.[57]

Such a free-ranging "no where" subject was simultaneously alienated and free. For, in the words of Tuan, "place is security, space is freedom." Or, put another way, space is freedom without security. It is vagrancy.[58]

The ambiguously "free" space of vagrant subjectivity would have been most intensely occupied by perpetual itinerants in early modern England: not only wandering beggars or rogues but also migrant laborers (who might at any time resort to begging or theft) in the process of continually shifting from place to place, relationship to relationship, job to job. But what about those other subjects on the margins of vagrancy (im)proper? — those housed but socially and psychically displaced apprentices and servants, or those many poor householders just "getting by" (indigent husbandmen in the country; petty craftsmen and minor traders in the city) who often held more than one job, occasionally needed poor relief, and frequently were forced to move and change jobs? I would argue that the space of vagrant subjectivity — of speculating in displaced, serial identit(ies) — would also have been open, if not wholly available, to many of these poor. That is, the poor householder might very well have provisionally and/or partially experienced vagrant subjectivity if not vagrancy per se. Implicit in this claim is the argument that subjectivity itself need not be consistent or singular.

What I am proposing, in other words, is that we need to expand our thinking about early modern subjectivity so that its conceptualization itself becomes vagrant or multiple. In recent years, many models of subjectivity have been promulgated by cultural critics of the period: from the radical debunking of the older humanistic notion of Renaissance individualism or interiority (for example, by such Marxist critics as Francis Barker and Catherine Belsey) to the currently dominant reaffirmations of subjectivity, but only as dependent on social or political constructs (as variously argued by Stephen Greenblatt, Jonathan Goldberg, and myself, among others) to the latest "born-again" visions (such as Debora Kuller Shuger's religiously-construed subjectivity — which is fragmented or interior, dependent on whether the subject is Protestant or Catholic — or Katharine Eisaman Maus's God-based inwardness that cuts across religious lines).[59] Much of value is offered by these various interpretations, but two problems recur: (1) they tend to offer a universal or holistic version of the early modern subject when in fact that Renaissance "I" derives from consideration of a select pool of contemporaries who are white, male (Belsey is the notable exception here), and of the upper or at least educated middling sorts; and (2) such a universalized subjectivity (however differently defined) tends to be treated as if it were singular and consistent.

Might it not be more likely that, as Maus herself has suggested, subjectivity is in fact mobile and even inconsistent?[60] That is, to expand upon her point: depending on many variable general factors (status, wealth, age, religion, gender, locale), as well as on diverse shifting particular events in everyday living, might not one and the same subject experience, say, an intense withdrawal or interior wholeness at one moment, an entirely publicly or socially constructed identity at another, an overwhelmingly self-divided or internally fractured sensibility at another, or a sacral self securely grounded by a Godly "I/eye" at yet another? The poor worker whose family was crammed together into a one-room cottage or who shared his or her meager urban space with strangers within a small section of a tenement may have been denied any sense of a placed interior "I"; but s/he might still have lived through — however provisionally, partially, or ambivalently — a variety of changing, different "selves": perhaps as socially constructed, then as God-determined, or then — in the course of job diversity and mobility — as vagrantly multiple and displaced.

Indeed, to conclude with yet another hypothesis, I posit that the conception of subjectivity as itself mutable and manifold might well have been most available as a "thought" in the early modern period by those lower to lower-middling orders for whom vagrant subjectivity, as defined in this chapter — as provisional, manifold, mobile, and dispersed — was in varying degrees a lived experience. And those persons were by and large lowly urban dwellers, especially Londoners, though always capable of wandering far beyond the city walls.

Notes

1. *The Shirburne Ballads, 1585–1616,* ed. Andrew Clark (Oxford: Clarendon, 1907), pp. 6–7.

2. "Minister," of course, had both secular and religious meanings in the period. Secular meanings included in the *OED* are 1, "a servant or attendant," such as a server of meat and drink, and 3. "A high officer of state." Employable in both secular and religious ways is definition 2, "One who acts under the authority of another, one who carries out executive duties as the agent or representative of a superior." Definition 4 in the *OED* offers purely "ecclesiastical and religious uses" of the term.

3. A. L. Beier, *Masterless Men: The Vagrancy Problem in England, 1560–1640* (London and New York: Methuen, 1986), p. 89.

4. Beier, *Masterless Men*, p. 98.

5. Beier, *Masterless Men*, pp. 140–41.

6. Christopher Pye, "The Theater, the Market, and the Subject of History," *ELH* 61, no. 3 (1994): 501–3.

7. A. L. Beier and Roger Finlay, eds. *London, 1500–1700: The Making of the Metropolis* (London: Methuen, 1986), pp. 18, 19.

8. Beier, "Social Problems in Elizabethan London," *Journal of Interdisciplinary History* 9, no. 2 (Autumn 1978): 214.

9. Paul Slack, "Vagrants and Vagrancy in England, 1598–1664," *Economic History Review* 27 (1974): 363–66, and *Poverty and Policy in Tudor and Stuart England* (Cambridge: Cambridge University Press, 1991), pp. 68, 99; Beier, "Social Problems," pp. 220–21, and *Masterless Men*, pp. 52, 67–68.

10. *London, 1500–1700*, ed. Beier and Finlay, p. 20.

11. Ian W. Archer, *The Pursuit of Stability: Social Relations in Elizabethan London* (Cambridge: Cambridge University Press, 1991), p. 76.

12. Lawrence Stone, "Social Mobility in England, 1500–1700," *Past and Present* 33 (1966): 31.

13. Beier, "Engine of Manufacture: The Trades of London," in *London, 1500–1700*, ed. Beier and Finlay, p. 154.

14. Stone, "Social Mobility," p. 53.

15. William C. Carroll, *Fat King, Lean Beggar: Representations of Poverty in the Age of Shakespeare* (Ithaca, N.Y.: Cornell University Press, 1996), p. 141, n. 15 (see also pp. 142–43); Archer, *Pursuit of Stability*, pp. 1–2 (see also pp. 243–44).

16. Paul Griffiths, *Youth and Authority: Formative Experiences in England, 1560–1640* (Oxford: Clarendon, 1996), pp. 13, 40, 60. On masterless youths, see pp. 351–89.

17. Griffiths, *Youth and Authority*, pp. 351–89.

18. Beier, "Social Problems," pp. 213–14; *London, 1500–1700*, ed. Beier and Finlay, p. 50; Slack, "Vagrants," p. 366.

19. Beier, "Social Problems," p. 216.

20. Beier, "Social Problems," p. 215.

21. Griffiths, *Youth and Authority*, p. 330, n. 172.

22. Steven Rappaport, "Reconsidering Apprenticeship in Sixteenth-Century London," in *Renaissance Society and Culture: Essays in Honor of Eugene F. Rice, Jr.*, ed. John Monfassani and Ronald S. Musto (New York: Italica, 1991), pp. 239–61; see also his *Worlds within Worlds: Structures of Life in Sixteenth-Century London* (Cambridge: Cambridge University Press, 1989), pp. 311–15. Archer also questions Rappaport's findings (*Pursuit of Stability*, p. 15).

23. Beier, "Social Problems," pp. 215–17. See also Steven R. Smith, "The Ideal and Reality: Apprentice-Master Relationships in Seventeenth-Century London," *History of Education Quarterly* 21 (1981): 449–59, esp. 457, and his "The London Apprentices as Seventeenth-Century Adolescents," *Past and Present* 61 (1973): 151–53; Ilana Krausman Ben-Amos, *Adolescence and Youth in Early Modern England* (New Haven: Yale University Press, 1994), pp. 100–108; Archer, *Pursuit of Stability*, pp. 216–18; Griffiths, *Youth and Authority*, pp. 290–350; and Michael MacDonald and Terence R. Murphy, *Sleepless Souls: Suicide in Early Modern England* (Oxford: Clarendon, 1990), pp. 252–55.

24. Beier, "Social Problems," p. 210; see also Ben-Amos, *Adolescence and Youth,* pp. 218–19.

25. Slack, *Poverty and Policy,* pp. 94–95.

26. Ben-Amos, *Adolescence and Youth,* pp. 82–83. Ben-Amos has a habit of ending the youth's story with placement as an apprentice, but, given the large drop-out rate, in many cases such placement would be but a stage in a continuous process of displacement.

27. Beier, *Masterless Men,* p. 90.

28. Joan Thirsk, *Economic Policy and Projects: The Development of a Consumer Society in Early Modern England* (Oxford: Clarendon, 1978), p. 6.

29. *Orders Appointed to be executed in the Cittie of London, for setting roges and idle persons to worke, and for releefe of the poore* (London, n.d.); probably printed in 1582 or 1586. See also Thirsk, *Economic Policy,* pp. 65–66.

30. Thirsk, *Economic Policy,* p. 172; see also pp. 3, 7–8, 110–11, 148, and esp. 155–57.

31. Jeremy Boulton, *Neighbourhood and Society: A London Suburb in the Seventeenth Century* (Cambridge: Cambridge University Press, 1987), pp. 72–73.

32. Beier, *Masterless Men,* p. 88.

33. *Statutes of the Realm,* 14 Eliz. I, c.5. The matter of who was to be counted as a vagrant, Slack notes, was "a topic much disputed in the Commons in 1571 and 1572"; *The English Poor Law, 1531–1782* (London: Macmillan, 1990), pp. 12, 20.

34. Archer, *Pursuit of Stability,* pp. 244–45.

35. Archer, *Pursuit of Stability,* p. 244.

36. Steve Hindle, "Exclusion Crises: Poverty, Migration and Parochial Responsibility in English Rural Communities, c. 1560–1660," *Rural History* 7, no. 2 (October 1996): 41.

37. Letter to Burghley (1596), reprinted in Frank Aydelotte, *Elizabethan Rogues and Vagabonds,* vol. 1, Oxford Historical and Literary Studies (Oxford: Clarendon, 1913), pp. 168–73.

38. Boulton, *Neighbourhood and Society,* p. 115; Hindle, "Exclusion Crises," p. 131.

39. Boulton, *Neighbourhood and Society,* p. 115. Jonathan Barry, Introduction to *The Middling Sort of People: Culture, Society and Politics in England, 1550–1800,* ed. Jonathan Barry and Christopher Brooks (New York: St. Martin's, 1994), p. 17; definition, p. 2.

40. Jean-Christophe Agnew, *Worlds Apart: The Market and the Theater in Anglo-American Thought, 1550–1750* (Cambridge: Cambridge University Press, 1986), p. 41.

41. Rappaport, *Worlds within Worlds,* p. 333.

42. Beier, "Vagrants and the Social Order in Elizabethan England," *Past and Present* 64 (1974): 4.

43. "Register of Passport for Vagrants, 1598–1638," in *Poverty in Early-Stuart Salisbury,* ed. Paul Slack (Wiltshire Record Society, Devizes, 1975), pp. 34, 37. So, too, the 1572 vagrancy act classifies as vagrant anyone who "can gyve *no reckninge* howe hee or shee dothe lawfully get his or her Lyvinge" (14 Eliz. I, c.5; my emphasis).

44. Smith, "London Apprentices," pp. 157–61; see also his "Ideal and Reality," pp. 449–59; and, on the range of apprentice literature as well as its political significance, Mark Thornton Burnett's recent book, *Masters and Servants in English Renaissance Drama and Culture* (New York: St. Martin's Press, 1997).

45. Ben-Amos, *Adolescence and Youth,* p. 206.

46. Griffiths, *Youth and Authority,* pp. 114–15.

47. See Stephen Greenblatt's *Renaissance Self-Fashioning: From More to Shakespeare* (Chicago: University of Chicago Press, 1984) and "Invisible Bullets," in *Shakespearean Negotiations: The Circulation of Social Energy in Renaissance England* (Berkeley: University of California Press, 1988), pp. 21–65.

48. See Agnew, *Worlds Apart,* esp. pp. 52, 99, and 101–48.

49. Judith Butler, *Gender Trouble: Feminism and the Subversion of Identity* (London and New York: Routledge, 1990), pp. 134–41.

50. Christopher Hill, *The World Turned Upside Down: Radical Ideas during the English Revolution* (New York: Viking, 1972), pp. 32–40; *London, 1500–1700,* ed. Beier and Finlay, p. 21.

51. Steven Mullaney, *The Place of the Stage: License, Play, and Power in Renaissance England* (Chicago: University of Chicago Press, 1988). Peter Clark notes that "trading was virtually free in the streets of London"; *The English Alehouse: A Social History, 1200–1830* (London: Longman, 1983), p. 202.

52. Yi-Fu Tuan, *Space and Place: The Perspective of Experience* (Minneapolis: University of Minnesota Press, 1977); Michel de Certeau, *The Practice of Everyday Life,* trans. Steven Rendall (Berkeley: University of California Press, 1984); Henri Lefebvre, *The Production of Space,* trans. Donald Nicholson-Smith (Oxford: Blackwell, 1991).

53. Andrew McRae, "The Peripatetic Muse: Internal Travel and the Cultural Production of Space in Pre-Revolutionary England," in *The Country and the City Revisited: England and the Politics of Culture, 1550–1850,* ed. Gerald MacLean, Donna Landry, Joseph P. Ward (Cambridge: Cambridge University Press, 1999), pp. 41–57.

54. de Certeau, *Practice of Everyday Life,* p. 103.

55. *The Book of John Fisher, Town Clerk and Deputy Recorder of Warwick (1580–88),* ed. Thomas Kemp (Warwick: Henry T. Cooke and Son, n.d.), p. 106.

56. "Simulacra and Simulations," in *Jean Baudrillard: Selected Writings,* ed. Mark Poster (Stanford: Stanford University Press, 1988), pp. 166–84.

57. *All the Works of John Taylor the Water Poet,* pub. 1630 (London: Scolar Press, 1973), p. 99.

58. Tuan, *Space and Place,* p. 3.

59. Francis Barker, *The Tremulous Private Body: Essays on Subjection* (London: Methuen, 1984); Catherine Belsey, *The Subject of Tragedy: Identity and Difference in Renaissance Drama* (London: Methuen, 1985); Greenblatt, *Renaissance Self-Fashioning;* Jonathan Goldberg, *James I and the Politics of Literature: Jonson, Shakespeare, Donne, and Their Contemporaries* (Baltimore: Johns Hopkins University Press, 1983); Patricia Fumerton, *Cultural Aesthetics: Renaissance Literature and the Practice of Social Ornament* (Chicago: University of Chicago Press, 1991); Debora Kuller Shuger, *The Renaissance Bible: Scholarship, Sacrifice, and Subjectivity* (Berkeley: University of California Press, 1994); Katharine Eisaman Maus, *Inwardness and the Theater in the English Renaissance* (Chicago: University of Chicago Press, 1995).

60. Maus, *Inwardness,* pp. 29–30; following this reasoning, Maus makes a distinction between "subjectivity" and "inwardness," which, she argues, are not always commensurate.

PART IV

DIVERSIONS
AND DISPLAY

Foreign visitors with privileged access, like Frederic Gerschow, companion to Philip Julius, the duke of Stettin-Pomerania, toured palaces, described their treasures, and termed London splendid. William Harrison and Fynes Moryson, by contrast, emphasized that the city's edifices did not present a uniform street facade, that domestic wealth was not exhibited in outward show, and that, in the words of Moryson, "all the magnificence of London building is hidden from the view." The essays in this section begin with structures — country houses, playhouses, urban palaces — but turn also to the objects, activities, and values that constituted London's unargued "splendor."

The Elizabethan country house is not the most obvious object of analysis for a study of "material London"; Wollaton, Hardwick, Longleat, and Worksop rose in splendid isolation from their imparked grounds. But, as Alice T. Friedman maintains in "Inside/Out: Women, Domesticity, and the Pleasures of the City," these most familiar artifacts of English society circa 1600 were, in fact, "bastions of court culture set within the rural landscape but separate from it." The very isolation of the country house worked to segregate its inhabitants from country people, reinforcing the London character of their lives. "The experience of London and of its culture of display" dictated how country gentry built their houses, what they wore, and what gifts they gave. Even though Sir Francis Willoughby preferred to live in Nottinghamshire, London was the focus of his arts patronage and the source of his design ideas, skilled craftsmen, luxury goods, specialty foods, and funerary monuments. His wife, however, irrevocably strained the marriage with her frequent stays in the city. For, Friedman states, "the country house as an institution rested heavily on rules of etiquette and concepts of leisure which required upper-class women to remain behind the newly constructed walls of the country estate." In this, the consumer culture was complicit, for women could own London luxury items without being in London. But London's *amusements* were not transferable, and therein lay the trouble for Lady Willoughby. In her youth Lady Anne Clifford complained bitterly about being exiled to rural Kent; when in her age she turned her back on London, Friedman suggests, it was precisely because the city, its goods, and its diversions were temptations even for this strong-willed woman.

For men and women of all classes, a principal pleasure of London was playgoing. In "The Authority of the Globe and the Fortune," Andrew Gurr presents a revisionist history of the way in which that pleasure came to be institutionalized around 1600, with London established as the "natural, proper, settled, and approved place" for players. Until 1594, itinerant players had used innyards and market squares. In that year, however, two companies were officially allocated the Theatre and the Rose, to be succeeded between 1599 and 1600 by the Globe and the Fortune. Even at the earlier date, neither structure was what players would have wanted in an acting space. By 1594, they had already had extensive experience of performing in schools and guildhalls, and, while outdoor theaters held the advantages of natural light and huge capacity, indoor theaters had taught them the commercial value of enclosed spaces where all viewers had to be paying customers. By the early seventeenth century, interiors were the playing places of choice in Bristol, York, Oxford, and elsewhere; only in London were there permanent open-air theaters. What set London apart was its competing centers of authority, with Lord Mayors making annual attempts to have playing banned, but with the Lord Chamberlain anxious for the companies to provide the court with Christmas entertainment. He was able to offer protection in suburban locations. Gradually, outdoor theaters acquired their own authority, as Gurr details. A repertoire of plays written for these spaces militated against their radical redesign. When Shakespeare's company acquired the Blackfriars in 1608, they could have moved indoors for good; they did not. When the Globe burned in 1613, they rebuilt it. They continued to perform in the place that now seemed like "home."

Linda Levy Peck writes that in 1600 London lagged behind the rest of Europe architecturally. By 1625, however, England's aristocracy had fully embraced Continental culture. In "Building, Buying, and Collecting in London, 1600–1625," she argues that the turning point was 1603. Under James, aristocratic culture was British, as distinct from English; urban, through the construction of London palaces as well as country houses; gendered, with women and court favorites playing significant roles as patrons and style setters; European, in the adoption of influences from France, Italy, and the Netherlands; and imperial, with houses built to British standards in Bermuda and Ireland. "What it meant to be noble in the seventeenth century," Peck concludes, "was significantly different from what it had meant a century and even decades before." Although gentlemen in London were encouraged by the Crown to settle and shop in the west end, in fact those who did not live in palaces along the Strand took lodgings in various wards of the city. Living in close proximity to craftsmen, merchants, and traders, theirs was an urban experience. For the elite, London was the home of the court, the source of luxury goods to send back to their country estates, and the site for social rituals of gift giving. Even so, the city did not keep pace with their developing taste for personal splendor. With no London art galleries, there was no infrastructure for importing the paintings, sculptures, and tapestries aristocrats had begun to collect. Ambassadors and agents were thus dispatched to the Continent on buying expeditions. The urban elite looked beyond London to create a London culture of display.

These essays trace paths of desire in early modern London. As Friedman shows, country houses could recreate the style of London and could import many of its goods, but they could not duplicate its pleasures. The behavior of elite women demonstrates that London remained an object of desire. According to Gurr, the actions of London censors introduced players to the advantages of closed playing spaces, but then the peculiar politics of the city denied them their desire. For this dissatisfaction there were compensations, and what London took with one hand it gave back, in unexpected ways, with the other. Peck describes London as the great style setter and taste maker, but she also demonstrates that the desires aroused by the city exceeded the city. Material London proved out the most basic anthropological theory of consumption: desire is never satisfied. It always has its discontents.

12

Inside/Out

Women, Domesticity, and the Pleasures of the City

Alice T. Friedman

A cluster of contradictions underlies the emergence of the English country house as a social and architectural institution in the last decades of the six-teenth century, not least of which is the growing importance of London in the lives of landowners and their families. For London was not only home to the court and the hub of a network of power and influence which stretched the length and breadth of the country, it was also England's most splendid mar-ketplace and the center of social life, a place teeming with activity in which public rituals and private dramas were played out in full view of discerning strangers. The experience of London and of its culture of display heightened anxiety about the power of things not only to communicate status but to *confer* status on their owners, causing men and women in the country — as else-where — to rethink their wardrobes, their houses, and the furnishings of their rooms.[1] Tastes and appetites formed in and by the city, however distant, were the engines which drove the process of change in the country, and the "country house" — physically located in the country and rooted in local traditions, yet shaped by the culture, the social norms, and the material world of London and the court — was created in response to these new, urban experiences.[2]

Thus the apparently straightforward term "country house" obscures the multiple functions of the architectural type and oversimplifies the image of the highly complex culture it embraces. Awareness of these contradictions is a recurrent theme in a number of artistic movements and forms associated with the late Elizabethan and Jacobean periods, including the "country house poem," as Raymond Williams pointed out long ago in *The Country and the City*.[3] Works like Jonson's "To Penshurst" celebrate country tradition in terms and images which are calculated to call attention to their opposites. Indeed, London-based artistic tastes and the depredations of court fashion loom ghostlike over the opening lines, through a series of negations:

Thou art not, Penshurst, built to envious show,
Of touch, or marble; nor canst boast a row
Of polish'd pillars, or a roofe of gold:
Thou hast no lantherne, whereof tales are told;
Or stayre, or courts; but stand'st an ancient pile . . .

(ll. 1–5)[4]

As a number of critics, notably Don Wayne and Leah Marcus, have argued, Jonson's poem, and those of other writers in this genre, can be understood within the context of fragmentation in Jacobean society caused by the erosion of traditional customs and allegiances, the increasing alienation of the rural populace, and the growth of London — not simply in physical size but as a pervasive presence in people's lives. Hence Jonson's emphasis on the calming presence of the landowner who maintains a household and dispenses hospitality in the country, an image again invoked through comparison, with which the poem ends:

Now, Penshurst, they that will proportion thee
With other edifices, when they see
Those proud, ambitious heaps, and nothing else,
May say, their lords have built, but thy lord dwells.

(ll. 99–102)[5]

Jonson problematizes activities and themes which recurred with regularity in the lives and relationships of real individuals and families as they moved back and forth between the country and the city. Emphasizing visual culture and consumption of goods, his writing goes to the heart of experiences which confronted his contemporaries, whether they were courtiers, country-house builders, or casual visitors to the city. Jonson's "To Penshurst" thus provides a lens which brings key questions into focus. What, for example, is the value of tradition — in local customs, in relationships or, indeed, in building materials and styles? What is the value of novelty or the meaning and purpose of acquiring and displaying new things? Finally, what is "lordship" and how does one establish and maintain authority in a changing society?

This last set of questions had far-reaching implications for political and economic relationships, particularly in a society ruled by a woman, but it also pointed out the instability of traditional notions of gender. Just as the authority of the lord over his tenants was called into question by new opportunities for economic and physical mobility in the late sixteenth century, so, too, was the power of the husband over his wife challenged by the new freedoms offered by the city. Profound changes in the ideology of gender among men and women of the upper classes are suggested by recurring tensions in the day-to-day negotiations of married life, by individual womens' movements between the country and the city, and in the division of labor and power between couples.

Further, the culture and etiquette of the country house itself suggests an effort to absorb and neutralize gender conflict: just as it relied on the importation of urban culture to the country in order to stem the flow of its life's blood to the city, and just as it depended on the palliative effects of traditional charity and hospitality to blur troubling distinctions of class, so the country house as an institution rested heavily on rules of etiquette and concepts of leisure which required upper-class women to remain behind the newly constructed walls of the country estate. These rules served the double function of safeguarding privileges of class and suppressing privileged women's new freedoms of movement.[6]

The examples which follow focus on the activities of country-house builders and their families as consumers of goods, visitors to London, and occasional participants in the life of the court. The first cluster of these, presented here in the greatest depth, are all drawn from the lives of one socially ambitious upper-gentry couple, Sir Francis and Elizabeth, Lady Willoughby of Wollaton in Nottinghamshire.[7] Born into a solid gentry family with connections to the Tudor court, Sir Francis achieved notoriety as the builder of Wollaton Hall (fig. 12.1) in Nottinghamshire, a substantial and flamboyant country house designed by Robert Smythson between 1580 and 1588. The house was paid for out of the profits from rents and coal mining on Willoughby's extensive Warwickshire and Nottinghamshire estates, and represented the culmination of two decades of energetic business activity and arts patronage in the 1570s and 1580s. Although his financial and political interests kept him connected to the London-based legal system and to the court, Willoughby preferred to remain in the background and was never a major player in London circles. His social, economic, and political life revolved around his country estates and local interests. Yet, with the exception of transient players and musicians who came to the house at Wollaton, all of his patronage focused on London-based artists and writers.

Looking at the portraits of husband and wife (figs. 12.2 and 12.3) which were painted by the court painter George Gower in 1573 and then transported from London to Wollaton, we are immediately reminded of the centrality of this contact between the country and the city in the sitters' lives.[8] Most obvious is the existence of the fashionable portraits themselves, commissioned by the couple during a period of residence in London. In style and manner they

12.1. Wollaton Hall, Nottinghamshire (photo: City of Nottingham).

are entirely consistent with Gower's other work for aristocratic and gentry patrons with ties to court circles. Further, the costumes of the two sitters clearly depend on the London market both for materials and fashionable style. Sir Francis's black doublet is decorated with aglets of gold, and the ruff around his neck is fastened with a golden chain which hangs over it; Lady Willoughby is more elaborately dressed—indeed, her portrait cost 20 shillings to Sir Francis's 10, an indication of how much more difficult it was to paint. She also wears a gown decorated with jewels, both pearls and gold beads; her hat, obviously designed as part of the pink, black, and white ensemble, has a band of pink silk ribbon, decorated with gold jewels and topped with pink and white feathers of various kinds. It goes without saying that none of these materials were locally produced or bought. Even without the evidence of the Willoughbys' account books from the 1570s—which record their London journeys (and those of family and servants) and the rich array of silks, velvets, and linens they bought—we are conscious of the sitters' links to London markets and fashions.[9]

12.2. Portrait of Elizabeth, Lady Willoughby by George Gower (1572). Collection of Lord Middleton, Birdsall.

This cosmopolitan orientation and wealth are further elaborated in the portrait of Lady Willoughby by the presence of a large jewel on her bodice made from gold, enamel, and baroque pearls in the shape of a merman in a basket; it is probably Italian and bears a certain similarity to the "Canning Jewel" in the Victoria and Albert Museum in London.[10] The market for such gems was limited, and they could only be purchased from a few agents or exclusive goldsmith shops. The Willoughbys' household accounts from this

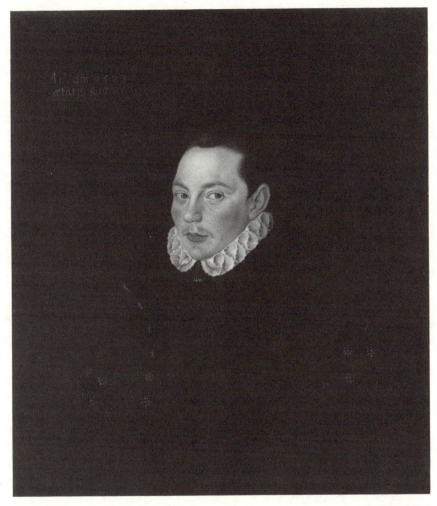

12.3. Portrait of Sir Francis Willoughby, by George Gower (1572). Collection of Lord Middleton, Birdsall.

period record numerous purchases of such luxuries in the city: books, paper, pictures, and musical instruments also appear, as do payments to the grocer for spices and foodstuffs, including five hundred oranges and three hundred lemons in one delivery, and purchases of Italian velvet, "Levant" taffeta, lace, silk thread and ribbon, and other fabrics.[11] Monthly entries record the cost of bringing these goods back to Wollaton and of sending servants to London to buy them.

A second category of payments in the accounts represents both the importation of services by London specialists and dispensing of gifts and patronage to guests. Thus in 1565 we find a letter from Sir Francis's brother-in-law Sir Matthew Arundell, who was often in London at the court (since his wife, Willoughby's sister, was a lady-in-waiting to the Queen), in which he writes that he is still hoping to find and hire someone who can both play and sing; payments are made in the 1570s to a professional musician who plays upon the virginals. Throughout the accounts, nonresident musicians, players, itinerant scholars, beggars and assorted visitors are rewarded.[12] Further payments are made to two London doctors who cared for Lady Willoughby during her frequent illnesses—one surgeon who seems to have been in residence at Wollaton and one physician who frequently makes the trip from town. Other indications of specialists being hired include a payment "for the platt maker's board that came from London to measure the groundes in May 1573."[13]

Thus it comes as something of a shock to discover that the Willoughbys were still living in the old manor house in the town of Wollaton during this period. That earlier residence in the valley, at the foot of the hill on which Smythson's Wollaton Hall would be built, was made up of a cluster of ordinary-looking houses and agricultural service buildings which seem quite incongruous with the new London-made luxuries. The gates of the house opened directly onto the main street of the town, providing easy access to laborers, tradespeople, and visitors.[14] Movement between the house and the town was thus frequent and casual, and the physical boundaries between social classes, while present, were permeable. Although a set of household orders written by Willoughby in the 1570s lays out the rules for the proper service of meals by servants in the great hall and chamber, distinctions of wealth and status were not yet paralleled by architectural formality, monumentality, or clearly defined spatial enclosure. Separation from the life of the country people would occur in the 1580s with the construction of the new "country house." For the women of the family, this change in environment would mean greater restrictions on behavior and mobility, in particular a withdrawal from informal contact with townspeople and from the physical environment of the town itself.

Visits to the city by the Willoughbys and their extended periods of residence represent a far more ambiguous picture. Like many wealthy landowners of his time, Sir Francis sometimes traveled to London to look after his business and legal interests, and he seems also to have owned a number of properties in and around Holborn. One of these was a substantial house known as "The Castle" in Lincoln's Inn Fields which he inherited from his father, a Knight of the Body under Henry VIII, but about thirty other properties on both sides of Holborn are listed in documents recording receipts of rents.[15] These included twelve tenements on the Staple Inn side. Holborn was an area outside the city walls, on the far northwestern side of the densely inhabited city, but for Willoughby's purposes, and no doubt for his father's as well, it was desirable for its proximity to the Inns of Court, which stood between Holborn and the river. The character of the buildings in the area, with houses and shops along the street front and courtyards behind, suggest both Willoughby's interest in income-producing properties and his desire to avoid the hothouse environment of the fashionable districts around Westminster.

What little evidence we have about where Willoughby stayed during his visits to London suggests that he favored this area but for the most part rented accommodations from others rather than setting up housekeeping in any of his own properties. This would have taken the properties off the rental market, and Willoughby's visits to town were, in any case, never extended. On the occasion of his daughter's wedding in 1581, for example, he seems to have stayed at his cousin's house in Lincoln's Inn, generally referred to as "The Grange," where he was attended by eleven men; three others stayed at the White Hart Inn nearby.[16]

Lady Willoughby's visits to London are more problematic, since she first went to town in 1573 as a result of her need to be near her doctors, and then made it clear that she wanted to stay on alone, contrary to her husband's wishes and, of course, to the conventions of family life and feminine propriety. She, too, stayed in rented or borrowed accommodations. Things seem to have begun amicably enough. In June 1573, we find Sir Francis apologizing for not being able to join her in town and asking his cousin to escort her there.[17] In 1574, there is a light-hearted letter in which Lady Willoughby thanks her husband for some venison that he sent up to her, and in which she writes, "she has sent him a hat (which she chose for him herself) which is of the newest fashion . . . a very good fashion for him, because it is not high crowned, so that when he rides a hunting he may go under the bushes and never pull it off."[18] By 1575, however, Lady Willoughby's habits of travel began to cause friction between the couple. We find Sir Francis writing to his wife's servant to inquire about the details of the excessive charges for her stay in town and asking if he knew how long she intended to remain. His concerns were both financial and social; while he complained of the costs of maintaining a separate household, he also noted that it looked bad for his wife and the mother of his children to be living in London alone: as he put it "London standing in the eye of the world, it would not stand great with her credit to be still riding in the streets."[19]

Numerous handbooks of advice counseled against such behavior and cautioned upperclass women to avoid both the town and the sort of common servingman whom one might meet in the street or as Grace Mildmay put it, "any of lyke disposition, whose ribald talk and ydle gesture and evill suggestions were dangerous to our chaste ears and eyes to hear and behold."[20] Clearly the city was no place for a gentlewoman alone; her business was in the country with her husband and children, a place in which the principal entertainments were the frequent rounds of visits, card playing, music making, and reading which are recorded with such regularity in the account books and books of advice.

Women's experience of and pleasure in the city's bounty was to be mediated through distance; they might own the rich jewels and plate produced by Cheapside goldsmiths (so lavishly suggested by the so-called "Cheapside Hoard," discovered in 1912 and thought to represent a jeweler's stock) or wear the rich fabrics displayed in the mercers' shops, but physical presence in the streets — let alone shopping for themselves — was not acceptable.[21] This not only limited their opportunities to socialize but also presented them with a difficult contradiction: display of fashion and jewels was increasingly important to social status, but the opportunities for such display away from the court were increasingly limited, regimented by the slow pace of life in the country.

These precious objects connected their owners to London and the life of the court; they could also cause problems. This was indeed the case with a small portrait of the Willoughbys' Nottinghamshire neighbor Sir Thomas Stanhope which came into Lady Willoughby's possession in 1579.[22] The portrait was enclosed in a jeweled case and meant to be worn as a brooch or pendant; it was of a type familiar on London and Continental markets and only available from artists and jewelers of the highest quality. Rumors about a secret love affair between Lady Willoughby and Stanhope had circulated among servants and neighbors for some time, but had been successfully dispelled until she was observed wearing the jewel. When Sir Francis demanded that she give it up, she refused. In a letter to Lady Willoughby's sister, Stanhope tried to explain that he had in fact bought the jewel for his wife in London, but since Lady Willoughby had also asked him to buy her some diamonds there, he had sent the jewel to her, saying that if she liked it she should keep it and return the picture. What effect this letter had on Sir Francis is not known, but it was not long after this that he and his wife were formally separated and, by a judgment of the Queen, he was obliged to pay a yearly allowance of £200.[23]

The highly charged meaning of circulating London-bought objects between the city and the country is made clear by two further incidents, both involving Bess of Hardwick, the builder of Hardwick Hall (1591–97) in Derbyshire, another of Smythson's impressive country houses. Like the Willoughbys, Bess and her fourth husband, the earl of Shrewsbury, argued about authority within their marriage and about her responsibilities towards him as wife and mother. Each of them maintained an entourage of servants and each moved between his or her country houses in the Midlands and London, although the earl had a much more significant presence in town, owning properties at Chelsea and in Dowgate Ward in the City.[24] Their difficult marriage erupted in a number of skirmishes and pitched battles, one of which produced a long list of silver and household items which the earl demanded she return to him and her answer to him, which consisted of terse annotations to the list.[25] Next to each item she noted its condition and/or its whereabouts: she could return *none* of them, she said, as some of the pieces were broken, some sold, some pawned or "laid to gage" and some given away; one item on the list, described as a "great bason and ewer fashioned like a ship, gilt and embossed . . . 100 pounds" was annotated by Bess as follows: "Bought by the Earl of purpose for the countess to give away, which she did as his lordship well knoweth."[26]

Gift giving of all kinds was an important sign of loyalty and respect on the country estate: hospitality was matched by gifts of produce or livestock from the tenants (an image invoked in "To Penshurst") and expensive gifts of plate or jewels were exchanged among neighbors or family members. As is well known, gift giving at the court of Queen Elizabeth, particularly at the New Year, was the occasion for the production of many splendid garments, paintings, jewels, and embroideries, but the swiftly changing styles of the court had to be respected, even by those in the country. Thus we find that Bess of Hardwick, a frequent seeker of royal favors, sought advice from a friend more than once about the right gift for the Queen; on one occasion in 1561, recorded in a letter in the Folger Library, she was counseled by her friend Lady Cobham to embroider some sleeves but not to have them made up: "for that the fasshuyne ys much altared senes youw wer heyr."[27]

Fashion consciousness extended beyond costume, painting, and decorative arts to architecture, landscape design, and monumental sculpture. The distinctive appearance and siting of a country house like Wollaton, completed in 1588, or Hardwick Hall (1592–97) signifies not only the presence of elite culture but also of London-based workmen (Robert Smythson among them) and even foreigners.[28] Isolated from the town and protected by a vast park and ornamental gardens (fig. 12.4), these houses seems to be bastions of court culture set within the rural landscape but separate from it. While undoubtedly connected to their region, to local culture, and to the town, both houses (and their households) looked beyond the country to the city. In style and conception, Wollaton and Hardwick are sophisticated buildings which draw heavily on Continental sources for planning, design, and sculptural imagery. They are linked to a cluster of country houses — which includes Longleat and Worksop,

12.4. Wollaton Hall, by John Griffier (ca. 1705). Collection of Lord Middleton. Photo courtesy of the Paul Mellon Centre for Studies in British Art, London.

among others — commissioned by an elite group of patrons connected to the court. Moreover, Wollaton's London connections are immediately apparent in the carved ornament, strapwork, and figural sculpture which covers the house. No local craftsman could have carried out work of this quality, and although we cannot attribute specific carvings to individual hands, the names of London-based craftsmen do appear on the building accounts.

Funerary monuments carved by these artists were also a highly prized London purchase. Tombs of all types, with and without life-sized effigies, were produced in great numbers, and the work of Netherlandish craftsmen based in London (including Garret Johnson, Richard Stevens, Maximilian Colt, and others as yet unidentified) was much sought after.[29] These monuments were carved in London and shipped in pieces to locations all over the country, then reassembled on site, sometimes with the help of local laborers. Willoughby himself commissioned a monument in London, which still survives on the wall of the village church at Wollaton, as a memorial to his father and mother; Bess of Hardwick's tomb monument in Derby Cathedral was designed by Smythson himself.[30] Thus while burial in London, with elaborate funeral rites (pre-

12.5. Tomb of the earls of Sussex, by Richard Stevens, in Boreham, Essex (1589). Photo: National Monuments Record.

ferably in the evening), throngs of mourners, and a tomb in Westminster, remained the *most* prized form of commemoration, particularly for women, internment in the local village church with a high-priced, London-made monument became the norm for the gentry and aristocracy (fig. 12.5). Though some men and women did turn to local craftsmen, hoping to get inexpensive copies of up-to-date styles, they paid a heavy price when their discerning neighbors saw the awkward carving and evident provincialism of the monuments that were produced (fig. 12.6).

For the Willoughby family, keeping up with London fashion proved more difficult following Sir Francis's death in 1596. Under the stewardship of the Willoughbys' daughter Bridget and her husband Sir Percival, the house and its inhabitants seem somehow less cut off from their roots in the country. While no less capable of putting up a fashionable front if they had to—they too commissioned portraits in London and shopped for luxurious fabrics and jewelry—this generation of Willoughbys reduced their contact with the court and abandoned any notion of following the London "season." Part of the reason for this was economic—Sir Francis had left his heirs heavily in debt,

12.6. Tomb of Thomas Fermor, by Richard and Gabriel Royley, in Somerton, Oxfordshire (1582). Photo: National Monuments Record.

and Percival Willoughby's frequent stays in London were entirely devoted to his business affairs — including a nine-month stay in the Fleet prison.[31] In part this has to do with Bridget's aspirations and temperament: while we find her asking her husband to bring oranges and lemons, fruit and spices from the London grocer, she is for the most part content with the ample supply of goods in the local markets and shows no signs of following fashion. During this period of its history, then, Wollaton Hall seems to have gone from being a country house to simply a house in the country, though this would change at the end of the seventeenth century.[32]

For others of this generation, however, London fashion and the life of the court remained matters of burning importance, but here again much depended on individual circumstances, particularly gender. Much has been written in recent years about Lady Anne Clifford (1590–1676), both as a diarist and as a patron of the arts, and she remains an excellent source of information, not only for her well-documented and long life, but also because of the breadth of her London and country connections.[33] Ever sensitive to the representation of status through both ritual performance and material display, Lady

Anne focused on the problematic boundary between the country and the city as the site on which she would construct an identity as a powerful figure of her time. Having spent her childhood in and around London and at court as the only daughter of the earl of Cumberland, and having lived her married life at Knole as the wife of the earl of Dorset, and at Wilton as the wife of the earl of Pembroke, it is not surprising that Lady Anne Clifford would have acquired a highly developed sense of urban and rural culture. She lived her entire life among men and women who traveled between London and their country estates, patrons of the arts who energetically sought out the best London goods and then expended considerable effort and money fitting out their country houses with the fruits of their shopping trips.

From an early age, Lady Anne Clifford understood fashion, and in her early twenties she became a patron of the arts in her own right, commissioning London-made monuments for her cousin Frances Bourchier in 1612 (erected in the Bedford family chapel at Chenies), for her mother in 1617 (erected in the village church at Appleby; perhaps by Maximilian Colt) and for the poet Edmund Spenser in 1620 (by Nicholas Stone, now destroyed), the last of which was placed in Westminster Abbey.[34] Her diary records her familiarity with the full range of London's bounty: clothes, jewels, books, pictures, food-stuffs, and every imaginable luxury.

Yet like Lady Willoughby, Lady Anne Clifford could be denied the pleasure of the city on her husband's authority when he chose to enforce it. In 1616 she was confined at Knole for refusing to yield her claims to her estates in Yorkshire and Cumbria. This agreement would have alleviated the strain on her husband's purse which his extravagant lifestyle demanded; thus he refused to let her join him in London unless she gave in. She wrote: "All this time my Lord was in London, where he had all and infinite great resort coming to him. He went much abroad to Cocking, Bowling Alleys, to Plays and Horse Races, and was commended by all the World. I stayed in the Country having many times a sorrowful and heavy heart, and being condemned by most folks because I would not consent to the Agreement, so as I may truly say, I am like an Owl in the Desert."[35] Whenever she was free to travel, Lady Anne moved among the houses of her aristocratic friends enjoying the London "season." In the fifty years which had passed since Lady Willoughby's time, much had changed. Great lords kept house in their city mansions; others rented or stayed with friends. Women played an active role in this society. In 1616, for example, Lady Anne, together with her husband, visited her longtime friends the earl and countess of Arundel, at their London house, where she says she "saw all the Pictures and Statues in the Lower Rooms."[36] That house, shown in Hollar's print, was typical of the London mansions of the period in being a

12.7. The Countess Pillar, in Brougham, Cumbria (1654). Photo: National Monuments Record.

disorderly collection of buildings gathered around a series of courtyards, and it bustled with exactly the sort of activity that Lady Anne so sorely missed in the country. Her diary and memoirs record a series of visits throughout the city: crisscrossing back and forth from Westminster to the Savoy to Somerset House and Bedford House along the river, from Austin Friar's near Bishopsgate, to Baynard's Castle, where she lived in the 1630s, Lady Anne participated actively in London society and in its culture of consumption.

Nevertheless, we know that when Lady Anne finally took possession of her northern estates as an independent landowner in the late 1640s, she turned her back on London. She focused instead on the country, adhering to local customs and traditional rituals, and resolutely insisting on renovation of her medieval castles — Brougham, Brough, and Pendragon in Cumberland, and Skipton in Yorkshire. Her patronage supported the work of local artisans. Nowhere in the many works of architecture and sculpture she commissioned in these years is there evidence of the work of elite, London-based craftsmen. The Countess Pillar, erected in 1654 to mark the spot on which she had last seen her mother (fig. 12.7), provides ample testimony to the change in her tastes. Even her own appearance was altered: she dressed in black and foreswore jewelry and ornaments. She turned to her Bible and to her books, enacting a life of seignorial generosity and stoic retreat, rejecting the court and embracing "a private country life" as she called it, in a highly self-conscious manner. Distance from London was certainly a factor in Cumbria, but in the 1660s we still read in her accounts of purchases at York of silver spoons and tankards "to give away," of payments to the man "that follows my law business at London," and of shipments from London of ribbon, marmalade, thirteen casks of Canary sack, and a pound of Virginia tobacco "for my own consumption."[37]

Lady Anne's withdrawal from the world of fashion was a deliberate gesture of rejection. Yet the memory of the city was very much present in the life she chose, even as she insisted on its absence. Thus we return again to Jonson and "To Penshurst," for, like the poem, Lady Anne's country life was constructed with one eye on the city — on the city and its culture within herself. In his funeral oration of 1676, Bishop Rainbow recalled that when a friend told her that she would love to go to London, quote "to glut her eyes with the sight of such happy objects and after give up her self to her country retirement," Lady Anne replied that, were she herself to go, she would need "spectacles (or blinkers) [like a horse] put before mine eyes, lest I should see and censure what I cannot competently judge of."[38] The bishop took this as an indication of the clarity of her rejection of the world, that she would leave others to enjoy such things without censure, but surely the opposite is true: a lover of the city, she shields her eyes because the sights were still a source of temptation to her, a woman whose tastes and desires were forged in the London of Elizabeth and in the country houses of consumers, newly awakened to the pleasures of the marketplace.

Notes

1. For parallel developments in Italy see Richard A. Goldthwaite, *Wealth and the Demand for Art in Italy, 1300–1600* (Baltimore: Johns Hopkins University Press, 1993). For consumption in England at a slightly later period see *Consumption and the World of Goods,* ed. John Brewer and Roy Porter (New York: Routledge, 1993). For tensions over status, see D. Cressy, "Describing the Social Order of Elizabethan and Stuart England," *Literature and History* 3 (1976): 29–44 and L. Stone, "Social Mobility in England 1520–1700," *Past and Present* 33 (1966): 49ff.

2. For the architectural history of this type see Olive Cook, *The English Country House* (London: Thames & Hudson, 1974), pp. 8–26, and Mark Girouard, *Life in the English Country House* (London and New Haven: Yale University Press, 1978), esp. chpts. 3 and 4. See also M. W. Barley, "Rural Housing in England" in *The Agrarian History of England and Wales,* vol. 4, 1500–1640, ed. Joan Thirsk (Cambridge: Cambridge University Press, 1967). For a view of the economic basis of these changes see Susan Cahn, *Industry of Devotion: The Transformation of Women's Work in England, 1500–1660* (New York: Columbia University Press, 1987).

3. Raymond Williams, *The Country and the City* (Oxford: Oxford University Press, 1973), esp. chpts. 3 and 4. See also William A. McClung, *The Country House in English Renaissance Poetry* (Berkeley: University of California Press, 1977).

4. Ben Jonson, "To Penshurst," in *Poems of Ben Jonson,* ed. George Burke Johnston (Cambridge, Mass.: Harvard University Press, 1962), pp. 76–79.

5. See Don Wayne, *Penshurst: The Semiotics of Place and the Poetics of History* (Madison: University of Wisconsin Press, 1984) and Leah S. Marcus, "Politics and Pastoral: Writing the Court on the Countryside," in *Culture and Politics in Early Stuart England,* ed. K. Sharpe and P. Lake (Stanford: Stanford University Press, 1993), pp. 139–60.

6. See Alice T. Friedman, "Architecture, Authority, and the Female Gaze: Planning and Representation in the Early Modern Country House," *Assemblage* 18 (Fall 1992): 40–61.

7. See Alice T. Friedman, *House and Household in Elizabethan England: Wollaton Hall and the Willoughby Family in the Sixteenth Century* (Chicago: University of Chicago Press, 1988).

8. Historical Manuscripts Commission, *Report of the Manuscripts of Lord Middleton Preserved at Wollaton Hall* (London: HMSO, 1911) (hereafter, HMC, *Middleton*) pp. 432, 434.

9. HMC, *Middleton,* p. 448. For London, see Philippa Glanville, "The City of London," in *The Cambridge Guide to the Arts in Britain,* ed. Boris Ford, vol. 4, *The Seventeenth Century* (Cambridge: Cambridge University Press, 1989), pp. 165–77.

10. See *Princely Magnificence: Court Jewels of the Renaissance, 1500–1630* (London: Victoria and Albert Museum, 1981).

11. HMC, *Middleton,* pp. 431–48. On p. 536 there is a letter in which Sir Francis Willoughby mentions that he is looking for "treble lutes fit for his purpose."

12. HMC, *Middleton,* pp. 528–29.

13. HMC, *Middleton,* p. 429.

14. J. H. Hodson, "The First Wollaton Hall," *Transactions of the Thoroton Society* 72 (1968): 59–67.

15. HMC, *Middleton,* pp. 321–22. For Staple Inn, see John Schofield, *The Building of London from the Conquest to the Great Fire* (London: British Museums Publications Limited in Association with the Museum of London, 1984), p. 153ff. See also his "Medieval and Tudor Domestic Buildings in the City of London," in *Medieval Art, Architecture, and Archaeology in London,* British Archaeological Conference Transactions (1984) (London, 1990), pp. 16–29. General surveys include Walter Besant, *London in the Time of the Stuarts* (London: A&C Black, 1903), and Norman G. Brett James, *The Growth of Stuart London* (London: G. Allen and Unwin, 1935).

16. HMC, *Middleton,* pp. 555–56.

17. HMC, *Middleton,* p. 535.

18. Letter described by Cassandra Willoughby, excerpted in "Extracts from Collections of Cassandra Willoughby, 1702," HMC, *Middleton,* pp. 536–37.

19. *HMC, Middleton,* p. 536.

20. Rachel Weigall, "An Elizabethan Gentlewoman: The Journal of Lady Mildmay circa 1570–1617," *Quarterly Review,* 215 (1911): 119–38, esp. 120. See also Philip Stubbes, *Anatomie of Abuses* (London, 1583), sigs. 9v, 47v–48v.

21. For the gendered experience of shopping, see Derek Keene, "Shops and Shopping in Medieval London," in *Medieval Art, Architecture, and Archaeology in London,* British Archaeological Conference Transactions (1984) 1990, pp. 29–46. For Lady Willoughby's problems with a jewel purchased in London for her by Sir Thomas Stanhope in 1579, see HMC, *Middleton,* p. 544.

22. HMC, *Middleton,* pp. 544–45.

23. HMC, *Middleton,* p. 552.

24. See Catherine Jamison, ed., *A Calendar of the Shrewsbury and Talbot Papers in Lambeth Palace Library and the College of Arms* (London: HMSO, 1966–71), MS 697, fol. 111; and Historical Manuscripts Commission, *Calendar of the Manuscripts of the . . . Marquis of Salisbury . . . Preserved at Hatfield House,* 24 vols. (London: HMSO, 1883–1976) (hereafter, HMC, *Salisbury*), vol. 12, pt. 3, 158–67.

25. For plate, see Philippa Glanville, *Silver in Tudor and Early Stuart England: A Social History and a Catalogue of the National Collection* (London: Victoria and Albert Museum 1990).

26. HMC, *Salisbury,* 3:160.

27. Folger X.d. (428) 16, cited in Janet Arnold, *Queen Elizabeth's Wardrobe Unlock'd* (Leeds: W. S. Manley and Son, 1988), p. 96.

28. Friedman, *House and Household,* chpt. 4.

29. See Nigel Llewellyn, *The Art of Death: Visual Culture in English Death Ritual ca. 1500–1800* (London: Reaktion Books, 1991), and Clare Gittings, *Death, Burial and the Individual in Early Modern England* (London: Routledge 1984). For Willoughby's patronage of London tomb sculptors, see Alice T. Friedman, "Patronage and the Production of Tombs in London and the Provinces: The Willoughby Monument of 1591,"

The Antiquaries Journal, 1985 (2): 390–401. See also Adam White, "Nicholas Stone and Early Stuart Sculpture," in *Cambridge Guide to the Arts,* pp. 267–75.

30. See *Architectural History* 5 (1962): catalogue number 1/6, p. 30.

31. A. C. Wood, *The Continuation of the History of the Willoughby Family by Cassandra, Duchess of Chandos* (Eton: Windsor, 1958), pp. 38–39.

32. Friedman, *House and Household,* chpt. 6. See Joan Thirsk, *Economic Policy and Projects: The Development of a Consumer Society in Early Modern England* (Oxford: Clarendon Press, 1978).

33. See Barbara Kiefer Lewalski, "Claiming Patrimony and Constructing a Self: Lady Anne Clifford and Her Diary," in *Writing Women in Jacobean England* (Cambridge, Mass.: Harvard University Press, 1993), pp. 125–52, and Graham Parry, "The Great Picture of Lady Anne Clifford," in *Art and Patronage in the Caroline Courts: Essays in Honor of Sir Oliver Millar,* ed. David Howarth (Cambridge: Cambridge University Press, 1993), pp. 202–19. See also R. Malcolm Smuts, *Court Culture and the Origins of a Royalist Tradition in Early Stuart England* (Philadelphia: University of Pennsylvania Press, 1987), esp. chpt. 3.

34. See Alice T. Friedman, "Constructing an Identity in Prose, Plaster, and Paint: Lady Anne Clifford as a Writer and Patron of the Arts," in *Albion's Classicism: The Visual Arts in Britain 1550–1650,* ed. Lucy Gent, Yale Center for Studies in British Art (New Haven and London: Yale University Press, 1995), pp. 359–76.

35. *Diaries of Lady Anne Clifford,* ed. D. H. Clifford (Far Thrupp, Stroud, Gloucestershire: Allan Sutton, 1990), p. 43.

36. *Diaries of Lady Anne Clifford,* ed. Clifford, p. 43.

37. Cumbria Record Office, MS WD Hoth/17; see 8 June and 5 August 1665; 14 February, 14 March, and 18 October 1666; and 30 April 1668.

38. Edward Rainbow, *Sermon Preached at the Funeral of Anne, Countess of Pembroke, Dorset and Montgomery* (London: R. Royston and H. Broom, 1677), p. 44.

13

The Authority of the Globe
and the Fortune

Andrew Gurr

My title, "The Authority of the Globe and the Fortune," is an anomaly and a paradox. In conventional thinking, the playhouses and the players of London had no authority whatsoever. They were the products of the sort of "liberty" that was at best merely tolerated by the authority of the Crown, and never even so much as tolerated by the authority of the City of London. What we think of now as their authority has only been acquired in the centuries since, a subsequent investment made largely in the interests of Shakespeare's plays, which have given this period a fascination that other periods have never secured. My title emphasizes that anomaly.

It also emphasizes a paradox within the anomaly, that these two playhouses acquired authority within their own territory thanks to certain acts of the government laid down by two long-serving Privy Councillors. This paradoxical but real authority is a point I wish to demonstrate. Because although these two theaters were not quite the first to be officially approved by the Privy Council, they were certainly the first London playhouses to be built with the backing of that official approval, to the specifications of the professional companies that expected to use them, a point which rightly has a special fascination for enthusiasts of the surviving "material" play-texts. The anomaly inside that paradox is that they were both the second-best choices for the players who first used them.

Up to 1594 the leading professional companies expected to travel indiscriminately and to play anywhere, using the city's inns in spite of the Lord Mayor's opposition. There is no evidence that they ever expected to make a long stay at any of the London playhouses, let alone anywhere else in the country, before May 1594. In that year two newly made and officially approved companies were allocated specific suburban playhouses. That new deal lasted through the 1596 crisis when one of the companies tried to build in the

Blackfriars liberty. The two companies only really developed a sense of London as their natural, proper, settled, and approved place in 1599 and 1600 when they built their own playhouses, the Globe and the Fortune. My second point about these two theaters is that their design must have been, in the view of the players, a distinctly retrograde step.

Despite this second point, the first owners did see the building of the Globe and the Fortune as events to celebrate. They were the only playhouses ever built, to my knowledge, which had a set of plays written for them that actually celebrated their new names.[1] Not only was all the globe a stage (in *As You Like It*) and Hamlet could be seen to wave at "this distracted Globe" all around him, but on the other side of the Thames, Henslowe commissioned two parts of *Fortune's Tennis,* and his company revived *Old Fortunatus,* which may have been the play that originally inspired the playhouse's name, for his new venue. They were places to celebrate. The Globe and the Fortune were the first London theaters to be designed and built for specific companies to use, and to use permanently, as their "home." That is the other kind of authority that they carry.

It is worth painting the frame for this narrative picture by first emphasizing how anomalous all the nine amphitheaters built between 1567 and 1614 really were. They were not the first playing-places set up in London: well before 1567 there were indoor places, at court, in the schools, and elsewhere, which had obvious advantages in everything but daylight and the huge audience capacity that the open theaters provided. You can, in fact, make a strong case for open-air playing-places being a retrograde step in the eyes of the professional players themselves, a harking back to the marketplace scaffolds that belonged to the centuries before Elizabeth. Elizabeth's famous proclamation of 16 May 1559, which ordered the local mayors and magistrates to license plays for performance, did the companies an extraordinary and unexpected service. Although designed chiefly for religious censorship, to check the amateur performance of guild plays, the annual Mystery cycles, the proclamation did mention the professional traveling companies, and in doing so it served them very well indeed — it brought them indoors.

Elizabeth's proclamation required local mayors to see and censor a play before it could be released to the populace. That order fortuitously gave the companies, for the limited period that the proclamation was in force, access to the biggest meeting room in every town for their performances. No mayor was going to stand in the town marketplace to see the play he had to censor. So performing inside guildhalls suddenly became standard practice for the professional companies. It was not popular with most mayors. There are ample records in the *REED* volumes[2] of how much allowing the players into the guildhalls cost the towns. Guildhall doors and windows were broken regularly during performances, as outsiders would try to get in or at least see in. Some towns even took their guildhall's window glass out before a performance. Produced by an edict from the central government, like most such edicts it was not an innovation likely to survive for very long. But while it lasted it transformed the professional players' idea of their business. What this access to the guildhalls did give the players, besides a venue with a roof, was for the first time perfect control over payment. Without paying at the door you could not get into the guildhall. Playing on specially erected scaffolds in marketplaces, a tradition which persisted in towns like Shrewsbury, was likely to be more costly and far less profitable because in such cases the only access to the audience's pennies was by taking a hat round.

Access to guildhalls first taught the professional companies the commercial value of an enclosed theater to play in. Payment for playing in courts or great halls came in a lump sum, not from the takings at the door. That innovation brought an early change — recognition that enclosed playing-places had financial advantages — which soon needed revision. Once the main point of the 1559 proclamation was superseded by the new licensing function of the Master of the Revels in the 1580s, hostility in mayoralties to players using their guildhalls grew markedly. That prompted another change. Once the proclamation was finally dead along with its author (i.e., after 1603) the players did not revert to marketplaces, but turned to local inns instead, and to indoor inn venues at that. A large room at an inn in Wine Street, Bristol was converted into a playhouse in 1604. Another in York was given the same function at about the same time, and a small town in Lancashire did the same. Inns like the Red Lion in Norwich, possibly an indoor but more likely an innyard venue, and the indoor King's Head at Oxford, became the standard resort for the traveling companies under the Stuarts. In some towns civic hostility made the companies do what they did in London and retreat to the town boundaries. Forced out of Cambridge, for instance, they played at nearby Chesterton. But even then it was almost exclusively the indoor venues, the local inns, that they used for their playing. Only in London from the 1590s were they invariably confined to the suburban locations and the open-air venues. In a real sense the Globe and the Fortune were retrograde steps in the eyes of the players. They would have preferred places like James Burbage's Blackfriars in 1596, if that adventurous scheme had worked as Burbage meant it to.

That is background to what happened in London in the 1590s. The main story is the Privy Council's attempt to regulate the professional playing companies between 1594 and 1600. It had many ramifications, from the social stigma of being a common player with a drum-and-trumpet system of advertisement (which led to the ban on the Blackfriars playhouse in 1596) to the happy accident that brought in five of the playing sharers as co-owners of the Globe in 1599. That latter piece of good luck made them the most secure company and helped to make them the most durable in town. What underlies all that is the novelty of the companies settling down into assigned and authorized playing-places in London in the 1590s and the drastic change of thinking which it all represents.

Sometime in that decade, London became "home" to the professional companies. Henslowe's famous letter written on 28 September 1593 about the collapse of Pembroke's Men has a phrase in it that marks the change. Henslowe wrote "as for my lorde a penbrockes wch you desier to knowe whear they be they are all at home and hauffe ben this v or sixe weackes."[3] By cutting short the following remarks about the players' having to pawn their playbooks and apparel, we can hear in Henslowe's casual phrase what he thought was the broken company's base. For all the long stints of traveling that every company still practiced because of the epidemics of plague and the Lord Mayor's hostility to playing, and in spite of the fact that the Lord Chamberlain had not yet designated any of the suburban playhouses for the approved companies to use, what Henslowe knew was that by 1593 the leading professional companies thought of being in London as "at home."

When did London become "home" for the players under Elizabeth? In the 1580s even a company as preeminent as the Queen's Men used a wide variety of playing-places in London. In their prime up to Tarlton's death in 1588, they are on record as using at least three inns and two different playhouses in London; in fact, they used every one of the known venues for playing in London, to which they added the Rose in 1594. A city license of 28 November 1583 allowed them to perform at the Bull and the Bell, one open and one roofed, "and nowheare els within this Cyttye."[4] They also played at the Theatre in about 1584, at the Bel Savage Inn in 1588, at the Curtain (according to *Tarlton's Jests*) and at the Rose early in 1594. Fifteen years after Henslowe's comment, in his *Apology for Actors* written in about 1608, Heywood could hail "my good friends and fellowes the Citty Actors"[5] as a group of workers permanently resident in London. That, however, was some time after the Lord Chamberlain had licensed the first two playhouses and King James had given royal patronage to three of the leading companies. The practice of one company staying at a single London playhouse to work for long periods of time was still a new one in 1593.[6]

Company tenure at London playhouses, whether city inns or innyards or the established suburban amphitheaters, was generally short-lived up to 1594. Strange's Company played at Henslowe's Rose from February 1592, when they first established themselves, for a total of barely six months through the twenty-one months up to August 1593, in spite of the fact that their leading player, Alleyn, married Henslowe's stepdaughter in October 1592.[7] Pembroke's had probably been using the Theatre across the river through the same period, which could hardly have been long enough to give either playhouse a firm identity as a "home" for the players. They still held entirely to the habit of moving regularly from one venue to another. They probably lacked the number of playbooks necessary to allow them a really long stay in any one venue. And they had those roofed guildhalls and inns in other towns and in the city of London itself to reflect on as better venues for playing than the open-air yards of the London suburbs. For all we know, the six months when Strange's used the Rose in 1592 was the longest unbroken stay that any company had maintained up to then at any amphitheater playhouse.

Their mobility at this time has many factors behind it. One of the least remarked of these factors was probably the most influential: their preference for playing indoors. The fame of Burbage's Theatre and Henslowe's Rose from 1594 can easily obscure for us the fact that they must have been the second-best places for playing in the eyes of the professional players. As constant travelers, access to the town and city guildhalls and to London's inns made outdoor performances their fall-back position under Elizabeth. By the 1590s they had ample experience to make them prefer playing indoors. Burbage's attempt to replace the Theatre in 1596 when its lease was dying with the Blackfriars confirms their preference.

Where does this put the early amphitheaters of Shoreditch and Southwark? The Queen's Men's venues inside the city included the Bel Savage, a converted innyard, but also at least two indoor places at inns. The idea of playing indoors in winter was certainly not first conceived when the King's Men acquired their Blackfriars hall in 1608. It was already standard when the Lord Chamberlain was prompted in October 1594 to ask the Lord Mayor if he would allow his new company, the Chamberlain's Men, to play at the Cross Keys inn. The players evidently did not wish to spend the whole winter playing only at the open-air Theatre. We do not know whether the Lord Mayor granted that request. But we do know that it was only after that time that the two officially approved companies started to play at the Theatre and the Rose all the year round. That was why Burbage built his Blackfriars hall playhouse in 1596. He designed it as a permanent replacement for the Theatre in the form of a new playhouse comparable to the roofed inns which the companies had been used to up to then, but free from the city's impositions in its "liberty." Burbage meant it not just for the winter season, but for all-year-round playing, as a complete replacement for his Theatre. That was his vision for the future of professional playing in 1596.

The open-air amphitheaters did have their advantages. They could take in far larger numbers than any city inn, or even a guildhall, outside London. They had better lighting, thanks to natural daylight, than any indoor location. Above all they had the advantage of being out of the reach of the Lord Mayor. His recurrent hostility to professional playing is the main reason why the players must have found it difficult to think of London as their natural base for so long. The Privy Council deal setting up the two authorized companies of 1594, the Admiral's and the Chamberlain's Men, was part of a plan that included a final prohibition on playing at any inn or alehouse inside the city. The two Privy Councillors involved, the Lord Chamberlain and his son-in-law the Lord Admiral, must have agreed on this to appease the Lord Mayor. Exclusion from the city gave security to the two companies at a price which the players must not have enjoyed paying.

The fact that most players for whom records have been found were resident in the London parishes closest to the playhouses — Shoreditch, Bishopsgate, and Southwark — is not a substantial confirmation that they were "at home" there, because no searches have yet been made to identify whether any players lived in other towns. Most of the parish records about the players that have turned up come from the later years, when residence in London had become a practical necessity for all the leading players. It is true that many of the players in the large companies from the 1570s onward had families based in London. So far as we can tell from the limited entries that survive, a majority of them had wives and children and, hence, presumably regular housing in the city or its suburbs. The records that have been found are, of course, mainly about the most familiar names, whose interests must have based them in London more readily than any of the other towns that their companies regularly visited. Shakespeare is almost unique as a player with a family based at a long distance from London. Other early players (pre-1600) with wives and children living in London include Richard Allen, Edward Alleyn, Christopher Beeston, William Bird, both of the Robert Brownes (for all their Continental traveling), George Bryan, James Burbage, Alexander Cooke, Richard Cowley, Richard Darlowe, Thomas Downton, John Duke, Edward Dutton, John Dutton, Lawrence Dutton, Lawrence Fletcher, John Garland, Thomas Goodale, Robert Gough, Thomas Greene, John Harrison, John Heminges, Francis Henslowe, Thomas Heywood, Antony Jeffes, Humphrey Jeffes, William Johnson, Richard Jones, Ben Jonson, Edward Juby, Richard Juby, William Knell, Tobias Myles, John Nill, Robert Pallant, Augustine Phillips, Robert Shaw, Martin Slater, Richard Tarlton, and Robert Wilson. Despite having families in London, some of these players were chronic, if that's the right word, travelers, who toured with companies constantly in the years when the London base was firmly established under the Stuarts.

In the years when London was the obvious center of action no player whose identity is well known and whose name can be found in parish or other records had a residence listed anywhere but in the city or its suburbs. That unscrupulous traveler Martin Slater may be a special case. He was a perpetual tourist. He used different licenses, usually forged, to license his company's travel to places as far distant as Edinburgh in 1599. His different companies, or different licenses, are on record all over the country. He was noted by name as playing in five different towns between 1605 and 1625. Nonetheless, it was said in 1609 that he had a family in London consisting of ten dependents.[8] This seems to suggest that even the most compulsive of the traveling players felt himself to be at home in the metropolis for at least some of the time.

In the later years, after a place to play in London became a fixture, some of the more established players bought themselves houses just outside London. Augustine Phillips had established himself with house and lands by the Thames, London's greatest routeway, at Mortlake when he died in 1605. Henry Condell had a house in the outlying London village of Fulham in the 1620s. But none of these acquisitions, with the single exception of Shakespeare's purchase of New Place in Stratford in 1597, indicates an intention of living very far from the job in London.

It is likely that many of the players belonging to the companies that tried to secure a foothold in London in the 1590s would only have taken London lodgings while working there, as Shakespeare did. Richard Tarlton kept an inn in Gracechurch Street in the 1580s while he was a Queen's player, but his chief successor, Will Kemp, is recorded as living in "Samson's Rents" in Southwark in 1595, 1596, 1598, and 1599, and in Langley's New Rents in 1602. These records probably mean that, like Shakespeare, he stayed in lodgings while he had employment in London. There is no mention of a wife or children. Similar histories apply to Thomas Pope and Gabriel Spencer. Other parish records identify some "base-born" children whose fathers were players, suggesting that they were not family men, or at least not good family men. These include Will Sly and Edmund Shakespeare. But by the 1590s a clear majority of the players did have families, and their families all seem to have been based permanently in London. By the time Joan Alleyn came to re-use her stepfather's term — writing to her husband on 21 October 1603 to say that all the companies were now "Come hoame . . . at theyr owne houses"[9] — it was a normative statement. But it was not one that could have been made even fifteen years earlier.

What happened in the 1590s was largely a consequence of the long struggle between London's Lord Mayor and the Lord Chamberlain on the Privy Council, who was concerned to protect the professional companies so that they could perform each Christmas for his cousin the Queen. From the 1570s onwards every Lord Mayor wrote to the Privy Council asking that plays be banned from the city. Charles Howard as Lord Chamberlain in 1584 made an agreement with Guildhall that only the new company, the Queen's Men, would be allowed to play at the city's inns. The court *Remembrancia* from March 1584 to January 1587 are missing, but the Lansdowne papers have a partial record of the decisions made in that period. They include a petition that the Queen's Men sent to the Privy Council appealing against pressure laid on them by the city fathers, together with the responses to it from the Lord Mayor and from Howard as Chamberlain. Howard's "remedies" for the city's grievances included setting specific limits on the times of day for playing, and most specifically declaring "That the Quenes players only be tolerated, and of them their number and certaine names to be notified in your Lps. lettres to the L. Maior and to the Justices of Middlesex and Surrey. And those her players not to divide themselves into several companies."[10] The city inns where the Queen's Men would be allowed to play were specified. The Lord Mayor of that year was appeased at least in part by the Council's refusal to allow any company other than the Queen's to play inside the city limits.

Playing at the city inns was the cause of constant nagging by the Lord Mayor to the Council until nearly 1600. Howard was in a peculiarly advantageous position to deflect the Lord Mayor's complaints and to set up a new arrangement that affirmed James Burbage's wisdom in originally building his playhouse out in the suburbs. Howard was Lord Lieutenant of Middlesex, where the Theatre and Curtain stood, and on the Commission for magistrates of Surrey, where the Rose and the baiting-houses stood. It was easier for him to protect the suburban playhouses from the Lord Mayor's anger than the city inns. In May 1594 he and his father-in-law Henry Carey (successor as Lord Chamberlain) devised a plan which both appeased the Lord Mayor and satisfied the Council's need to keep the players on hand in London. The Queen's Men had divided and declined as leaders of the pack of officially patronized professional companies. Several patrons of leading companies died in late 1593 and early 1594, putting their players at risk. So the Lord Chamberlain and his son-in-law set up two new companies as replacements for the Queen's Men, each giving his name as patron to one of them.[11] To that year's Lord Mayor they offered a more substantial concession over playing than Howard originally had made to his predecessor when he was Lord Chamberlain in 1584. The two new companies were now to be barred along with all others from ever playing inside the city. They were allocated instead to the playhouses in the suburbs where Howard had control over the local magistrates. One went to the Theatre in Middlesex, the other to the Rose in Surrey. No other playhouses were to be licensed for players to use.

The evidence for this is inferential, but it is entirely consistent. Had the players still been as free as before to use the inns, the Lord Chamberlain would not have had to ask the Lord Mayor in the following October to let his new company play indoors at the city's Cross Keys Inn. The Privy Council's next plague ban (later in 1594) had new phrasing, not specifying playing "in & about London" as before, but now only playing "within the libertyes of the Cyttye." These liberties included the Clink on Bankside where the Rose was located.[12] The next Privy Council Order banned playing "in the places usuall about the citty of London."[13] In September 1595 the Lord Mayor renewed his council's complaints against playing, now specifying not the city inns but "the Plaies . . . that ar daily shewed at the Theator & Bankside." He had stopped complaining about their presence inside the city. In July 1597 his renewed attack asked the Council "to direct your lettres aswell to our selves as to the Justices of peace of Surrey & Midlesex for the present staie & fynall suppressinge of the saide Stage playes, aswell as the Theatre, Curten, and banckside, as in all other places in and abowt the Citie." This was when the Theatre was closed, and the Chamberlain's Men had transferred to the Curtain, which is why the Curtain was now added to the specification. But it was also the time when Langley's unlicensed Swan was in trouble with the returned Pembroke's Men and *The Isle of Dogs*. It was an opportune moment to renew the complaint about playing generally.

For all the reference to the extra playing-places in the Mayor's letter of July 1597, it is clear that the Rose and the Theatre were by now the only approved places for London playing. We need not go here into the reasons for the July 28 order of that year from the Privy Council to demolish all the playhouses. What we should register is the renewal in February 1598, with a new Lord Chamberlain, Henry Carey's son, now the patron of his father's company and required to do his father's job in running London playing, of the authorization for just the two companies. This I believe was, as before, Howard's doing. "Whereas licence hath bin graunted unto two companies of stage players retayned unto us, the Lord Admyral and Lord Chamberlain," the authorization begins and goes on to issue a ban on a third company then trying to get a foothold. Two years later it was Howard who issued the warrant of January 1600 allowing the Fortune to be built. Two months after that the Council wrote to the Middlesex magistrates to stop a new playhouse going up near Cripplegate. Howard, George Carey, and Cecil signed another authorization for the Fortune addressed to the Middlesex magistrates in April. They had a clear policy to limit the number of licensed playing-places and, thereby, to protect the two companies that had been set up in 1594 to guarantee the annual Christmas revels.

Finally, on 22 June, the Council reaffirmed its whole policy in a heavy document which shows, among other things, evidence that it was undoubtedly composed by a committee. It was much interlined and corrected. London was to have only two companies and only two playhouses. The demolition of the Theatre and the replacement of the Rose by the Fortune meant that the approved two were now to be the Fortune and the Globe. The order declares weightily that "The Lordes and the rest of hir Majesties privie Councell, with one and full Consent, have orderd in manner and forme as followeth." The exact terms were set out thus:

First, that there shall bee about the Cittie two howses and noe more allowed to serve for the use of the Common Stage plaies, of the which howses one shalbe in Surrey in that place which is Commonlie called the banckside or there abouts, and the other in Midlesex. And foras muche as there Lordshippes have bin enformed by Edmond Tylney Esquire, hir Majesties servant and Master of the Revells, that the howse now in hand to be builte by the said Edward Allen is not intended to encrease the number of the Plaiehowses, but to be in steed of an other, namelie the Curtaine, Which is either to be ruined and plucked downe or to be putt to some other good use, as also that the scituation thereof is meete and Convenient for that purpose. Yt is likewise ordered that the said howse of Allen shall be allowed to be one of the two howses, and namelie for the house to be alowed in Middlesex, soe as the house Called the Curtaine be (as yt is pretended) either ruinated or applied to some other good use. And for the other allowed to be on Surrey side, whereas [there Lordshipps are pleased to permitt] to the Companie of players that shall plaie there to make there owne Choice which they will have, Choosinge one of them and noe more, [And the said Companie of Plaiers, being the Servantes of the L. Chamberlen, that are to plaie there have made choise of the house called the Globe, yt is ordered that the said house and none other shall be there allowed]. And especiallie yt is forbidden that anie stage plaies shalbe plaied (as sometimes they have bin) in any Common Inn for publique assemblie in or neare about the Cittie.[14]

This is the key statement of late Elizabethan policy over professional playing. It is the fullest version of the policy that was first laid down by Howard and Carey together in May 1594. A subsequent letter to the justices of Middlesex and Surrey dated 31 December 1601 refers back to it, saying "about a year and a half since . . . wee did carefullie sett downe and prescribe an order to be observed concerninge the number of playhowses and the use and exercise of stage plaies, with lymytacion of tymes and places for the same."[15] A similar letter went to the Lord Mayor.

All these documents bear the mark of Charles Howard, the Lord Admiral, not his cousin and client Tilney, the Master of the Revels, or George Carey, the new Lord Chamberlain. Howard is the consistent factor in all the negotiations between the Council and the city from 1584 to 1601. In the six years after he and Henry Carey established the Lord Admiral's and the Lord Chamberlain's Men, it was above all his support for the two companies that secured them their place "at home" in London, and it was that support which gave them the right and guaranteed them the resources to build their own new playhouses, the Fortune and the Globe.

From May 1594 the Rose and its opposite the Theatre, replaced through reluctant necessity in April 1597 by the Curtain, were the undisputed homes for the two London companies that the Privy Council authorized. Each was built by an entrepreneur. The Rose was originally financed by Philip Henslowe as an amateur enthusiast of playing, with help from a grocer, John Cholmley, who got in return the exclusive right to sell his produce to the playgoers. What Henslowe's connection was with any of the early companies of players we do not know. We don't even know if his playhouse was used much between 1587 when it was built and the start of his "Diary" in 1592. The only evidence for any early playing there is a Privy Council letter of 29 October 1587 to the Surrey magistrates about playing on the sabbath. This most probably applied not to the old Newington Butts playhouse in the south, but to the new Rose on Bankside. It notes that the violation was "especiallie within the Libertie of the Clincke and in the parish of St. Saviours in Southwarke,"[16] where at that time the only playhouse was the Rose. But otherwise there is no evidence of anyone playing there, no contemporary references of any kind. Its early use must have been fairly casual and intermittent.

What are the implications of all this? The security of a "home" base for the professional companies from 1594 is a matter of some historical value. But it also has a role to play in the story of the major surviving records, the play-texts, and the question of how much their composition was determined by the venues they were written for. Because the Rose and the Theatre were the first playhouses which the companies could have expected to use constantly, the plays written specifically for them have a distinctive value when we try to discover any information about their original staging. Given the preference the companies had for the indoor venues inside the city, we can say that no play could ever have been written for performance at any specific playhouse until the Rose and the Theatre took in their two new companies in 1594. There is no doubt that the plays composed for the two companies between 1594 and 1600 were designed for their fixed and official playing-places and the distinctive features of their stages. The new stability these two open-air theaters enjoyed as the "home" base for their companies is affirmed by the remarkable infrequency of records for either company doing any traveling in the years up to 1603. Until 1594 there was no reason for any writer to exploit any known features of any playhouse, because he would expect the play to be as mobile as the companies. That consideration gives a certain potency to the Rose and the Theatre, but much more to their successors, the Globe and the Fortune. That is their real modern authority.

About the Rose there is ample evidence to show the large scale of exploits it achieved with its new authority between 1594 and 1600. But at thirteen years old in 1600, it was still surprisingly young to be replaced by the Fortune. Its small size compared with its rival the Theatre as a near neighbor may be one reason for that, and the establishment of the rival company building the Globe on the model and scale of the Theatre may have been another. One wonders if, once the exigencies of having no theater of their own had forced the Burbages to move south of the river for their new site, some word may not also have been spoken from on high about returning one of the playhouses north once the other had moved south, to keep the distribution balanced between Surrey and Middlesex. The relative size of the Theatre and the Rose, one ninety-nine feet in outside diameter and the other only seventy-four (as the archaeologists found in 1989) need not be an issue here. What is worth considering is whether the confidence that the players now had in the late 1590s led them to design their new playhouses in any significantly different ways from the designs of James Burbage in 1576 and of Henslowe in 1587, and for that matter of Francis Langley on Bankside with the Swan in 1595.

We know that the Globe's framing timbers for its polygonal "scaffold" were old, and we also know that the use of a second-hand scaffolding of oak timbers restricts, more than a little, the scope for imaginative new designs. There was in any case a necessary conservatism in both new structures. In 1599, despite James Burbage's plan of three years earlier to replace the Theatre with a roofed hall playhouse, the Privy Council's decision to keep playing in the suburban amphitheaters prevailed. So both the young Burbages and Alleyn and Henslowe were constrained to follow the aging and conservative designs of the older playhouses. In any case, their stock of plays was designed for that kind of theater. But what advances might they have imposed on the old designs, particularly their stages?

We know that the Fortune contract, laid down for the builder who had just finished the Globe, said that it should be a self-conscious equivalent to the Globe. In its own way that affirms the owners' submission to the Privy Council's decrees. Slightly smaller, given its rectilinear site, the Fortune probably had the same number of auditorium bays as the Globe in its scaffolding — twenty: five on each of the four sides of the square, making each bay almost exactly the size of the Rose's fourteen, at ten-feet six-inches deep, and similar in size if rather smaller in capacity, because of its corners, to the Globe's twenty.[17] Its contract explicitly set out similar specifications for its decor. The only difference was the highly conspicuous one of its being square against the roundness of the Globe, surely at least in part a deliberate ploy to differentiate the one from the other.

Two initial questions about these new theaters need to be asked. One is whether, with a tiring house and stage built free of the gallery scaffolding, the designers were not liberated to make a stage that did incorporate some of the innovations dreamed up in the great years since 1576. Back in 1567 the Red Lion appears to have had a stage and a tiring-house design with a "turret" that stood largely independent of the gallery framing. The planners for the new Globe had to struggle with the basic anomaly inherent in the design, of fitting a two-level structure of stage and tiring house, starting with a stage platform five feet above ground level and a second-level balcony and lords' rooms, into a frame which supplied a tiring house behind the stage that had three levels. Even with the stage floor at five-feet high, as the Red Lion specifies, some foundation infilling, and a "heavens" over the stage reaching down a little lower than the gallery roofing, it still leaves the best part of twenty-six vertical feet of the *frons* to be matched up to the thirty-two feet of total height that the Fortune's three galleries took up. And if you expect to have a gallery accessible to the stage — for Arthur in *King John* to jump from and pretend to kill himself, for Romeo to climb up to, or even for King Richard to speak to Bullingbrook from before making his descent to the "base court" of the stage platform — you cannot easily locate it at the second gallery level of the frame, eighteen feet above the stage platform.

Early plays like these in the company repertoire must have influenced the Globe's stage design to some extent because the players must have expected to revive the plays. That is one consideration: that Shakespeare's long tenure in the company and the fame of his plays which made them apt for regular revivals must have augmented the conservatism with which the design problems were approached in 1599. But the designers were otherwise remarkably free to order what they wanted. The problem of floor levels alone provided the builders with a good reason for building the whole tiring house and its extrusion, the stage platform, as an integral structure that was distinct from the gallery scaffolding, however it might be attached to it. The tiring-house area in any case had to be walled off from the adjacent galleries at both levels. One or two hints that the gentry who occupied the lords' rooms made their entry through the tiring house, as the gallants did who sat on stools on the stage at the indoor playhouses, would seem to confirm that the tiring house was walled off, which is roughly what we might expect, to ensure the security of the company's expensive costumes if nothing else. Only the skeletal frame of the galleries at the back of the tiring house would impose itself on the design of the tiring house. The *frons scenae* with its balcony and entry doors did not have to be integral to the gallery scaffolding.

So the design was, on the one hand, constrained by the existing repertoire of popular plays like *Richard II* and *Richard III, Romeo and Juliet,* and the three plays with Falstaff in them. On the other hand, flaws in earlier designs could now be rectified, and innovations both backstage and front could be introduced. For evidence about such possible innovations we have to look to the texts of the plays written for the Globe and the Fortune, and more directly to the Fortune contract.

First, however, there is another initial question, the old one about auditorium entry. It does make good sense to have access stairways on the outside of a galleried playhouse so that latecomers have to enter the galleries from the back, instead of from the yard through the front ranks of spectators, as the system identified by Lambarde and Thomas Platter required. That would be a tangible and beneficial advance on the old system of entry because it would reduce conflict between early arrivals and latecomers and also reduce the number of gatherers. Separate gatherers were needed at the Rose because Henslowe took his rents from the gallery takings, as did Langley at the Swan. The Globe company did not need to keep the takings separate because the same consortium ran both the company and the playhouse. The same gatherers could collect takings and rents for both sharers and householders. But there is evidence in the Hope contract that the Swan had a stair turret or turrets, at least by 1614, and James Lusardi claims that the Utrecht drawing of the Theatre of 1576 shows that it had stair turrets.[18] That evidence appears to invalidate the idea that they were an innovation in 1599 and takes stair turrets off the list of likely innovations at the Globe and the Fortune. We have to wait to find out more about the auditorium entry systems until the rest of the Rose's foundations can be excavated and, perhaps, eventually the Globe too.

The Fortune contract shows little direct sign of the players' intervening over its design. It does specify a distinct "Stadge and Tyreinge howse to be made, erected & settupp within the said Frame, with a shadowe or cover over the saide Stadge," but it then refers to "a plott thereof drawen" which has not survived. The stage is to be forty-three feet across and should extend to the middle of the fifty-five foot yard, and "to be in all other proporcions contryved and fashioned like unto the Stadge of the saide Plaie howse called the Globe," which is not much help, except that it does suggest that evidence from the six surviving Fortune plays ought to have demands for staging fitting those in the Globe plays, and vice versa.

This is not the place for that kind of analysis. The needs for staging the Globe plays were delicately analyzed by Bernard Beckerman more than thirty years ago.[19] I would alter some of the plays he identified as Globe plays from

1599 to 1609, and I would reinterpret some of his readings over certain features, most notably the trap and the question of flying properties from the heavens. But that project awaits further study, not least a mass of fresh experimentation using the stage of the new Globe in Southwark.

The Globe and the Fortune are well worth the archaeology, even if at present they are unlikely to get very much of it. To confirm that, it may be worth reasserting a point that runs rather strikingly counter to my initial suggestion that the open-air playhouses must have been seen by the players as a retrograde step. This point has been made before, but it bites particularly sharply here. Shakespeare's company did acquire the Blackfriars after all in 1608 and could have gone indoors for good then. But something about the Globe in its first ten years had them hooked. In those early years the Globe acquired its own authority with the players who used it. As early as August 1608, as soon as they retrieved their lease at the beginning of that longest of closures for plague, the two Burbage heirs chose to allot shares in the Blackfriars playhouse among their fellows who were already part-owners of the Globe. From the start they planned to use both theaters, one for summer and the other for winter. It was an incredible extravagance, to leave one playhouse empty, especially once the number of companies wanting London playhouses increased to six, as it did with the creation of two new royal children's companies in 1610 and 1611. Six companies, five playhouses, and one company hogging two of them meant that two companies were short of a permanent place to play in the second decade of the seventeenth century. The King's Men's policy decision of 1608 was selfish and not advantageous commercially. But they stuck to it, and one reason must be that they had grown to like the open-air Globe.

By the time the Globe burned down in the summer of 1613 they must have known that they could get a higher income from playing exclusively at the Blackfriars. Yet they still liked their amphitheater enough to pay to have it rebuilt more expensively than ever. By then the crisis in playhouse availability was even more intense, the Porter's Hall indoor project having been squashed by the Privy Council, and there must have been a thought in some of the King's company backers' minds in 1614 to hire out one of their two playhouses to other players. But they hung onto the Globe. That choice, costly and selfish as it was, testifies to the power of sentiment and tradition in the company housekeepers. It also affirms the perhaps surprising popularity and presumably efficiency of the Globe as a machine for playing in. Above all, it gives the two amphitheaters, the Globe and its square counterpart the Fortune, the authority of being the first coerced, misshaped but effective homes for the only approved companies of 1599 and 1600 through that incredibly fruitful first decade of the seventeenth century.

There is a final anomaly, and even a paradox, in this story. The King's Men chose to preserve their two playhouses for their one company against all the economic arguments, as a collective decision. They were free to do so because in a heavily capitalistic management system where all the other playing companies were backed by entrepreneurial impresarios, they were unique in maintaining a wholly sharing cooperative system. They were both tenants and landlords of their own properties, sharers and housekeepers in the company and the playhouses. They financed themselves. Henslowe at the rival playhouse had done the more traditional and authoritarian thing, working as impresario-financier, monarch of the companies he ran, along with his managerial son-in-law. It was a system that as it developed clearly favored the impresario capitalist over the collaborative playing team.

But working for the impresarios, players of the other companies looked enviously at the Globe company's sharing system. In 1618 the Fortune company signed an agreement with their landlord Alleyn that bought them shares in his playhouse, effectively replicating the Globe system at the Fortune. The King's Men had become a model for their rivals in things other than their plays. For the Fortune company, their imitation did not last beyond 1622 when the Fortune burned down. It was a worse loss than the Globe in 1613, not because the Fortune company could not get another playhouse, but because the Fortune burned at midnight, and so took all the playbooks and costumes with it; whereas the Globe, burning down during a performance of *Henry VIII,* had enough bright sparks on hand to save all of the company's vital assets from the fire. Such a rescue act must be what saved the half of the Shakespeare plays that were not yet in print for posterity and kept the company going. The Fortune company had less luck. Their playhouse was rebuilt with money from financiers, not the players, and throughout its subsequent history, like that of all the London playhouses other than the Globe and Blackfriars, it remained in the hands of the impresarios.

The anomaly of the Globe company becomes a paradox when their management system is studied. From 1603 they ran under the patronage of the highest figure in the land, Britain's most well-argued autocrat. And yet this best, most privileged, longest-living, and most prosperous of all the early Stuart companies, the only one carrying the name of the Stuart kings, ran for forty-eight years as the most democratic and cooperative organization in the whole of England. Its consistent financial success in the face of the impresario system that ruled its rivals began accidentally at the Globe in 1599 in material London. The paradoxical authority of the Globe helped to develop the ultimate paradox: the most anti-authoritarian system of management that ever ran in early modern England, with the king's own name as its cover.

Notes

1. Jonathan Hart, *Theater and World: The Problematics of Shakespeare's History* (Boston: Northeastern University Press, 1992), pp. 231–32. Hart notes that the Globe and the Fortune were both given emblematic names.

2. *Records of Early English Drama,* general ed. Alexandra F. Johnston (Toronto: Toronto University Press, 1979–).

3. *Henslowe's Diary,* ed. R. A. Foakes and R. T. Rickert (Cambridge: Cambridge University Press, 1961), p. 280.

4. E. K. Chambers, *The Elizabethan Stage,* 4 vols. (Oxford: Clarendon Press, 1923), 4: 296.

5. Thomas Heywood, *An Apology for Actors* (London: 1612), sig. A3r.

6. For the question of how quickly the companies can be seen from outside as becoming London-based, see also William Ingram, *The Business of Playing: The Beginnings of the Adult Professional Theater in Elizabethan London* (Ithaca: Cornell University Press, 1992), p. 14.

7. The six-month stay was from late January to June 1592, and then January to early February 1593.

8. Slater's travels, so far as they appear in the various *REED* records, are noted in Gurr, *The Shakespearean Playing Companies* (Oxford: Clarendon Press, 1996), under the various company records, pp. 217, 237, 312, 330, 336, 390, 391, 410, and chpt. 3. His domestic records are cited in Mark Eccles, "Elizabethan Actors IV: S to End," *Notes and Queries* 238 (1993): 165–76, esp. 171.

9. *Henslowe's Diary,* p. 297.

10. Chambers, *Elizabethan Stage,* 4: 302.

11. This story is told in more detail in Gurr, "Three Reluctant Patrons and Early Shakespeare," *Shakespeare Quarterly* 44 (1993): 159–74.

12. There is reason to be skeptical of the emphasis that Stephen Mullaney puts on the freedom to play only in the "liberties"; see *The Place of the Stage: License, Play, and Power in Renaissance England* (Chicago: University of Chicago Press, 1988). The Lord Mayor's jurisdiction was not so easily defined. But there can be no other reason for the Council to specify "libertyes."

13. The documents cited here are transcribed in Chambers, *Elizabethan Stage,* 4: 316–34.

14. *Acts of the Privy Council of England,* ed. J. R. Dasent, 32 vols. (London: HMSO, 1890–1907), 30: 395.

15. *Acts of the Privy Council,* 30: 466.

16. *Acts of the Privy Council,* 15: 271.

17. John Orrell, "The Architecture of the Fortune Playhouse," *Shakespeare Survey* 47 (1994): 15–28.

18. James P. Lusardi, "The Pictured Playhouse: Reading the Utrecht Engraving of Shakespeare's London," *Shakespeare Quarterly* 44 (1993): 202–27, esp. 215–20.

19. *Shakespeare at the Globe, 1599–1609* (New York: Macmillan, 1962).

14

Building, Buying, and Collecting in London, 1600–1625

Linda Levy Peck

Lionel Cranfield, a major London merchant engaged in the importation of Italian silks, velvets, and taffeta in the 1590s, tripled his wealth between 1598 and 1601, accumulating a net worth of £6,600.[1] As a sign of his prosperity and prospects, Cranfield decided to build in Wood Street, just off Cheapside, where he had his business. But Cranfield had problems with his builders. On 19 November 1603, Thomas Gardiner wrote of the need to finish "a botcher's beginning: . . . For the columns that bear your new building must be removed one foot further outward and a new foundation made, for he hath left the jetty so great the joists sink already . . . If Mr. Thornton, whom Mr. Stowe commended to you, had not taken the work in hand . . . your charge and work before had been spoiled." The "botcher" had cut a window "so far under the size . . . that it would not serve for neither of hall nor parlour window . . . the making of the stairs to that building shall not be done except you will come up for one hour to see and hear the opinion of Thornton . . . He would have the parlour chimney set where the buttery door is . . . It will grace the parlour and the door for the stairs to go out of the parlour where the chimney is or thereabouts."[2]

Such a homely letter suggests that in building his house at Wood Street Cranfield did not engage an architect but, like most contemporary owners, relied on his own ideas and those of his builders.[3] Thornton, recommended by John Stow (the famous author of the *Survey of London*), had rescued a bad job, ennobled the parlor and provided the taste the builder—or was it the owner?—lacked.[4]

Cranfield's problems in Wood Street should be contrasted with his next major building project. In 1621 Cranfield, now Master of the Court of Wards and soon to be named Lord High Treasurer of England, decided to enlarge and add a park to Beaufort House, the Chelsea mansion he had recently acquired for £3,000 and which had once belonged to Sir Thomas More.[5] To design the extension he hired Inigo Jones, the Stuart court's favorite architect, who was just completing the Whitehall Banqueting House. Cranfield's taste for Italianate architecture burgeoned. In 1624 Sir Henry Wotton, former ambassador to Venice and shaper of the Jacobean taste for Italian and Italianate art, sent Cranfield his new book *The Elements of Architecture,* in which he extolled the virtues of Vitruvius, Alberti, and Palladio, and the classical style.[6] Thus Wotton cited Palladio's views that the "principal Entrance was never to be regulated by any certain Dimensions but by the dignity of the Master; yet to exceed rather in the more, than in the lesse, is a mark of Generosity, and may always be excused with some noble Emblem, or Inscription, as that of the Conte di Bevilacqua, over his large Gate at Verona."[7] All that survives today of Cranfield's building is Jones's elaborate gate which the Earl of Burlington rescued and incorporated into his own eighteenth-century neoclassical Chiswick House, that epitome of the Palladian revival (fig. 14.1). Taken together, these moments in Cranfield's building, virtually bracketing the reign, suggest significant changes in cultural display during the reign of James I.

Yet what was new? London had been an important metropolis and entrepot since Roman times, as well as the site of government and of the ecclesiastical elite since the Middle Ages. As its overall population quadrupled from 50,000 in 1550 to 200,000 in 1630,[8] it was frequented by gentry in term and Parliament time, and, as F. J. Fisher pointed out in his seminal article of 1948, it had become the site of conspicuous consumption in the sixteenth century.[9] In 1599 Thomas Platter, a German traveler to England, noted that "this city of London is so large and splendidly built, so populous and excellent in crafts and merchant citizens, and so prosperous, that it is . . . esteemed one of the most famous in all Christendom. . . . Most of the inhabitants are employed in commerce; they buy, sell and trade in all the corners of the globe . . . In one very long street called Cheapside dwell almost only goldsmiths and money changers on either hand, so that inexpressibly great treasures and vast amount of money may be seen here."[10]

If London was already a large and wealthy city by 1600, the Stuarts and the court they began to create in 1603 could claim no credit. Indeed, Simon Thurley has emphasized that the Stuarts did little building themselves in the early seventeenth century, especially compared to the French and Spanish monarchs.[11] Although they planned to rebuild Whitehall, Jones's Banqueting Hall was the only part completed. Indeed, the most important single event of the sixteenth and seventeenth centuries, whether for labor or for changed land

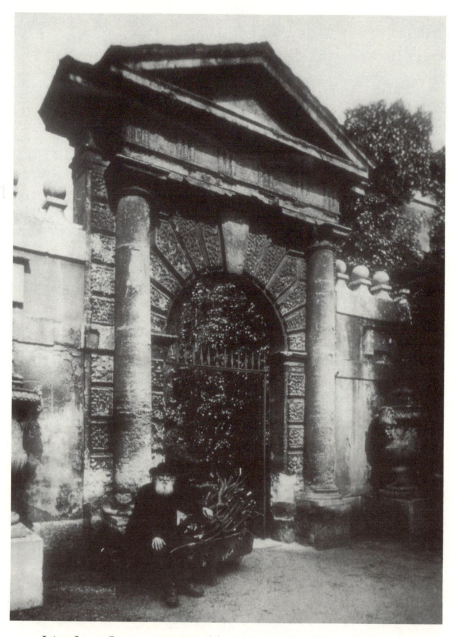

14.1. Inigo Jones Gate, commissioned by Lionel Cranfield, now part of Chiswick House.

usage, was the dissolution of the monasteries in the 1530s. The dissolution put 25 percent of the land in the hands of the laity by the end of the seventeenth century and opened up substantial areas of London for development. Did anything really change, then, between Cranfield's building in Wood Street and his building in Chelsea — and if so, what?[12]

Consumption is both a symbolic and practical act.[13] Cranfield's changing pattern of consumption was not unusual among the Jacobean elite. While wealth in Britain had gradually expanded from the fifteenth century with occasional hiccups, the forms of Jacobean expenditure changed in important ways. In 1600 the English elite lagged fifty years behind their Continental counterparts both in wealth and display. But, by 1625 that elite had embraced the material culture of Italy, France, and the Netherlands.

In Renaissance Italy, Richard Goldthwaite writes, "The humanist Matteo Palmieri exalts splendor as the quality . . . needed to enhance one's life with beauty . . . including the house, its furnishings and other appurtenances." Splendor and magnificence were matched virtues: "whereas magnificence is manifest in public architecture, splendor expresses itself in the elegance and refinement with which one lives his life within buildings."[14] This was the "world of goods" to which the British elite increasingly turned in the seventeenth century.

As I have argued elsewhere, the accession of James VI of Scotland as James I of England brought the creation of a new royal court, new conceptions of kingship and of empire, the construction of a new elite, and the evolution of a new relationship with Europe. This political rupture with the Elizabethan past now found new cultural expression: the Earl of Northumberland defended himself against charges of treason in 1605 by claiming that he was too busy to plot treason: "examine but my humors in buildings, gardening and private expenses these two years past."[15] He lent his collection of Latin, Italian, and French architecture books, including Vitruvius ("the father of all the rest"), Sebastiano Serlio, Wendel Dietterlin, and Leon Baptist Alberti, to Sir John Holles — "Palladius you have already." Sir John Holles replied sententiously that "the pleasure of building, being a more permanent work [was] many times better than getting of children or other posterity."[16]

Let me emphasize what was new by making four points. First, the elite created by the accession of James I was new and British: it was made up of Socts, members of great noble families like the Howards and the Percies, whose ambitions were unfulfilled by the Elizabethan regime, and Elizabethans who had successfully negotiated the transition to the accession of a foreign monarch, most notably Robert Cecil, earl of Salisbury. Second, Jacobean aristocratic culture was significantly urban.[17] Even such important studies as those of Lawrence Stone have suggested that the English aristocracy differed from their Continental counterparts: while the French built city palaces, the English built country houses.[18] Yet in the early seventeenth century, the English nobility increasingly built city palaces. Third, the construction of Jacobean culture was shaped by gender in two respects. In the first respect, women continued to be important consumers linking London and the country. Because they often organized the shopping, they often made the consumption decisions.[19] Several notable women were active patrons of the new culture: Queen Anne, for whom Inigo Jones designed the Queen's House in 1616; Lucy Harrington, countess of Bedford,[20] who spent much of her time at court while her husband, the earl of Bedford, was in the country, and who battled the earl of Arundel for pictures; and Catherine Knollys, countess of Suffolk, an important court broker. Indeed, Alatheia Talbot, countess of Arundel, was the first English person to commission Rubens, sitting for her own portrait in Antwerp in 1620.[21] Jacobean culture was shaped by gender in a second way. The role of favorite, while not new, became more important under King James; the king's favorites, Robert Carr, earl of Somerset, and George Villiers, duke of Buckingham, became proponents of the new taste. Carr's collections were put together by Dudley Carleton, who succeeded Wotton in Venice, and Arundel and Buckingham used brokers like Balthazar Gerbier, Daniel Nys, and Nicholas Lanier to buy pictures and sculpture.[22] Perhaps as a result, the purveyors of the new taste — ambassadors, brokers, merchants, antiquary-dealers — explicitly insisted that the new type of collecting was *not* effeminate. This made it appropriate to a nobleman of the ancient nobility such as the earl of Arundel and his peers, as well as to the favorites. Fourth, an important strand of Jacobean culture was European and imperial. Classical architecture had perhaps reached Bermuda as early as 1619,[23] and by the 1630s Thomas Wentworth built a marble-columned mansion in Jigginstown, Ireland, which cost £22,000. Its frontage of 360 feet made it larger than both Hatfield House and Longleat.[24]

In England the first changes in elite consumption occurred as the wealthy drew on Continental models and Continental books. English manuals came later. Indeed, in the case of architecture the first work published in England in the sixteenth century, *First and Chief Groundes of Architecture* by John Shute in 1563, was drawn extensively from the work of the Italian architect Sebastiano Serlio.[25] When such a shift in practice takes place, the local infrastructure may not yet be in place to support it. In 1600, where was the architect, where was the shop, where was the auction house in which to buy the new objects? And how did one know what to collect?

The Crown's role in creating this new aristocratic urban culture was complicated. It allowed the development and building of the New Exchange and of Covent Garden, continued to promote monopolies for the importation of new industries, developed plans for the rebuilding of Whitehall Palace, and commissioned Jones' Banqueting Hall with Rubens' ceiling designed in conscious imitation of the cycle the painter had done for Marie de Medici. Prince Henry and Anne of Denmark began their own collections. Yet, royal policy, as Paul Slack has suggested, moved simultaneously in two different directions: on the one hand, ordering gentry to return to their counties and, on the other hand, encouraging the development of the West End of London as an aristocratic living and shopping area.[26] In 1661 Sir Balthazar Gerbier, advisor to the duke of Buckingham forty years earlier, published his book *On the Importance of Magnificence in Building*. By this time there was little new; after all, the Florentine architect Alberti had said much the same thing in the fifteenth century, and the English elite had been building, buying, and collecting in the new style for fifty years. It did signal, however, the triumph of these ideas of magnificence and splendor despite the upheaval of the Civil War and Commonwealth.

Building

The country house has become such an icon of English aristocratic life that we forget that in the early seventeenth century the English aristocracy were increasingly building or renting houses in London, and that by the end of the seventeenth century, as Susan Whyman has shown in her study of the Verneys, country gentry were spending as many as nine months a year in London. Great ecclesiastical statesmen of the Middle Ages had lived in great inns in the city.[27] By the sixteenth and seventeenth centuries, these residential patterns had been secularized, much as they had been in fifteenth-century Florence. Although Burleigh and Leicester rebuilt London houses, Elizabethan nobility and officeholders were likely to rent housing during term time. That changed with the accession of King James. John Adamson points out that the most significant building of the period 1603–25 was a series of great palaces along the Strand.[28] In addition there was Syon House in Putney and the creation of new squares such as Covent Garden and of new market places such as Robert Cecil's New Exchange, a competitor to Sir Thomas Gresham's Royal Exchange. The earl of Bedford's real-estate venture was specifically designed to meet the needs of the new elite: he engaged Inigo Jones to produce a new aristocratic townhouse designed specifically for an urban gentry. After James I decided not to go on progress around the countryside, as Elizabeth had done, London became even more of a magnet for those who would serve the king for reward and for those who catered to elite tastes.

"Location, location, location" were the watchwords for the seventeenth century (as well as for the present day). Did you live near work—that is, if a merchant, in the city, if a courtier, near the court? Or did you live near the shops, near Cheapside, Paternoster Row, or the new West End? Or near transportation—that is, the river Thames? The court nobility also metaphorically lived above the shop, since access to court helped to define status, power, and wealth.

The Howards, whose power in the late fifteenth and sixteenth centuries had rested on their great land holdings in East Anglia and on the military and political skills of the second and third dukes of Norfolk,[29] illustrate the changing projection of noble life, at once urban and Italianate. Among the new elite that James's accession swept into power or elevated were Henry Howard, earl of Northampton; his nephew Thomas Howard, earl of Suffolk; and his great-nephew Thomas Howard, earl of Arundel, who was restored to his titles if not to the East Anglian estates which were shared between his great uncle and cousin.[30] The houses of these three Jacobeans—Northampton House, Audley End, and Arundel House—reflect not only Howard ambitions but also the changing court culture. Northampton built his palace on the Strand diagonally across from the Whitehall Tilt yard;[31] it was the largest London house built in the Jacobean period. Audley End, built by his nephew Suffolk at the same time, was the largest country house constructed in the Jacobean period. We do not know who designed either. John Adamson points out that initially Northampton House did not take full advantage of its site on the river but imposed itself on the viewer with its 162 feet of frontage on the Strand, proclaiming by its size and proximity to the court the power of the lord who resided within. If the framework of the house was not innovative, its contents were splendid. When Northampton died in 1614, the house was inherited by Suffolk, and the countess of Suffolk bought the earl's household stuffs for £5,000 from his trustees: "the like whereof then could not elsewhere be gotten."[32]

One striking aspect of the building boom of the first decade of the seventeenth century was that some of these aristocratic palaces were *remodeled* within decades from the 1630s through the Civil War, Commonwealth, and Restoration, as the English nobility got a better handle on continental style. They were rebuilt not because they were in poor repair but because they were old-fashioned. When Northampton House came into the hands of the Percies, earls of Northumberland, they rebuilt it first according to the designs of Inigo Jones in 1642 and secondly of John Webb, Jones' associate, in the 1650s.[33] Magnificence and splendor, building and its furnishings, went hand in hand. Moreover, when John Evelyn visited Northumberland House in 1658, he admired the Earl's pictures; these included a Titian (which Northumberland bought from Van Dyck, who like Rubens was not only a painter but a collector and dealer), paintings by Andrea del Sarto, Georgione, and da Vinci, as well as "divers portraits by Van Dyck."[34] Howards and Percies living on the Strand collecting pictures from the Rialto? The descendents of those overmighty subjects who had challenged the monarch had reshaped aristocratic identity and now challenged each other as connoisseurs.

The courtiers' buildings on the Strand were visual assertions of power that proclaimed access while not requiring their inhabitants to live in the palace itself. Maria Rodriguez-Salgado points out that Philip II of Spain had encouraged his nobility to build near the palace in Madrid, adding to the court's splendor and, more practically, providing lodging for visiting dignitaries.[35] Indeed in such a theatrical culture, some of these buildings surrounding the English court were stage sets. For instance, when the duke of Buckingham took over York House on the Strand, he used it apparently for elaborate receptions rather than daily living.[36] Henry Peacham wrote of York House in Buckingham's day that "the galleries and rooms are ennobled in the possessions of those Romans heads and statues which lately belonged to Sir Peter Paul Rubens, knight, that exquisite painter of Antwerp."[37] There were also ceilings painted by Gentileschi. In the 1640s, much like Buckingham, Northumberland kept his art collection next door at York House, which he rented.[38]

If consumption is important, so, too, is diffusion. The most important architects of the era besides Inigo Jones were the Smythsons. In 1609 and 1618–19 the Smythsons, father and son, came to London to sketch the new buildings going up on the Strand. Smythson drew the New Exchange, the Earl of Northampton's new house, and the pergola added to Fulke Greville's house in Holborne, a fashion that he noted had been imported from Italy (fig. 14.2). These fashions were then incorporated in the country houses of the Cavendishes for whom the Smythsons worked.[39]

In asserting that this new elite and the culture it produced was urban, we should not focus only on the great Strand palaces which only a few could afford. The new elite lived in many wards of the city and its suburbs, whether in their own houses, in inns, or in furnished lodgings, alongside, and in many cases boarding with the tailor, the barber, the scrivener, the apothecary, and the grocer.[40] Some of the Scots lived in the city: the earl of Argyle bought Devonshire House, which had belonged to the Harringtons, sometime after 1604, and the marquis of Hamilton owned it until his death in 1625. In response to the proclamations of James I and Charles I directing the nobility and gentry to return to their homes in the country,[41] inquiries revealed gentry living in many of London's wards, often claiming that they were the king's servants or in town to pursue law suits.[42] However, the returns to inquiries between 1632 and

14.2. "The Front of Bathe House: Sir Foulke Gryvelle's: in Houlborne, 1619," sketched by Robert Smythson. Reproduced by permission of the librarian, British Architectural Library / Royal Institute of British Architects.

1635 document gentry, whom we traditionally define as country gentlemen, with no country home at all.[43] Sir John Suckling of Norfolk and his family lodged in the house of William Sharowe, tailor, in Fleet Street,[44] and "Sir Fulke Greville . . . for his abode in the country he has none we can learn."[45] Sir Christopher Darcy even claimed downward mobility: he was a younger son, the little land that he owned was let to farmers, and he had married into the family of a London doctor.[46]

Lionel Cranfield, who had been impeached shortly after Wotton sent *The Elements of Architecture* to him in 1624 and who was removed from office as lord treasurer, had to sell his Chelsea mansion. He now lived in St. Bartholomew the Great parish during term time, renting part of the earl of Holland's house. He had other houses for his family in Covent Garden and Lincoln's Inn Fields. He continued to buy paintings by Van Dyck and frames by Nicholas Stone, and he hired carpenters, plasterers, bricklayers, and joiners to work on his house in St. Bartholomew's.[47] Confined to the Tower for fifteen years because of complicity in the Gunpowder Plot, the ninth earl of Northumberland was finally released and developed close ties to the court of Queen Henrietta Maria. In January 1634–35, the common council in Farringdon Ward Without, St. Brides certified that "the Earl of Northumberland has taken Dorset House in Salisbury Court for five years and has been resident there one year . . . and he and his family were last in the country at his mansion house at Petworth and at Syon in Middlesex." Even when the Howards and Percies went to the country they were not far from London. In sum, whether they built great palaces on the Strand or took rooms with the tailor in Fleet Street, the English nobility and gentry were increasingly urban, and they intermingled with the London populace. Even palaces like Northumberland House were surrounded by the victualler, the sadler, and the vintner.[48]

Buying

Thomas Platter had noted in 1599 that London was filled with shops. The early seventeenth century saw a significant increase in the importation of luxury goods, including textiles, wine, and food such as pepper and dried fruits. While the value of imports to London was the same in 1600 as it had been in 1560, by 1620 it was 40 percent higher. For example, in 1560 the trade in imported silk fabrics had a value of £29,864; by 1622 it had more than doubled to £79,530.[49] The growth in demand for luxury goods stemmed from several sources: faster population growth among the nobility and gentry than among the rest of the population; the increase in agricultural rents allowing those with property more disposable income; and the increase in honors and titles, so that more people not only aspired to but also practiced the life of the gentry. As Christopher Clay points out, the symbols of aristocratic status had changed. While the gentry kept fewer servants and spent less on funerals, they increased the number and variety of their material goods, including chimney pieces, plasterwork, furniture, hangings, carpets, pictures, plate, glassware, clothing, and coaches. "The very rich," Clay writes, "always retained a fondness for imported goods."[50] Although the Royal Exchange was a little smaller than "the one in Antwerp," Thomas Platter reported that "all kinds of fine goods are on show; and since the City is very large and extensive merchants . . . meet together in this place where several hundred may be found assembled twice daily . . . buying, selling, bearing news, and doing business generally."[51]

    In the early seventeenth century, Robert Cecil, earl of Salisbury, built the New Exchange on the Strand. Designed by Inigo Jones (fig. 14.3), opened by King James, and commemorated with a masque by Ben Jonson, the New

14.3. The New Exchange, by Inigo Jones (drawn 1618–19). Reproduced by permission of the Provost and Fellows of Worcester College, Oxford.

Exchange celebrated the luxury trade. Peace with Spain in 1604 had fostered an expansion of English trade and a change in focus from the northern ports in Germany to the Mediterranean. English merchants sailed to Russia, the Baltic, the Mediterranean, North Africa, the Indian Ocean, and America in the search for luxury goods.[52] At the opening of the New Exchange, the royal family, the Queen, Prince, Duke of York, and Lady Elizabeth were presented with goods from India and China. Leases were granted to sellers of "clothes, books, fancy goods, perfumes, and other personal articles on expensive leases."[53] The market for these goods was nationwide.

The creation of the Royal and New Exchanges can be documented; the process of shopping is less easy to recreate. When we do analyze shopping, we find close links between London and the countryside, revealing the integration of a national economy. London was the center for the most important purchases of the well-off.

In May 1613 John Eaton, servant to the earl and countess of Cumberland, sent goods worth close to £140 to York. He assured the countess that he had followed instructions and "beaten down the prices." "After wee had sought and searched almost all the shops in Cheapside . . . I found that the first shope we were at . . . was Mr. Barnes . . . where wee had as good or better choyce than elsewhere, we could not mend our marketts nor save a penny in the pound of that wee were demanded here, in any of the places wheresoever we went."[54] The earl of Bath, whose country house was hundreds of miles closer to London, had his sheets made and his musical instruments mended in the country.[55] But the earl and countess of Cumberland turned to the metropolis for clothing and furnishings for houses and stables in the North, and their neighbors had their watches fixed in London.[56]

Material London was central to the ritual of gift giving which permeated early modern society. A country neighbor who had just come from the capital sent the earl of Cumberland the greatest rarities he could find in London, "such novelties as were fit for Noble personages": a citron, two oranges, and six lemons. (He asked for a buck in return to make merry with his neighbors.)[57] At the time of the earl of Somerset's wedding to Frances Howard in 1613, everyone of note was expected to give a gift. John Taylor wrote to the earl of Cumberland that "the king declared . . . plainly that he thought no man did love him that did not show his love at this time to my Lord of Somerset . . . Mr Dackombe (now Master of Requests) and Mr Ashton took up £100 worth of plate in silver dishes and presented them unto him in your Lordship's name in a very good fashion. . . . they did it out of their loves. . . . he took it very thankfully from your Lord. Never were there so many and so great gifts presented to a Subject before. He was presented and feasted by the

City." In exchange, Somerset promised to aid Cumberland's claims to Bewcas-tle.[58] In this case the gift giving was entirely organized in London, where the plate was purchased and presented to the favorite. Moreover, the fictive nature of contemporary gift giving, in which gifts should theoretically be freely given without expectation of recompense,[59] is fully displayed. Cumberland merely had to pay the bill—which was more difficult.[60] As Taylor wrote ruefully, "Nor do I yet see how to pay it."

But though our subject is London, it is impossible to locate consumption only in the capital. Goods circulated in the wares of merchants, in the ex-change of gifts, and in the train of families as they moved back and forth from city to country. Thus the Spencer inventory for Althorp taken in 1610 listed "plate brought from London the 10th of June 1611," including a cup with the Spencer arms and six silver trencher salts, three bigger than the others, with the Spencer arms and crest at every corner.[61] Contemporary inventories show us the importance attached to silver plate (the equivalent of ready cash), linen, tapestries, and pictures which were sent from one house to another to provide the appropriate "splendor" for aristocratic life.

At home the Crown promoted the luxury trade. Tapestries continued to be important and Cardinal Wolsey's were much prized and recycled. At the same time, King James established the tapestry factory at Mortlake on the out-skirts of London to replace imports of Low Countries tapestries. The most fa-mous series were taken from a set of Raphael cartoons purchased by Charles I for the purpose of "translating" them into English tapestries. Many sets were produced for sale to the English elite.[62]

But what was the infrastructure for the purchase of Italian pictures? Just as there was little English literature on architecture, there were no shops in which to buy the Tintorettos and Bassanos that courtiers now clamored for. In the Netherlands by the 1620s, if not earlier, there were galleries—we have paintings of their interiors—but these seem to have come late to England. Instead we have ambassadors like Sir Henry Wotton and Dudley Carleton putting together collections for English courtiers, and agents such as George Gage, Lanier, and Gerbier, buying work on the Continent.[63] Indeed, Van Dyck celebrated Gage's role as "shopper" for fine art in his famous triple portrait in which Gage is shown viewing a painting with a sculpture nearby.[64]

Collecting

The collections of favorites and of office-holders in the late sixteenth century were of two types. The first was that of Sir Walter Cope, a version of the "wunderkammerer" on the Continent, with all sorts of exotic clothing and furnishings such as "an African charm made of teeth . . . Beautiful Indian plumes, ornaments and clothes from China. Shoes from many strange lands," or wonders of natural history such as "the horn and tail of a rhinoceros . . . described as a large animal like an elephant" and "a unicorn's tail" and "Flies which glow at night in Virginia instead of lights since there is often no day there for over a month."[65]

More often, the collections were made up of portraits of the monarch and great officials of England and, if the collector was eminent enough or had the right connections, portraits of foreign leaders. Thus, in the inventory of 1596 of Lettice Knollys, countess of Leicester,[66] we find portraits of the prince of Orange and his wife and son, and Mary of Hungary, regent in the Netherlands. Such portraits of the leaders of the Low Countries were probably acquired when the earl of Leicester led the English forces in the Netherlands in the 1580s. There were also seven small Flanders pictures and eight maps. This inventory certainly does not reflect the earl of Leicester's complete collection.[67] In fact, it may reflect Lettice Knollys's own taste several years after Leicester's death. In this inventory there is no portrait of Queen Elizabeth, although there are portraits of Robert Cecil, members of the Knollys family, the countess's relatives, portraits of women friends, and an unfinished painting perhaps of Lettice herself. The same manuscript provides "a note of the late Earl of Essex, his goods" which includes armor, jewels, and books but no pictures.[68]

In contrast, James's favorites collected Italian art. Until the recent work of A. R. Braunmuller and Timothy Wilks, the young Scottish favorite of James I, Robert Carr, earl of Somerset, had not been known as an art collector. But the inventory of Carr's goods taken after his fall in 1615 shows a full-fledged collection of Italian High Renaissance and Mannerist pictures put together for him, just before his fall, by Dudley Carleton who succeeded Wotton in Venice.[69]

When James made his first and only trip back to Scotland in 1617 his entourage included the earl of Arundel. Descended from Dukes of Norfolk who had distinguished themselves on the battlefield, Arundel was neither a military leader nor a county magnate with hundreds of retainers and tenants. As we have seen, Arundel was a connoisseur. Arundel House, on the Strand, was of course the most important site for the appropriation of Italian and classical culture because Arundel was the most important collector of the period. His London house, with an extension designed by Inigo Jones, became famous as its owner hoped it would for the antique marbles, sculpture, and European painting that he and his wife Althaea Talbot collected on their

14.4. Portrait of Thomas Howard, earl of Arundel, by Daniel Mytens, in his sculpture gallery, Arundel Castle. Reproduced by permission of the National Portrait Gallery, London.

travels especially in Italy (fig. 14.4). They were avid consumers and directed their agents to scour the Continent from the Netherlands to Constantinople for pictures, marbles, books, and furniture.[70] They also ensured that their collections would be available to a wider audience, first through John Selden's publication of Arundel's marbles and secondly by opening the house "that all gentlemen of Vertue or Artes which are honest men may allways be used, with curtesy & humanity when they shall come to see them."[71]

Arundel's will, drafted before the trip to Scotland, places his collections at the heart of his aristocratic identity. Arundel asks his young son James to "succeede me in my love & reverence to Antiquities & all things of Art, I give unto him all my statues & pictures whatsoever with all inscriptions or monuments of stone which I desire he may take soe much a love unto as that he may increase those I leave . . . which (God knoweth) I have gathered with soe much travaile & chardge, I give him all my bookes manuscriptes. . . . that he may delight in learning & languages, fit for a nobleman." Dedicating his collections to the fame of his family, Arundel hoped "to inflame the Heyres of my House with the love of things vertuous & noble."[72] While Arundel accompanied the king to Scotland, the countess of Arundel gave a banquet for Sir Francis Bacon, Sir Julius Caesar, the Master of the Rolls, and two judges. "It was after the Italian manner, with four courses and four tablecloths, one under another."[73]

When did Jacobeans become connoisseurs? Arundel made his crucial visit to Italy with Inigo Jones from 1613 to 1614, which set the pattern not only for his collecting but for others at the Jacobean court and, as we have seen, Carleton put together an entire collection for the earl of Somerset in 1615. The duke of Hamilton, the Scottish Privy Councillor and English courtier, put together an important collection of pictures by his death in 1625, in which there were few portraits but paintings by Rubens, "old Tintoret," Bassano, Bruegel, and Caravaggio.[74] Such collections, as well as their massive building projects, are more signs — as was Arundel's will — that what it meant to be noble in the seventeenth century was significantly different from what it had meant a century and even decades before.

Yet at the beginning of the seventeenth century, the English were still uneasy about their interest in arts and collecting, even those who were its keenest promoters, such as the diplomat Sir Henry Wotton and the English ambassador in Constantinople Sir Thomas Roe. Thus Wotton concluded his work *The Elements of Architecture* of 1624 defending ornament: "Against which (me thinks) I hear an Objection, even from some well-meaning man; that these delightful Crafts may be divers ways ill applied in a Lord. I must confess indeed, there may bee a Lascivious and there may be likewise a superstitious use, both of Picture and of Sculpture."[75] Wotton was concerned that interest in art and architecture would be thought popish or morally corrupt, identified presumably with English views of Counter Reformation Italy.

Roe, however, was concerned that collecting might be thought effeminate. He wrote to Arundel from Constantinople in 1621 that he was sending him ancient coins, "rare peeces of white corall" for his fountains; and a piece of "Priam's palace in Troy for its antiquity." He had found out how to get ancient marbles from Delphos, which in due course Arundel received, but manuscripts were more difficult. Marvelling at what was available in the Turkish empire, he wrote: "I find the gentlest arts and sciences rather despised and neglected, than worn out; as if they were meanes to soften and civilize those natures, whose end and proposition is warr, blood and conquest: . . . I think they would here follow the precept of a barbarous Goth, Not to destroy, but leave and deliver them to us for our corruption to divert us from the thought or use of arms: But they are absurdly mistaken; for civility and knowledge doe confirm, and not effeminate good and true spirits."[76] Roe's discussion resembles the debate in Spain about whether or not peace softened the spirit of the nation and whether or not it would be better to go to war.[77] It is significant — and unusual — to see it applied to collecting.

In conclusion, what was the larger political and economic significance of the cultural changes that I have been charting? Politically, paintings, sculpture, fountains, gardens, and triumphal arches were integral parts of the performance of royal and aristocratic power in early modern European courts. The new British court, increasingly based in London, copied, imported, and at times, as at Mortlake, tried to produce or reproduce international style. Art and luxury objects increasingly became the medium of exchange between ambassadors and favorites, between clients and patrons. Such practice had already taken place between the court of Spain and the courts of Italy. Philip II had sent both architect and gardener to look at palaces and gardens in France, Italy, and the Netherlands as he settled on Madrid as the capital for his court.[78] While foreign artisans had moved to London in large numbers in the late sixteenth century in the wake of the religious wars in France and the Netherlands, many of the luxury goods coveted in the early seventeenth century continued to be produced abroad and imported. Interior decoration was borrowed from the French; gardens were crafted by the Mannerist Simon Caux; paintings and sculpture were imported from Italy and the Netherlands.[79] The economic significance of this new culture lies in the important change in the pattern of consumption among the nobility and gentry. This change parallels that documented by Goldthwaite for Italy between 1300 and 1600 and provides the basis for the culture of gentility documented by Lois Carr and Lorena Walsh in Old and New England.[80]

The Jacobean court established the pattern for aristocratic building, buying, and collecting for the rest of the century and laid the basis for the creation of a European court culture in Britain. Thirty years after Thomas Platter's visit to London, Rubens wrote in 1629 that "this island seems to me to be a spectacle worthy of interest of every gentleman . . . not only for the splendor of the outward culture, which seems to be extreme . . . but also for the incredible quality of excellent pictures, statues and ancient inscriptions which are to be found in this court. . . . Certainly in this island I find none of the crudeness which one might expect from a place so remote from Italian elegance."[81]

Notes

I am grateful to Stanley Engerman for his comments on an earlier draft of this chapter.

1. Menna Prestwich, *Politics and Profits Under the Early Stuarts* (Oxford: Oxford University Press, 1966), pp. 30, 55.

2. The "botcher" had complained to his company but they acknowledged his error. Gardiner concluded "Yet I pray you come to London on Monday. You need stay but to see the work and know your opinion. The little parlour shall be shortened according to your mind." Historical Manuscripts Commission, *Calendar of the Manuscripts of Major-General Lord Sackville, preserved at Knole,* vol. 1, Cranfield Papers, 1551–1612, ed. A. P. Newton (London: HMSO, 1940), pp. 59–61.

3. The most popular pattern books were those of Cornelius Bos (1540s), Jan Vredeman de Vries (1563), Abraham de Bruyn (1584). John Schofield, *The Building of London: From the Conquest to the Great Fire* (London, British Museum Publications Ltd. in Association with The Museum of London, c. 1984), pp. 6–11.

4. For a discussion of the increasing importance of the parlor as well as the position of the buttery and hall in the seventeenth century see Frank E. Brown, "Domestic Space in Seventeenth-Century London," *Comparative Studies in Society and History,* 25 (1986): 558–90.

5. Beaufort House had belonged to Robert Cecil and he had planned to rebuild it. See W. H. Godfrey, *The Parish of Chelsea, part 2* in *Survey of London* (London: London County Council, 1913), 4:18–27. While Cranfield was wealthier in 1621 than in 1603 he was able to buy Beaufort House for £3,000, about what he valued the Wood Street properties at. See Prestwich, *Profits and Politics Under the Early Stuarts,* pp. 27, 384.

6. Sir Henry Wotton, *Elements of Architecture* (London, 1624). Addressing the sort of problem that Cranfield had at Wood Street he urged the construction of a model in pasteboard or wood: "In a Fabrique of some 40 or 50 thousand pounds' charge, I wish 30 pounds at least layd out before hand in an exact Modell; for a little misery in the Premises, may easily breed some absurdity of greater charge, in the Conclusion" (pp. 65–66).

7. Wotton, *Elements of Architecture,* pp. 119–20.

8. Schofield, *The Building of London,* p. 157.

9. F. J. Fisher, "The Development of London as a Centre of Conspicuous Consumption in the Sixteenth and Seventeenth Centuries, *Transactions of the Royal Historical Society,* 4th ser., 30 (1948): 37–50; Richard Goldthwaite argues the importance of

the city—Florence, Rome, Venice—as the engine of consumption in Italy, "The Empire of Things: Consumer Demand in Renaissance Italy," in *Patronage, Art, and Society in Renaissance Italy* (New York: Oxford University Press, 1987), pp. 153–76.

10. *Thomas Platter's Travels in England, 1599,* ed. Clare Williams (London: Jonathan Cape, 1937), pp. 156–57.

11. Simon Thurley, *The Royal Palaces of Tudor England* (New Haven: Yale University Press, 1993).

12. John Chamberlain commented that Cranfield's Chelsea mansion was a long way from Wood Street. Prestwich, *Politics and Profits Under the Early Stuarts,* p. 381.

13. Mary Douglas suggests that "consumption is a ritual process" and that goods are the visible parts of culture in *The World of Goods* (New York: Basic Books, 1979), pp. 65–72. See R. Malcolm Smuts, "Cultural Diversity and Cultural Change at the Court of James I," in *The Mental World of the Jacobean Court,* ed. Linda Levy Peck (Cambridge: Cambridge University Press, 1991), pp. 99–112, which stresses the importance of aristocratic households in the creation of Stuart culture; Smuts, *Court Culture and the Origins of a Royalist Tradition in Early Stuart England* (Philadelphia: University of Pennsylvania Press, 1987), and J. C. Robertson, "Caroline Culture: Bridging Court and Country," *History* 75 (1990): 388–416, which emphasizes the diffusion of court culture to the countryside.

14. Richard Goldthwaite, *Wealth and the Demand for Art in Italy, 1300–1600* (Baltimore: Johns Hopkins University Press, 1993), p. 249.

15. Quoted in Mark Nicholls, *Investigating Gunpowder Plot* (Manchester: Manchester University Press, 1991), p. 144.

16. Historical Manuscripts Commission, *The Manuscripts of His Grace the Duke of Portland, Preserved at Welbeck Abbey,* 10 vols. (London: HMSO, 1891–1919), 9:152, 115. Neither letter is dated. Mark Girouard suggests that Northumberland's letter dates from 1610 in *Robert Smythson and the Architecture of Elizabethan England* (London: Country Life, 1966), pp. 28–31.

17. This was a point made by Fisher, "The Development of London as a Centre of Conspicuous Consumption," pp. 37–50.

18. See Lawrence Stone, "The Residential Development of the West End of London in the Seventeenth Century," in *After the Reformation,* ed. B. C. Malament (Philadelphia: University of Pennsylvania Press, 1980).

19. See Jan de Vries, "Between Purchasing Power and the World of Goods: Understanding the Household Economy in Early Modern Europe," in *Consumption and the World of Goods,* ed. Brewer and Porter (London: Routledge, 1993), pp. 85–132. They were also important figures in the market itself. See British Museum, *Catalog of Prints and Drawings, Satires,* 1:31–33, no. 62, Hollar, "The Market Place." As to diffusion, Jan de Vries suggests that there was a steady increase in consumption from the early sixteenth to the nineteenth centuries and points to the significant role of women in the household economy in making decisions about consumption.

20. Karen Hearne, "Lucy Harrington, as Art Patron and Collector" (M.A. thesis, Courtauld Institute, 1990). Queen Anne also wanted Jones to make alterations to Somerset House where she resided. Raymond Needham and Alexander Webster, *Somerset House Past and Present* (London: T. Fisher Unwin, 1905).

21. David Howarth, *Lord Arundel and His Circle* (New Haven: Yale University Press, 1985).

22. See David Howarth, "Merchants and Diplomats: New Patrons of the Decorative Arts in Seventeenth-Century England," *Furniture History*, 20 (1984): 10–17; Howarth, *Lord Arundel and His Circle*.

23. I am grateful to Karen Kupperman for this point.

24. Hugh Kearney, *Strafford in Ireland* (Cambridge: Cambridge University Press, 1959, 1989), pp. 172–73, 178. See also M. Craig, "The New Light on Jigginstown," *Ulster Journal of Archaeology*, 33 (1970): 107–10, cited in Robertson, "Caroline Culture," *History* 75 (1990): 410 n.

25. E. Harris, *British Architectural Books and Writers, 1556–1785* (Cambridge: Cambridge University Press, 1990), p. 418.

26. Paul Slack, *From Reformation to Improvement: Public Welfare in Early Modern England* (Oxford: Oxford University Press, 1998).

27. See Caroline Barron, "The Aristocratic Town House in London, 1400–1600," unpublished conference paper, The Aristocratic Townhouse in London, Institute of Historical Research, University of London, July 15–17, 1993.

28. See John Adamson, "Princely Palaces: Aristocratic Town Houses, 1600–1660," unpublished conference paper, The Aristocratic Townhouse in London.

29. In addition Henry VIII married two of the third duke of Norfolk's nieces, Anne Boleyn and Katherine Howard.

30. Under Elizabeth, William and Charles Howard each served as Lord Admiral and Thomas Howard also served in the fleet against the Spanish Armada.

31. On the rebuilding of Northumberland House see Jeremy Wood, "The Architectural Patronage of Algernon Percy, 10th Earl of Northumberland," in *English Architecture Public and Private, Essays for Kerry Downes*, ed. John Bold and Edward Chaney (London: Hambledon Press, 1993), pp. 55–80; John Adamson, "Princely Palaces: Aristocratic Town Houses, 1600–1660."

32. Quoted in Anthony Upton, *Sir Arthur Ingram* (Oxford: Oxford University Press, 1961), p. 80.

33. See Wood, "The Architectural Patronage of Algernon Percy, 10th Earl of Northumberland."

34. Quoted in E. Beresford Chancellor, *The Private Palaces of London* (London: K. Paul, French Tribner, 1908), p. 54. He was not impressed with the new stairs. See also Christopher Sykes, *Private Palaces, Life in Great London Houses* (New York: Viking, 1986).

35. Maria J. Rodriguez-Salgado, "The Court of Philip II of Spain," in *Princes, Patronage and the Nobility: The Court at the Beginning of the Modern Age* (Oxford: Oxford University Press, 1991), p. 235.

36. See George Gater and E. P. Wheeler, *The Strand* in *Survey of London*, 18:54.

37. Henry Peacham, *The Complete Gentleman*, ed. Virgil B. Heltzer (Ithaca: Cornell University Press, 1962), p. 121.

38. Jeremy Wood, "The Architectural Patronage of Algernon Percy, 10th Earl of Northumberland." Quoted in *Survey of London*, 18:55.

39. Mark Girouard, *Robert Smythson and the Architecture of the Elizabethan Age*.

40. Oxford, Bodleian, Bankes MSS, parcels 14 and 62.

41. See Felicity Heal, *Hospitality in Early Modern England* (Oxford: Oxford University Press, 1990), pp. 119–20; 146–47. Heal cites James's 1616 speech in which he attacked "creeping Italian fashion," p. 119.

42. The church wardens tried to protect some of their gentry as an "ancient parishioner" . . . and "good benefactor to our poor."

43. Oxford, Bodleian Library, Bankes MSS 62/18.

44. Oxford, Bodleian Library, Bankes MSS 14/2.

45. Oxford, Bodleian Library, Bankes MSS 14/4.

46. Oxford, Bodleian Library, Bankes MSS 62/18.

47. Oxford, Bodleian Library, Bankes MSS 62/31. For Cranfield's accounts see National Register of Archives, Cranfield, A/389/1, Oct. 1630, "payment for work at Lord Middlesex's St Bartholomew's London; A462/4, receipts signed by Nicholas Stone.

48. *Survey of London,* 18:8.

49. Christopher Clay, *Economic Expansion and Social Change in England, 1500–1700,* 2 vols. (Cambridge: Cambridge University Press, 1984).

50. Clay, *Economic Expansion and Social Change in England 1500–1700,* 2:25. Schofield points out that plaster and papier-mache were introduced by Italian craftsmen. Surviving plaster ceilings include the Great Chamber at Charterhouse built by Thomas Howard, fourth duke of Norfolk, before 1572; Paul Pindar's house near Bishopsgate in 1599; and Prince Henry's room in Fleet Street ca. 1610.

51. *Thomas Platter's Travels in England, 1599,* ed. Williams, p. 157.

52. Clay, *Economic Expansion and Social Change in England, 1500–1700,* 2:123–26.

53. Lawrence Stone, *Family and Fortune* (Oxford: Oxford University Press, 1973). The orders for the government of the New Exchange specified that only these shops were allowed: haberdashers, stocking sellers, linen drapers, seamsters, goldsmiths, jewelers, milliners, perfumers, silk mercers, tiremakers, hookmakers, stationers, booksellers, confectioners, girdlers, and sellers of china, pictures, maps, and prints. Its hours were from 6 A.M. to 8 P.M. in summer and 7 A.M. to 7 P.M. in the winter (*Survey of London,* 18:96).

54. British Library (hereafter BL), Althorp MSS B2, John Eaton to Thomas Little, 16 May 1613.

55. BL, Eg. 4258, Steward's Account for the Earl of Bath, 1602–4.

56. BL, Althorp MSS, B2, John Eaton to Thomas Little, 16 May 1613.

57. See, for instance, BL Althorp MSS B1, Henry Arlington to Earl of Cumberland, 31 August 1601, Wakefield.

58. BL, Althorp MS B2, 31 Jan 1613–14.

59. See Linda Levy Peck, *Court Patronage and Corruption in Early Stuart England* (London: Unwin Hyman, 1990).

60. B.L., Althorp, 18 Jan. 1613–14, John Taylor to Francis Clifford, 4th Earl of Cumberland.

61. B.L., Althorp MSS A 26.

62. Wendy Hefford, "Cardinal Mazarin and the Earl of Pembroke's Tapestries," *Connoisseur,* 195, no. 786 (August 1977): 286–90; Laurence Martin, "Sir Francis Crane," *Apollo* 113, no. 228 (February 1981): 90–96.

63. Edward Chaney, "Two Unpublished Letters by Sir Henry Wotton to . . . Duke of Mantua," *Journal of Anglo-Italian Studies* (1991): 156–59. David Howarth, "Merchants and Diplomats: New Patrons of the Decorative Arts in Seventeenth-Century England," *Furniture History* 20 (1984): 10–17; Howarth, *Lord Arundel and His Circle.* Nevertheless, neither Arundel's nor Buckingham's collection can compare

with the collection of Philip III's favorite, the Duke of Lerma, who in the first decade of the seventeenth century had 2,000 pictures. See Sarah Schroth, "The Private Picture Collection of the Duke of Lerma," (Ph.D. diss., New York University, 1990).

64. As described by Jeremy Wood, Stuart Court Conference, Institute of Historical Research, September 1994.

65. *Thomas Platter's Travels in England, 1599,* ed. Williams, pp. 171–73. Platter said that many of these items had come from a trip to India. Cope also had a collection of coins and pictures.

66. Oxford, Bodleian Library, Eng. Hist. MSS c. 120, fol. 35ff. An inventory 23 April 1596 of goods of the Countess of Leicester and Sir Christopher Blount.

67. See "An Inventory of the Plate, Household Stuff, Pictures etc in Kenilworth Castle, Taken after the Death of Robert Earl of Leycester, 1588," in *Ancient Inventories . . . Illustrative of the Domestic Manners of the English in the Sixteenth and Seventeenth Centuries* (London, 1854).

68. Oxford, Bodleian Library, Eng. Hist. MSS. c. 120.

69. Folger Shakespeare Library, MSS L.b. 638; A. R. Braunmuller, "Robert Carr, Earl of Somerset, as Collector and Patron," in *The Mental World of the Jacobean Court,* ed. Peck (Cambridge: Cambridge University Press, 1991), pp. 230–250; T. Wilks, "The Picture Collection of Robert Carr, Earl of Somerset," *Journal of the History of Collections* 1 (1989): 167–177; Oxford, Bodleian Library, Eng. Hist. MSS c. 120.

70. See David Howarth, *Lord Arundel and His Circle.*

71. Quoted in John Newman, "A Draft Will of the Earl of Arundel," *Burlington Magazine* 122 (1989): 692–96.

72. Quoted in ibid.

73. Quoted in Percy Lovell and William McB. Marcham, *Survey of London,* vol. 17, pp. 49–50.

74. See inventory in appendix 3 in Hearne, "Lucy Harrington, As Art Patron and Collector."

75. Wotton, *Elements of Architecture,* p. 121.

76. Sir Thomas Roe, *The Negotiations of Sir Thomas Roe in his Embassy to The Ottoman Porte* (London, 1740). Sir Thomas Roe, "your lordships curiosity being unlimited."

77. I am grateful to John Elliott for this point.

78. See Jonathan Brown and J. H. Elliott, *A Palace for a King* (New Haven: Yale University Press, 1980).

79. Roy Strong, *Henry, Prince of Wales and England's Lost Renaissance* (New York: Thames and Hudson, 1986). Timothy Wilks, "The Court Culture of Prince Henry and His Circle, 1603–1613" (Ph.D. diss., Oxford University, 1987).

80. Lois Green Carr and Lorena Walsh, *Inventories and the Analysis of Wealth and Consumption in St. Mary's County, Maryland, 1658–1777* (Chicago: Newberry Library, 1977).

81. Quoted in Christopher White, *Peter Paul Rubens, Man and Artist* (New Haven: Yale University Press, 1987), p. 225.

PART V

BUILDING THE CITY

The most familiar images of London before the Great Fire are the densely detailed views of Visscher, Norden, Dankerts, and Hollar. Carefully superimposed labels encourage us to tour their drawings like visitors to the early modern city, encountering landmark after landmark: the Thames, London Bridge, the Tower, St. Paul's, St. Lawrence Poultney, Guildhall, the Royal Exchange, the borough of Southwark, the Bear Garden, the Globe theater. To attempt to move through the city as if at ground level, though, requires us to develop a higher level of resolution than even these bird's-eye views provide, through the recovery and juxtaposition of other forms of evidence.

In "The Topography and Buildings of London, ca. 1600," John Schofield assembles information from archaeological investigations, surviving structures, maps, and administrative records, among other things. In genre after genre of city building, his sources reveal that the dominant theme of the cityscape was growth. Civic construction included a new workhouse, new hospitals, and improved water systems. Following the Dissolution, many former religious properties were first converted into urban mansions and then, under the pressure of increased population, subdivided into tenements. Parish churches added galleries to accommodate larger gatherings, and new churches were built for religious exiles from the Continent. A marked characteristic of residential building was a small footprint and multiple stories, again in consequence of population density. Industry relating to the exchange of goods remained within the city, but the more noxious industries, typically those involved in the production of things, moved to the suburbs. In the greater region, new crops, pottery works, armament manufactures, and other industries also gave witness to the city's predominance. Schofield concludes that sixteenth-century London was materially transformed by the property that came available at the Dissolution. Further, the city was unique in England for its cathedral embellished with a Renaissance portico, Inns of Court, theaters, shipping facilities, administrative offices, and presence of the royal court. But none of these distinctions made it a Renaissance city. Even as London neighborhoods grew more defined — the west for politics and culture, the center for finance and law, the east for industry and shipping — they retained a social mix, with rich and poor intermingled. This was one of the markers of London's continued medieval character at the turn of the century.

Peter W. M. Blayney gives the detailed history of one London building project in "John Day and the Bookshop That Never Was." The printer Day, who maintained extensive business premises in Aldersgate, in 1572 sought also to establish a bookshop in St. Paul's Churchyard among other booksellers. Matthew Parker, archbishop of Canterbury, petitioned William Cecil, Lord Burghley, on Day's behalf. Parker stated that Day's Churchyard lease was already secured, that the shop was already fabricated (built "little and low"), that Day suffered materially from the delay in erecting it, and that he was hindered by the envy of other booksellers. Historians of early modern print culture, misled by Parker's deliberate understatement, have come to believe that shops in Paul's were something like stalls in an open market; instead, Blayney demonstrates, they were substantial permanent structures. Parker's reference to Day's lease from the bishop and dean was also a calculated misdirection, because the churchmen had no right to issue such a lease. The area known as Paul's Cross Churchyard did lie within the cathedral precinct, but it had originally been a ground for citizen assembly and it remained under the authority of the City. Parker's petition represents the attempt of one jurisdiction, the Church (the dean and chapter of St. Paul's, the bishop of London, and the archbishop of Canterbury), to seize control from another jurisdiction, the City (the mayor and aldermen), by enlisting the support of a third jurisdiction, the Crown (Secretary Burghley, the High Commission, the Privy Council, and the Queen). Evidently, however, the attempt failed and the mayor and aldermen of London retained their contested authority over Paul's Cross Churchyard, because Day's was a "bookshop that never was."

Jurisdictional conflicts were inevitable in a city that was simultaneously national capital, home for the court, and economic center of the kingdom. But there were controversies in the private lives of London citizens, too, especially in consequence of the city's booming population. In "Boundary Disputes in Early Modern London," I bring together the mid-sixteenth-century reports filed by a group called the London Viewers, the surveys of London properties drawn in the early seventeenth century by Ralph Treswell, and the 1590s property records of Londoner Nicholas Geffe. The London Viewers were a team of four men, each experienced in the building trades, who were appointed by the Lord Mayor to adjudicate disagreements among neighbors in the urbanizing city. Treswell's floor plans show residential buildings in situ, among their neighbors. The surveys thus provide visual evidence of many of the urban jeopardies the Viewers confronted: the cleaning and repair of shared privies; the maintenance of walls, fences, and setbacks; leakage from overhanging eaves and jetties; fair access to wells and streets; challenges to ancient agreements of partition; and new construction that blocked the light of older buildings or overlooked their private gardens. As records from elsewhere in England show, boundary controversies were not unique to London. Nor was it only in London that houses enlarged and compacted with changing family situations, household numbers, and personal wealth. But the spectacular demographic growth of the city certainly put new pressure on negotiations of space and ownership, and the reports of the Viewers suggest that early modern Londoners were called on to tolerate escalating levels of annoyance in their everyday lives. These stresses resonate in the personal accounts of Nicholas Geffe.

Blayney's chapter adverts to London's important role as the center of English print culture. But his essay, like the other two, looks beyond printed texts to other forms of evidence with their many contingencies of survival and of meaning. Schofield builds his long view of London through aggregation, amassing dissimilar categories of data into an intelligible whole. Blayney's approach is to contextualize a familiar record in such a way that it yields deeply revisionist meanings. My method is analogical, as I relate three different classes of document that, given the vagaries of manuscript production and preservation, do not precisely intersect in person, time, or place. All three essays suggest how much of London's material history remains to be discovered, as, through archaeological excavations, archival investigations, analytical reconsiderations, and theoretical repositionings, we continue (re)building the early modern city.

15

The Topography and Buildings of London, ca. 1600

John Schofield

The Growth of London and the Creation of Neighborhoods

The single theme that dominates the history and archaeology of London in the period 1500–1650, and beyond to the nineteenth century, is the growth of London and its consequences; in relation to the metropolis as a whole, to the country at large, and to the world outside. London's growth in the sixteenth and seventeenth centuries occurred mainly because of the centralization in London of the nation's political and economic life, and because of upheavals in provincial economies. In no other European country were these two processes so potently combined, so that London's resulting extraordinary growth contributed to England's being one of the most urbanized countries in Europe by 1650.[1]

In the City of London,[2] natural features of the topography had been disappearing under man-made constructions throughout the Middle Ages. The underlying natural contours continued to be smoothed out and valleys filled in or encroached upon, despite some civic efforts at maintenance of watercourses. The intramural course of the Walbrook stream which had divided the city into two halves and was already embanked by 1500, was largely covered over by 1600. Concern with the state of the Fleet Ditch, and attempts to deepen it and remove wharves and privies, continued throughout the sixteenth century without much success.[3] Land reclamation into the Thames, a notable feature of the Middle Ages, seems to have slowed down during the fifteenth century, in part because of the braking effect of more durable stone walls constructed by then on many riverside properties. Certainly most of the known sixteenth-century expansions are minimal. Perhaps because of the comparative lack of reclamation sites requiring large amounts of trade and domestic waste, patterns of rubbish disposal began to change after 1450; stone and

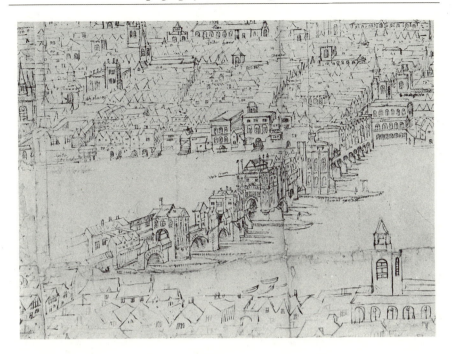

15.1. London Bridge and the nearby north bank of the Thames about 1540, from the panorama by Wyngaerde. The outer bridge gate in the foreground was decorated with the City arms and statues. Ashmolean Museum, Oxford.

brick cesspits had to be emptied when full, and the rubbish was now carted out of the city. Large-scale dumping into large and unsightly brickpits north of the wall at Moorfields, used in 1477 but no longer required, was encouraged in the early sixteenth century; recent archaeological excavation in the north part of Moorfields has found an exceptional array of sixteenth-century domestic and trade waste in the landfill. The town ditch was also filled up because the waterfront areas had stopped taking urban rubbish, making it one of the most fruitful archaeological zones for artifacts of this period.

Before the Great Fire of 1666, the City lay between two other zones, each with its own character: the West and East Ends. In outline by 1600, the West End functioned as a political and cultural focus around Westminster; financial and legal services were concentrated in the Fleet Street suburb and the City; and beyond to the east lay an area of industrial activity, warehousing, and maritime activities (though the last two were to develop mainly during the seventeenth century). This three-part division of London grew out of the topographical situation before 1500. Palaces, mansions, and inns for travelers

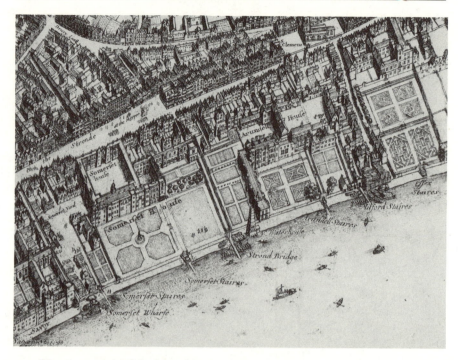

15.2. Mansions south of the Strand in 1658, a detail of the view of west central London by Wenceslaus Hollar. This shows Somerset House (1549) and Arundel House, with the gallery built, or more probably adapted, by Thomas Howard for his collection of classical sculptures in 1604–20. British Museum.

lay west of the City (fig. 15.2), attracted by the royal and parliamentary center at Westminster, and in the fifteenth century the riverside settlements east of the City began to expand to meet increased demands of the merchant fleets for ship repair and victualing services. The building boom of the late sixteenth century prompted by the dissolution of the monasteries, nearly all of which lay near the wall (whether inside or outside), contributed to the crystalization of these areas and to their different character. Land became available for building in many localities, but especially immediately outside the wall or between the City and Westminster.

New construction took on the growing character of the existing neighborhood around it, whether rich new housing or shantytown sprawl. Suburban areas also grew at different rates because each was responding to different needs and pressures. To the west, Westminster incorporated the manors of Ebury, Hyde, and Neyte in 1604, increasing its official size almost three times.[4] The architectural form of the square began in England with Lincoln's Inn

Fields, followed by the Duke of Bedford's development of Covent Garden, and William Newton's houses in Queen Street (though not a square, a much admired formal street development), all dating from the 1630s.[5] Development also took place north of the city, into Clerkenwell, and ultimately into Islington and south Hackney, though at a more gentle pace than expansion to the east or west. To the east, Stepney was an immense parish, composed of several isolated hamlets in marshland. With the growth of the navy in the sixteenth century, Blackwell and Ratcliffe, with Deptford, became important harbors. Land around Wapping was embanked and buildings spread along the river.

Development was also taking place south of the River Thames. Southwark, the largest of the medieval city's suburbs, had long had a separate character. Many of the activities there were unregulated. Though a few early theaters functioned briefly in and to the north of the city, it is probably no accident that the most important and enduring Elizabethan and Stuart theaters were established south of the river. In 1600 Southwark comprised two built-up zones, Borough High Street and the eastern triangular block of Bermondsey. Lambeth was a small village around the palace and ferry. This picture seems to have held to at least 1650 without major increase in urban area.

In 1597 Francis Bacon wrote an essay entitled "Of Travel." For the serious tourist, he said, "the things to be seen and observed are: the courts of princes . . . the walls and fortifications of cities and towns . . . antiquities and ruins; libraries, colleges, disputations and lectures, where any are; shipping and navies; houses, gardens of state and pleasure near great cities; armories, arsenals, magazines, exchanges, burses, warehouses, exercises of horsemanship; fencing, training of soldiers and the like; comedies, such whereunto the better sort of persons do resort; treasures of jewels and robes, cabinets and rarities."[6] We shall visit the City of London in 1600 in this chapter like tourists, but I also wish to highlight certain aspects to explain why the City looked as it did at the opening of the seventeenth century. These concern the growth of London from about 1550, and the consequential specification or hardening of different localities within the conurbation of the city and a few miles around; architectural features of London as a large, or even capital, city; the nature of industries in London (again, broadly defined) at this time; the effect of London on its region and hinterland within England; and, finally, the buildings and artifacts which were products of, or intended to promote, London's trade with Europe.

The evidence for post-medieval London comes from six main sources: records of standing buildings, either surviving or demolished; archaeological excavation; documentary records; panoramas, drawn surveys, plans and maps; contemporary descriptions; and later engravings, photographs, and other illustrations. The emphasis of this essay will be on the contribution of topographical and archaeological study, particularly the campaigns of urban archaeology since about 1970.

Walls, Civic Buildings, and Civic Spaces

The city wall of London had been repaired on a substantial scale as long ago as 1477, and by 1600 virtually all the defenses were approaching, or had passed, redundancy (fig. 15.3). Since 1471 no rebel or foreign enemy had tested the defenses (Wyatt's approach to the city in 1553 had not been a serious threat), so that London never had need of the colossal Renaissance bastions and moats which by 1600 were such a feature of many Continental cities, such as Antwerp (1567, to the designs of Luca Paciotto), Augsburg, or Vienna. From the first half of the sixteenth century, the city ditch of London was filled in over much of its remaining length by the encroachment of properties along extramural streets and by manufacturing facilities such as tentergrounds; at the same time piecemeal adaptations were making inroads into the wall and bastions from the inside.

During the sixteenth and early seventeenth century several of the gates were rebuilt in the Renaissance style evident all over Europe: Ludgate (1586), Aldgate (1608), and Aldersgate (1617). These gates, rebuilt if necessary after the Great Fire, were finally removed in the 1760s. In 1600 London Bridge, the main entrance to the city, was still encrusted with medieval houses and shops (see fig. 15.1). The drawbridge had ceased to function before 1500 and defeated all attempts by the Bridge corporation's engineers to make it work again; the problems seem to have been with the adjacent stone gate of 1426 not being able to take the strain of raising it. In 1600, the only recent development on the Bridge of any note was the building of a timber-framed structure of several stories across and over the bridge at about its midpoint, Nonsuch House, in 1563. Apart from a suggestion that this building came ready-framed from the Low Countries, it remains something of a mystery.

Other new institutional buildings during the sixteenth and early seventeenth century reflected new needs, largely without frills. The Guildhall chapel, college, and library buildings were forfeited at the Reformation, but the chapel was restored for civic religious services and later adapted for a law court.[7] London's principal prisons, the Fleet and Newgate Gaol, were notorious for their wretched conditions. The Fleet was a state prison which continued in use until 1844; evidence of its long history from the eleventh century until its closure has been gained from archaeological excavations by the Museum of

PUBLIC ARCHITECTURE.

15.3. A portion of the City wall of London, near St. Giles Cripplegate, drawn by J. T. Smith (1793). The parapet had been rebuilt with brick in 1477. Though this view is from the end of the eighteenth century, buildings had encroached up to the wall by 1600. London Guildhall Library.

London in the area in 1987–89, now being analyzed. Newgate and Ludgate were city prisons, the latter rebuilt in 1585 along with the gate. The sixteenth century also saw the city begin to grapple with the problem of poor relief, exacerbated by the tremendous inflow of immigrants; one action was to found a house of correction and workhouse in the former Bridewell Palace in 1553.

15.4. The west end of Cheapside in the engraving of a now lost painting of the coronation of Edward VI in 1547. This shows the procession passing Goldsmiths' Row, a long timber-framed block of shops built in 1491 decked out with rich tapestries. On the left side is the Eleanor Cross of 1290, which had (for the moment) survived the Reformation. Museum of London.

Excavations of 1978 found several parts of the original palace buildings, dated 1515–23, which clearly survived a century of adaptation up to the Great Fire. Parts were still standing in the early decades of the nineteenth century, when they were the subject of drawings.[8]

Most of the hospitals attached to the religious orders were dissolved between 1538 and 1547 (St. Thomas of Acre, Cheapside; St. Augustine Papey; Elsing Spital) and the hospital of St. Anthony of Vienne, Threadneedle Street, had ceased by 1565, but others survived: St. Bartholomew's Hospital was refounded in 1544 and the hospital of St. Mary of Bethlehem was not suppressed but granted to the City. By 1600 London had five hospitals to deal with the sick, impotent, and vagrants together, and this must be rated an important initiative within Tudor England. The architecture and interiors of these establishments before the seventeenth century are not known.

There were other civic improvements, for instance to the roads and especially to the water system. Pumps or conduits were established at Aldgate in 1535, Bishopsgate in 1513, Dowgate in 1568, Lothbury in 1546, and next to churches such as St. Mary Magdalen Old Fish Street in 1583 and St. Nicholas Cole Abbey, also in about 1583.[9] In 1582 a Dutchman, Peter Morice, established a system of pumps and pipes to take Thames water from near St. Magnus church on the Bridge into individual houses in the eastern part of the city, culminating in a public facility at the "four ways," the junction of Cornhill and Gracechurch Street, which seems to have functioned in some ingenious way with the running of the tide. By John Stow's time, twenty years later, the system was "now no such matter, through whose default I know not"; it had apparently fallen into disrepair.[10]

Like most sixteenth-century European towns of any size, London had a central space which contained its best shops, though it never had a municipal square. Cheapside, like Maximilian Strasse in Augsburg, remained the main street of London for public events and royal processions, for instance in 1547 (fig. 15.4) and 1638. In Cheapside (and shown in the corner of fig. 15.4) was the Eleanor Cross, built in 1290 by order of Edward I at one of the resting places of Queen Eleanor's coffin; it was constantly attacked by Puritans in the sixteenth century and eventually demolished in 1643.

At the west end of Cheapside lay St. Paul's Cathedral. At the Reformation the cathedral had suffered. The high altar was demolished and replaced by an ordinary table for the sacrament. Along the thoroughfare between the north and south doors, known as Paul's Walk, servants could be hired and lawyers received clients. Though Elizabeth I attended services in the cathedral several times and donated to its repair, the building gently declined. In 1561 the spire was struck by lightning and caught fire; it was afterwards taken down and not replaced.

Northeast of the cathedral was Paul's Cross, where royal proclamations, victories in war, and papal bulls were announced. The Cross, an octagonal pulpit with a lead roof, was used for open-air sermons and political speeches. Here, in 1527, Tyndale's translation of the Bible was publicly burned, as were the works of Martin Luther. Appropriately enough, Thomas Carlyle called Paul's Cross "the *Times* newspaper of the Middle Ages." The area around the Cross became a center of bookshops by 1600.[11] The Churchyard was an early center of publishing; here the works of Shakespeare and many others were sold, though the printing often took place elsewhere. It was also a central place for doing business, and foreigners might try to trade here without the permission of the City livery companies.

The cathedral's story can be taken forward a few decades to the Great Fire. Starting in 1633 and continuing until the Civil War of the 1640s, Inigo Jones added a classical portico to the west end and reclad the transepts and the choir in stone with classical details; fragments from this portico were discovered for the first time in 1996, used with other rubble in the foundations of the south-west tower of Wren's cathedral.[12] The Parliamentarians destroyed the statues of James I and Charles I on it, smashed windows, and stalled horses in the nave of the cathedral. Engravings of the exterior (including the portico) and the inside by Wenceslaus Hollar 1656–58 show the faded grandeur and melange of architectural styles then apparent. In 1666, the area was devastated by the Great Fire; but carved stones from arches and tombs of the pre-Fire cathedral continue to appear whenever Wren's crypt walls are pierced in building work. The medieval and Tudor cathedral, or parts of it, survive in jumbled form in the walls of the present crypt of 1668–88.

Religious Houses and Churches: Dissolution and Reformation

Though the cathedral survived the upheavals of the second quarter of the sixteenth century, almost all London's many religious houses did not. The fortunes of the buildings inside the monastic precincts can be described in two overlapping phases: (a) 1532–70, the era of the urban mansions and other prestigious uses of the precincts, and (b) 1560–1600, the period of the succeeding fragmentation of the precincts into many tenancies, comprising in some cases industrial premises and smaller-scale housing of the kind called "tenements" by Stow and other commentators.

By the end of the reign of Henry VIII, the majority of the monastic precincts had been transferred to courtiers or officials of the Court of Augmentations. Thus Austin Friars passed to Sir William Paulet, Lord Treasurer; and St. Bartholomew's Priory to Sir Richard Rich, Lord Chancellor. They may not have adapted well to domestic use as urban palatial complexes, and often their new owners moved elsewhere within the space of a generation and the buildings were subdivided for other uses. Only one of these mansions can be seen today: the Charterhouse, northwest of the city, rebuilt by Sir Edward North between 1545 and 1565 and by Thomas Howard, Duke of Norfolk from 1565 to 1571.[13] A second and larger monastic house, now physically destroyed but for two fragments inside a modern office block, is currently being studied: Holy Trinity Priory, Aldgate, the house of Augustinian canons founded in 1108. The priory was granted by Henry VIII to Thomas Audley in 1533, and the precinct can be reconstructed at the end of the sixteenth century due to the survival of a plan of the majority of the buildings by John Symonds, probably drawn about 1585 (fig. 15.5). An outline of the house of the dukes of Norfolk (Duke's Place is still the name of a nearby street) within the carved-up monastery buildings can be reconstructed from this plan, engravings of 1790–1825, and excavations of 1977–90.[14]

By the 1560s several of the former monastic precincts, including those containing noble residences, were used as the workplaces for industries, some run by immigrants from abroad, such as the production of glass by Jacob Verzelini in the hall of the Crutched Friars by 1575[15] and of delftware pottery by Jacob Jansen and other refugees from the Low Countries in the former Holy Trinity Priory, Aldgate by 1571.

Though the development of the precincts was usually haphazard and piecemeal, that at St. Bartholomew's Priory, Smithfield, was exceptional in that the priory had kept a large space open to the northeast of the church. Here was held Bartholomew Fair, in its heyday the greatest cloth fair in the country, since 1133. The third Lord Rich came into possession of the former priory in 1581, and he began to develop the area by laying out three streets which survive today as Cloth Fair, Middle Street, and Newbury Street; rows of houses, some of fashionable size and others partly or wholly in brick, lined the streets by 1616; construction was in progress from 1598.[16] Several buildings from this speculative venture remained until the early twentieth century. Houses of three or four stories with garrets encroached onto the site of the demolished nave of the priory church (the choir being kept for parochial use, ensuring its survival to the present day), and others were built against the choir and lady chapel to the east. In the open area northeast of the priory church, the Bartholomew Fair of Jonson's play was held by taking over the shops in the new houses for a week. Despite this requirement, many of the

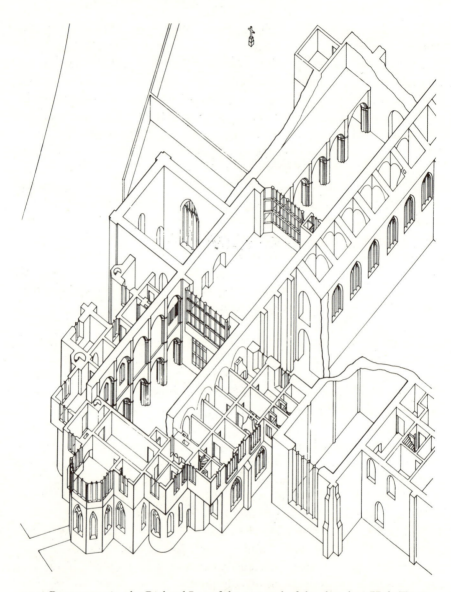

15.5. Reconstruction by Richard Lea of the east end of the church at Holy Trinity Priory, Aldgate, as adapted for noble and lesser housing by 1585 when surveyed by John Symonds. A prospect-house or gazebo fills the crossing, looking into the roofless choir and nave of the priory church; around the former are small houses with jetties sprouting from the Romanesque arches. Schofield and Lea, in preparation.

15.6. St. Ethelburga's church in Bishopsgate in 1739, by West and Toms. The shops from its front, a feature of church lands in the mid-sixteenth century, were removed only in 1932. The church was badly damaged by a terrorist bomb in 1993. Museum of London.

houses put up in this small block of streets in the two decades either side of 1600 were of substantial character and seem to have been at least respectable, as their situation next to a nucleus of superior residences in the larger stone buildings of the former priory would suggest. At the same time, the majority of them were only of one room in plan, though with several stories. The whole scheme is significant as being a private speculative property venture on a large scale fully forty years before the more famous, and probably more select, examples of Lincoln's Inn Fields or Covent Garden, further west.

The priory churches themselves had various fates, bound up with London's existing spectacular provision of religious buildings. Medieval London had 108 parish churches; though some were moderately large with three aisles and a Perpendicular tower, the majority were small, on constricted sites and often partially hidden from the street (fig. 15.6).[17] Nationally the Reformation had resulted in a drastic slimming of expenditure on churches, but the emphasis in London was not, as in towns like Winchester, Lincoln, or York, a matter of large-scale pruning of churches; here, there was only readjustment. At the Reformation three parish churches disappeared: St. Audoen and St. Nicholas Shambles[18] were subsumed into the new parish based on Christ Church Greyfriars, and St. Mary Axe parish was added to that of St. Andrew Undershaft. New churches were founded to serve the communities within the former monastic precincts at St. Anne Blackfriars (1597) and St. James Duke's Place (established on the site of the chapter house of Holy Trinity Priory in 1622, perhaps confirming use of that building as a church since the 1570s).

Strype's editions of Stow's *Survey* mention many new galleries and other embellishments in parish churches in the early decades of the seventeenth century, but this apparent burst of church building derives partly from the enthusiasm of Anthony Munday, who noted all the recent rebuildings in London churches in his continuation of Stow's *Survey* published in 1633. We therefore have a detailed list of repairs and extensions in the years 1609–32, which may have been incorporated without any further research by Strype. It is the case, however, that galleries were added to London churches from the 1580s, and that this must be an indication of rising numbers, at least among the church-going. In recent years pre-Fire masonry has been seen encased in Wren's external renderings at several churches, for instance the north aisle of 1503, surviving to full height, at St. Mary at Hill (revealed in 1984 and 1988), or at St. Vedast Foster Lane, where a pre-Fire south door to the church is now exposed, having been disclosed in recent cleaning.

In the suburbs, the pattern of church provision reflected the pressure of new population, and here new church work is significant. In 1580, as early as any City church, the medieval parish church at Stepney, out to the east, was given a gallery. St. Giles in the Fields, out to the west, was rebuilt (1623–25), and St. Mary Bermondsey, across the river to the south, was enlarged (1608–10). Chapels-of-ease were built in the expanding settlements on the Thames bank eastwards at Wapping in 1617 (parish 1694), at Poplar by the East India Company in 1654 (parish 1817), and at Shadwell in 1656 (parish 1669).

From the opening of the sixteenth century, also, London was attracting refugees and minorities who wished to have their own places of worship. By 1568 immigrants may have numbered 7 to 8 percent of the population of the metropolis. In the City, the Dutch congregation was recognized in 1550 and was granted the nave of the former Austin Friars in Broad Street. French Protestants occupied the chapel of St. Anthony's Hospital in Threadneedle Street, sharing the Austin Friars' burial ground. By the mid-seventeenth century London was a major center of nonconformist activity, and Baptists and Presbyterians met at locations all over the city and in its suburbs. There has been very little, if any, archaeological investigation of these places in and around the capital, which was their spiritual epicenter.

Houses and Other Forms of Secular Architecture

The population of the central urban area, based on the City, doubled between 1550 and 1650. How were these people housed? Most of the main developments of the period in domestic planning and construction at the level of ordinary citizen are known through documentary records and the survival of a handful of buildings, but archaeology has an important complementary role to play.

A body of data and a tentative typology of pre-Fire house plans have been provided by the drawn surveys of Ralph Treswell.[19] Four types (or sizes) can be distinguished: (1) one-room plan on each floor (though up to six stories high), (2) two-room plan (the most common), (3) three to six rooms in a plan, and (4) larger mansions (all courtyard houses). Before the Reformation many of these had belonged to either monasteries or parishes as chantry estates, and their surveyed state 1607–14 may reflect rebuildings by new owners in the second half of the sixteenth century.

One of Treswell's sites was excavated in Aldersgate Street in 1987 (indeed, it was his own house, on lease from Christ's Hospital), but only the base of one surveyed well was recorded for the period around 1600. The Treswell surveys are complementary to the archaeological information since the buildings he depicts formed strata which were removed in the nineteenth century for ubiquitous basements. On the waterfront south of Thames Street, deposits are deeper, and archaeological excavations of 1974–81 in the reclamation zone have produced the lower parts (often basements) of ordinary houses, cellars, and alleys of the fourteenth to seventeenth centuries.[20]

There was no serious fire in London between 1212 and 1666, partly no doubt a product of the regulations of the early thirteenth century which insisted on fire-break walls of stone between properties. This meant that the houses in the City were traditional in plan, though their appearance and size might change easily as the great majority were of timber framing. Two developments in the sixteenth century might be noticed in the planning of rooms and in decoration (especially woodwork and plaster, both externally and internally). First, there was a series of new ideas in taste and arrangement of rooms: in the early sixteenth century the closet and the study appeared in larger houses. The study may well have developed into the private library during the seventeenth century; books did not merit a special room in medieval or Tudor

London houses, though they did by the end of the seventeenth century. Another construction now recorded more frequently (its history in medieval houses in the capital is still obscure) was the gallery, a term which denoted a passage or corridor, a lobby or vestibule, a long room intended primarily for exercise and recreation, or a covered walk around one or more sides of a garden. Indeed, even when it was high up in a principal range, the gallery always bordered, or ended with a view of, the private garden; there are two examples of this in the clothworkers' houses surveyed by Treswell in 1612, in Billiter Lane and in Throgmorton Street.[21]

After Henry VIII, there was little if any royal lead in architectural matters between 1547 and 1603, and we have to look elsewhere for the leaders of style. Perhaps there were few to speak of; the world of Elizabeth's courtiers has recently been summed up as "Italianized architecture, Frenchified gardens and Flemish tapestries."[22] The decoration of well-to-do London houses included tapestries (see fig. 15.4) and painted hangings and wooden paneling in a small number of rooms (fig. 15.7). Both inside and outside, from about 1560, woodwork was carved into lively grotesques (fig. 15.8). At the end of the century, such as on the tomb of William Kerwin at St. Helen's Bishopsgate (1594), the decoration includes bunches of fruit more common in the middle of the seventeenth century. From the middle of the century, judging by evidence of engravings and surviving examples in towns around London, there were plaster ceilings in the best chambers, often the hall on the first floor of the compact urban house; and, from about 1580, emblems in plaster on the outside of the building.

Innovations in planning, and probably indulgence in exuberant or costly decoration, were, of course, largely confined to the houses of the nobility or the prosperous leading citizens. Their neighbors in smaller houses faced different problems. Though their homes probably had more fireplaces than similar houses in other towns, they had grave problems of shortage of space. The small urban property, often forming a frontage to a street with a large house behind, grew upward. The flat lead roof and balconies appeared to provide a little more air. Stairs and staircases were developed to articulate this growth in both small and medium sized houses. And in so doing, by 1600 the stairs were often coming up directly from the street or from an alley, breaking the house into two separate worlds of trade and private lives.

Within the old City itself, there was no social segregation into rigidly divided areas of rich and poor quarters; this lack of differentiation, a feature of the medieval city, was still the case in 1638, at least among the classes which paid tithes.[23] Poor streets or lanes were interspersed between the larger mansions or prosperous districts, as demonstrated vividly by the range of housing 1607–14 in the surveys of Treswell.[24]

15.7. A room in a house in Crutched Friars which escaped the Great Fire, drawn by J. T. Smith (1792). The paneling, fireplace, and ceiling are all circa 1600. Museum of London.

Trade and the crafts of London were still supervised, at least publicly, by the companies which had grown up from beginnings in the twelfth century. The sixteenth and seventeenth centuries were, however, a period of change for the livery companies. As their political and economic power declined, their roles as landlords and charitable trustees increased. Several company halls were rebuilt or augmented: for example, the Mercers in 1522, Salters in 1539, Coopers in 1543–47, Clothworkers in 1549 and 1594, Cordwainers between

15.8. Two sides of the courtyard of a house in Crutched Friars, drawn by J. T. Smith (1792); a display of wood carving in the grotesque style, but incorporating the badges of livery companies. Figure 15.7 must have been a chamber on one of the upper floors. Museum of London.

1559 and 1577, and Ironmongers in 1578. Smaller companies (such as the Embroiderers, Fletchers, or Innholders) now also acquired halls, with at least fifty having known sites by 1600. Many of these company halls preserved the plan-form of the medieval courtyard house, which the majority had been prior to acquisition.[25]

15.9. A cross section through the range formerly the nuns' dormitory at St. Helen Bishopsgate, drawn by W. Capon (before 1799, published 1817). Above the thirteenth-century undercroft is the hall of the Leathersellers' Company of 1610, with its fine plaster ceiling. The room still kept its medieval doorway to an adjacent building, shown on the right-hand side. Museum of London.

After 1530, some companies took advantage of the availability of land in the newly released precincts, for instance, the Leathersellers at St. Helen Bishopsgate. Here the church of the former nunnery was kept because it was also a parish church. The nuns' hall and other buildings to the north of the church, however, were sold, first to Sir Richard Williams, nephew of Thomas Cromwell, and in 1544 to Thomas Kendall, leatherseller, who bought at least the east cloistral range, composed of the former dorter and chapter house, on behalf of the Leathersellers' Company. They already had a hall, but they moved here and rebuilt the east side of the cloister in two stages: the upper part of the chapter house as a parlor in 1567 and the upper floor of the dorter as a fine hall in 1610 (fig. 15.9).

The almshouse first appears in London records in the second decade of

the fifteenth century, but the dissolution of the monasteries and of their charitable activity led to the necessity for more, as a corollary of sixteenth-century
Poor Law. New almshouses were established by prominent citizens through
their livery companies; not, as in the medieval period, as an adjunct of the
company hall, but on separate, often peripheral sites away from the city center
(e.g., the Drapers in Crutched Friars by 1535, Salters [through Ambrose
Nicholas] in Monkwell Street in 1576, and the Merchant Taylors in Hog
Street [near the Tower] 1593; others include the Clothworkers, Haberdashers, Ironmongers, and Painter-Stainers). Two sets of almshouses were surveyed by Treswell.[26] The earliest outside the City are those established by
William Lambarde at Greenwich in 1576, but they do not survive.

The Idea of Recreation and Its Consequence for Buildings

The gradual migration of the sites of almshouses to the countryside was a
consequence of urban growth, which turned fields into streets and gardens
into alleys. At the same time, and perhaps prompted by the speed and intensity
of that growth, the perimeter of the built-up area at any one time became a
zone expressly for the pursuit of recreation. By the second half of the sixteenth
century there were self-contained garden plots with summer houses on both
sides of extramural Bishopsgate. The northern side of the city was becoming a
recreational zone. From 1606 to 1616 the Moor, the boggy area, was finally
drained and laid out in walks as public gardens, a feature of other major
European cities later in the century. To the north was an area reserved for
archery practice. Cockpits and theaters were mostly in the suburbs beyond the
city (especially Shoreditch and Southwark), with notable exceptions being the
Fortune Theatre in Golden Lane (1600) and the Whitefriars Theatre (rebuilt
1629) or private theaters such as Burbage's in Blackfriars. Two Shakespearean
theaters, the Globe and the Rose, have been partly excavated on Bankside.[27]
Nor was theater the only spectacle on the Shakespearean South Bank: traces of
a bear-baiting ring and two bear skeletons were excavated at Skinmarket Place,
Southwark, in 1989.

Industries

Theaters had to share the suburbs with industrial complexes, some representing new industries. Extramural growth of an industrial character in sixteenth-
and seventeenth-century London has been attributed to the lower cost of rents,

greater space, the exclusion of certain noisome trades from practicing within the walls, and a failing craft control over the extramural areas. In the City about 1640, several trade groupings were located predominantly either inside or outside the walls. Thus merchants, officials, those in services, decoration/furnishing, and metalworking (from armorer to goldsmith) lived and worked largely inside the walls, whereas workers in clothing, leather, and the victualing trades were to be found outside. In general, during the period 1540–1700, those concerned with production of things lived primarily outside the walls, and those concerned with exchange of goods lived inside. Though some production still took place within the walls, for instance in the ex-monastic buildings described above, far more was developing especially in the northern, eastern, and southern fringes of London. An industry with medium-size plant requirements, dyeing, operated along the waterfront as it had in the Middle Ages.

In the sixteenth century the immediately extramural areas north and west of the City still provided grazing and cultivation space, but these activities were in time forced beyond the City to Islington and surrounding villages. Tentergrounds feature on the sixteenth-century views of the city. Heavy industries such as shipbuilding were being established downstream, and industrial activity mixed with residential development in the expansion of the East End.

Industries were to be a particular feature of the development of land south of the river in decades immediately after 1600. Foremost among the new industries, as revealed by archaeological work, was the making of a new kind of pottery already foreshadowed by Jansen and other innovators: tin-glazed wares. The dominant new demand was for pottery for display or decoration, for which the pretty, but hardly durable, tin-glazed wares were particularly suited. In the case of tin-glazed wares we see a burgeoning consumer-led business. The tin-glazed (delftware) industry was in the forefront of London's pottery production in the first half of the seventeenth century both in Southwark and to the southeast at Woolwich, where lead-glazed earthenwares were made in the sixteenth century, to be followed by a brief experimentation with stonewares in the first half of the seventeenth century. The introduction of tin-glazed wares to London seems also to have been a technological advance, combining the use of a new glazing technique, the blending of different sources to produce a clay with the necessary physical properties, a new direction in kiln design, and possibly a discrete step in the size of units of production and complexity of organization.[28]

Another new industry was making clay tobacco pipes. The first Virginia tobacco appeared in England in 1586, and the crop was cultivated commercially in Virginia from 1614. In the following century it was to become one of

England's major imports and re-exports. Unfortunately, due to a scarcity of makers' marks on pipes before 1600, the makers only become identifiable as individuals twenty or so years later. The clay tobacco pipe industry is one topic on the archaeological agenda of the near future.

London and Its Hinterland

Between 1520 and 1660 changes in the region's countryside reflected the needs of the capital. Farming patterns incorporated new crops and a more specialized, market-orientated outlook. Specialisms proliferated, such as hops and fruit, nursery and vegetable production, and fattening of cattle brought considerable distances from the provinces.

Several areas around the metropolis provided pottery during the period: especially Kingston, the Surrey/Hampshire borders,[29] Farnham, Farnborough, to the northeast at several sites around Harlow (Essex) and to the southeast at Woolwich; but the network of local trade between the City, its environs, and provincial towns has not yet been studied. Some pottery was coming in from the Midlands and Staffordshire. There was also industrial growth in the region: the first English blast furnace was established at Newbridge in the Weald in 1496, beginning the development of the area as the workshop of the Tudor armaments industry, and clothmaking and glassmaking were important in Surrey and Sussex.

In addition to professional services and central government, London did provide some things in return. It was the main provider for luxuries of all kinds to the region: according to Brian Dietz, "metropolitan professional services and an increase in social appetites, which only the capital could satisfy, emptied provincial pockets at a remarkable rate."[30] London was, therefore, the center of the coaching and goods transport systems, and most of the inns were situated outside the gates or in Southwark, where there was ample space for stables. Plans of several pre-Fire taverns and inns are found in the Treswell surveys.[31] Inns with origins in the medieval period, and with fabric probably of the sixteenth and seventeenth centuries, survived well into the nineteenth century to be recorded, and fragments have occasionally been found in excavations.

London As a Trading Center

London's preeminence in trade is reflected in a range of institutions and buildings or facilities. Though the number of official landing-places was increased

15.10. The courtyard of the Royal Exchange, drawn by Wenceslaus Hollar (1647). Museum of London.

to about a dozen in 1559, the chief quays were still Billingsgate and Queen-hithe (particularly for grain) as shown in the pre-Fire panoramas of Wyn-gaerde (ca. 1540) and Hollar (1647). But congestion may have been a rising problem; beginning in the fifteenth century wharves and docks in the suburbs along the waterfront east of the city were developing fast, especially at Lime-house and Blackwall. By 1600 the departure points for international voyages (and associated victualing and repairing) were the new suburbs downstream of the city, at Deptford, Wapping, and Ratcliffe; the monopoly of the medieval inlets was superseded.

The city's bid to be eminent in European commerce was demonstrated from 1566 to 1568 by the construction of the Royal Exchange in Cornhill (the street which, along with the nearby Lombard Street, was the center of foreign financial dealings in the medieval period), a project initiated by Sir Thomas Gresham and the City (fig. 15.10). The Royal Exchange was modeled on the bourse built in Antwerp in 1531 and was designed by Hendrick van Paesschen of Antwerp. The timber came from Gresham's manor of Battisford in Suffolk, but the stone came at least partly from Flanders. The complex comprised a quadrangle of arcades, with shops and storage compartments above, and a tower. It was destroyed in the Great Fire and its successor, built 1667–71 in similar form, was destroyed by fire in 1838. On the waterfront and downstream of the bridge, we know from a pre-Fire engraving that the medieval Custom House was rebuilt in 1559 as a turreted building. It was rebuilt by Wren partly on the same site after the Fire, but little evidence of either structure was recorded during excavations undertaken in 1974.[32]

Apart from the Steelyard in Thames Street, the Hanseatic compound on the waterfront (which seems to have had no overtly foreign architectural features), there were few other buildings in London before 1600 which were designed to serve or promote foreign trade. In 1555 and 1581 the Muscovy and Levant Companies were founded, and the East India Company was given its charter in 1600; but the distinctive buildings of the latter, based initially on merchants' houses but later including large warehouses, spread through the east part of the city and further eastward, outside the City, during the seventeenth and especially eighteenth centuries.[33] In 1600, the buildings which came as part of a colonial or commercial empire were still a thing of the future; though Walter Ralegh foresaw that England could become the most powerful nation in the world if she built up a great navy, this only happened when London merchants had greater influence with the national government, after 1640 and especially after 1688.

Conclusion

In this brief tour of London around 1600, we have surveyed the buildings and topography of the place, both of which are continuously being revealed by study of maps, documents, and work on archaeological sites throughout the present conurbation. From this survey, I propose three overall conclusions. The first is that expansion of London was aided by the dissolution of the monasteries. This was the fundamental change to the topography of London in the decades before 1600, and its many and fundamental effects were not yet fully worked through by the opening of the seventeenth century. Industries sprouted in the newly released areas, and a revolution in ownership of urban land allowed the boom in building throughout the city and its surrounding areas. These developments, which horrified Stow and his contemporaries (including the Crown), permitted a massive number of immigrants to stay, live, and work in London. These immigrant groups changed the social, industrial, and religious character of the capital forever.

Second, London buildings were occasionally exceptional because the place was so large and displayed features peculiar to a capital city: the great cathedral which was to receive its portico in 1633–40, the Inns of Court, and the large number of theaters. Its facilities for shipping were the largest in the country. And London meant government and the royal court, based at this period either in Westminster (Whitehall) or relatively nearby at Hampton Court.

Third, however, the City of London in 1600 was not a Renaissance city in its architecture, in comparison say to Paris, where large areas had recently been laid waste by bombardment and siege and thus created an opportunity for rebuilding. London was too built up. There were traces of the Low Countries, and especially Antwerp, in its buildings, but no style seems to have been prevalent. In 1600, London was a medieval city on the edge of spectacular expansion in the century to come.

Notes

1. *London 1500–1700: The Making of the Metropolis,* ed. A. L. Beier and R. A. P. Finlay (London: Longmans, 1986), p. 11.

2. In this chapter, the term "City" with an initial capital letter refers, according to context, to one of two things: either the corporate institution (now the Corporation of London) or the area within the City boundaries which lay a variable distance (up to half a mile) beyond the medieval walls. The term "city" without an initial capital letter indicates the space inside the walls.

3. John Schofield, *Medieval London Houses* (New Haven and London: Yale University Press, 1995), p. 6, fig. 49.

4. N. G. Brett-James, *The Growth of Stuart London* (London: Allen & Unwin, 1935), pp. 127–50.

5. Brett-James, *Growth of Stuart London,* pp. 151–86; John Summerson, *Georgian London* (Harmondsworth, Middlesex: Penguin, 1945; revised edition 1978), pp. 27–51.

6. Quoted in John Hale, *The Civilization of Europe in the Renaissance* (London: Fontana, 1993), p. 183.

7. Caroline Barron, *The Medieval Guildhall of the Corporation of London* (London: Corporation of London, 1974), pp. 40–42.

8. R. A. P. Finlay and B. R. Shearer, "Population Growth and Suburban Expansion," in *London, 1500–1700,* ed. Beier and Finlay, pp. 37–59; Derek Gadd and Tony Dyson, "Bridewell Palace: Excavations at 9–11 Bridewell Place and 1–3 Tudor Street, City of London, 1978," *Post-Medieval Archaeology* 15 (1981): 1–79.

9. For a review of the water supply in 1600, see Brett-James, *Growth of Stuart London,* pp. 53–56.

10. John Stow, *Survey of London,* ed. C. L. Kingsford, revised edition (Oxford: Oxford University Press, 1971), 1:18, 188.

11. Peter W. M. Blayney, *The Bookshops in Paul's Cross Churchyard* (The Bibliographical Society, Occasional Paper no. 5, 1990); and Blayney, "John Day and the Bookshop That Never Was," this volume.

12. John Schofield, Gordon Higgott, and Mark Samuel, "The Work of Inigo Jones at St Paul's Cathedral: Recent Discoveries," in preparation.

13. D. Knowles and W. F. Grimes, *Charterhouse: The Medieval Foundation in the Light of Recent Discoveries* (London: Longmans, 1954).

14. John Schofield, *The Building of London from the Conquest to the Great Fire* (London: British Museum Publications, 2nd edition, 1993), pp. 145–48; John Schofield and Richard Lea, *Excavations at Holy Trinity Priory, Aldgate*, in preparation.

15. J. Sutton and A. Sewell, "Jacob Verzelini and the City of London," *Glass Technology* 21, no. 4 (1980): 190–92.

16. Schofield, *Medieval London Houses*, p. 42; Roger H. Leech, "The Prospect from Rugman's Row: The Row House in Late Sixteenth- and Early Seventeenth-Century London," *Archaeological Journal* 153 (1996): 201–42.

17. John Schofield, "Saxon and Medieval Parish Churches in the City of London: A Review," *Transactions of the London and Middlesex Archaeological Society* 45 (1994): 23–146.

18. John Schofield, "Excavations on the Site of St. Nicholas Shambles, City of London, 1975–79," *Transactions of the London and Middlesex Archaeological Society* 48 (1997): 77–135.

19. John Schofield, *The London Surveys of Ralph Treswell* (London: London Topographical Society Publication, no. 135, 1987); Schofield, *Medieval London Houses*.

20. John Schofield and Tony Dyson, *The London Waterfront, 1200–1750*, in preparation.

21. Schofield, *Medieval London Houses*, pp. 84–86.

22. Hale, *Civilization of Europe*, p. 268.

23. *The Inhabitants of London in 1938, edited from MS 272 in Lambeth Palace Library*, ed. T. C. Dale (Society of Genealogists, 1931); Valerie Pearl, "Change and Stability in Seventeenth-Century London," reprinted in *The Tudor and Stuart Town: a Reader in English Urban History 1530–1688*, ed. Jonathan Barry (Harlow, Essex: Longman Group, 1990), pp. 139–65.

24. Schofield, *Surveys of Ralph Treswell*; Schofield, *Medieval London Houses*.

25. Schofield, *Medieval London Houses*, pp. 44–49.

26. Schofield, *Medieval London Houses*, p. 58.

27. Simon Blatherwick and Andrew Gurr, "Shakespeare's Factory: Archaeological Evaluations on the Site of the Globe Theatre at 1/15 Anchor Terrace, Southwark Bridge Road, Southwark," *Antiquity* 66 (1992): 315–33; Jean Wilson, *The Archaeology of Shakespeare* (Stroud, Gloucester: Alan Sutton, 1995); Julian Bowsher, *The Rose Theatre: An Archaeological Discovery* (London: Museum of London, 1998). Details of theater design in this period are not comprehensively covered by documentary evidence, and the results of these investigations are of importance to theater historians and actors.

28. A series of studies of the tin-glazed pottery industries of London is in preparation by the Museum of London. This series will include volumes on production sites, and hopefully on the sites of consumption (that is, groups of pottery found on excavations of domestic sites, usually in cesspits).

29. Jacqueline Pearce, *Border Wares* (London and Norwich: Stationery Office, 1992).

30. Brian Dietz, "Overseas Trade and Metropolitan Growth," in *London, 1500–1700*, ed. Beier and Finlay, p. 134.

31. Schofield, *Surveys of Ralph Treswell*; Schofield, *Medieval London Houses*, pp. 53–55.

32. Schofield, *Medieval London Houses,* fig. 21; Tim Tatton-Brown, "Excavations at the Custom House, Part II," *Transactions of the London and Middlesex Archaeological Society* 26 (1975): 103–70.

33. Christopher Evans, "Power on Silt: Towards an Archaeology of the East India Company," *Antiquity* 64 (1990): 643–61.

16

John Day and the Bookshop
That Never Was

Peter W. M. Blayney

On 13 December 1572 Matthew Parker, archbishop of Canterbury, wrote a letter to Lord Burghley. He began by reporting that Bartholomew Clerke had been commissioned to answer a recent Catholic polemic, adding that the intended printer, John Day, was having a new font of type cut to be used in that and other works. And having thus introduced the name of the printer who had been his protégé for several years, the archbishop turned to his second main topic.

Nowe, sir, daye hath complained to me that dwellinge in a corn[r], and his brotherne envienge him, he cannot vtter his book*es* wch lie in his hande ij or iij thousand pownd*es* worthe, his frendes haue procured of pawles a lease of a little shop to be sett vp in the Church yearde, and it is confermed, And what by the instant request of sum enviouse booksellers, the maior & Alderm*en* will not suffer him to sett it vp in the Church yearde, wherin theye haue nothing to doe but by power, this shop is but little and lowe & leaded flatt, and is made att his greate cost to the su*m* of xl or l[li], & is made like the terris, faier railed & posted fitt for men to stande vppo*n* in any triumphe or showe, & can in noe wise either hurte or deface the same. And for that you of the Councell haue written to me, and other of the Commission, to helpe daie &c. I praie yo[r] L: to move the Q: Ma[tie] to subscribe her hand to thes or such letters that all this entendement maye the better goe forward, wherein yo[r] H: shall deserve well both of Christes Churche & of the prince, and state.[1]

Three hundred and three years later, when Edward Arber published his transcript of the first of the Stationers' Registers in 1875, Parker's letter was one of the illustrative documents he included.[2] Few comparable descriptions of early bookshops have been printed, and none has been as readily accessible or as frequently quoted. If such a thing as a "usual modern conception of a typical Elizabethan bookshop" can be said to exist, therefore, it is hardly surprising that the image has been largely shaped by Parker's words — albeit partly obscured by Arber's misreading of "railed" as "vailed."

What creates the first and most lasting impression are the words "little and lowe & leaded flatt." Although the shop has not yet been set up, Day has nevertheless spent upward of forty pounds in having it "made att his greate cost." Rightly or wrongly, the reference to prefabrication may suggest a collapsible, transportable structure that could be set up almost anywhere. The records of Elizabethan London often refer to what are called the "stalls" of local booksellers. If one adds the usual modern misinterpretation of that word to the fact that so many of Day's supposedly envious "brotherne" were located in a cathedral churchyard, it is easy to understand why many people have imagined that the bookshops of St. Paul's resembled an open-air market.

Parker's letter is not, however, a document to be trusted at face value. If the archbishop has reported his complaint accurately, then Day was guilty not only of a bias that verges on paranoia but of a deliberate attempt to mislead his patron. It is difficult to believe that Parker, who had survived the reign of Mary Tudor to be appointed primate of England by Elizabeth, was too unworldly to notice any of the gaping holes in the logic of the story he was passing on to Burghley — or, indeed, that he was naive enough to imagine that Burghley was any more gullible than himself. But Parker, like Day, had an agenda. His interests were not quite the same as Day's, but he, too, wanted to overcome the opposition and to see the shop built. So of course it would be little and low, and fair and fit, and could in no wise hurt. And so, equally of course, the letter needs to be taken with one or more pinches of salt. But before I begin holding parts of it up to the light, and before I turn a more objective and more detailed description of the same shop, it will be useful to take a look at its intended surroundings.[3]

Speaking very approximately, St. Paul's Cathedral measured three hundred feet in breadth and six hundred in length, and stood in a roughly rectangular precinct measuring six hundred feet by more than nine hundred. The more cathedrals one has visited, the more likely one is to translate those dimensions into the image of a single building standing in an area of open ground surrounded by a wall. But as nature abhors a vacuum, Tudor London abhorred empty space: the City population had been growing rapidly for decades, and by 1572 the ground plan of the precinct resembled that pictured in figure 16.1. Most of the larger buildings in the churchyard — which included the parish churches of St. Gregory (at the southwest corner of the cathedral) and St. Faith (in the vault below the chancel) — were connected in one way or another with the ecclesiastical administration. But in addition to all the official and public buildings, in a narrow band fronting on most of the alleys, the street, and the open spaces, stood a variety of private houses, tenements, and shops.

What little open ground there was can be considered as three separate

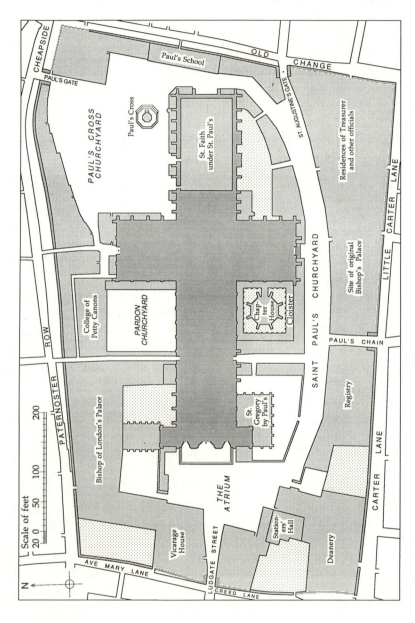

16.1. St. Paul's Churchyard in 1572.

parts. The street along the south side of the cathedral (itself named St. Paul's Churchyard) had once been a usable highway crossing the precinct from east to west. But by 1321 the dean and chapter had planted a post in the middle of St. Augustine's Gate, presumably to stem the flow of carts. The City fathers renewed their complaints about that post from time to time, but the ecclesiastical authorities prevailed until the Interregnum when, presumably after some enthusiastic sawing, the newly passable gateway was nicknamed Paul's Stump. The space outside the main doors of the cathedral was known as the Atrium or West Churchyard and was sometimes used for triumphs and shows of the kind that Parker suggests could be watched from the flat roof of a low bookshop. The largest open area in the precinct, though, was in the northeast, and was known variously as the North Churchyard, the East Churchyard, or (after the famous open-air pulpit that stood there) Paul's Cross Churchyard.

Before the thirteenth century the eastern half of that ground had not even been part of the cathedral precinct (fig. 16.2). It was the site of London's Folkmoot — the ground where the citizens used to assemble when summoned by a bell in the square tower, later called Jesus Steeple, that would eventually define the northeast corner of the churchyard. In 1256, however, the dean and chapter began work on an extended chancel which lengthened the Norman cathedral considerably, as shown. Although the City authorities must presumably have agreed to the necessary demolitions, which included the original parish church of St. Faith, by 1276 the dean and chapter had apparently decided that the precinct should be extended to match the new length of the cathedral. In that year, therefore, the mayor and aldermen made the first of what would become regular complaints about obstruction and enclosure in St. Faith's parish. Work on the final walling in of the enlarged precinct began in 1316, and when the citizens brought a string of grievances before the Justices Itinerant at the Tower five years later, their main complaint was that the Folkmoot and the bell-tower had been enclosed.[4] No details of the judgment are recorded, but it seems to have been something of a compromise. The dean and chapter did complete the precinct wall, and the post remained in St. Augustine's Gate, but at the same time it was evidently acknowledged that parts of the churchyard, including the streets along the south and east sides of the cathedral, belonged to the king and were under the jurisdiction of the City rather than the Church. And all indications are that although it had been enclosed, the Folkmoot too remained under the control of the City. Like a West Berlin inside East Germany, or a small village of indomitable Gauls in Roman Armoricum, the Folkmoot remained a scab of City authority that undoubtedly chafed the territorial instincts of the dean and chapter.

By 1572, what had once been the Folkmoot had become the heart of the

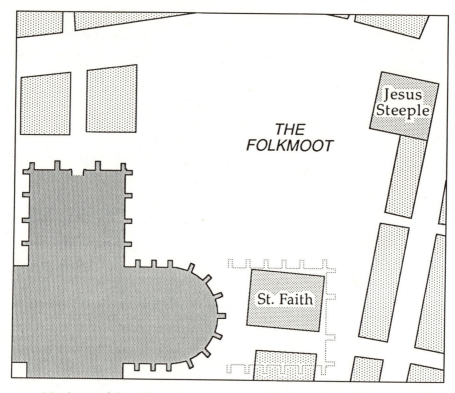

16.2. Northeast of the cathedral, ca. 1250, showing the planned extension of the chancel.

English book trade (fig. 16.3). There were bookshops and binderies in other parts of the cathedral precinct—and there were, of course, other parts of London where bookshops clustered—but Paul's Cross Churchyard was without parallel. Many of the buildings on the north side were tenements belonging to the bishop of London, and most of those were occupied by booksellers or binders by the early 1500s. After the Reformation had prompted a rapid expansion in the English trade in English books, the as yet undeveloped bays between the cathedral buttresses were leased out by the dean and chapter as building lots, and by 1572 only three bays in the Cross Churchyard remained empty. Some of those new buildings never became bookshops, but even those were rented to binders, claspmakers, or others associated in some way with the book trade. Meanwhile, in the late 1540s several dissolved chantry properties in the churchyard were also acquired by stationers and developed as bookshops. Seeing the trend, the petty canons in turn began to lease out

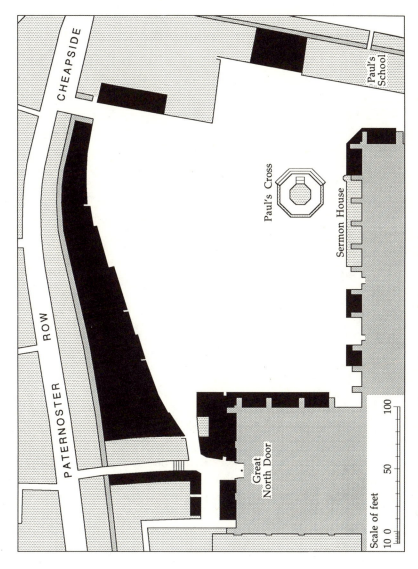

16.3. Paul's Cross Churchyard in 1572 (stationers' shops in black).

parts of their official residences near the Great North Door — again, mostly to stationers.

Among the plots newly developed by stationers was part of an old paved gallery, about six feet wide, along the southwest end of the alley that led from Paternoster Row to the Great North Door. When identified in a bookseller's address on a title page, the passage was called Canon Alley after the canons' residences that flanked it. Usually, though, it was known as Pissing Alley, because the paved gallery built over by John Walley in the 1570s had formerly been what was nostalgically referred to a few years later as "the Auncient pissinge place."[5]

Before a bookshop replaced it, what had stood at the east end of the chancel in the northernmost bay facing Paul's School was "a Cõmon privie . . . wherevnto the schollers of Powles schoole, and all the inhabitantes there aboutes vsed to resorte." It had been, in fact, the *last* resort — and thanks to the booksellers, by 1580 there were no public facilities of that kind left in the Cross Churchyard. By 1600, there were complaints about the state of the ground around the pulpit, which "lyethe more like a laystall then a Churche yarde to the great offence of many,"[6] a somewhat unexpected consequence of the spread of literacy.

St. Paul's Churchyard, then, bore no resemblance to a marketplace, nor were the bookshops at all like the little booths and stalls that many have envisaged. Even the buildings between the cathedral buttresses were at least two stories tall, and while a few of those in the outer ranges had three stories, most had four, not counting garrets. By the 1570s there were very few eligible properties in the Cross Churchyard itself still available to be taken over by booksellers, and few empty plots left against the cathedral walls — but there was still the Atrium, and a lot of street frontage between the two.

That, then, was the cathedral precinct in which John Day wanted a shop — and having introduced the churchyard, I must now say a few words about Day himself.

Although there were certain trades that could be practiced in London by almost any resident, most manufacturing trades and all retailing were restricted to those who were free of the City — freemen, their wives and children, or their widows. Once he had made the mistake of being born in Suffolk in 1522,[7] there were only two ways in which John Day could have become free of London, one of which was by serving an apprenticeship of at least seven years. This he declined to do. The only other way was to become free by redemption — to buy one's way in. But the freedom was highly coveted and the number of redemptions a year was small and controlled, so the process usually required not only money but also more influence than the young Day yet had.

On occasion, a City company whose fortunes and membership had seriously declined was allowed to take in a group of redemptioners.[8] Sometimes the new freemen included men of entirely unrelated trades who were prepared to pay a handsome bribe into the company's decayed coffers to become free of the City. The City authorities disapproved of such chicanery and sometimes forced offending redemptioners to translate into a more relevant company. That process involved paying a fee to the City authorities as well as to each of the two companies — but translation was anyway usually more of a benefit than a punishment.

In 1546 the Company of Bowstringmakers, or Stringers, was allowed to nominate twenty redemptioners[9] — an unusual number, suggesting either serious decay or mild corruption. None of the freemen is named in the surviving record — but four years later, no fewer than six Stringers were translated to other companies within the space of four months, and four of them (including John Day) were described as having originally been freed by redemption.[10] So although the record of Day's translation from the Stringers to the Stationers does not mention the fact, it is reasonably certain that he was a member of the class of 1546 — the year in which he began to print.

Day first met the future Lord Burghley — the recently knighted Sir William Cecil — at least twenty years before the archbishop wrote the letter to which I shall soon return. Cecil had been Somerset's secretary and had not only survived his master's fall but had become secretary first to the Duke's nemesis and successor, Northumberland, and then to the young king himself. In September 1552 Northumberland wrote to Cecil about Bishop John Ponet's newly written catechism: "I haue thought good to requier yo[u] to be a meane for the kinges ma[tes] lycens for the printinge of the same, And that this poore man, who hathe byn allwaies A furderer of godlie thinges, may by his highnes gracius goodnes be auctorised for the onlie printinge of the same for A certein space soche as shalbe thought mete by his ma[tie], wherin the poore man shal haue caus to pray for his highnes."[11] The supposedly poor man in question — Day, of course, who had in fact been a singularly successful printer and publisher for six years — duly received his grant four months later — with no term specified, and therefore for life. By then it included not only Ponet's catechism but also the king's own authorized one, any and all of the works of the best-selling Thomas Becon, and the ABC and little catechism. Poverty was never, in fact, John Day's most obtrusive characteristic.

And that brings us back, at long last, to Archbishop Parker and his letter. "Nowe, sir, daye hath complained to me that dwellinge in a corn[r], and his brotherne envienge him, he cannot utter his book[es] w[ch] lie in his hande ij or iij thousand pownd[es] worthe." The implication is clear: poor Day's warehouse is crammed with books because he can't sell them, and he can't sell them because his fellow stationers envy him and because his premises are so inconveniently situated. And if that is what Day really told Parker, he was stretching the truth far beyond its breaking point.

To begin with the "corn[r]": Day's business premises were rented from the City and were known as Aldersgate. Not "near Aldersgate," or "in Aldersgate Street," but Aldersgate itself: the gatehouse of one of the seven principal gates of the City, astride the main street leading out of London to the Great North Road. What Day occupied was not merely the original gatehouse but included extensions built against and over both the gate and the City wall beside it. Inside the wall at Aldersgate, as John Stow describes it, "on the East side, is the addition of one great building of timber, with one large floore paued with stone, or tile, and a Well therein curbed with stone, of a great depth, and rysing into the said roome, which is two stories high from the ground. . . . *Iohn Day* Stationer, a late famous printer of many good bookes, in our time dwelled in this gate, and builded much vpon the wall of the cittie towards the parish Church of Saint *Anne*."[12] For that so-called "corn[r]," Day paid the City the substantial ground rent of twenty-three pounds a year, and he apparently also rented an adjoining house from the parish of St. Anne.[13] Day was, in fact, under no illusions about the advantages of his location. Less than two years before Parker wrote to Burghley, some unspecified problem apparently made it seem unlikely that the Aldersgate lease would be renewed. Rather than greeting the news as a welcome opportunity to relocate, Day persuaded his most powerful patron, the earl of Leicester, to intercede with the City authorities on his behalf.[14] Some of his bookselling "brotherne" may have had good cause to envy him.

Day had, in fact, once had a retail bookshop just outside the churchyard in Cheapside, and had continued to run it during the early 1550s even after moving to Aldersgate.[15] When he gave it up, his career showed no obvious signs of imminent collapse — but then, Day's livelihood did not depend on being a retail bookseller: by profession he was a printer and publisher. As a publisher he acquired or procured texts from which he thought he could make a profit. In each case, when the time seemed ripe he had several hundred copies manufactured. Thereafter, the success of the venture depended on selling as many copies as possible at wholesale rates to as many retailers as possible — not on Day himself being one of the potentially hundreds of booksellers in England who might each sell a few copies, one at a time, to members of the public.

John Day was unusually good at what he did and acquired an impressive number of very salable works — including the *Psalms in English Meter* of Sternhold and Hopkins, which was far and away the best-selling English book of its era.[16] He was also one of the declining number of major publishers who owned a printing house and printed his books for himself. If he had paid someone else to print them — as many successful publishers did — the printer would typically have marked up his costs by 50 percent, and Day would then have marked up *his* costs by at least as much, and often more, when selling wholesale. By doing his own printing he made a double profit because he could mark up his costs by at least 125 percent and still remain competitive with comparable books. In the four years before Parker wrote the letter, Day printed ninety-five books and other items of which copies have survived. Six were official documents; the remaining eighty-nine were printed for himself. Forty-three of those — nearly half — were reprints, all but four of them reprints of books previously published by Day himself. Those figures are impressive enough in themselves, but what is truly astonishing is that while seven of the reprints were of books printed as recently as the previous year, no fewer than twenty-one were reprinted *in the same year* as the previous edition.

If Day really did have an inventory problem, therefore, he had only himself to blame: if he couldn't sell his books, he shouldn't have reprinted them so often. But the fact is that while stock worth two or three thousand pounds might have been a serious problem for a retail bookseller, for a publisher of Day's caliber it is no more than we should expect. Let us take a single case: Foxe's *Book of Martyrs*. Day's first edition of 1563 sold out in seven years, so we can confidently assume that the second edition of 1570 consisted of at least 1,200 copies. The third edition appeared only six years later, so the second edition presumably sold at an average rate of about 200 copies a year. At the time of Parker's letter, therefore, Day probably had between 700 and 800 copies in stock — and at a wholesale price of between 24 and 30 shillings a copy,[17] those copies were worth somewhere between £850 and £1,200. That one book would therefore have accounted for a substantial fraction of Day's reported inventory. Furthermore, he did eventually gain a foothold in Paul's Churchyard, when he took over a shop in the Atrium in or before 1576. After his death, an employee who had worked for him there reported that during Day's last years "his vnbounde book*es* were rated to be wourthe three thowsand poundes and better besydes his bounde bookes in his ij° Shoppes wo'th . . . three or foure hundreth poundes."[18] Instead of reducing his inventory, then, after finally acquiring a churchyard shop, Day apparently increased it.

The fact that his initial complaint was a blatant sham ought not to matter: churchyard leases were not allocated charitably according to need, and it is unlikely that he had to skate quite so close to perjury in order to obtain one. As Parker tells us, "his frendes haue procured of pawles a lease of a little shop to be sett vp in the Church yearde, and it is confermed." That much at least is true, and it is only the suspicion aroused by the previous sentence that makes me wonder whether Parker was merely being self-effacing, or whether he had a deeper reason for hiding behind the anonymous plural, "his frendes" — for it was Parker himself who did the procuring. Leases issued by the cathedral authorities were copied into the Dean's Registers, which have survived. Day's twenty-one-year lease, dated 7 December 1571, was issued jointly by the bishop of London and the dean and chapter (an unusual fact, to which I shall return), and specifies that it was granted by "the saide Bisshoppe and Deane and Chapito^r of one assent and Consente at the instaunce and requeste of the moaste reverende ffather in god Matthewe Archbisshoppe of Canterberye."[19]

More important, the lease includes details that allow us to quantify Parker's idea of "little and lowe" — which, while evocative, is hardly precise. After specifying the exact position of the northeast corner of the site, the lease continues: "And so from the saide poynte or corner cominge directly westwarde xxiiij^{ty} ffoote in lengthe and also from the saide poynte or corn*er* com*m*inge directlye Southwarde xxiiij^{ty} ffoote in lengthe and xij ffoote in breadthe by and thoroughe bothe the saide lengthes and either of them." On this plot (fig. 16.4), Day is permitted to build "fayre and bewtyfull buyldinges" (a later clause will in fact require him to covenant for a single building),

Provided Allwaies that the same buyldinges shall not at the grounde encroche nerer to any buyldinge or Shoppe nowe nere adioyninge to the saide plott then by the space above appointed [i.e., 24 feet] nor shall in the hiest parte of the roofe exceede in heigth in any parte above twelue ffoote from the grounde except it be in garnisshinge with turned post*es* and rayles whiche shall not excede three ffoote in heigthe above the roofe, nor the saide Buyldinges shall excede in breadthe above twelue ffoote from the owtesyde of one wall to the owtesyde of the other wall.

Most shops today can be recognized as shops by their display windows. What typified a shop of the 1570s, though, was an external wooden counter fixed to the wall below the widow. This was known variously as a stall, a stall board, or a shop board, and was often hinged so that it could be closed up like a horizontal shutter across the lower half of the window. Unless the whole window was protected by a large overhang, it would be surmounted by a larger board that served as an awning to protect the stall. This was known as a penthouse, or pentice, and in some cases was also hinged to cover the upper half of the window. Interestingly, and very unusually, the 1571 lease gives details. Day is permitted to make "Appentices for defence ageinste wether and heate as also ffoldinge Shopp bordes to fall owte warde from the saide Buyldinges with convenient stoopes post*es* and Steyes to beare the saide

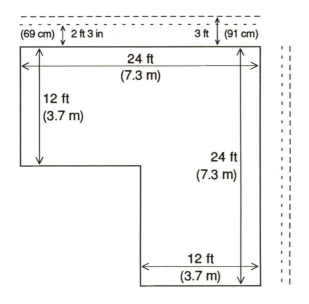

16.4. The proposed ground plan of John Day's bookshop.

Shopp bordes when they be Lett Downe. . . . Provided allwaies that the sayd ffoldinge Shoppe bordes shall not conteyne in bredthe any of them above three quarters of a yarde nor be lett Downe vppon the Sabboth or other hollydayes but onely vppon workingdayes And that the sayd Appentices or any of them shall not extende or reache oute from the saide Buyldinges above one yarde."

There is no way of knowing how Day would have arranged the two main frontages, but I doubt that either of them would have had a single, twenty-four-foot stall. For the sake of a guess, therefore, in each frontage I have imagined a central door flanked by seven-foot stall boards. Figure 16.5 is a very simplified and very conjectural reconstruction seen from the east, directly opposite one of the windows, which is closed. The other is nearly open, with the pentice up, the shop board partly down, and a completely conjectural set of "stoopes postes and Steyes" unfolding into place below it.

While the lease is very explicit about the folding of the shop boards, nothing of the kind is said about the pentices. Perhaps, then, they were to be fixed—but I have imagined them folding down to complete the closure of the windows. And for times when all four shopwindows are closed up, I have added a small window above each door for illumination. For the sake of simplicity I have also imagined that Day's carpenter has not yet finished turning

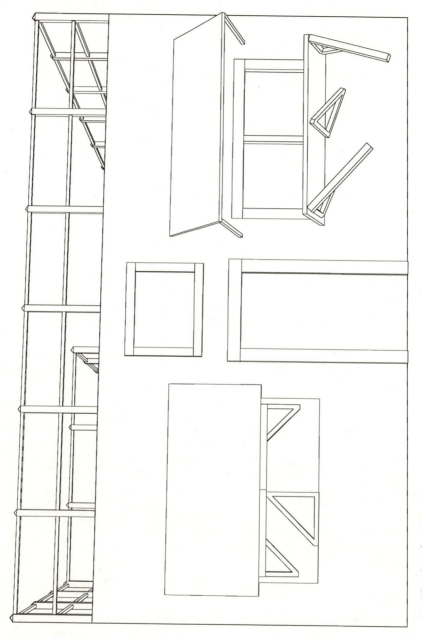

16.5. The shop from the east.

the last of the decorative posts for the roof, so the rails are temporarily supported by plain square ones — which coincidentally happen to be easier to draw.

In figure 16.5 the shop is seen from an eye-height of five feet six inches and a distance of about forty-five feet. Had the building ever existed, this view would have been impossible, because we could not have backed more than twenty-four feet away from the window. Let us therefore sidle south along the frontage opposite until we can get an undistorted view from the southeast in figure 16.6. The far window is now completely open for business and the other is being opened. For reasons that will soon become apparent I have declined to conjecture anything at all about the south wall, so we need not dwell on this view. Since there is another business frontage on the north side, the view from the northeast is more impressive. Parker's phrase was obviously both subjective and relative, but figure 16.7 is not quite what I expect from the words "little and lowe."

The shop would, of course, have been much smaller than Day's other premises: the annual rent was to be 13 shillings and fourpence (two-thirds of a pound), while for his so-called corner at Aldersgate he was paying £23. It would also have been undeniably lower than the two-, three-, and four-story buildings occupied by most of the other churchyard booksellers. Parker, of course, is hardly to blame for any false deductions we may have made from the fact of prefabrication. This was clearly not to be a collapsible or transportable structure, but Day could easily have spent a sizable sum on it before it was actually put in place. Woodwork such as doors, window frames, shop-boards, pentices, posts, and rails could all have been made up in advance. And even for a much larger building, it would not have been unusual for the whole timber frame to have been cut and assembled in a carpenter's yard to make sure that everything fit, and then to have been marked and dismantled for reassembly on the final site. But however many excuses we make for the archbishop, it remains fair to call his description, at the very least, deceptive.

But the shop was never built. "And what by the instant request of sum enviouse bookesellers, the maior & Aldermen will not suffer him to sett it vp." On 2 April 1572, about four months after the lease was sealed, the Court of Aldermen heard some kind of dispute between Day and the Stationers' Company. Unfortunately, the clerk skipped at least one line of his notes when copying the entry into the Repertory, but it is unlikely that any crucial information was lost. "Item this daie the matter betwene m^r Day & his companie for the buyinge of all m^r Daies bookes suche as now he haith or hereafter shall [here there is a gap in the sense] that they shall talke together betwene this & the next courte & make reporte there what they shall agre on And in the meane

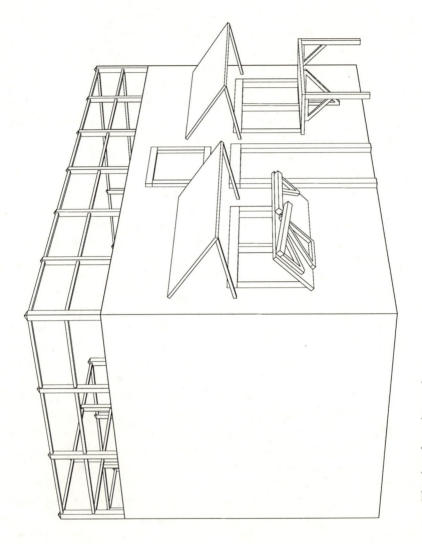

16.6. The shop from the southeast.

16.7. The shop from the northeast.

tyme Day not to go in hand with buyldinge of his shoppe in pawles churche yerd."[20] Even more unfortunately, these events occurred during a five-year gap in the Stationers' Company records, so we have no other account of this controversy. Day held several very lucrative royal patents, the most recent of which included an automatic ten-year monopoly on any new book written or compiled at his own charges.[21] The dispute referred to in the Repertory probably concerned a projected Company purchase of those patents — but I have no idea which party might have been the unwilling one. What *is* reasonably clear is that the mention of the churchyard shop was something of an afterthought, seemingly unconnected with that disagreement.

At this point the paper trail vanishes for over two years. The Court of Aldermen presumably handed both matters over to a delegate or a subcommittee, and never again considered them in full court. Nothing more was recorded in the Repertory, and I have found no clues in the Journal of the Common Council. Seven more months elapsed before Parker wrote to Burghley, and three months later the Privy Council duly wrote to the mayor and aldermen on Day's behalf[22] — but neither that letter nor any consequent action is mentioned in the City records.

It is, however, unlikely that Day and Parker can be trusted any more on the subject of "sum enviouse bookesellers" than on Day's supposed hardship. The cast of characters is just too large and distinguished for a mere squabble between stationers. On one side we have the Lord Mayor and the aldermen of London. On Day's side we have the dean and chapter of St. Paul's, the bishop of London, and the archbishop of Canterbury. In seeking Lord Burghley's support Parker invokes both the High Commission and the Privy Council, asks him to recruit the Queen herself, and says that if Burghley does so he'll "deserve well both of Christes Churche & of the prince, and state." Quarrels among booksellers rarely escalate quite that far. If the mayor and aldermen had been acting in the interests of the duly appointed printer to the City, Parker's account might have seemed more plausible — but the City Printer was John Day himself, so it seems unlikely that his supposed rivals could have turned the City authorities so completely against him.

My last quotation from Parker's letter was an incomplete sentence, and in the part I omitted the archbishop makes what I believe to be a very revealing comment: "And what by the instant request of sum enviouse bookesellers, the maior & Aldermen will not suffer him to sett it vp in the Church yearde, wherin theye have nothing to doe but by power."

In Parker's view, then, the City fathers have no jurisdiction in the churchyard "but by power": that is, unless so empowered by the rightful governors of the cathedral precinct, namely the ecclesiastical authorities.[23] There were undoubtedly parts of the churchyard in which the Church could indeed overrule the City both in theory and in practice. But the precinct also contained ground that former bishops and deans had long recognized and explicitly described, when granting leases for neighboring properties, as "the cōmon way," "the cōmon highe waye," or "the kinges heighway"[24] — and there was also the former Folkmoot.

It seems unlikely that Parker was simply unaware of the City's traditional rights and privileges in Paul's Cross Churchyard. Presumably, then, his open denial of those rights was a calculated attempt to abolish them rather than a display of ignorance. Perhaps the mayor and aldermen had angered him by exercising their prerogative tactlessly or high-handedly. In March 1569 they had torn down the old sermon house — a gallery built against the cathedral where they used to sit to hear the sermons at Paul's Cross — and had built a larger one in which their wives could join them. At the same time they considered the feasibility of moving the Paul's Cross pulpit one yard to the east.[25] Nothing in the City records suggests that the aldermen considered it necessary to consult the cathedral authorities on either occasion — but six months later they sent a committee to the churchyard to view a new building that *they* considered to be an encroachment, "and to move my lorde Busshopp of London for the stayinge and reformacōn thereof."[26]

The Day lease may therefore have been a deliberate retaliation, designed to show those aldermen once and for all whose churchyard (in Parker's opinion, at least) it really was. The bishop and dean issued the lease jointly because neither of them had ever claimed jurisdiction over that particular plot of ground before — and when they specified that they were doing so at Parker's "instaunce and requeste" they were presumably attempting to cover themselves. But if either they or the archbishop hoped that the City might perhaps have forgotten the origins of the Cross Churchyard, their timing was conspicuously unfortunate. Less than eight weeks before the lease was granted, an unusually large public assembly had been convened at the Guildhall on 15 October 1571 to be addressed by the recorder of London, William Fleetwood. Present were the Lord Mayor, the aldermen, the Common Council, the wardens of all the companies, and "a great multitude of other Citizens." And in his opening paragraphs, Fleetwood reminded all present that in 1219, and again in 1222, Henry III "dyd at the place which we now call Paules crosse assemble a Folkemote of the Citie of London, so called bicause it is a metyng and callyng together of the Folke that is the people, the gouernours and the worshypfull and honest inhabitauntes of this Citie."[27] While it is remotely possible that neither the archbishop nor the bishop knew that the citizens had so recently and publicly been reminded of the site of their ancient Folkmoot,

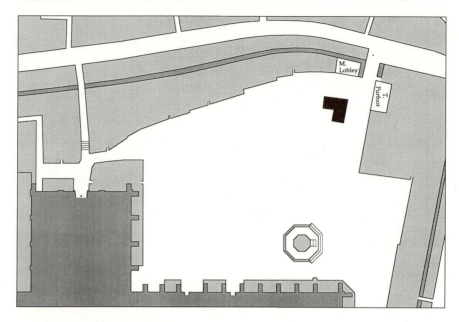

16.8. The intended site of John Day's shop.

John Day himself knew only too well—because he had just printed and published the text of Fleetwood's oration.

There was nothing at all subtle about the challenge implicit in the Day
lease. The intended site of the shop was defined by measurement from a
specified point: "that is to saye the Northe easte poynte or corner of the
said Plott towardes the North easte gate there Leadinge into the vpper ende
of Chepesyde distante at the grounde xxiiij^ty ffoote from the Shoppe late
Mighell Lobleyes and lykewyse xxiiij^ty ffoote from the Shoppe now Thomas
Purfootes."[28] Location, location, location. As figure 16.8 clearly shows, that
would have been not so much a bookshop as a street corner. The lease was in
fact a territorial claim that said, loudly and clearly, "We of the cathedral acknowledge the existence of a street, twenty-four feet wide, along the existing
frontages—but the rest is ours." Envious booksellers had nothing to do with
it: the mayor and aldermen *had* to oppose what they would rightly have seen
as the thin end of a wedge (fig. 16.9); the tip of an iceberg (fig. 16.10); the first
move in a campaign of encroachment that could have meant the end of Paul's
Cross Churchyard as a public space.

Exactly how the matter played out is uncertain, but the City authorities
had evidently prevailed by June 1574. On the tenth of that month the Court

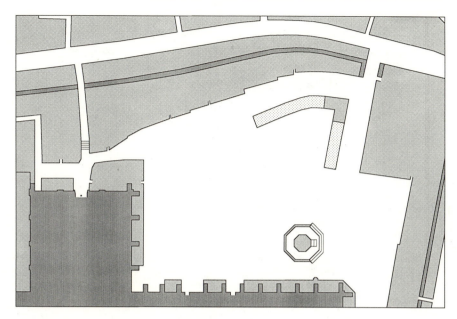

16.9. Day's shop as the thin end of a wedge.

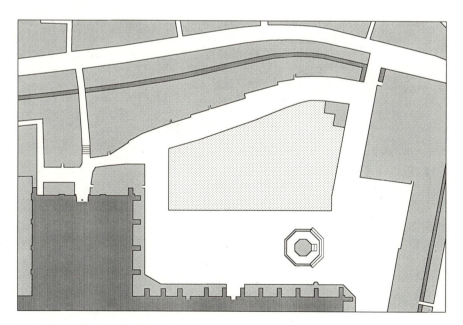

16.10. Day's shop as the tip of an iceberg.

appointed a committee of two aldermen and the Chamberlain to "take payne to procure or gett some shopp or other conuenyent place in Paules church-yarde for Iohn Daye Stacyoner to kepe his shopp to sell bookes in."[29]

Sometime between that date and 1576, with or without the committee's assistance, Day finally secured the lease of premises in the churchyard: the "Long Shop" in the Atrium near the northwest door of the cathedral, vacated in 1573 by William Jones. The controversial corner shop near Paul's Gate was never built — and when I last walked across the intended site, it was still un-developed.

Notes

1. British Library, MS Lansdowne 15/50.

2. *A Transcript of the Registers of the Company of Stationers of London; 1594–1640 A.D.,* ed. Edward Arber (London: n.p., 1875–79; Birmingham: n.p., 1894), 1:454.

3. Most of the following description of the cathedral precinct and the shops in it is condensed from Peter W. M. Blayney, *The Bookshops in Paul's Cross Churchyard* (London: The Bibliographical Society, 1990).

4. Guildhall Library (hereafter GL), MS 25,121/1756.

5. GL, MS 25,630/2, fol. 151v; MS 9537/9, fol. 48r, no. 27.

6. GL, MS 9537/9, fol. 57r.

7. C. L. Oastler, *John Day, the Elizabethan Printer* (Oxford: Oxford Bibliographical Society, 1975), p. 4.

8. For example, Corporation of London Records Office (hereafter CLRO), Repertory 8, fols. 163v (fourteen Weavers, 1531), 281v (five Minstrels, 1533); Rep. 11, fol. 284v (twelve Weavers, 1546); Rep. 12, fol. 349r (fourteen Blacksmiths, 1551), etc.

9. CLRO, Rep. 11, fol. 312v.

10. CLRO, Rep. 12, fols. 200r (John Day, 11 February 1550), 234v, 240v.

11. Public Record Office, SP 10/15, no. 3 (fol. 5r). In the revised *Calendar of State Papers, Domestic Series, 1547–1553* (1992), C. S. Knighton wrongly identifies the "poore man" as Reyner Wolfe (p. 257 n).

12. *A Survey of London* (1598: STC 23341), sig. C7r (ed. C. L. Kingsford [1908], 1:34).

13. CLRO, Rep. 16, fol. 70v; Oastler, *John Day,* p. 30.

14. CLRO, Rep. 17, fol. 112r (1 March 1571).

15. A. W. Pollard and G. R. Redgrave, *A Short-Title Catalogue of Books Printed in England, Scotland, and Ireland, and of English Books Printed Abroad, 1475–1640,* 2nd ed., rev. W. A. Jackson, F. S. Ferguson, and Katharine F. Pantzer (London: The Bibliographical Society, 1976–91), 3:52; Oastler, *John Day,* p. 31.

16. The revised *Short-Title Catalogue* lists more than 500 editions before 1641.

17. A Company regulation of 1598 limited the wholesale price of an unillustrated book set in either pica or english type at two sheets a penny (*Records of the Court of the Stationers' Company, 1576 to 1602, from Register B,* ed. W. W. Greg and E. Boswell [London: The Bibliographical Society, 1930], pp. 58–59). That rule is admittedly twenty-

eight years of Elizabethan inflation later — but given its unusually large pages and its illustrations, the cost per sheet of the 1570 *Martyrs* (STC 11223) must have been well above average. A complete copy contains almost 600 sheets (Leslie Mahin Oliver, "Single-Page Imposition in Foxe's *Acts and Monuments*, 1570," *The Library*, 5th series, 1 [1946–47]: 49–56, p. 51), and if wholesaled at exactly two sheets a penny, would have cost a retail bookseller just under 25s.

18. Oastler, *John Day*, p. 32.

19. GL, MS 25,630/2, fols. 405r–6r.

20. CLRO, Rep. 17, fol. 296v.

21. *Calendar of the Patent Rolls, Elizabeth*, VI, no. 1181; see also IV, no. 675.

22. *Acts of the Privy Council*, VIII, p. 89.

23. I am grateful to David Harris Sacks for drawing my attention to the apparent meaning of "by power." *OED* records comparable senses (Power *sb.1* 4.b. and 5), but not this particular idiom.

24. For example, GL, MS 25,630/2, fols. 155v (Buck), 171r (Jugge), and 415v (Norton) respectively.

25. CLRO, Rep. 16, fols. 447r, 448r, 481r.

26. Ibid., fol. 521v.

27. Fleetwood, *The Effect of the Declaratiō Made in the Guildhall* (1571: STC 11036), sig. A2r.

28. GL, MS 25,630/2, fol. 405v.

29. CLRO, Rep. 18, fol. 223r.

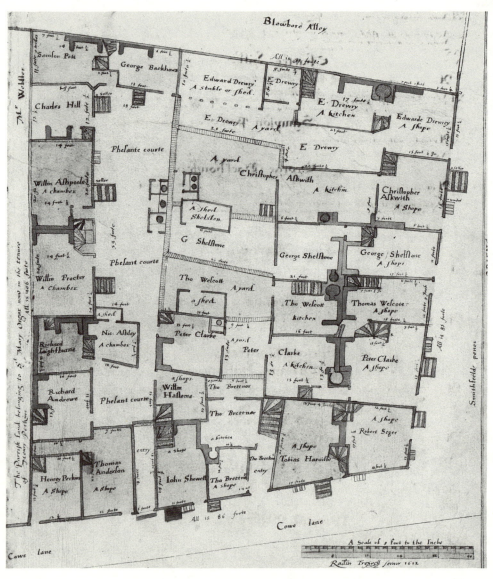

17.1. Tenements on Smithfield and Cow Lane. Clothworkers' Hall Plan Book, 41; Schofield, no. 46, fig. 50 and plate 5. By permission of the Court of The Clothworkers' Company.

17

Boundary Disputes in Early Modern London

Lena Cowen Orlin

Almost always, the first thing to be said about early modern London (and now in this volume the last thing, as well) is that it experienced an astonishing growth in population. To rehearse the numbers put forward by David Harris Sacks in the first chapter: there were perhaps 50,000 London residents in 1500; 200,000 in 1600; and more than 500,000 by 1700. In 1500, London was matched or exceeded by sixteen urban centers in Europe; in 1600, only Naples and Paris were larger; by 1700, London was the single most populous European city.[1] In 1500, London was four times larger than any other city in England; in 1600, fifteen times larger; in 1700, twenty times larger. Of course such statistics are estimations, and of course they are arguable; other authors in this collection offer other statistics. But the steep rate of London's growth is undeniable. This essay attempts to make material the abstract numbers of demographic calculations and to illustrate some of the consequences of urban density for the everyday lives of sixteenth- and seventeenth-century Londoners. In other chapters, David Harris Sacks, Alan Sinfield, Ann Jones and Peter Stallybrass, Andrew Gurr, and Peter Blayney have already made reference to the London of competing nexuses of power and authority: the City administration, the royal court, the ecclesiastical hierarchy, and the rising class of those wealthy from trade. But the conflicts experienced on a regular basis by the greater number of Londoners undoubtedly had to do with their next neighbors, with boundaries and fences, shared chimneystacks, common cesspits, blocked windows, waste disposal, rainwater drainage, and building maintenance. The population explosion put the most common domestic functions under uncommon pressure.

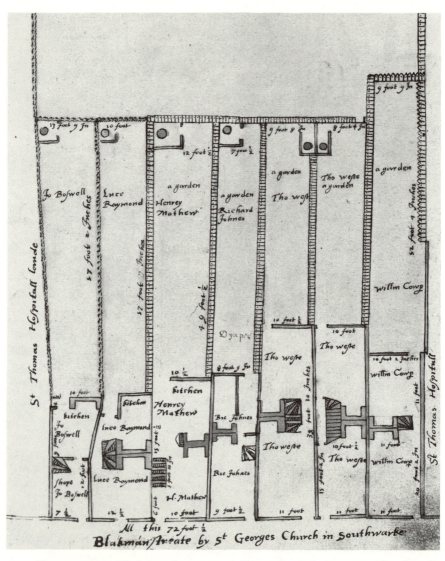

17.2. Tenements on Blackman Street (now Borough High Street) in Southwark. Christ's Hospital Evidence Book, 5; Schofield, no. 49, fig. 53. By permission of The Governors of Christ's Hospital.

The London Viewers and Ralph Treswell's London Surveys

In "The Topography and Buildings of London, ca. 1600" (see Chapter 15), John Schofield provides a comprehensive overview of the built city. In earlier publications, Schofield has also made available the remarkable set of London plans drawn by Ralph Treswell during the first decades of the seventeenth century.[2] Treswell, a painter-stainer by trade, was hired to survey a number of properties, including country estates.[3] But the commissions Schofield has made best known were those for Christ's Hospital and the Clothworkers' Company. Both institutions were endowed with a number of tenanted residential properties in London. Treswell drew ground-level floorplans of each residence or cluster of residences, establishing the relationships among houses, yards, gardens, and outbuildings (fig. 17.1). He named and measured ground-floor rooms. In text accompanying most drawings (instanced in figs. 17.4 and 17.8), Treswell also named associated upper-level rooms, regularly giving their measurements, often identifying the rooms they stood over, usually indicating whether they contained chimneys or houses of office. The houses of early modern London could rise three, four, five, even six and seven stories.[4]

A plan for multiple residences in Southwark (fig. 17.2) introduces the elements of Treswell's design vocabulary with particular legibility (the area was less densely built-out than neighborhoods across the Thames). Each building is two rooms deep, and the general pattern seems to be for a shop at streetside and a kitchen behind. In all but one instance, a chimney stack with back-to-back openings heats both rooms; John Boswell, however, had an unheated shop. In each case there are stairs, presumably to the upper levels (although in one instance, that of Henry Mathew, a cellar seems also to be accessed internally). The most common type of stairs has steps turning around a newel post. Shop frontages vary from seven-and-a-half to twelve-and-a-half feet. Behind each house is a garden. The property tenanted by Boswell is bounded by a hedge; elsewhere there are fences. Edging William Cowper's lot is one section of stone wall, probably part of St. Thomas Hospital, adjacent. At the far end of all but one of the gardens—Cowper's—is a privy. Because this survey lacks Treswell's usual description of the upper stories, we do not know for certain what the sanitary arrangements were for those living in the property tenanted by Cowper; elsewhere, though, it seems to have been the case that those who did not have outdoor privies did have indoor houses of office (as Treswell preferred to call the facilities when they were placed inside and above ground level).

At the time this plot was surveyed (in 1611), Thomas West had secured

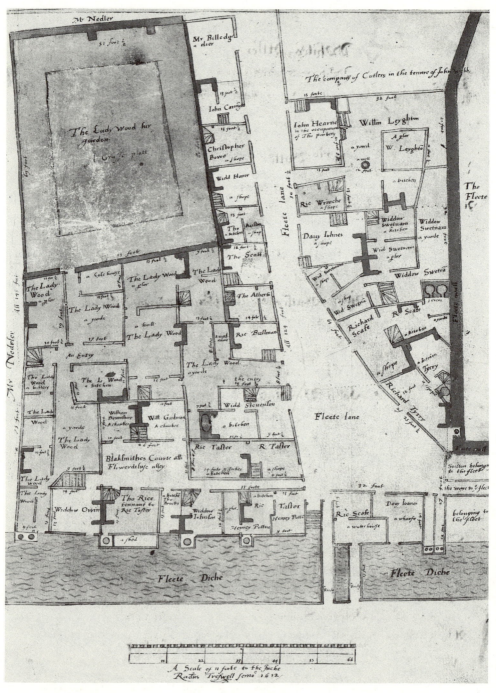

17.3. Tenements on Fleet Lane. Clothworkers' Hall Plan Book, 47; Schofield, no. 22, fig. 26 and plate 10. By permission of the Court of The Clothworkers' Company.

control of two of the properties. His joint tenancy probably averted what might otherwise have been a source of some difficulty: two adjoining privies sharing a single cesspit. It was one thing when privies had Fleet Ditch to empty into (fig. 17.3 shows four common privies and five private ones placed over the Ditch). Shared cesspits in the city, however, could cause problems that brought them to the attention of the London Viewers.

The London Viewers were a group of four men, generally men from the building trades, commissioned by the City to adjudicate property disputes. Reports filed formally by the Viewers remain from the early to mid-sixteenth century in the collections of the Corporation of London Records Office. (Records after 1558 are lost, with some scattered exceptions in the 1620s and 1630s and in the occasional copy kept privately by one of the parties to a dispute.) In her edition of the surviving reports deposited with the City, Janet Senderowitz Loengard describes the Viewers' procedures.[5] The reports were commissioned by and addressed to the mayor and aldermen of London. For most cases there were a plaintiff and a defendant; in some instances, however, the Viewers undertook a "party" view requested jointly. Many reports ended with the boiler-plate caveat that their determinations might be reversed should any written "evidence" of past property negotiations be forthcoming. Lacking such documents, the Viewers worked according to the "custom of the city," from their knowledge of building practices, and by gathering oral histories. In one case from 1536 they emphasized that they had conducted "deliberate examination of the oldest men and longest dwellers within the said wards now living" (no. 121); in another they specified that they consulted not only both parties but also "ancient men" (no. 233).[6]

The Viewers' findings constitute a complementary order of evidence to that presented in Treswell's surveys. Together, the Viewers' reports and Treswell's surveys register the stresses of life in London as it urbanized. In 1546, for example, the Viewers reported on the case of Thomas Carmardon, plaintiff, and George Asshe, defendant. They found "two jakes adjoining together," one belonging to Carmardon and one to Asshe, with "an old stone wall between" the jakes. The wall was crumbling. The Viewers determined that the wall should be rebuilt two-feet thick in its original position, so that each party might independently "cleanse and carry away the ordure or dung that is within his ground" (no. 202). In 1550, they reviewed the construction work of grocer William Lane, who shared a cesspit with vintner Myles Ayer and who had taken the initiative to "part" the vault with a brick wall: "As it is now made, is nothing wronged," the Viewers approved (no. 270). In 1556, confronting men with more than one complaint, the Viewers suggested that they might consider "severing" the vault of a shared cesspit to avoid future controversy in at least this one respect (no. 368). In a case where three "tunnels," or privy shafts, served a single cesspit, the Viewers concluded that the pit should be "made clean by all the three lessees thereof at their costs and charges"— meaning that the costs should be equally divided (no. 267).

Some arrangements were more complicated, however. Treswell's survey of a cluster of properties on Knightrider Street (fig. 17.4) shows the subdivision of what in the mid-sixteenth century had been a single messuage called the White Hart.[7] By the time of the 1611 survey, there were large drinking rooms occupied by Abraham Fryth and smaller shops and properties tenanted by John Welshaw, Thomas Alcoke, Robert Rowse, Thomas Chilton, George Eakins, and a man surnamed West. One consequence of subdivision is shown in Alcoke's privy, sited behind his chimney with every appearance of having been carved out of Rowse's single ground-floor room (the room is identified in the accompanying text as a shop). One flight up, Rowse had a hall, a chamber, and a kitchen. Some of these rooms were positioned over properties belonging at ground level to others. According to Treswell, Rowse's second-floor chamber had "a funnel of a privy out of the room above," that is, a shaft from a privy on the third story. In fact, the plan shows two shafts running behind Alcoke's privy, meaning that there may have been three stools belonging to at least two different residents feeding a single cesspit.[8]

The situation is much like that examined by the Viewers in 1542, a case of two drapers, Henry Dolfyn and John Dymock, whose interior privies had a shared cesspit (no. 170). Dolfyn had only one stool feeding the pit; it was located in his own chamber. Dymock had three stools, one in his own chamber, one in his maidservants' chamber, and one in his manservants' chamber. The pit could be cleaned and its accumulations removed only through the house of Dolfyn, the one-stool man. Removal of the waste, said the Viewers, "was to him and all his house a great nuisance [noyaunce] being no less than xxx [thirty] ton." They ruled that the three-stool man, who suffered no trouble, should bear all the expenses of cleaning and removal, as also the cost of rebuilding the median wall which had to be broken in the process.[9]

A detailed account of expenses from 1575 suggests something of the extent of the "nuisance" involved. In this instance, only sixteen tons were carried away by two "night men," Mychaell Owyn and Edwarde Downes, and their crew. Their pay was 32 shillings (2s. per ton). The owners of the property also provided ten pounds of candles (2s. 3 ½d.); bread, cheese, beer, and ale for twelve men for two nights (5s. 4d.); and juniper to refresh the pit (3d.). Then there were charges for brick, mortar, and the services of a workman to reconstruct the funnels of the privy (22d.). Because this was not a shared cesspit, it was not necessary to rebuild a median wall. But, whether coin-

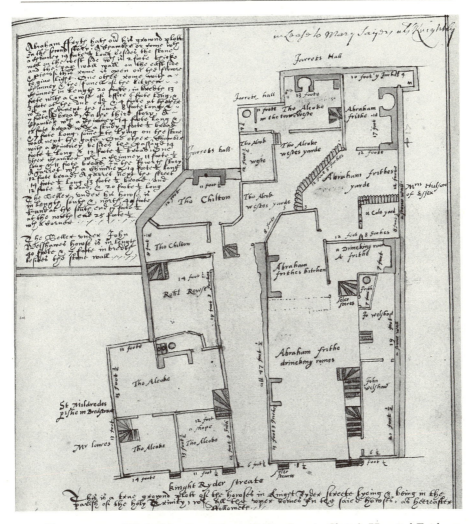

17.4. Tenements on Knightrider Street (now Trinity Lane). Christ's Hospital Evidence Book, 9; Schofield, no. 43, fig. 47. By permission of The Governors of Christ's Hospital.

cidentally or necessarily, the project also involved "paving the little yard the same time," which, with materials, the transport of materials, and labor, totaled nearly three pounds more. An overseer seems also to have been called for "to watch to see the tons filled" both nights (16d.; this entry suggests that for privy cleaning, *tons* refers to containers or barrels, not a measurement of weight). Finally, there was the cost of "making clean the house" afterward (2s.). As elaborate as this undertaking evidently was, it involved only

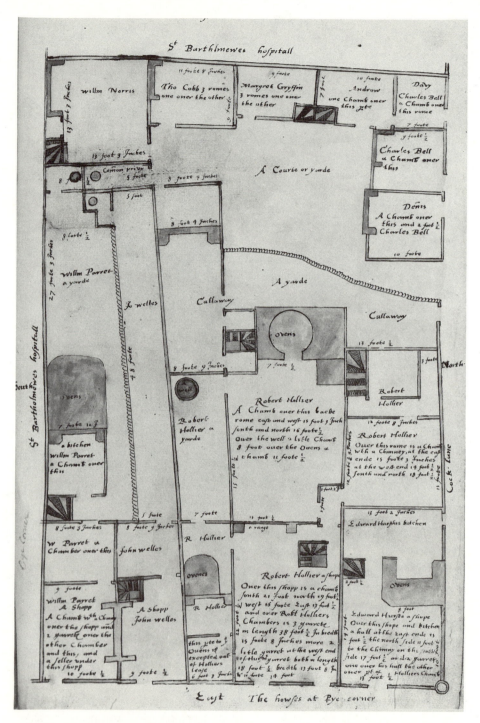

17.5. Tenements at Gittspur Street and Cock Lane (known as Pye Corner). Christ's Hospital Evidence Book, 17; Schofield, no. 25, fig. 29 and plate 7. By permission of The Governors of Christ's Hospital.

single ownership and was thus comparatively straightforward — except for some indication in the records that the house may have been robbed while its vault was open.[10]

The Viewers also dealt with the placement of privies, like those Treswell seems to show in his survey of properties along Giltspur Street and Cock Lane, an area dominated by large commercial ovens (fig. 17.5). Of particular interest in this survey is a group of three privies, one belonging to William Parret, one to John Welles, and the third a "Common privy" off a common yard. To trace the property line between the Parret and Welles lots is to conclude that all three privies fall within what we might have expected to be the bounds of Parret's yard. The situation may have been like that encountered by the Viewers in 1547, when John Haynes was found to have "encroached" within the grounds of Oswolde Docwraye to build his privy. The Viewers ruled that Docwraye should be able to "have and enjoy his own ground" without Haynes's privy on it (no. 214). But Treswell's survey of the Parret and Welles lots is just as likely to illustrate a situation like that entertained by the Viewers in 1550: "a little house with a jakes on the west side of the house of defendant lying toward the house of plaintiff," which privy house "belonged to defendant's house long before the parties purchased their houses." The Viewers concluded: "we say it ought still so to continue" (no. 269).

This last finding represents a common theme in the Viewers' reports: old and sometimes eccentric property agreements were rigorously enforced long after the original parties to them were gone. Thus their practice of consulting the "oldest men and longest dwellers." Many boundaries had been determined not by a logic of space but instead through a process of negotiation and redistribution. While Welles's privy seems to encroach on Parret's yard, it should also be noted that Parret's yard is wider than the rear footage of his house would seem to justify — perhaps in order to allow ready access to the wood that would have been stored in his yard and that would have been needed to heat his massive ovens. Indeed, it may be that Parret (or an earlier tenant) had been allowed to usurp some of his neighbor's yard in exchange for the corner taken out to serve as his neighbor's privy.

The business of establishing boundaries was as complicated as in a Viewers' case from 1555, when ironmonger Robert Hicks seems to have been challenged for the very posts at his front door. In the end, the Viewers gave him clear ownership of the eastern post, on which his door was hung, and allowed him eight inches' worth of the western post (no. 361). Haberdasher Edmund Bragg was fortunate enough to have deeds that proved to the Viewers that gentleman John Gilman had violated property lines both in laying claim to Bragg's garden and also in building a chimney and shed on other

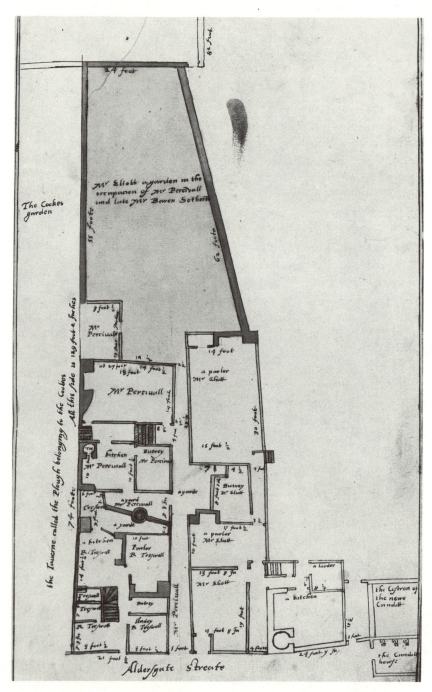

17.6. Tenements on Aldersgate Street. Christ's Hospital Evidence Book, 10; Schofield, no. 1, fig. 4. By permission of The Governors of Christ's Hospital.

Bragg grounds (no. 371). With boundaries that migrated over time (through the necessary give-and-take of coexistence) and more often than not without documentation, it is no wonder that so many Viewers' reports called for the building and repair of "lawful" and "sufficient" fences. Without the fence between Abraham Frith's yard and the yard tenanted by Thomas Alcoke but occupied by West (see fig. 17.4), and without the fence between Calloway's yard and an off-street court (see fig. 17.5), respective property lines would have been impossible to trace.

On the subject of fences, the Viewers were interventionist. In 1555, for example, they themselves pounded a nail into a brick wall and set a stake in order to mark the extremities of a fence to be built "line right and plumb" (no. 412).[11] They can be presumed to have known that clear property divisions would avert some future complaints to the city. The records of City officials who enforced the *Assize of Nuisance,* medieval precursors to the Viewers, tend to be more forthcoming with detail for certain kinds of urban distress, and thus they may expand our understanding of some of the Viewers' concerns. When fences fell into ill repair in the fourteenth century, pigs, dogs, cocks, hens, oxen, cows, men, women, children, and vagabonds were variously said to have entered into private gardens, with the result that fruit was stolen and herbs, grasses, and other plants were trampled. A case of 1345 indicates that there was a sense of general danger as well as personal damage: a vacant and unfenced plot was said to be a place where "malefactors and disturbers of the king's peace and robbers lurk there by night and waylay passersby, attacking, beating and wounding them and stealing their goods."[12]

Even as they called for clearly demarcated property lines and enclosed grounds, though, the Viewers could not allow fences and other structures to be obstructive. The diagonal boundary off Aldersgate Street which looks so awkward when shown schematically (fig. 17.6) in fact served two purposes. First and most obviously, it allowed for the joint use of a well set midway in the yards of a Percival and a Treswell.[13] Such a well came to the attention of the Viewers in 1550; it was determined that the cost of necessary repairs should be shared by those who shared the well (no. 290).[14] But, second, and at least as important, the angle at which the Treswell and Percival yards were subdivided also gave Percival passage to and from the street. The right of access is one that the Viewers ratified in 1551, when they concluded that clothmaker William Wall had unfairly prevented waterbearer George Cholmeley from making entry to his house through a passage eighteen-feet long and nearly four-feet wide (no. 311). For Thomas Kendall in 1547, the problem was the door of William Kynge's neighboring butcher shop that opened into his entry (no. 212); for fishmonger William Hollingworth in 1550, it was the table that skinner Roger

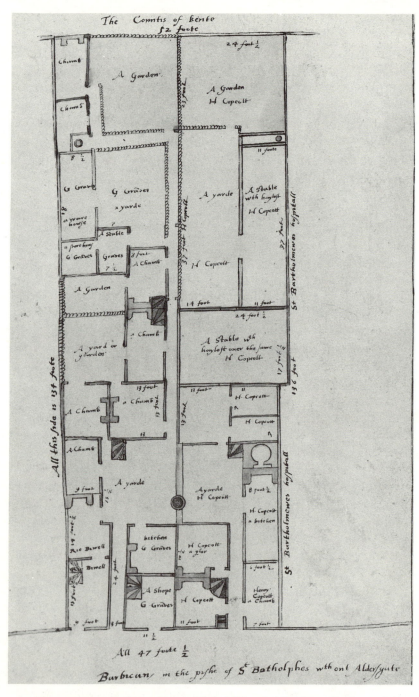

The Comtis of Kente
52 foote

17.7. Tenements on Barbican Street. Christ's Hospital Evidence Book, 21; Schofield, no. 4, fig. 7. By permission of The Governors of Christ's Hospital.

Lewe set out, blocking his entry (no. 288). The Viewers ruled that Kynge had to stop up the door and Lewe had to move his table.

In 1549 the Viewers upheld all the property rights claimed by merchant tailor John Apsley, except for a passage to Jefferey Hamlyn's house which ran through Apsley's tenement. Hamlyn was still to have his access (no. 239). In response to a joint request for review, the Viewers declared that fishmonger Thomas Lucas owned the right to lay out his merchandise under ironmonger Christopher Draper's very jetty (cantilevered overhang). But Draper in his turn had the right to pass through Lucas's yard to his own cellar. This was no small matter to Lucas; the Viewers specified that Draper's "recourse" included portage of Draper's goods, whether by horse, cart, carriage, or "recarriage" (no. 217). With increasing density, there was sometimes no happy compromise in the matter of access — as admitted in a 1549 case. The Viewers agreed with plaintiff Mistress Beatrice Bodley that she had the right of secure entrance to her garden. Observing a door of John Rauf's that opened into an alley alongside it, they remarked: "We think that there may evil inconveniences grow by it if that door do stand there." But they were forced nonetheless to conclude that "[this] door we cannot deny him" (no. 257).[15]

Each room in Treswell's surveys is identified not only generically (a hall, a parlor, a study) but also in terms of ownership. Treswell repeats the name of an owner as many times as that owner had ground-floor rooms. The fact is that where boundaries were not natural or logical, one tenancy could not immediately be distinguished from another by means of common sense. When Treswell fails in his double system of identification, his maps become unreadable, as is the case in an incomplete survey from Barbican Street, with no text for the upper-level rooms and a string of ground-level rooms with no owners' names (fig. 17.7). Richard Bewell and G. Graves seem to share a yard; both have doors opening onto it. But then there is a group of five chambers opening off either the yard or a passageway leading from it. To whom do these chambers belong? The numbers 5 and 6 in chambers at the top of the plan might suggest that four of the unnamed rooms were Graves's chambers 1, 2, 3, and 4, encircling an open area. If that's the case, though — that is, if Graves's rooms enclosed the whole — there would seem to have been no need for the fence between one "garden" and another "yard or garden" in that open area. Presumably, the area was divided between Bewell and Graves, and both had points of access. But we require the owner's label, placed serially and multiply, in order to be able to trace the perimeter of a "house" in these conditions.

Things might have gone more smoothly in London if all housing was as planned and artificial as, for example, David Smith's six tidy brick almshouses for six poor widows (fig. 17.8).[16] The units were not uniform because of the

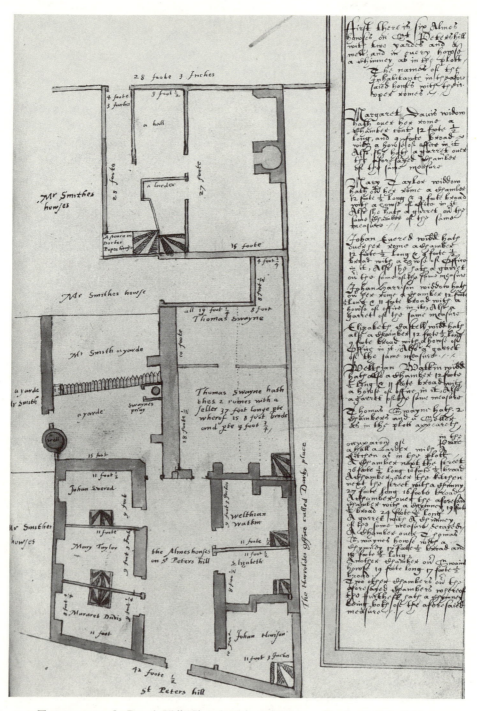

17.8. Tenements on St. Peter's Hill. Christ's Hospital Evidence Book, 16; Schofield, no. 34, fig. 38 and plate 8. By permission of The Governors of Christ's Hospital.

shape of the lot. But they were highly regularized, and each residence was perfectly self-contained: a ground-floor chamber, heated, with stairs up to the jettied upper-level chamber with its own house of office, and, at the third level, a garret noted by Treswell to be "of the same measure" as the second-level chamber. If one looks a little farther toward the widows' neighbors, however, the rule of rational property division ceases to operate. It is not only a matter of Smith's property (only sketchily indicated because it did not belong to Christ's Hospital), which seems to surround and invade the houses and grounds of Swayne and Price; it is a matter of merged buildings as well as misshaped yards. To the west of Swayne and at the top of the plan, Price (as identified in the text accompanying the plan) had a ground-level hall, larder, entry, and kitchen. Swayne had ground-floor rooms only. The two stories overhead were tenanted by Price. Somewhat mysteriously, the survey also labels a stair as belonging to "Doctor Pope's house." Since the text makes no additional reference to Pope, it is likely that his rooms were over the property identified at ground level as "Master Smith's houses." Meanwhile, no matter how rationalized the design of Smith's almshouses was, their occupants apparently shared a well with those in Smith's house and perhaps the residents in Swayne's and Price's dwellings, in addition. This well was only twenty feet from Swayne's privy.[17]

Back on Giltspur Street and Cock Lane (see fig. 17.5), there is another lateral sharing out of space, in this case among eleven separate tenants. At the top of the plan Charles Bell had a building in which he held both ground and second floors. In another bay to one side, he had the ground floor but someone named Dennis had the upper floor. To Bell's other side, a man named Andrew Davy had the ground floor and Bell had the upper floor. Davy also had the two stories of the next building around the corner. Meanwhile, as indicated at the bottom of the plan, William Parrot had rooms over the house shown as tenanted by John Welles; Edward Hurste had a garret and a room over the chambers of Robert Hollier; and Hollier's property, already irregularly shaped as it fanned out from its fourteen-foot street frontage, had a streetside parcel exempted for a purpose that Treswell does not specify. All we know is that "this part . . . is excepted out of Hollier's lease."[18]

Treswell notes that John Welles' fourth-floor garret (see fig. 17.5) and Price's third-floor garret (see fig. 17.8) were "decayed." Where space was shared, so were maintenance problems. When in 1550 disagreements between Benett Jackson and George Smyth came to the attention of the Viewers, there were common posts, gutters, windows, and privy cleansing to review. But there was also the fact that the floor of Smyth's chamber was rotting from water damage, imperiling Jackson's chamber directly below. The Viewers ordered that Smyth should repair his floorboards and keep them dry, while Jackson should keep the walls and foundation below in good repair (no. 272).[19] Sometimes the Viewers found harm as well as neglect: glazier Christofer Jackson suffered water damage because cooper Stephen Gybson had removed two lead drainage pipes (which the Viewers ordered him to restore, no. 301), and baker John Martyn broke Faith Patenson's brick wall while stacking wood against it (he was told to rebuild it, no. 255). Occasionally the jeopardies were general, as with old walls in danger of collapsing on any passerby (no. 188), chimneys ready to fall (nos. 189, 206), and two houses that needed structural repairs so that "either house may stand upon himself," no longer "tied together with bolts and dogs of iron" (no. 164). In a few instances, the Viewers gave deadlines for repairs and provided estimates of the costs involved (nos. 189, 344). Londoners were living in sufficiently close proximity that any one person's property maintenance was of immediate and material concern to neighbors above, below, and alongside.[20]

On a plan for a section of Pancras Lane not reproduced here (see Schofield, no. 33), it is especially ominous to read Treswell's note that "over here is building," because difficulties always seemed to follow new construction. There were property violations, like goldsmith Humfrey Jones building an extension to his house on ground belonging to his neighbor John Bell (no. 377), or weaver John Holmes encroaching on common ground (no. 304). There were also complaints of immediate damage: stone walls broken for the insertion of timber support beams (no. 175); roof tiles pulled down (no. 332); gutters spoiled and chimney tops crushed (no. 285); entries removed (no. 278); in one case, an entire bay window carried away (no. 286); in another, the side of a building stripped off (no. 175). All of these injuries the builders were required to put right. In 1555, John Leeke, esquire, evidently consulted the Viewers in advance of building. They gave Leeke explicit measurements to follow and warned him that he should be prepared to repair any "hurts" or "harms" occasioned by his construction (no. 360). When John Thatcher built a house in front of that of Christopher Nycolson, he took care to provide a passage for Nycolson to reach his house. Unfortunately, at three feet, ten-and-one-half inches wide, the passage was deemed insufficient by both Nycolson and the Viewers (no. 258).[21]

Nycolson also complained that Thatcher's new house left no ground for the runoff of his rainwater. Others objected when rainwater dripped from new buildings onto their old houses or lands. This was what "eavesdropping" could mean in sixteenth-century London. In 1554, the Viewers recorded that a nine-and-a-half-inch strip of land alongside the property of mariner William Tow had been set aside for brewer Richard Westraw's eavesdropping; Westraw's right to that ground was upheld (no. 352). The Viewers could require builders to tear down and start again with a setback sufficient to prevent eavesdropping; they could also require builders to modify overhangs or jetties.

There were, furthermore, multiple petitions against overlooking — when the windows of a new building permitted a view into an old garden — for gardens registered concerns for privacy with particular sensitivity.[22] In 1538 the widow Joanna Thorpe built in her back garden, next to the garden of Master William Ermystede. The Viewers, noting that Thorpe already had sufficient light from some windows, declared that the four windows overlooking Ermystede's garden should "be set in with a loupe so that there can be no sight thereby into the garden, or else to be clean stopped up" (no. 129). There was also the 1549 case of William Lambkyn, who had three windows looking into Peter Grene's grounds. The windows had once been boarded up, but Lambkyn had removed the boards. Here, the judgment of the Viewers was Solomonic. For the lower parts of windows on both stories of Lambkyn's house, boards were to be nailed flush against the window to prevent anyone in Lambkyn's house from looking into Grene's property. For the higher parts of his windows, boards were to be affixed some distance out from the house, sixteen inches out at the lower story and eighteen inches out at the upper story. These upper boards still "cut" the view, but at the same time they permitted light to enter Lambkyn's house (no. 260).[23]

There was a general consensus that light was necessary, especially for the work that was performed in these shops and houses, and this made the problem with overlookings more acute. Thus, access to light was usually upheld: grocer Christopher Basse was allowed to build the pentice over his shop large and high only as long as it did not block the light of his neighbor, the merchant tailor Robert Davyson (no. 267). In one instance from 1552, however, a man was given the right to block his neighbor's light at will. Since the Viewers do not in this instance give their rationale, it is impossible to tell whether there was a justification in tradition or whether the status of the builder — it was Sir William Sydney — decided the matter (no. 317).[24]

In one of the earliest surviving reports from the sixteenth century, the Viewers maintained the integrity of an empty strip of property, nearly eighteen feet long and just over seven feet wide, "reserved unbuilded for the light of both" adjoining occupants, the parish church of St. John Zachary and the Company of Waxchandlers (no. 6). This was in 1509 or 1510; it seems to have been the same strip of land that the Viewers revisited in 1544. The parson and churchwardens presented their copy of the earlier view as they complained that the waxchandlers had constructed a brick wall on the "void ground." In addition, they charged that the waxchandlers had built ovens over the church's

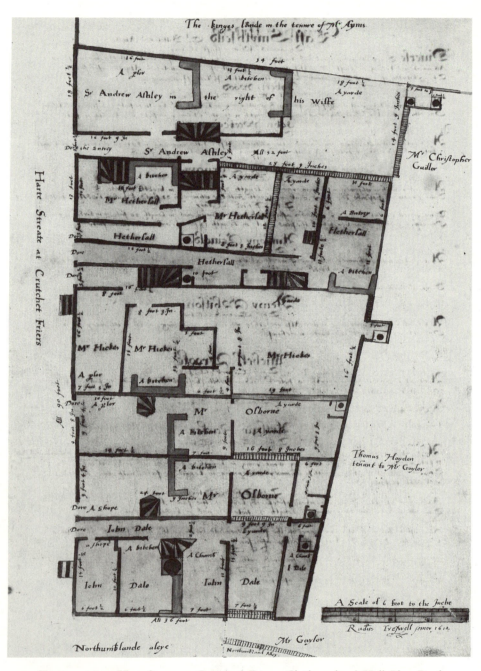

17.9. Tenements on Hart Street at Crutched Friars. Clothworkers' Hall Plan Book, 17; Schofield, no. 18, fig. 22. By permission of the Court of The Clothworkers' Company.

underground vault. The Viewers agreed that both wall and ovens should be removed (no. 183). Although the trail of formally deposited certificates in this dispute ends here (with the loss of all the Elizabethan reports), a record book maintained by the parish church of St. John Zachary indicates that the controversy continued. According to "A View by the City Viewers in 26 March 1565," copied in the record book, the wall and the ovens still stood, and the churchwardens again presented their evidence, a copy of the 1544 ruling. Again the Viewers called for the offending structures to be removed and again the dispute escalated: this time, the right of the church to five little "shops or houses" was also maintained.[25] The long dispute of the church and the guild is a salutary reminder that the Viewers did not always—or even often—resolve the grievances that occasioned their visits. Their reports document material damage, not long-simmering antagonisms and resentments.

New construction and the subdivision of old buildings made room for the influx of migrants to London. A 1597 report that has survived only among the property documents of the Company of the Propagation of the Gospel in New England records the Viewers' analysis of a warehouse and a number of surrounding rooms which, they concluded, had "in times past been a great mansion house, and is now divided into sundry parts."[26] In many other cases, however, the memory of less crowded conditions remained painfully fresh. On Hart Street, for example, Treswell draws "seven tenements sometimes but five lying all together" (fig. 17.9). Master Osborne's property, two tenements "sometimes but one," was divided neatly and symmetrically, with matching doors, stairs, and chimneys for occupants William Wilcockes and Nicholas Stevens. But a tenement owned by Master Heathersall, again two tenements "sometimes but one," was divided more messily and confusingly, with Henry Joyner occupying a streetside kitchen with yard behind, and Phillep Hole occupying a ground-level kitchen, buttery, and yard at the rear of the property, accessed by a long entryway from the street. Hole undoubtedly had windows overlooking Joyner's yard—and perhaps those of his neighbors Andrew Ashley and Mr. Hicks, as well.[27]

Similarly, the property surveyed on Threadneedle Street was originally one house (fig. 17.10). By the time it came to the Clothworker's Company, it had two tenants. Thomas Collins had a cellar that ran not only under his own shop but also under Harwood's buttery and yard. In an analogous situation, the Viewers prevented Ellice Lewys and her son Robert from reclaiming the space directly under "a parcel" of their own house because it had been deeded to Thomas Wygett at his purchase of the property; the Lewyses had to rebuild the vault wall they had broken through to create a door (no. 376). Grocer Thomas Alsoppe also tried to regain control of the cellar under his house, but,

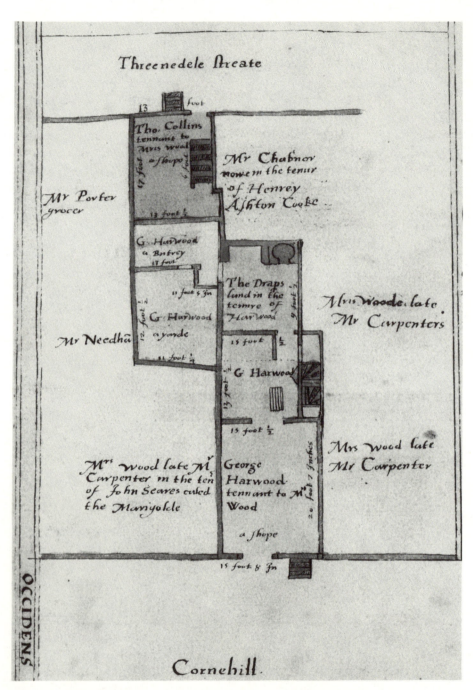

17.10. Tenements on Cornhill and Threadneedle Street. Clothworkers' Hall Plan Book, 21; Schofield, no. 17, fig. 21. By permission of the Court of The Clothworkers' Company.

again, the Viewers declared that custom prevented him. There was an "old door" from the Lady Dame Johanne Warren's house into the cellar, and possession remained in her hands (no. 370).

Treswell's survey of a plot at West Smithfield and Cow Lane (see fig. 17.1) numbers twenty separate tenancies and is dense with shared yards, walls, chimney stacks, and privy shafts. The site seems to cry out for visits from the Viewers, and it may well have seen cases like that of Stephyn Cobb, who became impatient with the water pipe running from Edmond Perye's house through his own kitchen. He removed it, only to be instructed by the Viewers to put it back (no. 261). Mercer Richard Smythe was told he had to live with the drains running through his bedchamber, but Thomas Blunte was advised, somewhat ominously, not to "annoy" Smythe "with no manner of corrupt water or any other thing going through it" (no. 293).[28] In 1554, the Viewers examined a gutter shared by merchant tailor Thomas Whytelocke and lorimer (bit-and-spur maker) Richard Dytcher. Dytcher had a door that opened over the gutter, "by reason thereof," it was observed, "the gutter is filled and the house annoyed with filth and the water course there descending stopped." The Viewers ordered Dytcher to make the door into a window so that the gutter could run clear. Dytcher counterclaimed that Whytelocke had built additional houses on his grounds and that the extra water drainage they produced "annoyed" him. Whytelocke was therefore ordered to convey independently the water coursing from his new buildings, "excepting only rain water" (no. 351). It was "the manner and custom of London" that "every man ought to bear his own water" (see, for example, nos. 236 and 237), but even the Viewers had to admit that the old rules could not always be upheld in new conditions like those at West Smithfield.

Long Views and Short

To complete the picture before us, several qualifying perspectives must be considered. Some go in the direction of lessening the impact of this account of the Viewers' reports and Treswell's surveys. For example, first, the experience of shared cesspits, chimneystacks, and drains was not *universal* in early modern London. The social integration described by Linda Levy Peck and John Schofield (in Chapters 14 and 15) is also shown in Treswell's surveys, where the wealthy can sometimes be found living cheek-by-jowl with shopkeepers and craftsmen (see fig. 17.3 for one example). But that doesn't mean that they weren't fairly well insulated from many urban jeopardies. And while some Viewers' cases show the gentry in contention with their "lesser" neighbors,

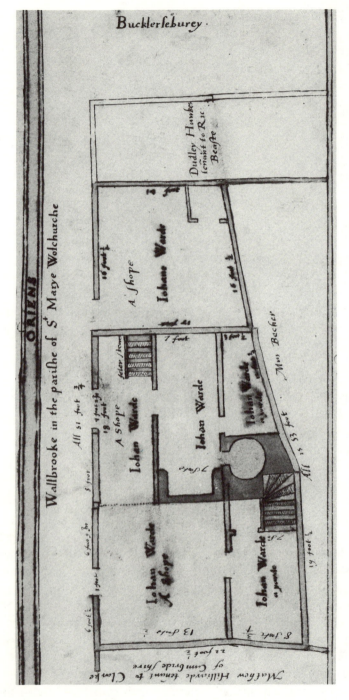

17.11. Tenements on the west side of Walbrook. Clothworkers' Hall Plan Book, 25; Schofield, no. 45, fig. 49. By permission of the Court of The Clothworkers' Company.

they may have filed petitions concerning tenanted properties rather than their own living quarters. My guiding interest here is in encountering something of the lives of the middling sort, but there were other populations and other experiences.

Second, amid all the Viewers' reports concerning aging structures and damaged premises, the complaints occasioned by building works remind us that many Londoners, like English men and women elsewhere, were involved in improving their properties, expanding, glazing, plastering, wainscotting, and in some instances, as Peck shows, achieving personal splendor. Similarly, for all the instances Treswell gives us of shrinking personal spaces and physical encroachments, he also allows us a glimpse of the heady opportunities available in London's commercial arenas. Besides the "seven tenements sometimes but five" and "two tenements now divided into three," there are also "two tenements sometimes three, but now used as one" (fig. 17.11). Here, Johanne Ward (or a predecessor) had succeeded in arrogating to her own use what had once been three separate properties. There remained three shop doors onto the street, three cellars, and two yards behind, but the tenement had in other ways been rationalized for its single tenant of record. Floor space had been reclaimed, for example, with only one set of stairs to serve the three cellars and one set accessing the upper levels. The continued partitioning of the yard probably had its uses; one area would have been reserved for wood to stoke the nearby oven. Above, there were a hall, a chamber, a parlor, a kitchen, and a buttery; on the third floor, three chambers and a closet; and, on the fourth, three garrets. Perhaps because of their one-time division, the second and third floors were more generously provided with chimneys than most London dwellings of this size; the residents of the engrossed tenements must have enjoyed the added comforts of their upward mobility. While the story of early modern domestic architecture outside London is one of an increasing number of rooms, with all the related consequences of more space, specialized functions, and arguably higher levels of privacy,[29] in London the prevailing trend ran in the opposite direction, as newcomers crowded into the city and subdivided its buildings. But this general trend had its exceptions, of which Johanne Ward was one.

Third, the sense of shared spaces and moveable borders that arises from Treswell's surveys was by no means unique to London. In Ipswich in Suffolk, to cite one telling example, William Melsopp provided for his three children by giving half his house to Samuel, half to William, and a back tenement to Susan, asking his sons to share "in common" the orchard, pump, privies, and shed, while bequeathing to Susan other yards and orchards.[30] Meanwhile, in Colchester in Essex, Richard Northey left his son Ralph his house with its

stable and a garden. According to his will, the stable was bought from Cuth-
bert Mutton, the garden from John Martyn, the passageway to the garden
from Thomas Roo, and the well from Robert Frankum. Describing the patch-
work of his property, Northey also noted that his son would have to build a
fence to the lately annexed well to demarcate what was probably a counter-
intuitive property line.[31] Other documents from other regions of England
reveal similar negotiations: property shrinking and enlarging as houses were
divided to accommodate more than one child, house room made for an elderly
widow or an incompetent sibling, and chambers made partible then subsequently reabsorbed with the deaths of those sojourners.

Fourth, none of the hazards outlined here was unique to London in this
time period. Derek Keene has documented the population explosion of the
medieval city (see Chapter 3), and the records connected with violations of
the *Assize of Nuisance* indicate that there were similar growing pains in these
earlier centuries, with neighbors complaining against neighbors about fetid
cesspits, construction damage, and overlookings. Diane Shaw emphasizes that
these cases reveal Londoners in "unwanted encounters with their neighbors'
smells, eyes, and ears."[32] Such encounters were not frequent features of the
later Viewers' reports. There were occasional instances of filth and water being
cast out of windows onto neighboring property (nos. 119 and 361), and
one — this from a gentleman — protesting the "infection of evil and contagious
air" from a neighbor's privy (no. 142). But when carpenter Thomas Cosyn
broke the brick coping of the Fleet wall to look over into the Fleet garden, and
when he raised the level of his land the better to see over the wall, the Viewers
considered damage done to the wall by the broken copings and an altered
water table; nothing was made of the fact that he had used dung to raise his
land (no. 171; see also fig. 17.3). Schofield points out that, by contrast, the
complaints of the sixteenth century more often concerned the "delineation of
boundaries" among city dwellers "who increasingly had to rub shoulders with
each other."[33] This does not mean that offenses to the eye, ear, and nose would
not have multiplied in these circumstances. Rather, medieval and early modern
grievances were probably sufficiently similar that many differences between
the reports of the two bureaucracies were a matter of convention more than
anything else; each had its own formulas, its own rhetoric.

Other larger perspectives, though, work against these moderating notions. Thus, fifth, while the London Viewers' reports constitute a convenient
slice of London's documentary history of property disputes, it is only a slice.
There were other avenues for redress of grievance, even in the City administration. For example, the records of the Carpenters' Company for 1601 show two
members of the company called to Silver Street by the mayor. They reported

that a two-story building had been raised a story-and-a-half higher and that
the new third story had an excessive, two-foot jetty that needed to be cut back
by eight inches. This was very like a Viewers' report but was not processed
through that bureaucracy.[34] There were also many disputes that were settled
without recourse to city officials, as in a 1609 instance documented in the
vestry minute book of the parish church of St. Bartholomew Exchange. William Woolley's new house encroached on the churchyard by four inches and
had two bay windows over the churchyard; the parson and churchwardens
made an "agreement of toleration," allowing the construction to stand so long
as Woolley and his successors paid the church an annual fine of twelve pence.[35]
It is not possible fully to recover how often this sort of "toleration" was
achieved privately and without any documentation. We do know, though, that
when negotiations failed, disputes could come also to the various law courts.
Some cases with other legal grounds necessarily grew out of the ill will generated among neighbors in crowded conditions. All told, the Viewers' reports
represent a fairly small percentage of the boundary disputes in early modern London.

Sixth, even in a survey like that in West Smithfield (see fig. 17.1), Treswell
fails to convey in full London's density. Depicting only tenants of record, he
does not tell us how many persons occupied each tenement. His text offers
hints; for one property, for example, he refers to a single chamber "divided
into diverse parcels wherein dwell diverse widows."[36] And there are other
classes of records, like Nehemiah Wallington's diary, that show a householder
with two bedchambers, one garret, a wife, children, and servants taking in first
a widow and her two children, then another relative.[37] Generally, though, we
know too little about how many Londoners may have shared a bedchamber—
or a bed. And of course Treswell takes no account at all of vagrant and displaced persons, whose living conditions Patricia Fumerton so evocatively describes (in Chapter 11). It is not in the nature of Treswell's enterprise to help
us with this important area of individual experience in early modern London.

To be sure, our understanding of particular historical phenomena should
always be modulated by an attempt to enlarge our field of vision. It is necessary
in this case to take on board the long temporal views of London provided from
the medieval perspective by Derek Keene and Diane Shaw and from the modern perspective of London's later, even more congested history. It is also necessary to maintain a broad awareness of the situations in other English towns
and cities. But for early modern Londoners, comparisons with former times
and other places were unlikely to have been mitigating factors—they would
not have had ready access to or much interest in such comparisons. Shared
cesspits, chimneys, and gutters; buildings partitioned side to side or up and

down; jetties and eavesdroppings and overseeings; blocked entries, restricted access, and property encroachments; neglect, damage, and inconsiderate behavior were real and immediate to them in ways that comparative history tends to suppress. To recover their perspectives, nothing is more eloquent than the personal chronicle, and, in fact, London's records provide us with one — a manuscript account completed by Nicholas Geffe around 1593.

The Case of Nicholas Geffe

On the front cover of Geffe's record book, his coat of arms is drawn beneath the boldly printed word "LONDON."[38] Geffe had acquired various lands in Essex, most notably Barking Abbey, but this little volume compiled information on his London properties, including the London estate of the dissolved abbey of Glastonbury, houses in the parish of St. Antholin Budge Row, and a tenement in Cheapside. Geffe narrates a long title search conducted in his effort to secure Glastonbury Place, details some of his costs for renovating that property between 1582 and 1593, copies in various leases and other legal documents, and also makes note of controversies with his neighbors.

One brief annotation indicates the kind of negotiation that could be conducted without resort to the Viewers or any other outside party. On 27 April 1590, Geffe writes, "I gave my neighbor Coker leave to rest the one end of his frame of the shed leaning toward Richardson's cellar upon my brick wall." The Viewers were frequently called by Londoners who did not want new structures built on old boundary walls, but not in this instance. This does not mean that Geffe's relations with his neighbors were always amicable, however. On at least two occasions, Geffe found himself in the sort of dispute that might have proceeded to the Viewers. His notes seem to register the arguments he made or planned to make in his own defense, apparently for a third-party audience. Because of the loss of the Elizabethan Viewers' reports, we cannot know whether these City appointees constituted his audience. But in any case, the Viewers approached a controversy as outsiders to it, and we have hundreds of instances of their methods and practices. Geffe's account is a unique report by a party to a dispute, made, perhaps, as he prepared himself to answer the complaints of his neighbors.

The first case concerned the wall around Geffe's garden. He had apparently pulled down some of the brick coping at the top of the wall. A financial record in the account book lists £3 17d. paid "for heightening the south wall of the garden in two places," and this must have been the project at issue, for the old coping would have been removed before the addition of new courses of brick or stone. When his neighbors complained about the damage to the wall, Geffe set out to prove that the wall was not theirs, as they claimed, but his alone. First, Geffe notes similarities between the piece of wall in dispute (on the south side of his garden) and another piece not bordering the same neighbor's property, "which is never wrought nor used but toward him that owneth the wall." Third (painstaking as he is in itemizing his arguments, Geffe here either misnumbers or omits a point), there are holes in the wall only "towards my garden," not the neighbor's. These "holes," which appear often in medieval records, were elsewhere called "arches" and sometimes "cupboards," intended, as Geffe details, "for the bestowing of things." The medieval *Assize of Nuisance* specified that every boundary wall should be three feet thick, with any arch one foot deep, so that neighbors on both sides could have arches with one foot of wall remaining between them. As Geffe observes, in his wall these storage spaces exist only on his side, "and it is not like that if the tenants had made the wall that they would so have provided for the owners of the garden [i.e., Geffe's garden] and not for themselves." Fourth, his wall has a "white stone, wherein stood the abbot of Glastonbury's arms," as is also true of the wall on the north side, Geffe's ownership of which is not in dispute. Fifth, the walls on both sides of the garden are of a "likeness." Sixth, the side of the wall facing Geffe's garden is ornamented with "crosses made in both the walls of gray bricks and the checker work," a design known as "diaper work" which is formed by the use of contrasting bricks. The decorative masonry is on Geffe's side of the wall only, which "[proves] the owner of the garden made both the walls and beautified them." Finally, Geffe notes that "the wall continueth just in one form on both sides all the length of the Abbot's garden." Geffe seems to have proceeded to his dispute without any written documentation concerning his ownership of the wall, but he marshalls the physical evidence forcefully.

In a second case, Geffe notes that on 10 August 1590 he "pulled down [his] kitchen chimney." According to his account for that year, the charge for "making" it "new" was ten pounds. On this occasion, Geffe admits that in rebuilding the chimney "I jutted out further than in truth it stood before" by some two-and-a-half feet. "Some took occasion to say that I had built upon the City ground," he writes, "to whom I answered that I have not." Again, Geffe methodically itemizes his answers to the complaint, demonstrating that, for all its greater size, the chimney still stood entirely on his own ground. First, with reference to the boundaries of the property, Geffe records that the abbot had "a liberty within the rails . . . and further than his own ground his liberty extended not." Second, the kitchen had ovens as well as a chimney: these ovens jutted out as far as Geffe's new chimney does, and the ovens were "never impeached." Third, the abbot had a pale or fence "time without all memory," which Geffe argues must have been set on the abbot's ground. Passage between the fence and the old rails was so narrow and "annoyed" that "hardly . . . any man could pass. . . . Which annoyance the City would never have tolerated if the pale had been raised or set upon the City's ground. And further than the pale and the place where the pale stood the Chimney is not set out." Geffe's arguments are clear here, but so is the fact that he cared little for the "annoyance" he caused those passing by his house. His account demonstrates, if others have not, how easily the complex history of London properties could be exploited to individual ends, and how readily both parties to a controversy could feel fully justified in their conflicting positions.

Geffe does not record the outcome of these disputes; all that survives is evidence of the application of his intelligence and attention to property matters. The volume as a whole is thus an account of his investments, intellectual and emotional as well as financial, in his chief London property. Geffe opens with the long story of how painstakingly he ascertained that the apparent heir to the property was legally entitled to lease it, searching rolls, cross-questioning the heir, reviewing probate documents. His first expense for Glastonbury Place, in 1582, was £200 for the lease; in 1583 he paid another £100 to extend his tenure. Even before that extension, he began a long and substantial series of improvements to the property: installing a pump, adding windows, building two new chambers and a hothouse, wainscotting several rooms and paving the yard, having verses painted to decorate the great chamber, heightening the garden walls, rebuilding the kitchen chimney, creating storage for wine, and in various ways claiming the house for his own. Geffe's account book offers ample witness of the ways in which he set about making his house his castle, as every man was said to have been entitled to do in this age.

The proverb "a man's house is his castle" had many colloquial and metaphoric incarnations, but it is generally interpreted as explicated by Edward Coke in ruling from the King's Bench in 1605 that "the house of every one is to him his Castle and Fortress, as well for defence against injury and violence, as for his repose."[39] It is ironic, given the material circumstances of London dwellers, that this was a prevailing cultural ethos of the period. Under the influence of Ralph Treswell and the London Viewers, the phrase no longer seems only or even primarily to express any confidence in or conviction about physical safety and emotional security. Not even Nicholas Geffe, a gentleman, was exempt from the conditions and contentions of material London. The dream of the castle that circulated in the sixteenth- and seventeeth-century city may, in fact, attest to a frustrated yearning for clear boundaries and impregnable perimeters.

Notes

I am grateful to David Wickham, archivist of Clothworkers' Hall, for the opportunity to consult the Treswell drawings in the Clothworkers' Plan Book; to the staff of the London Guildhall Library for the Treswell drawings in the Christ's Hospital Evidence Book and other documents, including Nicholas Geffe's account book; and to the staff of the Corporation of London Record Office for the Viewers' reports. I am greatly indebted to John Schofield for providing photographs of the Treswell drawings and to the Court of The Clothworkers' Company and The Governors of Christ's Hospital for permission to reproduce them here. Early versions of this chapter were presented in a conference at the Folger Shakespeare Library, the Sixteenth-Century Studies Conference, and the "Maps and Society" lecture series at the Warburg Institute. I am grateful to audiences on those occasions and to Kathleen Lynch, Tony Campbell, and Catherine Delano Smith.

1. London's position relative to the rest of Europe holds true only if Constantinople is omitted from consideration, although by 1550 the growth of that city had leveled off, and by 1750 London had matched it. See A. L. Beier and Roger Finlay, eds., *London 1500–1700: The Making of the Metropolis* (London: Longman, 1986), fig. 1 (p. 3).

2. I was introduced to Treswell's plans in *The London Surveys of Ralph Treswell,* edited by John Schofield (London: London Topographical Society, 1987). Although I silently expand Schofield's abbreviations and introduce some material from the Clothworkers' Plan Book and the Christ's Hospital Evidence Book that he omitted, I am deeply indebted to his edition throughout. For the convenience of the reader, Treswell's plans are identified by the numbers given in his edition; e.g., "Schofield, no. 22."

3. Treswell's 1602 bill for surveying Colne Engaine in Essex survives; see Guildhall Library, MS 13569. The job took him and his assistant sixteen days, including travel time, and he charged 10s. a day for their time and labor, for a total of £8. With the use of two horses, feed for the horses, and a man to fetch the horses, the total bill was £9 4s. 6d. For more on Treswell's career, see Schofield, *London Surveys.*

4. Treswell terms the story above ground level the "second" level. I follow his usage, which coincides with American rather than modern British practice.

5. I was introduced to the Viewers' reports by Loengard's edition of them, *London Viewers and Their Certificates, 1508–1558: Certificates of the Sworn Viewers of the City of London* (London: London Record Society, 1989). Although I silently expand her abbreviations, make some corrections (where my reading of the secretary hand employed differs from hers), and more thoroughly modernize her quasi-modernized text, I rely throughout on her edition and refer to it as the readiest point of access to these documents. It should be noted that, due to recataloguing in the Corporation of London Records Office, the numbers Loengard cites for the "C" file (Misc. MSS, Box 91) are no longer accurate, but I give them for the convenience of the reader consulting her edition. In this discussion, I emphasize the Viewers' reports from the last twenty or thirty years for which they are available as a way of minimizing, to the extent possible, their unavoidable chronological disjunction with Treswell's surveys.

6. For an example of the use made of their knowledge of construction, see no. 36, where the Viewers judged a church wing to be of "one building and builded at one

season" (see also no. 215: "it is all one whole frame"). In 1530 they recorded a case in which the defendant had torn down so many buildings that there was little left "that might lead them to any further knowledge." They concluded that neighbors should be questioned (no. 89).

7. See Schofield for a review of the history of the property, p. 126.

8. In Treswell's surveys and in the Viewers' reports, a standard size for a privy seems to have been four- or five-feet wide and six- or seven-feet long; Alcoke's was presumably extended in length to make room for the privy shafts from above. See Viewers' report no. 209 in which Mistress Hawt is to be allowed "the space of 7 foot of assize in length and 4 foot of assize in wideness or breadth" for her privy. See also no. 325, in which it is said that Francis Barney "ought of right to have the jakes 4 ft. 6 in. one way and 6 ft. the other way." In another Treswell survey showing a ground-floor privy with a shaft from a house of office above, the privy measures nine-feet long and four-feet wide (see Schofield, no. 36). In Viewers' report no. 320, a "tunnel" or privy shaft is specified as being 21 inches in breadth.

9. See no. 209 for a tenant with one stool paying one part and a tenant with three stools paying three parts; there was no "nuisance" involved. See also nos. 267, 288, 323, 333, and 383.

10. Guildhall Library, MS 16988/2, Register of the Company of Ironmongers. It is not clear from this account whether the job was performed at the company hall or some other property owned by the company. The last entry grouped with this account records forty shillings paid to one George Whalley "for so much as he had certain things stolen out of his house in the day time." If his was the house involved, the suggestion is that "night work" could also make a house vulnerable to theft. See also Donald Lupton's character of "Scavengers and Goldfinders," which refers to the use of candles "in the night" and to burdens carried "out into the fields"—except when they were dumped into the Thames (excerpted in *London in the Age of Shakespeare: An Anthology*, ed. Lawrence Manley [University Park: Pennsylvania State University Press, 1986], p. 329).

11. In 1549, the Viewers measured out three separate fences that were required to set off the garden of mercer Edward Cloxton—and, they specified, all three had to be completed by 1 August (no. 242). In 1552, they allowed one John Wyseman, esquire, to "cut away or dig up all such roots, boughs, or trees or any other thing" that prevented him from building his fence (no. 334). See also nos. 125, 235, 246, 273, 275, 276, 291, 294, 387, and 400.

12. See *London Assize of Nuisance, 1301–1431: A Calendar*, ed. Helena M. Chew and William Kellaway (London: London Record Society Publications, vol. 10, 1973). From a number of entries detailing personal damage, see especially nos. 34, 63, 66, 293, and 524. For personal danger, see no. 394 (which is quoted above) and also no. 250. It cannot always be assumed that medieval and early modern issues were identical, however. For the first half of the fourteenth century, for example, there were multiple complaints about cesspits being dug too near neighbors' foundations, spilling sewage into cellars and rotting walls. One remedy was removal, but one was a containing wall of sufficient thickness, 2½ feet if made in stone and 3½ if in earth. As such walls were built, proximity ceased to be an issue; instead, complaints commonly ran that the walls were too thin. For a representative sample, see *London Assize* nos. 2, 69, 110, 191, 219, 414, and 426. By the sixteenth century, however, cesspit walls were in place and the

ground of complaint shifted (but see *London Viewers* [no. 171] for an unusual exception in 1542, a withdraught next to the Fleet wall "without any wall . . . to defend the ordure of the withdraught").

13. "R. Treswell" may be the surveyor himself; as Schofield suggests, it is also possible that he is Treswell's son. In either case, the identification brings home that Treswell had immediate personal experience of urban density in early modern London.

14. See other instances of shared wells in figures 17.7 and 17.8.

15. See also nos. 327, 345, and 385.

16. The almshouses were endowed by Elizabeth I's embroiderer in 1584 for poor widows fifty-six years or older who had been resident in the parish or ward at least twenty years; see Schofield, p. 108.

17. The last point, regarding the close proximity of well and privy, is one I owe to Schofield (private correspondence).

18. For other overlapping spaces, see figure 17.4, with Thomas Chilton having one chamber over West's shop and another over Rowse's hall, and with West having a chamber over Frythe's kitchen as well as a "corner . . . being no part of this house but supposed to be of Jarrards Hall."

19. See also nos. 262 and 368.

20. In 1547, the Viewers spelled out that a landlord was to maintain "all the principals of the tenement." The tenant was responsible for repairs to "stone walls, brick, or tiling, where need is: both stone, brick, tile, lathe, nails, and workmanship. . . . timber, board for floors, quarter-board, and quarters for pentices that be broken, planks for the stable's doors or windows, as well for stuff as for workmanship. . . . daubing of the walls with lathe, nail, loam, and quarters where as the walls be broken, both stuff and workmanship. . . . gutters of lead . . . glass windows. . . . also for cleansing of the sieges and withdraughts" (no. 207). See also nos. 195 and 206. The subject of repair is a prominent concern in other classes of documents, like the records of parish churches and craft guilds, which conducted their own regular "views" of their tenanted properties.

21. Clothworker Thomas Armestronge called the Viewers in 1552, but their ruling went against him when he was ordered to repair "many of the tiles and other things of the house of defendant as he has broken down by reason of his building there" (no. 332). See also nos. 298, 307, 314, and 340.

22. For the medieval custom that windows overlooking a neighbor should be sixteen feet above ground, see *London Assize,* with dozens of instances of windows ordered blocked up because they allowed one household to see the "private business" of another. See also on this subject John Schofield, *Medieval London Houses* (New Haven: Yale University Press, 1995), p. 108.

23. See also nos. 103 and 357.

24. See also no. 279. Laura Gowing reports a 1611 Consistory Court case in which one woman's complaint about a new building blocking her light degenerated into the sort of name calling that proceeded to slander suits; see *Domestic Dangers: Women, Words, and Sex in Early Modern London* (Oxford: Clarendon Press, 1996), p. 117.

25. Guildhall Library, MS 9516. As a private copy of a Viewers' report, the survival of this document and its discovery are entirely fortuitous.

26. Guildhall Library, MS 7971. This box of documents contains private copies of three Viewers' reports, the first of which is cited. In 1598 the Viewers were called back

to the same property to sort out a dispute over the proper tenure of a warehouse and some rooms over it. In 1617 they reported on damage done to a house known as "the Service Tower" in consequence of construction.

27. See also Clothworkers' Hall Plan Book, no. 43 (Schofield, no. 47, fig. 51) for buildings at 77 Wood Street, with "Two tenements now divided into three."

28. Other cases suggested how this might be done: the pipe should be "either in lead or hard stone of Kent, being hollow gutter stone," and it should have "a sufficient grate of iron that nothing shall pass through the said water course but only except water" (no. 390). Again, medieval records are sometimes more specific about the water, refuse, and excrement thrown into gutters (see *London Assize,* especially nos. 243 and 566).

29. On this subject see Derek Portman, "Vernacular Building in the Oxford Region in the Sixteenth and Seventeenth Centuries," in *Rural Change and Urban Growth, 1500–1800,* ed. C. W. Chalklin and M. A. Havinden (London: Longman, 1974); John Schofield, *Medieval London Houses;* Victor Skipp, *Crisis and Development: An Ecological Case Study of the Forest of Arden, 1570–1674* (Cambridge: Cambridge University Press, 1978); and my "'The Causes and Reasons of all Artificial Things' in the Elizabethan Domestic Environment," *Medieval and Renaissance Drama in England,* 7 (1995): 19–75, esp. pp. 40–48.

30. Will abstracted by Marion E. Allen in *Wills of the Archdeaconry of Suffolk, 1620–24,* Suffolk Records Society no. 31 (Woodbridge, Suffolk: Boydell Press, 1989), no. 629. For the purposes of this discussion, I have oversimplified a will that is not fully self-explanatory, so complicated are the property arrangements.

31. Will abstracted by F. G. Emmison in *Essex Wills (England),* vol. 3 *(1571–1577)* (Boston: New England Historic Genealogical Society, 1986), no. 633.

32. Diane Shaw, "The Construction of the Private in Medieval London," *Journal of Medieval and Early Modern Studies,* 26, no. 3 (Fall 1996): 447–66.

33. Schofield, *Medieval London Houses,* p. 59.

34. Guildhall Library, MS 7784/1, no. 29.

35. Guildhall Library, MS 4384/1, p. 247. The bay windows were to be glazed to admit light but not fitted with casements that opened toward the churchyard.

36. Schofield, no. 40; see also Schofield, no. 39. The Viewers, too, addressed the division of rooms as well as of buildings (no. 277).

37. See Paul S. Seaver, *Wallington's World: A Puritan Artisan in Seventeenth-Century London* (Stanford: Stanford University Press, 1985), pp. 82–83 for Sarah Rampaigne and her children in 1635 and for Charles Rampaigne in 1646. See also Gowing for a Consistory Court case in which a man subdivided his shop by hanging some painted cloths with a bedstead behind (*Domestic Dangers,* p. 189).

38. Guildhall Library, MS 4159.

39. Edward Coke, Report on Semayne's Case (1605), translated into English in *Reports of Sir Edward Coke* ["The King's Bench Reports"] (London: 1658; Wing STC C4944), sig. Pp3r. For more on this proverb, see my *Private Matters and Public Culture in Post-Reformation England* (Ithaca: Cornell University Press, 1994), pp. 2–11 and 102–3.

Contributors

IAN W. ARCHER is Fellow, Tutor, and University Lecturer in Modern History at Keble College, Oxford. He is author of *The Pursuit of Stability: Social Relations in Elizabethan London* (1991) and of *The History of the Haberdashers' Company* (1991), as well as of several articles on early modern social history.

PETER W. M. BLAYNEY, an independent scholar living in Toronto, is the author of several studies of the London book trade in the sixteenth and early seventeenth centuries, including *The Bookshops in Paul's Cross Churchyard* (1990). He is currently working on a history of the Stationers' Company from 1501 to 1616.

ALICE T. FRIEDMAN is Professor of Art and Director of the Architecture Program at Wellesley College. Her publications include *House and Household in Elizabethan England: Wollaton Hall and the Willoughby Family* (1989), *Women and the Making of the Modern House: A Social and Architectural History* (1998), as well as articles on architecture, gender, and cultural history.

PATRICIA FUMERTON is Professor of English at the University of California, Santa Barbara. She is author of *Cultural Aesthetics: Renaissance Literature and the Practice of Social Ornament* (1991) and co-editor of *Renaissance Culture and the Everyday* (1999). She is at work on a book entitled "Spacious Voices / Vagrant Subjects in Early Modern England."

ANDREW GURR is Professor of English at the University of Reading and a director of the Globe project in London, chairing its research department. He has edited several plays for the Revels and the New Cambridge Shakespeare series. His books include *The Shakespearean Stage, 1574–1642* (1970, 1980, 1992), *Playgoing in Shakespeare's London* (1987, 1996), and *The Shakespearian Playing Companies* (1996). A book written in collaboration with Mariko Ichikawa, *Staging in Shakespeare's Theatres,* and an edition of the first quarto of *Henry V* are in press.

JEAN E. HOWARD is Professor of English and Director of the Institute for Research on Women and Gender at Columbia University. She is author of *Shakespeare's Art of Orchestration* (1984) and *The Stage and Social Strug-*

gle in Early Modern England (1994) and co-author, with Phyllis Rackin, of *Engendering a Nation: A Feminist Account of Shakespeare's English Histories* (1997). She is also an editor of *The Norton Shakespeare* (1997). She is at work on a book entitled "Theater of a City: Social Change and Generic Innovation on the Early Modern Stage."

ANN ROSALIND JONES, Esther Cloudman Dunn Professor of Comparative Literature at Smith College, has published *The Currency of Eros: Women's Love Lyric in Europe, 1540–1620* (1990) and, with Margaret F. Rosenthal, a translation, *The Poems and Selected Letters of Veronica Franco* (1998). Her essays on gender ideology and women's lyric have appeared in various collections, including *Rewriting the Renaissance* (1986), *The Ideology of Conduct* (1987), *Subject and Object: Reconstructing Renaissance Culture* (1996), and *Maids and Mistresses, Cousins and Queens: Women's Alliance in Early Modern England* (1999). Together, Jones and Peter Stallybrass have recently completed *Renaissance Clothing and the Materials of Memory,* forthcoming from Cambridge University Press.

DEREK KEENE is Director of the Centre for Metropolitan History, Institute of Historical Research, University of London. He is author of many essays on the social and economic history, topography, and archaeology of English towns, including studies of London from 600 to 1870. His book-length studies include *Survey of Medieval Winchester* (1985).

LENA COWEN ORLIN is Research Professor of English at the University of Maryland, Baltimore County and Executive Director of the Shakespeare Association of America. The author of *Private Matters and Public Culture in Post-Reformation England* (1994) and *Elizabethan Households: An Anthology* (1995), she is at work on a book entitled "Locating Privacy in Early Modern England."

GAIL KERN PASTER is Professor of English at George Washington University and editor of *Shakespeare Quarterly.* She has written *The Body Embarrassed: Drama and the Disciplines of Shame in Early Modern England* (1993) and co-edited *"Midsummer Night's Dream": Texts and Contexts* (1998).

LINDA LEVY PECK is Professor of History at George Washington University. She is author of *Northampton: Patronage and Policy at the Court of James I* (1982) and *Court Patronage and Corruption in Early Stuart England* (1990) and editor of *The Mental World of the Jacobean Court* (1991). She is currently working on a book entitled "Consuming Splendor: Britain in the Age of the Baroque."

DAVID HARRIS SACKS is Professor of History and Humanities at Reed

College. He is author of *Trade, Society, and Politics in Bristol, 1500–1640* (1985) and *The Widening Gate: Bristol and the Atlantic Economy, 1450–1700* (1991), co-editor with Donald R. Kelley of *The Historical Imagination in Early Modern Britain: History, Rhetoric, and Fiction, 1500–1800* (1997), and editor of Ralph Robynson's sixteenth-century translation of Thomas More's *Utopia* (1999). He is currently working on a book-length study of market culture and ethical discourse in early modern England.

JANE SCHNEIDER teaches anthropology in the Graduate School of the City University of New York. She is the co-editor, with Annette B. Weiner, of *Cloth and Human Experience* (1987) and is the author of several essays on cloth and clothing. Her anthropological field research has been in Sicily and has led to two books, co-authored with Peter Schneider: *Culture and Political Economy in Western Sicily* (1976) and *Festival of the Poor: Fertility, Decline, and the Ideology of Class in Sicily* (1996). A third book on Sicily is in progress, focusing on the mafia and the antimafia movement in Palermo. In 1998 she edited *Italy's Southern Question: Orientalism in One Country.*

JOHN SCHOFIELD is Curator of Architecture at the Museum of London. His publications on medieval and Tudor London include *The Building of London from the Conquest to the Great Fire* (1984, 1999) and *Medieval London Houses* (1995). He is currently working on aspects of seventeenth-century London houses.

ALAN SINFIELD teaches English and Lesbian and Gay Studies at the University of Sussex. His publications include *Faultlines: Cultural Materialism and the Politics of Dissident Reading* (1992); *"Macbeth": William Shakespeare* (edited for New Casebooks, 1992); *Cultural Politics — Queer Reading* (1994); *Political Shakespeare* (with Jonathan Dollimore, 2nd edition, 1994); *The Wilde Century: Effeminacy, Oscar Wilde, and the Queer Moment* (1994); and *Gay and After* (1998).

PETER STALLYBRASS is Professor of English and of Comparative Literature and Literary Theory at the University of Pennsylvania. With Allon White, he wrote *The Politics and Poetics of Transgression* (1986), and he has co-edited *Staging the Renaissance* (1991), *Subject and Object: Reconstructing Renaissance Culture* (1996), and *Language Machines: Technologies of Literary and Cultural Production* (1997). Together, Stallybrass and Ann Rosalind Jones have recently completed *Renaissance Clothing and the Materials of Memory,* forthcoming from Cambridge University Press.

JOAN THIRSK was, until retirement, Reader in Economic History in the University of Oxford and is general editor and part author of *The Agrar-*

ian History of England and Wales (8 vols., 1967–). She has written on the consumer society in *Economic Policy and Projects: The Development of a Consumer Society in Early Modern England* (1978). Her most recent book is *Alternative Agriculture: A History from the Black Death to the Present Day* (1997).

Acknowledgments

The contributors to this volume first gathered at a conference held at the Folger Shakespeare Library in the spring of 1995. "Material London, ca. 1600" convened under the auspices of the Folger Institute and with funding from the National Endowment for the Humanities. Thanks are due to Folger director Werner Gundersheimer, director of academic programs Barbara Mowat, and librarian Richard Kuhta. Barbara Ashbrook, in NEH's Division of Education, was, as always, generous with intellect and enthusiasm as well as funding. In the face of an unprecedented registration, the Folger Institute staffers who brilliantly staged the conference included then program administrator Kathleen Lynch, program coordinators Carol Brobeck and Rebecca Willson, and administrative assistant Amy Adler. Also providing extraordinary support were the Folger Reading Room staff, headed by Elizabeth Walsh; the guard staff, headed by King David Johnson; and the special events staff, headed by Anita Fox Sperling. Thanks are also extended to Folger reference librarian Georgianna Ziegler, curator of books and exhibitions Rachel Doggett, and curator of manuscripts Laetitia Yeandle, especially for their contributions to a Library exhibition, "Elizabethan Households," mounted in connection with the conference. Planning for the conference was undertaken in consultation with members of the Folger Institute's Central Executive Committee. Sheila ffolliott and David Harris Sacks were especially helpful in the planning process.

There was a sense of occasion about the "Material London" conference that cannot be recaptured here. For that, we would have to find some way of representing the vital contributions made by the session chairs: Susan Amussen, David Bevington, Richard Helgerson, Donald R. Kelley, Lawrence Manley, Karen Newman, and Phyllis Rackin. We would have to reproduce the closing remarks by Sheila ffolliott, which called for audience participation and rallied energetic discussion. Most of all, we would have to summon up that audience, over three hundred strong, who made this a lively collaborative process on a grand scale.

The collegial spirit with which each of the authors approached the conference continued through the compilation of this volume. The editor is also grateful for the unexpected felicities of working with Jerome E. Singerman, Ellen Fiskett, Noreen O'Connor, Alison A. Anderson, and all the staff at the University of Pennsylvania Press.

Index